Leslie Alan Dunkling

Editor: Beatrice Frei
Design and layout: Jean Whitcombe and Alan Hamp
Cover design and illustrations throughout: Robert Heesom

First published in hardback, 1974
Second edition in limpback, 1983
Revised and updated edition, 1986
Revised, updated and expanded edition, 1989

Published in Great Britain by Guinness Publishing Ltd,
33 London Road, Enfield, Middlesex

Set in Rockwell 9/11
Photoset by Ace Filmsetting Ltd, Frome, Somerset
Printed and bound in Great Britain by
Hazell Watson & Viney Ltd, Member of BPCC plc, Aylesbury, Bucks.

British Library Cataloguing in Publication Data
Dunkling, Leslie
The Guinness book of names.—Rev. and updated ed.
1. Names
I. Title
929.9'7

ISBN 0-85112-327-9

CONTENTS

Acknowledgements 4

Preface 5

1 **What's in a name?** *Introduction* 7

2 **First names first** *First name origins* 22

3 **Fashionable names** *First name fashions* 38

4 **Naming the baby** *First names – reasons for choice* 50

5 **The family name** *History of surnames* 63

6 **Making a name for yourself** *Psychology of surnames* 84

7 **Eking out names** *Nicknames* 93

8 **A local habitation and a name** *British place names* 105

9 **Names take their places** *New world place names* 117

10 **Neighbourly names** *Street names* 127

11 **Signing a name** *Pub names* 138

12 **Home-made names** *House names* 149

13 **Trading a name** *Trade names* 160

14 **No end of names** *Magazine names, pop group names, animal names, flower names, apple names, ship names, train and locomotive names, lorry names, dog names, cat names, yacht names* 169

15 **Name games** *Place name games, name anagrams, name rebus, name variations, name collecting, name stories, name poems, name jokes* 182

Bibliography 194

Names Index 197

ACKNOWLEDGEMENTS

This book could not have been written without the helpful advice, comments and friendly assistance of a great many people. It is unfortunately not possible to mention by name the three thousand or more correspondents who have written to me in the last few years about names of one kind or another. Many of them are members of The Names Society; some are authors of books listed in the Bibliography; many others are members of the public who responded to newspaper appeals for information. I am most grateful to all of them.

A special word of thanks must go to C. V. Appleton, who made available to me the results of his very extensive first name researches.

Very specific help with the book has also been given by Adrian Room, Beatrice Frei, Richard Luty, Anne Kirkman, Alec Jeakins, Gordon Wright, Rev Peter Sutton, John Field, Dr Kelsie Harder, Elsdon C. Smith, Gillian Skirrow, Professor Edwin Lawson, Dr Terrence Keough, William Gosling, Dr Cleveland Evans, Helen Vnuk, Jodi Cassell, Kathleen Sinclair, Cecily Dynes, J. Bryan III, Muriel Smith, A. A. Willis, Darryl Francis, Philip Riley, Pauline Quemby, George F. Hubbard and Harvey Türkel.

My wife, Nicole, has in her own way made it possible for the book to come into being. The poet was right: *a gode womman is mannys blys.*

GUINNESS

This Irish family name is a shortened form of **Mac Guinness** or **Maguinness,** also found as **Mac Genis, Magennis, Maguiness, Magennies, Maginniss.** It was earlier **Mag Aonghusa** or **Mag Aonghuis,** 'son of Angus'.

Angus in turn is a Gaelic personal name which was probably *Oino-gustu-s* in its earliest form, 'unique choice one'.

The usual Scottish form of the name is **MacInnes,** though it also occurs as **Mackinnes, Mackinness, MacGinnis, MacAngus** and **Macansh.**

Mac, Gaelic 'son', is sometimes (wrongly according to the purists) contracted to *M'* or *Mc* in writing. In parts of Scotland, eg Arran, it is pronounced *Ac* by Gaelic speakers. The change to *Mag* before a vowel is a feature of Irish Gaelic. The Welsh equivalent is *Mab* or *Map*, usually shortened to *Ab* or *Ap* and still further to *B* or *P*. Thus **Mab Evan** becomes **Ab Evan,** then **Bevan. Map Howell** becomes **Ap Howell,** then **Powell.**

PREFACE

'A preface,' wrote Isaac Disraeli, 'being the entrance to a book, should invite by its beauty. An elegant porch announces the splendour of the interior.'

It's a fine thought, but 'splendour' is not really what I want to offer in this book. Instead I have tried to bring together a mixture of information, entertainment, ideas and enthusiasm. The last of these I can at least guarantee to be present. Few authors can so have enjoyed immersing themselves in a subject, and I hope this will be clear on every page.

As for information, I asked myself at the outset what my potential reader would want to know about names. I thought he would certainly be interested in first names and surnames, in where those names came from and what they originally meant. In chapters on those subjects, therefore, I briefly summarise the historical and linguistic facts, and give the origins of as many names as possible. But I must say that, though I understand the interest in name origins, I think they are almost irrelevant in modern life. Far more to the point, it seems to me, is the consideration of why certain first names come into fashion or go out of fashion; why parents choose one name rather than any other at a given point in time; what associations are aroused in people's minds by certain names. There are a host of similar topics that concern the psychological and sociological aspects of names. I discuss such matters, having first presented firmly based tables of name frequencies that make a sensible discussion possible.

In these areas I try to offer a fresh approach, not merely to collate what is already in print. The usual books on first names are in any case very disappointing. I find no trace in any of them of an objective attempt to establish which names are currently being used. As a result they contain long articles about names such as Griselda and Letitia, while vital names such as Tracy, Joanne and Sharon are virtually ignored.

To complete the survey of personal names I deal with nicknames in a separate chapter. Nicknames have an inbuilt liveliness which makes them of special interest. The names are entertaining in themselves, whatever one says of them.

I thought my potential reader would next be interested in place names, and accordingly I turn in that direction. The interpretation of early English place names is a matter for the specialist, the scholar who has devoted a great deal of time to the study of certain languages and cultures. I received a preliminary training in philology, and my main hope is that this will have enabled me to interpret the findings of the experts without too much distortion. The place names of the New World have also been well studied by historians and linguists, and once again I summarise their work.

Personal and place names are the concern of a major part of this book, but the interest of names really does not end there. The rest of the book is concerned with street names and pub names, house names and trade names, boat names, locomotive names, animal names, and still more names. *All* names are fascinating, and I try to explain why. In this latter section of the book the scales are slightly loaded in favour of entertainment rather than information, especially in the chapter on 'Name Games'.

Finally, I include at the end of the book a Bibliography which mentions books such as the one from which I borrowed my opening quotation, Isaac Disraeli's *Curiosities of Literature*. It is there because among dozens of other interesting essays it contains those on the 'Influence of a Name', the 'Orthography of Proper Names', 'Names of Our Streets' and 'Political Nicknames'. Disraeli was clearly a names enthusiast: I hope there are many more like him.

Leslie Alan Dunkling

What *is* a name?

'The word(s) that someone or something is known by.'
Longman Dictionary of Contemporary English

'A proper name is a noun used in a non-universal function, with or without recognizable current lexical value, of which the potential meaning coincides with and never exceeds its actual meaning, and which is attached as a label to one animate being or one inanimate object (or to more than one in the case of collective names) for the purpose of specific distinction from among a number of like or in some respects similar beings or objects that are either in no manner distinguished from one another or, for our interest, not sufficiently distinguished.'
Ernst Pulgram *Theory of Names*

'The name of a thing is its soul.'
F. M. Cornford *From Religion to Philosophy*

Naming Names

Names are usually defined more specifically by referring them to the set of names, or nomenclature, to which they belong. Thus we speak of a place name (toponym), house name (econym), first name (Christian name, forename, given name), etc.

Names can also be differentiated by origin. By primary origin every name is either:

a) descriptive, ie formed of a word or words which describe in some way what is being named,
b) converted, ie a word or words arbitrarily associated with what is being named and given name status,
c) invented, ie a newly-formed word or words, or group of letters, or combination of letters and numbers, of no known previous meaning, brought into being as a name.

Once a name exists it can be:

d) transferred, ie borrowed from one naming system for use elsewhere, as with Hamlet when used to name a cigar. There is a special set of names available for transfer to any group of persons or objects—see Number Names on page George (19).
e) linked, ie extended by the addition of another element, as Johnson from John,
f) blended, ie joined partly or totally with all or part of another name, as in the house name Patalan, where Patricia and Alan live.

1 What's in a name?

The most famous comment on names in the English language occurs in Shakespeare's play, *Romeo and Juliet*:

> What's in a name? that which we call a rose
> By any other name would smell as sweet.

Juliet's beautiful speech, which in context is a passionate plea for what is known to be a lost cause, is often misinterpreted. Juliet does not believe what she says even as she says it, and Shakespeare certainly did not believe it. He gives quite a different answer to his own question many times in his plays and poems. With his usual genius, however, he makes Juliet ask herself a timeless question which has an infinity of answers. The innumerable sub-editors who have echoed the question at the head of a thousand columns simply acknowledge the fact. We must also acknowledge it, and attempt to find some answers.

A name's meaning

A name has different kinds of meaning. To most people, for instance, **Romeo** means the character in Shakespeare's play. The name is so generally associated with that romantic young lover that it can be used humorously to describe any such person. The original meaning of the name Romeo, which probably indicated a pilgrim to Rome, is quite another matter.

> *. . . all bearers of the Forsyte name would feel the bloom was off the rose. He had no illusions like Shakespeare that roses by any other name would smell as sweet. The name was a possession, a concrete, unstained piece of property, the value of which would be reduced some twenty per cent at least.*
>
> John Galsworthy *In Chancery*

Names can have public meanings and private meanings. **Lamorna,** for example, is a place name. This simple fact about the name is a general meaning which is implied by its presence on a map or in a gazetteer. To somebody who was born in Lamorna, or who lives there, the name obviously means far more. It conjures up immediately memories and associations. The name has an extended, particular meaning as well for many married couples, since Lamorna happens to be well-known as a honeymoon resort.

Some of those honeymoon couples transfer the name Lamorna to their houses, for it is often seen over porches in British suburbs. When such a transfer has taken place, a further extension of meaning is possible. A young couple who hope to have a house of their own one day see a house which is called Lamorna. For them that house is everything they dream about. Perhaps they fall in love with the name itself, with its form and sound. When they call their own house Lamorna some years later they may still be unaware of the name's public meaning as a place in the south-west of England. For them it has only a secondary, private meaning.

An even commoner example of secondary meaning occurs when parents use a particular name for their child to commemorate a friend or relation. In their minds the name is associated with the person who bore it, with that person's character and personality. The name means to them what that person means to them, rather than what a dictionary might say about the name's origin.

A name's origin

Just as many kinds of meaning are possible, so different kinds of name origins may be described. Primary origin refers to the way in which the name first becomes a name. For instance, if in the middle of a dark wood there is a clearing where the sun streams down, that spot might well be described by those who know it as 'the bright clearing'. A thousand years ago those words would have looked more like 'the sheer lea'. Such a description was applied to a place in southern England, and the general description gradually became a particular name. 'The sheer lea' is still so called today, though it has a slightly different pronunciation and is written **Shirley.**

But once such a name has come into being it can be transferred constantly from one entity to another. We spoke of Lamorna becoming a house name. By a similar process of transfer, Shirley became a surname. Then, as frequently happens with surnames, it began to be used as a boy's first name. In 1849 Charlotte Brontë wrote a novel in which the *heroine* was called Shirley, because:

> 'Her parents, who had wished to have a son, finding that . . . Providence had granted them only a daughter, bestowed on her the same masculine family cognomen they would have bestowed on a boy, if with a boy they had been blessed.'

The name was nevertheless rarely used for girls for many years, but in 1880 another transfer of the name occurred which was to prove helpful. The Reverend W. Wilks, who lived in the vicarage at Shirley, cultivated a new kind of poppy in his garden. He had grown it at Shirley Vicarage, so he quite naturally called the new flower Shirley. Soon afterwards it became fashionable to give girls flower names, such as Daisy and Violet, and Shirley was now a candidate that could be considered. The final step was for Shirley Temple to come along in the 1930s and associate the name with an ideal little girl and international stardom. Shirley quickly became one of the most popular names for a girl. It enjoyed a brief spell in the limelight before retiring to a more modest position, but it is certainly established permanently now as a girl's name. For many people it must be that first and foremost, and some may be quite unaware of its place name, surname, boy's name and flower name connections.

With **Shirley,** then, we see how the principle of secondary origin applies. Names are passed from one naming system to another, just as words are passed from one language to another. It would be well to consider how many naming systems, or nomenclatures, surround us.

Name density

On a normal day—which can itself be identified by many different names—most of us meet a number of people who are known to us by name. We may know, and use, their first names, surnames or nicknames which are drawn from different, but overlapping, systems. We will also meet people whose names we do not know, and here we may have to make use of personal name substitutes. Professional titles such as 'driver', 'officer', 'waiter', are given temporary name status, or we use a general term such as 'sir'. Lovers are also fond of using name substitutes. A correspondent once told me that her fiancé addressed her variously as 'chunkie', 'porky', 'sloppy', 'floppy', 'big softie', 'hot chops', 'cuddly duddly', 'tatty head', 'rumble tum', 'kipper feet', 'twizzle', 'lucky legs' and 'lucky lips'.

In our newspaper (named) we will read of many more people who are known to us by name, but whom we have never met. We will read, too, of places all over the world, most of whose names are familiar to us though we have not been to them.

'. . .'tis the same age our little bye would have been if we had had one six years ago. If we had, Jawn, think what sorrow would be in our hearts this night, with our little Phelan run away. . . .'

'Ye talk foolishness,' said Mr McCaskey. ''Tis Pat he would be named, after me old father in Cantrim.'

'Ye lie!' said Mrs McCaskey, without anger. 'Me brother was worth tin dozen bog-trotting McCaskeys. After him would the bye be named.'

O. Henry *Between Rounds*

Name magic

Paris! Paris!! Paris!!!
The very name had always been one to conjure with, whether he thought of it as a mere sound on the lips and in the ear, or as a magical written or printed word for the eye.

George du Maurier *Trilby*

I have a passion for the name of Mary,
For once it had a magic sound to me.

Lord Byron *Don Juan*

thy name reminds me
Of three friends, all true and tried;
And that name, like magic, binds me
Closer, closer to thy side.

H. W. Longfellow *To the River Charles*

'Who hath not owned, with rapture-smitten frame,
The Power of grace, the magic of a name?'

Thomas Campbell *Pleasures of Hope*

'Foxy?'
'Yes, Piet?' Their simple names had a magic, the magic of a caress . . .

John Updike *Couples*

'I am your father.'
God knows what magic the name had for his ears . . .

Charles Dickens *Barnaby Rudge*

The accidental affinity or coincidence of a name, connected with ridicule or hatred, with pleasure or disgust, has operated like magic.

Isaac Disraeli *Curiosities of Literature*

When we leave our houses, which usually have number names but may have other names, we walk through named streets. In a town we will pass shops which have names and which are crammed with named products. In the country we will be passing named fields and natural features.

If we live near the sea, or near a river (named), we may be exposed to ship or boat names. In some parts of the English-speaking world we will almost certainly see the traditionally well illustrated names of public houses.

Our job or profession will bring us into contact with still more names. They may be the names of other companies, or the names of products. If these products are simply components, not usually seen by the public, they may well have code names consisting of letters and numbers. The form will have changed, but these are still names.

Every occupation has its accompanying nomenclatures. The professional gardener must cope with vast numbers of plant names. A builder uses not just bricks but particular kinds of bricks that have names. A librarian becomes familiar with an ever-increasing number of names, though in his case they masquerade as book 'titles'.

All this only hints at the true name density which surrounds us. To stay with books for a moment, you are reading now a page that is identified by a number name, which has words printed by named type-faces **(Rockwell** and **Palatino)** on named paper **(Longbow).** The ink that has been used also has a name **(Onyx 2).**

A similar situation exists everywhere. Almost any generic term, even a word like 'table' or 'chair', conceals a naming system. A named chair may sound strange, but a company that manufactures chairs presumably makes several different models. A salesman from such a company might refer to the chair you are sitting on as an **Elizabethan,** say, or a **K52.** The simple word 'chair' would be meaningless on his order-forms.

So it is with specialists of all kinds. A man who works in a wholesale fruit market is probably surrounded by apples, but it is unlikely that he uses that word. He deals in boxes of **Coxes,** say, or **Granny Smiths.**

Such names differ from those that identify people, places, houses, boats and the like. They do not individualise, but serve to distinguish members of one group from those of another. There is obviously an important difference between generic names, such as **King Edward** for a potato, and what we may continue to call proper names, such as **Edward King** when it identifies an individual.

He kept reciting the names of cider apples:
'Coccagee and Bloody Butcher,
Slack-ma-girdle,
Red Soldier and Lady's Finger,
Kingston Black, Bloody Turk,
Fox Whelp, Pawson, Tom Putt,
Bitter Sweet and Fatty Mutt.'
His deep, rich fruity voice made them sound like poetry.

Humphrey Phelps *Just Around the Corner*

Proper names are more important than generic names from one point of view, since man has always tended to bestow an individual name on something that he considers to have a personality. In the past a fighting man was quite likely to name his sword, because he looked upon it as a friend who helped him in times of trouble. Soldiers in the Second World War named their tanks and trenches in a similar way. Many modern car-owners bestow an individual name on their vehicles, and that by no means exhausts the possibilities of this personalised naming. One thinks of the characters in P. G. Wodehouse's *Buried Treasure* who name their moustaches, and of 'Tickler', the cane used by Mrs Joe Gargery on Pip in Dickens' *Great Expectations*. In rural areas local folk-tales can lead to the naming of individual trees, such as 'The Kissing Tree' which grows near the house of J. B. Priestley.

The 'name-print' theory

Linguists know that no two speakers of a language use the language in quite the same way. Because of where and when they were born they use one dialect or another; because of their educational, professional and social backgrounds they know and use different words, or use the same words in different ways. Every speaker of a language has a personal dialect, an idiolect, which is like his linguistic finger-print. Similarly, one can safely say that no two people know and use the same body of names. We have all what might be called an onomastic finger-print, a 'name-print'.

This fact is sometimes exploited in general-knowledge tests. Candidates are shown a list of personal names, for example, and are asked to say whether the people concerned are engineers or writers, musicians, scientists or whatever. Properly applied, such a test can reveal very efficiently in which areas a candidate is well read, and how specialised his knowledge is.

An individual's 'name-print'—to use this playful term for a moment as shorthand for a highly complicated concept—is constantly changing. We hear a new song on the radio, see a new film, read a new book, and we add to our store of names or change the private meanings of old ones. We have no means of counting how many names a person knows at any one time, any more than we can count how many words he knows, but one's subjective impression is that whereas our store of words increases very slowly after the age of eighteen or so, we continue to add to our store of names at a steady rate all our lives. As we get older we are able to use our general vocabulary to talk of more and more specific entities—named entities. One wonders whether we reach a point where we know more names as such than words.

Here is a typical name-based quiz. Identify fully the literary characters whose unusual first names are listed below:

1 **Hercule**	5 **Peregrine**	8 **Rawdon**
2 **Kimball**	6 **Pollyanna**	9 **Rhett**
3 **Lorna**	7 **Phileas**	10 **Robinson**
4 **Mycroft**		

ANSWERS

1 Hercule Poirot in various Agatha Christie stories. 2 Kimball O'Hara in Rudyard Kipling's *Kim*. 3 Lorna Doone in R. D. Blackmore's novel of that name. 4 Mycroft Holmes, brother of Sherlock in the Conan Doyle stories about the great detective. 5 Peregrine Pickle in the novel of that name by Tobias Smollett. 6 Pollyanna Whittier in the Pollyanna stories by Eleanor H. Porter. 7 Phileas Fogg in Jules Verne's *Around the World in Eighty Days*. 8 Rawdon Crawley in William Thackeray's *Vanity Fair*. 9 Rhett Butler in Margaret Mitchell's *Gone With the Wind*. 10 Robinson Crusoe in Daniel Defoe's novel of that name.

Previous name studies

At first sight there appears to be general recognition of the importance of names because so much has been written about them. Elsdon C. Smith, in his excellent bibliography of works on personal names, listed nearly 3500 books and articles. That was in 1952, and he extends the list with newly published works and new 'discoveries' every year in *Names*, the journal of the American Name Society. An updated bibliography, *Personal Names and Naming*, compiled by Edwin D. Lawson, was published by Greenwood Press in 1987.

Geographical names have also received an enormous amount of attention, but there the matter virtually ends. It is possible to find the occasional books that deal with street names, house names, pub names, field names, ship names, pet names, nicknames, plant names, locomotive names and the like, but they are relatively few and far between. Details are given of as many as possible in the Bibliography at the end of this book.

What is serious about the situation is that statements about names, by writers on language and similar topics, invariably refer to personal and place names only or pay the merest lip-service to the existence of other nomenclatures. The position is thus very similar to the one that pertained 400 years ago in language studies, when it was only considered necessary to study seriously a handful of the world's languages. It was assumed that all other languages followed the same pattern as those few, and the then minor languages such as English were forced into a mould which was itself based on a misunderstanding.

Names—naming

As it happens, we cannot even claim that personal and place names have been thoroughly studied, in spite of the number of books about them. It is not just that a high proportion of those books are merely imitative, and often inaccurately so. Those studies which are sound and which make a real contribution to our knowledge are almost exclusively concerned with name origins. The psychology of naming has been made the subject of many short articles, but psychologists have on the whole left the field clear to the philologists.

A rare exception to this rule is *Nicknames: Their Origins and Social Consequences*, by Jane Morgan, Christopher O'Neill and Rom Harré, published in 1979 by Routledge and Kegan Paul. There is also a chatty book by Catherine Cameron called *The Name-Givers* (Prentice-Hall, 1983). But these two works are as nothing compared to the vast number of books on the subject published by philologists.

The result of this has been to give—in my own opinion—a totally wrong emphasis to name studies. The interpretation of philological data is obviously valuable for historians and the philologists themselves, but the interpretation of what the choice of names, for example, tells us about human thought processes would be equally valuable to scholars in many other fields.

To study the naming process one must have access to the namers as well as the names. The philologists have dominated name studies for so long that a myth seems to have grown up that only historically based name studies are academically respectable. We need to know about names *and* naming, just as when we study a language we need to know its vocabulary and its grammar. The one is virtually useless without the other.

The world of names

Because of the situation described above, our opening question: 'What's in a name?' can only be partly answered in this book. Just as an early cartographer, who wished to draw a map of the world, had very unevenly distributed information at his disposal, so a writer on the world of names is faced with an unbalanced situation. If a naming system is thought of as a country, then a few have been thoroughly explored and mapped—though in a specialist way. Others are almost virgin territories where one may wander for the first time. What follows must therefore be only a sketch-map at times—a first report. I hope that my traveller's tales will encourage others to visit these lands and fill in the details.

Any other name

'That which we call a rose', says Juliet, in Shakespeare's *Romeo and Juliet*, 'by any other name would smell as sweet'. Roses have hundreds of 'other names', as it happens, identifying the different varieties. I give below a personal selection of names taken from the useful publication *Find That Rose*, compiled by Angela Pawsey for the Rose Growers' Association.

Abundance
Ace of Hearts
Adam
Admired Miranda
Agatha
Agnes
Air France
Albertine
Alexander
Alexia
Allgold
Aloha
Alpine Sunset
Amanda
Amberlight
Amelia
Angela Rippon
Angelina
Anna Ford
Antonia
Apricot Brandy
Apricot Silk
Apricot Sunblaze
Ashwednesday
Aunty Dora
Aurora
Australian Gold
Autumn Fire
Autumn Sunlight
Baby Darling
Baby Gold
Babylon
Baby Masquerade
Ballerina
Baltimore Belle
Bashful
Battle of Britain
Beautiful Britain
Beauty Secret
Bees Frolic
Belle Amour
Belle Blonde
Black Beauty
Black Lady
Blesma Soul
Blessings
Blue Moon
Blue Peter
Blush Damask
Bobbie Charlton
Bonfire Night
Bonnie Scotland
Bonsoir
Boule de Neige
Bountiful
Breath of Life
Bridal Pink
Bright Smile
Buff Beauty
Burning Love
Busy Lizzie
Butterfly Wings
Can Can
Carefree Beauty
Carla
Carmen
Carol
Celeste
Celina
Cha Cha
Chanelle
Charmian
Cheerfulness
Chicago Peace
Chorus Girl
Cinderella
Claire
Clarissa
Cleo
Compassion
Congratulations
Coral Dawn
Coralie
Coralin
Cordelia
Cornelia
Cymbaline
Danse du Feu
Dapple Dawn
Dearest
Deep Secret
Dian
Dimples
Disco Dancer
Dopey
Doreen
Double Delight
Dreamgirl
Dreaming Spires
Dreamland
Easter Morning
Eiffel Tower
Eleanor
Eminence
Emma
English Holiday
English Miss
Eroica
Escapade
Ethel
Evangeline
Evensong
Eyepaint
Fairy Prince
Father's Day
Felicia
Fervid
Fiona
Fire Princess
First Love
Flora
Forever Amber
Forgotten Dreams
Fragrant Cloud
Francesca
Frenzy
Gabriella
Geraldine
Glenfiddich
Golden Promise
Golden Showers
Golden Wings
Goldilocks
Grandpa Dickson
Grandpa's Delight
Grouse
Grumpy
Gypsy Jewel
Hannah
Happy Thoughts
Heaven Scent
Heidi
Helga
Her Majesty
Highlight
Honeymoon
Hula Girl
Iceberg
Ilona
Indian Sunblaze
Intrigue
Invitation
Irish Mist
Irish Modesty
Isabel
Jaquenetta
Jet Trail
Jocelyn
Joy Bells
Just Joey
Kathleen
Katie
Kim
King's Ransom
Lafter
Laura
Lavinia
Leander
Leda
Lilli Marlene
Lindsey
Lovers Meeting
Lucetta
Maiden's Blush
Manuela
Margaret
Marlena
Martha
Mary
Mary Rose
Masquerade
Maxima
Meg
Melinda
Mercedes
Mermaid
Message
Michele
Mimi
Minnehaha
Mischief
Monique
Moon Maiden
My Valentine
Nevada
Nymphenburg
Oh La La
Oklahoma
Olive
Only You
Ophelia
Orange Sensation
Orange Sunblaze
Oriana
Orient Express
Peace
Peek A Boo
Penelope
Perdita
Piccadilly
Pink Panther
Polly
Prima Ballerina
Queenie
Rosina
Rosy Cheeks
Royal Romance
Royal Smile
Ruby Wedding
Satchmo
Saul
Scarletta
Schoolgirl
Scintillation
Shepherd's Delight
Sherry
Shona
Silver Jubilee
Silver Lining
Sleepy
Smarty
Sneezy
Soraya
Stars 'n Stripes
Stella
Summer Wine
Sun Blush
Sunset Song
Sunsilk
Super Star
Susan
Sweet Promise
Tallulah
Tatjana
Tender Night
Thelma
The Queen Elizabeth
Thisbe
Topsi
Tranquility
Twinkles
Velvet Hour
Violette
Wedding Day
Whisky Mac
Yesterday

A lady who was flattered to have a rose named after her changed her mind when she saw the description of the rose in a gardener's catalogue. Against her name it said: 'shy in a bed but very vigorous against a wall.'

Naming the day

In theory every day of the year can be identified by the name of one of the saints allocated to it by the Roman Catholic Church. Use of such saints' names, however, is not always popular. One Anglican vicar who wrote to his bishop, heading the page 'St Timothy's Day' received a terse reply on a sheet headed 'Wash Day'.

In *The Egoist* George Meredith writes:

'There's a French philosopher who's for naming the days after the birthdays of French men of letters, Voltaire-day, Rousseau-day, Racine-day, and so on.'

'We might give alternative titles to the days, or have alternating days, devoted to our great families that performed meritorious deeds upon such a day.'

'Can we furnish sufficient?'

'A poet or two would help us.'

'Perhaps a statesman.'

'A pugilist, if wanted.'

'For blowy days . . .'

Meredith was no doubt referring to Auguste Comte, 1798–1857, the founder of Positivism. As part of his 'religion of humanity' Comte proposed dedicating the birthdays of those who had furthered the progress of human beings.

It would be an interesting exercise, no doubt, to name the days of the year along the lines proposed. We might also revive for our onomastic calendar some of the day-names that have been used in the past. I give a selection below, but have dealt more fully with nearly a thousand named days in *A Dictionary of Days* (Routledge, 1988).

Admission Day The day on which American states celebrate the anniversary of their admission to the Union.

Advent Sunday The first Sunday in Advent, ie 30 November or the Sunday nearest to it.

Alamo Day 6 March. The Mexicans slaughtered the defenders of Alamo Fort, Texas, in 1836. Amongst those killed was Davy Crockett, who had gone to help the Texans.

Alexandra Rose Day 26 June. Introduced by Queen Alexandra (1844–1925) in 1912 to celebrate her fiftieth year in England. The money collected goes to hospitals.

All Fools' Day 1 April. The traditional day for playing practical jokes.

All Hallow(s) Day 1 November. *All Saints' Day.*

Allhallowmass 1 November. *All Saints' Day.* 'We had kept Allhallowmass with roasting of skewered apples . . .' R. D. Blackmore, *Lorna Doone.*

All Saints' Day 1 November. Also known as *All Hallow(s) Day, Allhallowmass, Hallowmas.*

All Soul's Day 2 November. A day of prayer for the souls of all the departed.

Annunciation *Lady Day.*

Anzac Day 25 April. A holiday in Australia and New Zealand commemorating the landing of their troops in Gallipoli during the First World War.

Apple and Candle Night A local name for *Hallow-E'en*, eg in Swansea.

April Fools' Day 1 April. *All Fools' Day.*

Arbor Day A day on which trees are planted, usually observed in April in the USA.

Armistice Day 11 November. Commemorating the signing of the armistice in 1918 to end the First World War. In Britain it is now *Remembrance Day* (also in Canada). In the US it has become *Veterans Day* and is now associated with the Vietnam War.

Ascension Day The Thursday forty days after Easter, on which Jesus ascended to heaven.

Ash Wednesday The first day of Lent. Pope Gregory the Great sprinkled ashes on the heads of penitents on this day.

Assumption 15 August. Commemorating the death of the Virgin Mary.

Australia Day 26 January or the following Monday. Formerly *Anniversary Day, Foundation Day.*

Balaclava Day In military slang, formerly a term for pay-day.

Bank Holiday In Britain the last Monday in August, formerly the first Monday in the same month.

Banian Day Sometimes *Banyan Day.* A day on which no meat is eaten. Used, for example, in Jamaica, where it often becomes Ben Jonson's Day, and by sailors. The reference is to a Hindu sect.

Bastille Day 14 July. The bastille, or prison, in Paris was stormed by revolutionaries in 1789.

Battle of Britain Day 15 September.

Beltane One of the old Scottish quarter days, occurring on *May Day* (OS).

Binding Monday The day following *Low Sunday*, from the custom whereby women bound the men with ropes and demanded a forfeit before releasing them. The day following was *Binding Tuesday* when the men bound the women.

Black Friday Applied variously to an examination day at school, the breaking up of the General Strike in 1926, and especially to 24 September 1869, when the Wall Street panic began.

Black Monday *Easter Monday.* Also the first Monday back at school after the holidays.

Blue Monday The Monday before Lent, when churches were decorated in blue. A later meaning was any Monday on which workmen preferred to drink rather than report for work.

Bonfire Night *Guy Fawkes' Day.*

Bounds Thursday *Ascension Day.* The parish bounds were traditionally traced on this day.

Boxing Day 26 December. Formerly the day on which Christmas boxes, containing money, were distributed among servants and tradesmen.

Bunker Hill Day 7 June. Also known as *Boston's Fourth of July.* Commemorating a famous battle in 1775.

Burns' Night 25 January. Scots honour their national poet, Robert Burns, 1759–96.

Bye Day An irregular and informal meet of hounds which is not mentioned on the hunt fixture card.

Cake Day 31 December. From the custom of giving children oatmeal cakes in Scotland.

Canada Day 1 July.

Candlemas Day 2 February. The feast of the purification of the Virgin Mary, celebrated with many candles in the churches.

Cantate Sunday *Rogation Sunday.* The introit for the day begins with the Latin word *Cantate*, 'sing'.

Care Sunday The fifth Sunday in Lent.

Carling Sunday *Care Sunday.* 'Carling' became the name for peas which were formerly eaten on this day.

Carnival Thursday The Thursday before *Shrove Tuesday.*

Childermas 28 December. Commemorates the slaughtering of the Holy Innocents by Herod.

Christmas Day 25 December.

Christmas Eve 24 December.

Circumcision 1 January.

Cobblers' Monday A Monday taken as a holiday. Cobblers were said to be unsure of which day to celebrate the feast of their patron saint, St Crispin. To be sure of not missing it, they celebrated it every Monday.

Collop Monday The Monday before *Shrove Tuesday*, the last day on which 'collops', or slices of meat, were eaten before Lent. Also known as *Shrove Monday.*

Columbus Day The second Monday in October, or 12 October. A US holiday commemorating the landing by Columbus in the Bahamas, 1492.

Commemoration Day At Oxford University, an annual celebration in memory of founders and benefactors.

Commonwealth Day 24 May originally, when it was known as *Empire Day.* Now second Monday in March.

Confederate Memorial Day Celebrated on different days in various southern states of the US to commemorate the war dead.

Corpus Christi The Thursday after *Trinity Sunday.* The words are the Latin for 'body of Christ.'

Cussing Day Formerly a dialectal name, eg in Somerset, for *Ash Wednesday.* Impenitent sinners were publicly cursed on this day.

Day of Atonement *Yom Kippur.*

D Day Now the day on which any planned operation is due to begin. Originally 6 June 1944, when British, American, Canadian, French and Polish soldiers landed on the beaches of Normandy during the Second World War.

Decimal Day 15 February 1971. The day on which Britain changed to decimal currency.

Decoration Day Same as *Memorial Day*, when graves are decorated with flowers.

Defenders' Day 12 September. A holiday in Maryland commemorating an unsuccessful attack on Baltimore by the British in 1812. It inspired Francis Scott Key to write the words of 'The Star-Spangled Banner'.

Derby Day The day in Summer when the famous horse race is run on Epsom Downs in England, or when one of its namesakes is run in Kentucky, Santa Anita or elsewhere. Until 1891 the English Parliament adjourned on this day.

Devil's Night The night before *Hallow-E'en.* The term is used in Michigan and elsewhere, but seems to be unknown in other parts of the US.

Dingaan's Day 16 December. A South African anniversary, now officially known as *Day of the Covenant.* It commemorates a victory in 1838 and is usually marked by sporting events.

Distaff's Day *Rock Day.*

Dog Days Days between 3 July and 11 August, formerly considered to be the hottest and unhealthiest days of the year. The name links them to the heliacal rising of the Dog Star.

Dominion Day 1 July. An earlier name of *Canada Day.*

Easter Day *Easter Sunday.* 'Easter' derives from the name of a pagan goddess whose festival was celebrated at this time of the year.

Easter Monday The Monday following *Easter Day.* A day of parades, bonnets and the distribution of Easter eggs.

Easter Sunday *Easter Day.*

Egg Saturday The Saturday before *Shrove Tuesday*, when eggs were formerly eaten. The day following was also known as *Egg Sunday.*

Ember Days Days of fasting appointed by the Council of Placentia (1095). They were the Wednesdays, Fridays and Saturdays following a) the first Sunday in Lent; b) Whitsunday; c) 14 September; d) 13 December. The four Fridays were called *Golden Fridays.*

Empire Day 24 May. This was Queen Victoria's birthday, which had been celebrated as a holiday for 60 years. After her death it became Empire Day, later *Commonwealth Day.*

Encaenia The day on which the anniversary of a church's dedication is celebrated.

Epiphany 6 January. From a Greek word basically meaning 'to show', with reference to the showing of the child Jesus to the Magi.

Fasten Tuesday A Northern English name for *Shrove Tuesday*. The Monday is also known as *Fasten's E'en*.

Fat Monday The Monday before *Shrove Tuesday*, which is known as *Mardi Gras*, 'Fat Tuesday' in e.g. New Orleans.

Father's Day UK: variable, usually early June. US: third Sunday in June.

Feast Day A saint's festival, eg that of the patron saint of a local church.

Feast of Stephen 26 December.

Field Day Originally a day when troops were reviewed. Figuratively, a day of exciting events. In the US often a sports day at a school or college.

Fireworks Day *Guy Fawkes' Day*.

First Day *Sunday* for the Society of Friends, who wished to avoid references to pagan gods or objects of worship. *Monday* became *Second Day*, and so on.

Flag Day 14 June in the US, though the date may vary in some states. In Britain a general term for a day on which flags are sold to raise money for charity (*Tag Day* in the US).

Foundation Day A former name of *Australia Day*.

Founder's Day 29 May at the Royal Hospital in Chelsea, London. Applied to any day on which the founder of an institution such as a university is commemorated.

Fourth (of July) see *Independence Day*.

Fourth of June The birthday of George III and *Speech Day* at Eton College.

Frabjous Day A wonderful day, according to Lewis Carroll, in *Through The Looking Glass*.

Furry Day 8 May. 'Furry' is probably connected with 'fair'. A Cornish festival enlivened by dancing.

Gala Day In general terms, a day of local celebration. Also the occasion for a quip by Rufus T. Firefly (Groucho Marx) in *Duck Soup* when told that it was a gala day. 'A gal a day is enough for me. I don't think I can handle any more.'

Gang Monday The Monday in Rogation Week. 'Gang' means going', and refers to processions that took place. The same week had *Gang Tuesday* and *Gang Wednesday*.

Gaudy Day A day of celebration and relaxation at Oxford and Cambridge universities.

Glorious Twelfth 12 July. The day on which Orangemen celebrate the Battle of the Boyne.

Golden Friday See *Ember Days*.

Good Friday The Friday before *Easter Day*, the anniversary of Christ's death. 'Good' is used in the sense of 'holy'.

Gooding Day 21 December. A day when alms were collected.

Gowkie Day Also *Gowkin' Day*. Scottish terms for *April Fools' Day*.

Grand Day An alternative for *Gaudy Day* in the Inns of Court.

Green Thursday *Maundy Thursday*.

Grey Cup Day Mid-November. The Canadian football final between teams from east and west.

Groundhog Day *Candlemas*. The popular US legend is that if the groundhog (woodchuck) can see his shadow on this day, there will be six further weeks of winter.

Gule of August 1 August. The 'Oxford English Dictionary' is unable to explain the origin of this ancient term.

Guy Fawkes' Day 5 November. In Britain the day on which Guy Fawkes' attempt to blow up the Houses of Parliament in 1605 is remembered with bonfires and fireworks.

Hallow-E'en 31 October. The eve of *All Hallows Day*. 'Hallow' means 'to make holy'.

Hallowmas *All Hallows Day*.

Handsel Monday The first Monday of the year, the day on which 'handsel', a gift or present which was meant to bring good luck, was given in Scotland.

Hock Monday The second Monday after Easter. Women bound the men with ropes and demanded payment to release them. 'Hock' is probably from a word meaning 'derision'.

Hock Tuesday The day following *Hock Monday*, when the men had their revenge on the women.

Hogmanay 31 December. The word is of disputed origin. Used mainly in Scotland.

Holy Cross Day 14 September.

Holy Innocents' Day *Childermas*.

Holy Rood Day *Holy Cross Day*.

Holy Thursday *Ascension Day*.

Hospital Day 12 May. Florence Nightingale's birthday. A day on which hospital rules are relaxed.

Huntigowk Day *April Fools' Day* in Scotland.

Inauguration Day 20 January following a presidential election in the US.

Independence Day 4 July. A US holiday, commemorating the adoption of the Declaration of Independence in 1776.

Ivy Day 9 October. An anniversary celebrated by some Irishmen related to the death of Charles Stuart Parnell.

Labor Day First Monday in September in the US.

Labour Day 1 May.

Lady Day 25 March. The Annunciation of the Virgin Mary. It is claimed that the British postal authorities once correctly delivered a letter addressed only to '25 March'. The recipient was a certain Lady Day, wife of a judge.

Laetare Sunday *Midlent Sunday*.

Lammas Day 1 August. Originally the 'loaf mass', at which the loaves made from the first ripe corn were consecrated.

League of Nations Day 10 January. Observed from 1920 to 1946.

Leap Day 29 February.

Lincoln's Birthday 12 February, or the first Monday in February. A public holiday in the US in honour of President Abraham Lincoln, 1809–65.

Long Friday *Good Friday*.

Love Day A day appointed for the settlement of disputes. Children born on such a day were sometimes named Loveday.

Low Sunday The Sunday following *Easter Day*.

Loyalty Day 1 May. US Veterans attempted to establish this title to combat what they saw as Communist propaganda disseminated on *May Day*.

Mad Thursday The Thursday before *Shrove Tuesday*.

M-Day A day when mobilisation is to begin. This is a military term similar to *D Day*.

Martinmas 11 November.

Maundy Thursday The Thursday before Easter. 'Maundy' is a 'mandate', or command, from the Latin version of John 13:34—'A new commandment I give you, that you love one another'. Originally princes washed the feet of poor people on this day. In Britain the king or queen distributes specially minted Maundy money.

May Day 1 May. The great rural festival of former times, now *Labour Day* in many countries.

Memorial Day The last Monday in May, or 30 May. A US holiday in memory of the war dead. Also called *Decoration Day.*

Michaelmas 29 September.

Midlent Sunday Also known as *Mothering Sunday.*

Midsummer's Day 24 June.

Mothering Sunday Originally the Sunday in the middle of Lent, now confused with *Mother's Day.*

Mother-in-Law Day 5 March. Initiated by the editor of a local newspaper in Amarillo, Texas, in 1934. It was observed by some families that year but does not seem to have caught on.

Mother's Day The second Sunday in May.

Nameday The feast day of the saint whose name one bears. Celebrated in many countries rather than the birthday.

Ne'er Day *New Year's Day*, Scottish.

Nettle Day *Oak-Apple Day.* In many parts of England children sting with nettles those who are not wearing a sprig of oak leaves.

New Year's Day 1 January.

New Year's Eve 31 December.

New Zealand Day 6 February.

Nickanan Night *Shrove Monday*, Cornish.

Nippy Lug Day Friday following Shrove Tuesday in parts of northern England. Children nip or pinch one another's ears.

No Smoking Day The custom of designating one day a year No Smoking Day appears to be taking hold in English-speaking countries.

Nut Monday The first Monday in August. A local British holiday.

Oak-Apple Day 29 May. The day on which Charles II was restored to the English throne. Oak-apples or oak leaves were worn to commemorate the incident when he hid in an oak tree to escape his pursuers (in 1651).

Open Day A day when members of the public can visit what is normally a closed institution.

Orange Day *Glorious Twelfth.*

Palm Sunday The Sunday before Easter. The palms in the church commemorate the palms strewn before Christ as he rode into Jerusalem.

Pan-American Day 14 April.

Pancake Day *Shrove Tuesday.*

Passion Sunday The fifth Sunday in Lent, the beginning of Passion Week.

Patriots' Day The third Monday in April. Celebrated in Maine and Massachusetts in commemoration of battles at Lexington and Concord in 1775.

Pentecost The seventh Sunday after Easter. 'Pentecost' is from Greek 'fiftieth (day)'.

Pinch-Bum Day *Oak-Apple Day.* A variant of the *Nettle Day* custom.

Plough Monday The first Monday after 6 January, the day on which farmers traditionally resumed their ploughing after the Christmas holiday.

President's Birthday *Washington's Birthday.*

Primrose Day 19 April. The anniversary of the death of Benjamin Disraeli, Earl of Beaconsfield. Queen Victoria sent a wreath of primroses, inscribed 'His favourite flower'.

Pulver Wednesday *Ash Wednesday.* From Latin *pulver* 'dust'.

Purification *Candlemas Day.*

Puss Sunday First Sunday in Lent. From Gaelic *pus* 'scowl'. In parts of Ireland unmarried people are thought to scowl on this day because they feel sorry for themselves. Sometimes such people are marked with chalk on their backs.

Quasimodo Sunday *Low Sunday.* The introit for the day begins *Quasi modo geniti infantes*– 'As newborn babes'.

Red Letter Day Now any day of special significance. Originally a holy day marked on a church calendar in red.

Refreshment Sunday *Midlent Sunday.*

Remembrance Day 11 November. Formerly *Armistice Day.*

Rock Day 7 January. A 'rock' was another name for the distaff, the stick on which flax was wound when spinning.

Rogation Sunday The fifth Sunday after Easter, the beginning of Rogation Week. 'Rogation' is from a Latin word meaning 'to ask'.

Rood Day *Holy Cross Day.*

Rosh Hashanah The Jewish New Year's Day.

Royal Oak Day 29 May. See *Oak-Apple Day.*

Sabbath Day Originally Saturday, now generally Sunday. Sabbath means 'rest'.

Sadie Hawkins Day 9 November, though now used of any day when the girls invite the boys to a dance. Introduced in the Li'l Abner strip cartoon in 1938 and now commonly celebrated in the US.

St Agnes' Eve 20 January. If young maidens fasted on this day they were said to dream of their future husbands. John Keats wrote his famous poem *The Eve of St Agnes* in 1819.

St Crispin's Day 25 October. The Battle of Agincourt was fought on this day in 1415, as Shakespeare reminds us in his *Henry V.*

St David's Day 1 March. Welshmen wear leeks to proclaim their nationality and honour their patron saint.

St Distaff's Day 7 January. The day on which the distaff side of the family, the women (who used distaffs for their spinning) resumed work after the Christmas holiday.

St George's Day 23 April. The feast of the patron saint of England.

St Lubbock's Day At one time a slang expression in England for a Bank Holiday. The reference was to Sir John Lubbock, whose Bank Holiday Act was passed on 25 May 1871.

St Patrick's Day 17 March. Irishmen wear the shamrock, a plant with trifoliate leaves which St Patrick used to illustrate the Trinity, and which became the national emblem of Ireland.

St Pompion's Day Also *St Pumpkin's Day, Thanksgiving Day.* 'Pompion' was an earlier form of the word 'pumpkin'. Pumpkin pie is invariably eaten on this day.

St Swithin's Day 15 July. Ancient lore says that it will rain for forty days if it rains on this day.

St Valentine's Day 14 February. The day of the 'immortal go-between', as Charles Lamb called him. The modern custom of sending Valentine cards dates from the early nineteenth century, but there were much earlier traditions which involved drawing the name of a sweetheart by lot on this day.

Salad Days Days of youthful inexperience.

Seventh Day Saturday for the Quakers, Seventh Day Adventists, etc.

Sheer Thursday *Maundy Thursday.* The 'sheer' means 'to shine', though early commentators thought that clergymen were meant to shear their hair on this day.

Shrove Tuesday The day before *Ash Wednesday*, or the beginning of Lent. The three days before Lent began are known as Shrovetide, because people were 'shriven'—they confessed their sins and were absolved.

Simnel Sunday *Mothering Sunday.* Simnel cakes were traditionally eaten on this day.

Speech Day A day when prizes are distributed at a school or college after speeches by dignitaries.

Sports Day Another day in the school calendar, normally near the end of the summer term, set aside for sporting events.

Spring Holiday An official British description of the holiday taken on 1 May or the first Monday following.

Spy Wednesday The Wednesday before Easter, the reference being to Judas. An Irish expression.

Still Days Between Maundy Thursday and Easter Day, when bells were not rung.

Tag Day The US term for *Flag Day* in Britain.

Thanksgiving Day The fourth Thursday in November (USA) or second Monday in October (Canada). A holiday on which thanks are given for divine goodness.

Thanksgobble Day *Thanksgiving Day.* A humorous American reference to the turkeys consumed at Thanksgiving.

Three Kings' Day *Epiphany.*

Today Day 'This very day' in Jamaica.

Trafalgar Day 21 October. Commemorating Lord Nelson and the Battle of Trafalgar, 1805.

Trick or Treat Night *Hallow-E'en.*

Trinity Sunday The Sunday following *Whit Sunday.*

Turkey Day *Thanksgiving Day.* Not an official term, but much used by radio/tv commentators.

Twelfth See *Glorious Twelfth.* The reference is sometimes to 12 October, the opening of the grouse-shooting season.

Twelfth Night 6 January. Formerly the day on which the pastrycooks excelled themselves with their fancy cakes, displaying them in their shop windows. Gentlemen who gathered to look at the displays were likely to have their coat-tails nailed to the shop-front, a traditional sport for boys on this day.

Tynwald Day 5 July. A day of celebration on the Isle of Man.

Union Day 31 May. Celebrated in South Africa.

Up Helly A' The last day of Yule, or *Twelfth Night.* Celebrated in the Shetlands.

Valentine's Day *St Valentine's Day.*

VE Day 8 May 1945. The day on which the Allies accepted Germany's surrender in the Second World War.

Veterans Day *Remembrance Day.*

Victoria Day *Empire Day.*

VJ Day 15 August 1945 (US 2 September). The day on which the Japanese surrendered to the Allies, bringing to an end the Second World War.

Waterloo Day 18 June. Commemorating the Battle of Waterloo in 1815.

Washington's Birthday The third Monday in February, or 22 February. A US holiday in honour of President George Washington, 1732–99.

Whit Monday The seventh Monday after Easter. 'Whit' is 'white'.

Whit Sunday The seventh Sunday after Easter.

Wrong Day Usually mid-July. A time of celebration in the town of Wright, Minnesota.

Xmas Day *Christmas Day.* The 'X' represents the Greek letter *chi.*

Yom Kippur The Hebrew 'day of atonement' observed on the tenth day of Tishri.

Days which are special for one reason or another continue to be named. A few recent examples are listed below:

Big Bang Day 27 October 1986. This was a day of significant change at the London Stock Exchange, marking amongst other things the end of fixed commissions on stock exchange transactions. The financial centres often name particular days. **Contango Day,** which probably corrupts **Continuation Day,** is an established term in London.

Comic Relief Day 5 February 1988. Less formally known as **Red Nose Day.** This was a day of fund raising for charities where light entertainers donated their services on radio and television, while people in pubs and clubs throughout Britain told jokes in order to raise money. Plastic red noses were also sold and were worn at many a fund-raising event.

Super Tuesday 9 March 1988. The day on which primary elections took place in fourteen Southern and border states, as well as in six other states, in the run up to the election of the new American president. It was originally an attempt to give the 'South' a coherent say in national politics.

A selection of names turned words

Amp the usual form of *ampère*, from the name of André Ampère, 1775–1836, a French scientist.

Aphrodisiac from the name of the goddess of love, Aphrodite.

Atlas In Greek mythology Atlas was made to support the heavens on his shoulders. A 16th-century map-book showed him supporting the globe on its cover, and caused his name to be transferred.

Bakelite Synthetic resin invented by Leo Hendrik Baekland, 1863–1944, a Flemish chemist.

Begonia in honour of Michel Bégon, 1638–1710, a Frenchman known for his patronage of science.

Bloomers associated with Mrs Amelia Bloomer, 1818–1914, who wrote and lectured on women's rights.

Bobby Robert Peel, 1778–1850, was Home Secretary when the Metropolitan Police Act was passed in 1828.

Bowdlerise from the name of Dr Thomas Bowdler, 1754–1825, who edited (some would say vandalised) Shakespeare so that the poet could 'with propriety be read aloud in a family'.

Boycott The Irish Land League treated Charles Boycott in this way in 1880.

Braille the system of raised-point writing for the blind was invented by Louis Braille, 1809–52, himself blind from the age of three.

Caesarian Julius Caesar is usually said to have been born by means of what we now call a 'caesarian operation'. His name derived from a word meaning 'cut'.

Cardigan from the name of James Thomas Brudenell, 1797–1868, the seventh earl of Cardigan, who led the famous charge of the Light Brigade at Balaclava in 1854.

Casanova Giovanni Jacopo Casanova de Seingalt, 1725–98, an Italian adventurer was the original philanderer.

Cereal from Ceres, an Italian goddess of agriculture.

Chauvinistic Nicolas Chauvin of Rochefort was exaggeratedly loyal to Napoleon's France.

Collie probably from Colin, a popular first name in Scotland where these dogs originated.

Colt a pistol patented by Samuel Colt in 1835.

Cretin a Swiss dialect form of Christian, and therefore derived from Christ.

Dahlia Anders Dahl was a Swedish botanist in the 18th century. The flower was discovered in Mexico by Humboldt and named in Dahl's honour.

Dandy a form of Andrew.

Diddle Jeremy Diddler is a character in *Raising the Wind* (1803) by James Kenney. He is a cheat and swindler.

Diesel After its inventor Rudolf Diesel, 1858–1913, a German.

Eroticism from Eros, name of the Greek god of love.

Fuchsia for Leonhard Fuchs, 1501–66, a German botanist.

Gardenia for Dr Alexander Garden, Vice-President of the Royal Society, who died in 1791.

Guillotine invented by Joseph Guillotin, 1738–1814, a French doctor. His surname ultimately derives from Guillaume 'William'.

Guy from Guy Fawkes, whose first name appears in many European languages and may derive from 'wood, forest'.

Hooligan probably derived from an Irish family who lived in Southwark, London, actually named Houlihan.

Jacket from French jaquette, 'peasant's coat'. Peasants were often addressed as Jacques, the popular form of Jacob, regardless of their true names.

Jemmy pet form of James.

Jockey from Jock, Northern form of Jack.

Jovial based on the name of the god Jove.

Lynch either from Lynch's law, after Charles Lynch, 1736–96, who presided over unofficial courts in Virginia, or from Lynch's Creek in South Carolina where groups of unofficial law-enforcers gathered.

Mackintosh patented in 1823 by Charles Mackintosh ('son of the chieftain').

Magpie the 'mag' is ultimately from Margaret and was added to the name of the bird.

Marionette a little Marian or puppet, ultimately from Maria.

Maverick Samuel Maverick neglected to brand his cattle. A maverick became a 'rover or stray', applied metaphorically to people as well as cattle.

Mesmerise Franz Anton Mesmer, 1734–1815, an Austrian physician, pioneered this early form of hypnotism, based on a false theory of animal magnetism.

Nicotine Jacques Nicot took some tobacco plants back to France in 1561. Nicot ultimately derives from Nicholas.

Ohm for Georg Simon Ohm, 1787–1854, a German physicist.

Pasteurise a method of sterilising milk, discovered by Louis Pasteur, 1822–95.

Platonic from the name of the Greek philosopher, Plato.

Saxophone invented by a Belgian named Adolphe Sax, about 1840.

Silhouette originally a portrait rapidly traced on a wall, following a person's shadow. Satirically applied to Etienne de Silhouette, French Minister of Finance in 1759.

Teddy bear alluding to Theodore (Teddy) Roosevelt, 1859–1919, a great bear-hunter in his spare time.

Trilby ultimately from the name of George du Maurier's fictional heroine Trilby in the novel of that name.

Volt from the name of the Italian physicist Count Alessandro Volta, 1745–1827.

Wellingtons named in 1817 after the Duke of Wellington.

Yankee probably from Jan (John) Kes, referring to the original Dutch inhabitants of New York.

Number Names

If we say that there are seven days in a week we are using the number seven and are concerned with quantity. If we decide to identify the days in the week by calling them One, Two, Three, Four, Five, Six and Seven, then each of these becomes a number name.

Number names are a kind of free-floating set of names that can be used in any of the thousand and one nomenclatures that need to be established temporarily or permanently. There is a strong prejudice against using them for anything that has human connections, and some people feel insulted if they are identified in this way. Yet number names are probably the most efficient we have, with many advantages over other kinds of name. For instance:

a number name positively identifies a unique entity—natural duplication and transfer do not arise within a given nomenclature;

number names have a highly convenient shorthand form which is recognised internationally;

they are usefully descriptive, often, in the sequential information they give about what is being named;

they follow a regular, simple pattern of formation which is readily understood.

The computer that calculates my pay knows me as 1199062, and I am quite happy to acknowledge this particular pseudonym—or 'numbernym,' as I should perhaps call it. That is not to say that I would like to be identified, on the cover of this book, for instance, as 1199062. For all its imperfections, the name that I bear because of parental whim and historical accident seems more appropriate, but that is only due to social convention. Noël Coward indicated the way things could go. When Lawrence of Arabia became an airman, Coward wrote him a letter which began 'Dear 338171, or may I call you 338 . . .'.

The full advantages of number names can be demonstrated by substitution. It is a convention that we identify the pages of a book by number names. When a different kind of name is substituted, we realise what we have lost. This page I have called George, in honour of my father, but if I were to name every page in honour of relations and friends, much as that might please them, where would it leave my readers? Imagine being asked to refer to page Ethel or Nicole. Alphabetical order would help, but that would still be clumsy compared to numerical sequence.

This example is meant to seem absurd, but the fact is that in an average town we tolerate a system of street names that is even more ridiculous. A few street names give vague help in locating the streets concerned, as when all the streets named after poets or admirals are grouped on the same estate, but one might argue that this is only a help to a minority of well-educated people. We could probably change all that and devise number name systems that would effectively relate streets to each other in any given town, but we will not do it, of course. Nor are we likely to interfere with the charmingly haphazard situation that exists with our first names and surnames, our place names and trade names. We will allow simple efficiency to reign only in unimportant nomenclatures, such as the pages of a book. Number names will no doubt continue to be the norm in that context, but remember that you did once read a page named George.

Invented names

Journalists have long been in the habit of amusing themselves and their readers by inventing personal names. Sometimes the jokes are visual, as in a name like *C. A. Boose*. Initials are popular, leading to names like *M. T. Head*. Social and professional titles may help the name along: *Miss Fitt, Miss Print, Miss Trust: Sir Parr Stitt, Sir Tenly Knotte, Sir Vere de Pression, Sir Taxe*. We read of the clergyman who is a *Canon Ball*, the soldier who is a *Private Part*, and so on. Even academic letters after a name have been brought into the fold, to create a *Reverend Fiddle D.D.*

The names listed below are mostly phonetic puns and make use of first names that have not been invented for the occasion. Most of the examples are the inventions of writers, a few have been borne by real people whose parents were determined to display their sense of humour at all cost.

Aaron C. Rescue
Adam Swindler
Agnes Day
Al E. Gater
Alf A. Bett
Amanda Lynn
Amelia Rate
Ames Hyer
Anita Room
Ann Cuff
Annie Seed
April N. Paris
Arty Fischel
Barry D. Hatchett
Bea Holden
Bell E. Acres
Ben Dover
Bennie Factor
Bess Toff
Beverly Hills
Bill A. Dew
Bing O. Winner
Blaise A. Weigh
Bonnie Scotland
Bunny Warren
Caesar High
Candy Kane
Carole Singer
Celia Later
Cherry Blossom
Chester Minit
Chris Cross
Claud N. Scratcht
Cliff Hanger
Constance Noring
Coral Ireland
Crystal Ball
Dan D. Lion
Dawn O'Day
Delia Cards
Diane Decay
Dick Tate
Dinah Mite
Don Key
Doris Shutt
Doug Pitts
Douglas Firr
Drew A. Head
Duane Pipe
Dustin Downe
Earl E. Bird
Eileen Dover
Ella Vater
Emma Nate
Erna Living
Ernest N. Devour
Esther Bunny
Etta Carrott
Eva Brick
Evan Keel
Faye Sake
Felix Cited
Ford Carr
Frank N. Stein
Freda Slaves
Gail Blows
Gay Cavalier
Gerry Atrick
Gladys Canby
Gilda Lily
Gloria Mundy
Gottfried Atlast
Gustave Wind
Haile Delighted
Hank E. Panky
Hans Zoffer
Hazel Twigg
Hedda Hare
Heidi High
Helen Hywater
Herbie Hind
Hiram Young
Holly Wood
Honey Potts
Honor Bright
Hope N. Prey
Horace Cope
Hugh Raye
Ida Down
Igor Beaver
Ima Hogg
Iona Mink
Iris Tugh
Isabel Tolling
Isla White
Ivor Headache
Jack Pott
Jay Walker
Jean Jerale
Jerry Bilder
Jim Nasium
Joan Novak
Joe King
Joy Rider
Jules N. Gold
Justin Thyme
Kay Oss
Ken Tuckie
Kirsten Swore
Kitty Hawk
Laura Norder
Lee Vitoff
Leighton Early
Levy Tate
Libby Doe
Lionel Rohr
Lisa Wake
Lois Price
Lori Driver
Lorne Mowers
Lotta People
Louis Dorr
Luke Warm
Lynn C. Doyle
Marius Quick
Mark Well
Martin Gale
Mary Christmas
Maud Lynne
Max E. Mumm
May B. Dunn
Mel N. Colley
Melody Lingerson
Mercy Lord
Mike Howe
Miles A. Head
Minnie Buss
Moira Less
Molly Coddle
Mona Lott
Moses Law
Mustapha Fixe
Nat E. Dresser
Neil N. Prey
Nick O. Teen
Noah Zark
Nora Bone
Olive Green
Oliver D. Place
Ophelia Legge
Orson Buggy
Owen Moore
Paddy Fields
Pat Ernal
Patty Cake
Paul Bearer
Pearl E. Handle
Penny Nichols
Persis Fuller
Peter Owt
Phil Landers
Piers Inside
Polly C. Holder
Poppy Cox
Reg Oyce
Rex Cars
Rhoda Camel
Rick O'Shea
Robyn Banks
Rose Dew
Rosetta Stone
Rosie Bottom
Ruby Port
Russ Tinayle
Sally Forth
Salome Downe
Sandy Beech
Sara Endipity
Sarah Nader
Scarlett Feaver
Sean Locks
Serge A. Head
Shirley U. Care
Sonny Enbright
Stan Dupp
Sue E. Seidl
Tanya Hyde
Teddy Bear
Titus Zell
Tom Katz
Tommy Gunn
Topsy Turvey
Troy Waite
Tudor Pyne
Upton O. Goode
Valentine Card
Victoria Falls
Wade Moore
Walter Loo
Wanda Toofar
Warren Peace
Will Power
Willie Nilly
Yul B. Allwright

Converted names

The names listed below have all been officially bestowed as first names. One or two of them may be accidental mis-spellings; others may be transferred family names. Most are clearly *ad hoc* conversions from words to first name status.

Admiral
Alias
Almond
Alpha
Amorous
Anchor
Angel
Anon
Apple
Aria
Ark
Arrow
Autumn
Baby
Berry
Beta
Blossom
Blue
Bold
Bonus
Boy
Brained
Bridge
Briton
Buster
Butter
Captain
Charisma
Colonel
Coma
Corky
Corona
Coy
Crocus
Danke
Dark
Despair
Diamond
Doctor
Dolphin
Duke
Dusty
Ebony
Elder
Elderberry
Elm
Emit
Energetic
Esquire
Evangelist
Fairly
Farewell
Fateful
Feather
Fiancé
Free
Freedom
Friar
Friend
Gem
General
Gentle
Gipsy
Gladness
Glory
Golden
Halcyon
Handy
Happy
Helm
Heron
Home
Hymen
Ivory
Jade
Jeans
Jewel
Joie
Jolly
Junior
Just
Kaiser
Khaki
Laddie
Lady
Last
Lavender
Liberty
Lilac
Little
Lord
Lovey
Low
Lucky
Ma
Magnet
Major
Maudlin
Mayday
Medium
Meek
Memory
Midsummer
Mimosa
Mine
Mister
Murder
Mystic
Nova
Oak
Ocean
Omega
Only
Orange
Other
Owner
Peace
Pepper
Pheasants
Pickles
Pinkie
Pleasant
President
Princess
Quaver
Queen
Rabbi
Rainbow
Rainy
Ramble
Raper
Raven
Rice
Rosebud
Saffron
Sapphire
Savannah
Senior
Sergeant
Sham
Shared
Shed
Silver
Silvery
Sir
Slim
Smart
Snowdrop
Sonny
Squire
Star
Stranger
Sunny
Sunshine
Swift
Syren
Tempest
Thistle
Thorn
Treasure
True
Vale
Vest
Virgin
Worthy

Miss Pleasant Riderhood is a character in *Our Mutual Friend*, by Charles Dickens.

'Possessed of what is colloquially termed a swivel eye—she was otherwise not positively ill-looking, though anxious, meagre, of a muddy complexion, and looking twice as old again as she really was'.

'Why christened Pleasant, the late Mrs Riderhood might possibly have been able at some time to explain, and possibly not. Her daughter had no information on that point. Pleasant she found herself, and she couldn't help it. She had not been consulted on the question.'

2 First names first

"Call me Anne
it sounds so much better
than Ann"
GREEN GABLES

It seems to be a universal habit, and one as old as language itself, for human beings to name one another. The regular pattern today among the English-speaking peoples is for a child to be given at least two names at birth, a *first name* and a *middle name*. Of these the first name is normally by far the more important, and not just because it is the descendant of the original single personal name with which our remote ancestors were content. It is our first name that most of us will respond to throughout our lives and come to look upon as part of ourselves. It is therefore natural for us to ask such questions as:

where did our first names come from?
what did they originally mean?
which names do we make most use of today?
why do parents choose one name rather than another?
how should we ourselves choose a name for a child if we are given that responsibility?

What is a first name?

We shall be attempting to answer all the above questions in the next three chapters, but the apparently simple question: 'What is a name?' becomes surprisingly complicated when we come to the **Catherine/Katharine** kind of problem. Are we to treat such spelling variants as one name, or should we separate out each variant and refer to it as a new name? There is also the matter of diminutives. As everyone knows, names like **Margaret** have given rise to pet forms such as **Madge, Peggy, Greta, Maisie** and the like. Should all these be considered as separate names?

As we begin to answer such questions we see the widely differing viewpoints of the historically-based names student and the student who is more interested in the sociological and psychological aspects of names. For the etymologist Catherine and Katharine were originally the same name, as were Margaret and all its diminutive forms. Since he is concerned with origins, the etymologist takes all forms of a name in his stride provided he can explain why they occur.

But from another point of view the change of a single letter in a name is quite enough to differentiate it from all others. No one would convince a **Francis** that his name was the same as **Frances,** although an etymologist would be justified in bracketing them together. My own etymological training is instantly forgotten when someone writes my name as **Lesley** rather than **Leslie.** I do not easily forgive those who change my sex with careless orthographic surgery. The change from **Stephen,** say, to **Steven** may appear to inflict less damage, but no doubt those who bear one form of the name object to being given the other.

In cases such as **Tracy/Tracey** I find it hard to believe that parents are thinking of two names and carefully choosing between them. In my view they are choosing *a* name which happens to have genuinely variant spellings. I believe, therefore, that a modern researcher must fall back on his instinct as a native speaker and weigh up the relative importance of etymological, phonetic and orthographic factors. He must then decide in each case whether he is dealing with one or more names.

I once heard a father tell a registrar what name he wanted to give his daughter. He then surprised both the registrar and me by writing the name down as **Evon.** But it was the father who was surprised, not to say incredulous, when the registrar pointed out that the name was usually spelt **Yvonne.** He insisted on spelling it his way. All of us were thinking, it seems to me, of the same name, which is why I would personally bracket these two widely differing spellings as one name. I would also treat **Laurence** and **Lawrence** as one, though I admit that when another registrar recorded my son's name in the latter form my instinctive reaction was to tell her that she had written down the wrong name.

A single first name, then, like some words, can occasionally have more than one 'official' spelling: perhaps because it started out in one language and eventually came to English-speakers both in its original form and in that of another language; perhaps because two or more forms of it were fossilised at a time when spelling was by no means standardised; perhaps because it is a new name that has not yet settled into one spelling; perhaps because some parents think that a different spelling will add a touch of novelty; perhaps because of a parent's or registrar's ignorance. In the following chapters I shall be grouping names by their main spellings, indicating variations only when opinion seems to be genuinely divided.

As for diminutives, it is clear that they eventually reach a point where they achieve full name status in their own right. If a girl is given the name **Elizabeth,** but her family and friends subsequently come to call her **Betty,** we could describe Betty as a link nickname.

But since the end of the 18th century, many pet names have been officially bestowed as if they were separate names. In some cases the names really have taken on a life of their own. It is no longer true to say that **Sally,** for example, is simply the pet form of **Sarah,** though that is how the name came into being. **Betty** is also frequently given as a name and must therefore be treated separately on those occasions.

Jacqueline has been a popular name in recent times, but many parents find it difficult to spell. Below are some of the ways in which it has been officially recorded on birth certificates. Should each spelling be treated as a separate name, or is it right to say that all the forms are variants of the same name?

Jacalyn, Jackalin, Jackaline, Jaclyn, Jaclynn, Jacolyn, Jacqualine, Jacqualyn, Jacqualynn, Jacquelean, Jacquelene, Jacquelin, Jacqueline, Jacquelyn, Jacquelyne, Jacquelynn, Jacquiline, Jacquline, Jacqulynn, Jaculine, Jakelyn, Jaqueline, Jaquelline.

Origins of first names

Sally and **Betty** represent developments of older names, but how did the older names come into being in the first place? We can usefully establish several different categories: the names began either as descriptions, or converted phrases, or they were inventions. They were formed by linking in some way to an existing name, or they were transferred from another naming system.

Let us look at each of those categories in turn and consider some examples:

DESCRIPTIVE NAMES include generic descriptions such as **Charles,** 'a man', **Thomas,** 'a twin', and direct descriptions such as **Adam,** 'of red complexion', **Algernon,** 'with whiskers or moustaches', **Crispin,** 'with curled hair', **Cecil,** 'blind'. Activity descriptions occur, such as **George,** 'a farmer', as do provenance descriptions: **Francis,** 'Frenchman'.

Sequential description led to names like **Septimus,** 'seventh', and **Decimus,** 'tenth'. **Original** and **Una** probably came into being as descriptions of first children, and **Natalie** and **Noël** were certainly temporal descriptions for children born or baptised on Christmas Day. Many names may have been either morally descriptive—**Agnes,** 'pure', **Agatha,** 'good'—or were commendatory conversions.

CONVERTED NAMES include those which seem to have reflected parental reaction to the birth. **Abigail,** 'father rejoiced', is an instance, as are **Benedict,** 'blessed', **Amy,** 'loved'. Commendatory conversions such as **Felicity** and **Prudence** merge with what were almost certainly descriptive names applied first as personal names to adults and subsequently transferred to children. Many Germanic names appear to be of this type, but **Cuthbert,** 'famous bright', **Robert,** 'fame bright', **Bernard,** 'stern bear' and the like may often have originated as blends, making use of standard name elements.

INVENTED NAMES have often been introduced by writers. They include **Fiona, Lorna, Mavis, Miranda, Pamela, Thelma, Vanessa, Wendy.**

LINK NAMES were frequently formed with **Yahweh** as an element, as in **John, Joan, Joseph** and many others. **God** occurs in names like

'If you call me Anne, please call me Anne spelled with an "e".'
'What difference does it make how it's spelled?' asked Manilla.
'Oh, it makes so much difference. It looks so much nicer. When you hear a name pronounced, can't you always see it in your mind, just as if it was printed out? I can; and A-n-n looks dreadful, but A-n-n-e looks so much more distinguished.'

L. M. Montgomery *Anne of Green Gables*

Elizabeth, 'oath of God'. Other names could be the basis, as with **Malcolm,** 'a disciple or servant of St **Columba'.**

Diminutive link names, of the Sally/Betty kind, later became a common source of new names, as did feminine links. These are names like **Louise, Roberta, Henrietta,** etc., from **Louis, Robert** and **Henry.**

TRANSFERRED NAMES have often been surnames which were themselves transferred place names. Examples are **Clifford, Graham, Keith, Leslie, Percy.** River names that have ultimately become first names by a long process of transfer include **Douglas, Alma** and more recently, **Brent.**

By an interesting twist, 'middle name' has come to mean something for which a person is well-known. 'Like fishing?' says a character in *Main Street,* by Sinclair Lewis. 'Fishing is my middle name', is the reply.

Middle names

Before looking at the more common first names in detail we must also say something about middle names. Firstly, it is statistically normal these days for children throughout the English-speaking world to be given one first name and one middle name. Two or more middle names are more usual than no middle name. While there is legally no upper limit on the number of middle names that may be given, most parents draw the line after four.

It has been the convention until very recently to give boys a 'safe', traditional first name and to be slightly more daring with the middle name, but to do the reverse with the girls. In the past many parents, having allowed their romantic fancy to run riot with their daughter's first name, felt that they must be more sober with the middle name. 'If she doesn't like X,' they would say, mentioning some exotic invention that they happened to have come across, 'she can always use her middle name.' There are signs that boys are now being treated in a similar way.

It is difficult to say how many people do in fact drop their first names and make daily use of their middle names as the result of a conscious decision. This involves a dramatic change, unlike the situation in which others find themselves, where the official first name—often the same as the father's or mother's name—has *never* been used in speech. Such middle names carried out the function of first names from the beginning. Perhaps one person in eight has a middle name which *is* used, for whatever reason. For other people, particularly those with common surnames, they mostly help to identify individuals more precisely on official forms. From an American point of view they also provide the essential middle initial.

Two American correspondents whose parents were thoughtless enough, as they humorously put it, not to provide them with middle names have commented to me in the past about the difficulties thus created. J. Bryan III (who at least has an interesting personal-name modifier) reports that his fellow countrymen absolutely insist on giving him a middle initial, and almost any seems to do. Mike Martin became M. Martin NMI ('No Middle Initial') when he joined the Army, and to avoid this disgrace he later legally adopted the middle initial **W.** The 'W' was, like the **S** in Harry S Truman, a letter name rather than an initial, not standing for any particular name. Mike was happy with his 'W' until his driving-licence arrived with his name written Michael **W (only)** Martin.

In some areas, such as Scotland, it is a custom for the wife's maiden name to become the child's middle name. The surnames of noble families in particular have long been used as first or middle names, so the precedent is there. Camden, writing in 1605, remarked that many were worried about what was then a new trend, thinking it would cause great confusion if surnames mixed with first names, but we managed to absorb names like **Sidney, Howard, Neville** and **Percy** without difficulty. More recent transfers from surname to middle- or first-name status include **Scott, Cameron, Grant** and **Campbell**—the Scottish influence being very noticeable. Such names often begin with very restricted use, used as middle names only where there is a family connection. After a probationary period as middle names they are promoted to first names. General recognition follows when they are used as first names by those who have no family reason for doing so.

It is always important to distinguish between first names and middle names. Historically it was first names, as individual personal names, which came first, to be followed in the Middle Ages by surnames, a large number of which were themselves derived from first names. Middle names, occupying a highly ambiguous area between the two more important nomenclatures and borrowing heavily from both of them, have been with us from the seventeenth century only. In terms of their social and psychological importance they are also totally overshadowed by the names that surround them. Middle names constitute what is almost a separate nomenclature, useful for minor purposes such as pacifying relations who want their names to live on, or perhaps genuinely acting as tokens of respect to namesakes. First names have the vibrancy which comes from daily use: middle names, and perhaps rightly so, are more like family heirlooms, necessary to preserve if only in the attic. The metaphor may be apt in another way. We have spoken of the middle-name arena as a proving ground for new names, but it is used to put old names out to pasture. **John, George, Henry, Mary, Elizabeth, Frances, Ann(e)** and **Margaret** currently appear to fall into that category. Ann(e), especially, is now used ten times as a middle name for every one use as a first name.

Perhaps you don't know what school-children are like. They're little devils. It's enough for them to know that your middle name, if you have one, is odd—I am called Jock Maconochie Campbell—and they give you no peace at all.

L. P. Hartley *The Love Adept*

The central stock of first names

Having established our definitions of 'first name' and 'middle name', we may now turn to the question of how many first names there are in what might be called 'the central stock'. There is nothing to stop parents in the English-speaking countries giving *any* name to a child as its first name, but in practice the vast majority of parents make very great use in any one year of a relatively small number of names. In 1900, for example, the **Smiths** in England and Wales made really significant use of only 120 boys' names and 160 girls' names. In 1980 they made equally significant use—and by this we mean nine families out of ten made use—of 125 boys' names and 175 girls' names. In the case of the boys, about thirty 'new' names, such as **Barry, Craig** and **Darren,** had appeared by 1980, but twenty-five others had been left aside. The latter included names like **Edmund, Herbert, Horace** and **Percy.** Similarly, girls' names such as **Deborah, Janice, Joanne** and **Karen** were among the seventy or so 'new' names being used. The fifty-five names that had fallen by the wayside included **Annie, Winifred, Nellie** and **May.**

There is evidence of this central stock of names on all sides. In a supplement to the Registrar-General's Report for Scotland, 1958, the first names given to 52 882 boys and 50 204 girls that year were fully analysed. Every *spelling* of a name was counted as a separate name, whereas I would certainly have bracketed such pairs as **Ian/Iain, Brian/Bryan, Alastair/Alistair, Ann/Anne, Lynn/Lynne, Carol/Carole, Teresa/Theresa.** Even with each of these counted as a separate name, the hundred most frequently used boys' names accounted for 49 674 occurrences, or 94 per cent of the total. The top hundred girls' names accounted for 41 552 occurrences—83 per cent of the total.

This intensive use of a relatively small number of names in any given year is revealed by every survey based on *white* families. Black American families and the West Indians in Britain have different ideas about naming their children. They value individuality far more, and use a much greater range of names. A small percentage of them do follow white naming practices, and use the same names that are fashionable with white families. Another group may make use of what almost constitutes a central stock of names used exclusively by black Americans and West Indians.

But the basic point is that black parents in general are more prepared than white parents to invent new names, to draw them from a wider variety of sources and restore old names to use, all in an effort to ensure that their children do not meet others who bear the same name.

At the end of this chapter I have included a mini-dictionary of first names, identifying the names which I think make up the central stock at the moment and giving their origins. I have tried also to identify the names which are especially popular with black families and comment on their sources. In both cases, the names which form the central stock today are not those which would have formed it a generation ago. Fashions in first names are always changing, and in the next chapter we shall go on to look at those changes in detail.

Name usage

There are fashions in name usage just as there are fashions in names. At the moment, first names are used very readily at every level of society between people who scarcely know one another. This has been the case now for at least fifty years, but as every reader of Victorian novels is aware, the situation in the 19th century was quite different. The 'lower orders', as they were then called, used first names amongst themselves, but polite society had a strict code of conduct which made them almost superfluous. Gentlemen addressed one another as Sir, before progressing to Mr with the last name. Later, if they were of equal rank, they might move on to using the surname on its own. Wives often addressed their husbands as Mr Jones, or whatever, and received the compliment of Mrs Jones in return.

It was young lovers of the time who attached great importance to the use of their first names. 'I would have leaped into the valley of the shadow of death, only to hear her call me John,' says a young man in *Lorna Doone*. To be allowed to call the young lady by her first name was also a great privilege.

The change towards less formal name usage began in America, and possibly reflected Quaker ideas of equality. By the 1930s the situation was also changing in Britain. C. Northcote Parkinson suggested in an article some years ago that the Duke of Windsor may have been influential in making first name usage acceptable at the highest levels of British society, having been influenced himself by American ways.

Name usage these days is generally simple, though particular relationships can still cause problems. Many people worry about what they should call their mother-in-law, for example. They feel that Mother or one of its variants is unsuitable, while Mrs followed by the surname is too formal. Use of the first name may also not feel right.

This can also be the case in a different kind of relationship. D. H. Lawrence interestingly remarks at one point that Lady Chatterley and her lover Oliver Mellors never use each other's first names.

Scottish lairds are traditionally addressed by the names of their properties, a fact which James Boswell stressed in his *Journal of a Tour to the Hebrides*. He commented on the problem of a laird who should correctly have been addressed as **Muck.** As Boswell says, this 'would have sounded ill, so he was called **Isle of Muck,** which went off with great readiness'.

The **Fred** Society was founded in 1983 by Fred Daniel. Members, who include those whose first or middle name is Fred and women who are **Winifred** and **Frederica**, receive a newsletter, the *Fred Connection*. They can also purchase Fred Society T-shirts, bumper stickers, coffee mugs and 'Freddy bears'.

Over 3000 Freds have joined forces in order to combat the 'caveman-nerd' image that the name invokes. The society, said an Associated Press report in 1987, 'tries to fend off images fostered by television's Fred Flintstone cartoons and advertisements depicting Freds as bumbling clerks and fast-talking salesmen'. The latest insult is the use of a term by cyclists in California. The people who crowd the bike lanes and get in the way of serious cyclists are now known as 'freds'.

Interested Freds should contact Fred Daniel, who is based in Palm Desert, California.

Name calling

Most of us are addressed in a variety of ways during a normal day. Friends will probably use our first names, or pet forms of those names, but they may also use personal name modifiers. Instead of: '*John*, how nice to see you!' someone says: '*My dear John*, how nice to see you!' They may also use a personal name substitute, otherwise known as a term of address, or a vocative: '*My dear*, how nice to see you!' Strangers, unaware of our names, are particularly apt to make use of these name substitutes. The shop assistant uses *Sir* or *Madam*, the motorist who has just had to take avoiding action because we stepped into the road in front of him uses *You stupid idiot*!

The variety of terms can be illustrated by reference to a character in *Anglo-Saxon Attitudes*, a novel by Angus Wilson. The central character of the book is Gerald Middleton, Professor Emeritus of Early Medieval History. Other characters, in the course of the novel, address him as follows:

family members—*Daddy, Father, my dear Father*
intimate friends—*darling, little Middleton, old dear, old thing*
friends—*dear, duckie, Gerald, Gerald dear, Gerald my dear, Middleton, my dear, my dear boy, my dear fellow, my dear friend, my dear Gerald, my dear Middleton, my dear Mr Middleton*
students and colleagues—*Professor, Professor Middleton, Sir*
an acquaintance—*Mr Middleton*
an angry friend—*you damned traitor*

Note how a term of address that begins with *my* is likely to be friendly, whereas one that begins with *you* is normally unfriendly. *Old* is also a friendly word: *old man* or *old lady* is affectionate where *young man* or *young lady* is probably reproving.

Friend, used as a term of address, is not necessarily friendly, any more than *pal* in an utterance such as: 'What's it got to do with you, *pal*?' The face value of any term can be reversed by the tone in which it is said.

As an experiment, try recording the different terms of address that others use when speaking to you. You might also note how many terms you use when addressing others, according to their status, age, sex, etc. Above all it is your attitude to the person you are speaking to which will decide what kind of name, name modifier or name substitute you use. (For a more detailed survey of this subject, see my *Dictionary of Terms of Address*, Routledge 1989.)

Mrs. Millamant: And d'ye hear, I won't be called names after I'm marry'd; positively I won't be called names.
Mirabell: Names!
Mrs. Millamant: Ay, as *wife, spouse, my dear, joy, jewel, love, sweetheart*, and the rest of that nauseous cant, in which men and their wives are so fulsomely familiar . . .
William Congreve *The Way of the World*

The central stock of boys' names

The following names for boys appear to be those mainly being used by English-speaking parents in the late 1980s. Brief indications are given as to the source, language of origin and original meaning of each name, but many explanations can only be offered tentatively.

Aaron biblical; Hebrew or Egyptian; origin unknown.
Adam bibical; Hebrew; 'red skin (or earth').
Adrian papal; Latin; 'of the Adriatic'.
Alan Norman; Celtic, origin unknown.
Albert Germanic; Old English/German; 'noble bright'.
Alexander historical; Greek; 'defending men'. **Alec/Alex** occur.
Alistair (most popular modern spelling) Translated; Gaelic form of *Alexander*.
Andrew biblical; Greek; 'manly'.
Anthony saint; Latin; origin unknown. **Antony** earlier and historically more correct.
Ashley surname/place name; Old English; 'ash wood or clearing'.
Austin saint; Latin *augustus*, 'venerable, consecrated'.
Barnaby biblical; Hebrew; 'son of encouragement'. Also as **Barnabas.**
Barry descriptive (?); Gaelic; based on 'spear'.
Benedict saint; Latin; 'blessed'.
Benjamin biblical; Hebrew; 'son of the south', ie 'the right hand'.
Bernard Germanic; Old English/German; 'brave as a bear'.
Bradley surname/place name; Old English; 'broad clearing'.
Brandon surname/place name; 'hill on which broom grows'.
Brendan saint; Gaelic; origin uncertain.
Brent surname/place name/river name; 'holy river' or 'high place'.
Bret(t) surname; Old French; 'a Briton'.
Brian historical; Celtic; origin uncertain. Also **Bryan.**
Cameron surname; Gaelic; 'crooked nose'.
Carl anglicised *Karl*, German form of *Charles*.
Chad saint; Gaelic; of uncertain meaning.
Charles historical; Germanic; 'a man'.
Christian commendatory; Latin; 'Christian'.
Christopher saint; Greek; 'bearing Christ'.
Clifford surname/place name; Old English; 'ford by a slope'.
Clive surname (historical); Old English; 'dweller by the cliff'.
Colin diminutive; Latin *columba* ('dove') or from *Nicholas*.
Conrad saint; Old German; 'bold counsel'.
Craig surname; Middle English; 'dweller by the crag'.
Dale surname; Old English; 'dweller in the dale'.
Damian saint; Greek; based on 'to tame'. Also **Damien.**
Daniel biblical; Hebrew; 'God is judge'.
Darren surname (?); origin uncertain.
David saint; Hebrew; 'beloved'.
Dean surname; Old English; 'dweller in a valley'. Also Latin; 'son of the dean'.
Denis, Dennis saint; Greek; 'of Dionysos,' (god of wine).
Derek Germanic; Old German; 'ruler of the people'.
Desmond surname; Gaelic; 'man from south Munster'.
Dominic(k) saint; Latin; 'of the Lord'.
Donald Celtic; Gaelic; 'world mighty'.
Douglas surname; Gaelic; 'dark blue' (originally a river name).
Duane, Dwayne surname; Irish; of uncertain meaning.
Duncan surname; Gaelic; 'brown warrior'.
Edward royal saint; Old English; 'happy guardian'.
Edwin royal; Old English; 'happy friend'.
Eric, Erik Danish; Old Norse; based on 'ruler'.
Eugene saint/Papal; Greek; 'noble, well-born'.
Francis saint; Latin; 'a Frenchman'. **Frank,** the diminutive is as popular.
Frederick Germanic; Old German; 'peaceful ruler'.
Gareth literary; Welsh form of **Gerontius**; 'old man'.
Gary diminutive; from *Gareth* or *Gerard*.
Gavin literary; Celtic or Germanic; probably from **Gawain.**
Geoffrey Norman; Old German; based on 'peace'.
George saint; Greek; 'farmer'.
Gerald Norman; Old German; 'spear rule'.
Gerard Norman; Old German; 'firm spear'.
Giles saint; Greek; 'young goat'.
Glen(n) surname; Gaelic; 'dweller in the valley'. **Glyn(n)** probably derives from this name.
Gordon surname (historical); Gaelic; 'great hill'.
Graham, Graeme surname; Old English; origin disputed.
Grant surname; Old French; 'great'.
Gregory saint; Greek; based on 'to be watchful'.
Guy Norman; Old German; origin uncertain.
Harvey surname; Old French; 'battle worthy'.
Henry royal; Germanic; 'home ruler'.
Howard surname; Old German, 'heart brave', also 'high warden', also 'ewe-herder'.
Hugh historical; Germanic; 'heart, mind'.
Ian translated; Gaelic form of *John*.
Ivan translated; Russian form of *John*.
Jack pet form of *John*, influenced by French **Jacques** (*Jacob*).
James saint; Latin; form of **Jacob** 'let God protect' (Arabic).
Jamie diminutive; Scottish form of *James* and **Jimmy.**
Jared, Jarrod Hebrew; 'rose'.
Jason biblical; Greek; form of **Jesus** or **Joshua** 'Yah is generous' or 'Yah protects'.
Jeffrey see *Geoffrey*.

Jeremy, Jerry biblical; Hebrew form of **Jeremiah**, 'Yah raises up'.
Jesse biblical; Hebrew; 'man of Yah'?
Joel biblical; Hebrew; 'Yah is God'.
John biblical; Hebrew; 'Yah has favoured'.
Jonathan biblical; Hebrew; 'Yah has given'.
Joseph biblical; Hebrew; 'may God add (other children)'.
Joshua biblical; Hebrew; see *Jason*. **Jeshua** and **Jesus** are other forms of this name.
Julian saint; Latin; form of **Julius**, possibly 'downy (beard)'.
Justin saint; Latin; 'just'.
Kane surname; Gaelic; 'warrior'.
Karl German form of *Charles*.
Keith surname; Celtic; 'wood'.
Kenneth saint; Royal; Gaelic; usually taken to be 'handsome'.
Kevin saint; see *Kenneth*.
Kieran saint; Irish; 'little dark one'.
Kirk surname; Norse; 'dweller near a church'.
Kristopher modern form of *Christopher*.
Kurt pet name from *Conrad;* Germanic; 'bold counsel'.
Lance Germanic; 'land'.
Laurence, Lawrence saint; Latin; 'of Laurentum'.
Lee surname; Old English; 'dweller by the wood or clearing'.
Leighton surname/place name; Old English; 'place where leeks were grown' or 'bright hill'.
Leonard saint; Germanic; 'lion bold'.
Leslie surname/place name; Gaelic; possibly 'garden or court of hollies'.
Lewis royal; Germanic; 'famous fighter'.
Liam pet form of *William* in Ireland.
Lloyd Welsh 'grey'.
Louis see *Lewis*.
Luke biblical; Greek; 'of Lucania'.
Malcolm saint; Gaelic; 'servant or disciple of St Columba'.
Marcus Roman; Latin form of *Mark*. **Marc** is also becoming popular.
Mark biblical; Latin; possibly connected with Mars.
Martin, Martyn saint; Latin; 'of Mars'.
Matthew biblical; Hebrew; 'gift of Yah'.
Michael biblical; Hebrew; 'who is like the Lord'?
Nathan biblical; Hebrew; 'gift'.
Nathaniel biblical; Hebrew; 'God has given'.
Neil, Neal Irish; Gaelic; 'champion'.
Nicholas saint; Greek; 'victory of the people'.
Nigel Latinised form of *Neil*.
Noël descriptive; French; for a child born on 'Christmas Day'.
Norman Germanic; Old English/ German; 'northman'.
Oliver Norman; Old French; 'olive tree', but numerous other possibilities.
Owen literary; Welsh; taken to be from Latin **Eugenius,** 'well-born'.
Patrick saint; Latin; 'a nobleman'.
Paul biblical; Latin; 'small'.
Perry pet form of **Peregrine,** Latin 'wanderer, stranger'.
Peter biblical; Greek (translation of Aramaic); 'stone'.
Philip, Phillip biblical; Greek; 'lover of horses'.
Ralph historical; Old Norse; 'counsel wolf'.
Randal(l) historical; Old English; 'shield wolf'. **Randy** occurs.
Raymond Norman; Old German; 'wise protection'.
Reginald historical; Old English; 'powerful might'.
Reuben biblical; Hebrew; 'He has seen my misery'.
Richard Norman; Old German/ English; 'stern ruler'. **Rickie** is also used.
Robert Norman; Old English/German; 'bright fame'.
Robin diminutive of *Robert*.
Roderick Old Germanic; 'fame rule'.
Rodney surname; Old English; 'Hroda's island'.
Roger Norman; Old English/German; 'fame-spear'.
Ronald Scottish form of *Reginald;* Old English; 'powerful might'.
Rory Gaelic; 'red'.
Ross surname; Gaelic; 'dweller at the promontory'.
Roy descriptive; Gaelic; 'red'.
Rupert royal; Old German form of *Robert*.
Russell surname; Old French, 'red'.
Ryan surname; Irish; 'red'.
Samuel biblical; Hebrew; 'name of God'.
Scott surname; Old English; 'a Scot'.
Sebastian saint; Latin; 'man from the city of Sebastia'. The city name meant 'venerable'.
Shane from **Sean**; Irish form of *John*.
Shaun, Shawn translated; Irish forms of *Sean=John*.
Simon biblical; Hebrew variant of **Simeon,** 'Yah has heard', but in Greek Simon is 'snub-nosed'.
Spencer surname; Old French; 'dispenser of provisions'.
Stanley surname/place name; Old English; 'stone field'.
Stephen biblical; Greek; 'crown'. Also as **Steven.**
Stuart surname; Old English; 'steward'. Also as **Stewart.**
Terence Roman; Latin; origin unknown. Frequently in form **Terry.**
Theodore saint; Greek; 'God's gift'.
Thomas biblical; Aramaic; 'twin'.
Timothy biblical; Greek; 'honoured by God'.
Toby biblical; Hebrew; form of **Tobias,** 'Yah is good'.
Todd surname; English; 'fox'.
Tony diminutive of *Anthony*.
Travis surname; Middle English; 'a toll-collector'.
Trevor surname; Welsh; 'big village'.
Troy surname/place name; Old French; from 'Troyes'.
Vernon surname; Old French; 'alder tree'.
Victor saint; Latin; 'conqueror'.
Vincent saint; Latin; 'conquering'.
Walter historical; Germanic; 'rule folk'.
Warren surname; Old French; from 'La Varenne'.
Wayne surname; Old English; 'wagon-maker'.
Wesley surname; English; 'west field' or 'field with a well'.
William Norman; Old German; 'will helmet'. Also **Willie.**
Zachary biblical; Hebrew, 'Yah has remembered'.

Boys' names used by black American families

The names listed below have all been especially well used by black American families in recent years.

Alonzo pet form of **Alphonso;** royal; Germanic; 'noble + ready'.
Alvin surname; Germanic; 'noble friend'.
André French form of *Andrew;* Greek; 'manly'.
Antoine French form of *Anthony* or *Antony*; Latin; of unknown origin.
Arnold historical; Old German; 'eagle power'.
Bennie pet form of *Benjamin* or *Benedict*.
Bryant surname; 'descendant of *Brian* or *Bryan*'.
Byron surname; 'worker in a cowshed'.
Calvin surname; Latin/French; 'the bald one'.
Carlos Spanish form of *Charles*, 'man'.
Carlton surname/place name; 'settlement of free men'.
Cedric apparently a literary invention (Sir Walter Scott) of unknown meaning.
Clinton surname/place name; English; 'settlement on a hill'.
Corey surname; Irish; possibly connected with *Godfrey*, 'god peace'.
Cornelius Latin; 'horn'.
Cornell surname; 'man from Cornwall' or 'one who lived on a hill where corn was grown'. Several other origins are possible.
Curtis surname; French; 'courteous, well-educated'.
Damon a personal name which occurs in classical Greek literature, later used to denote a typical young lover. Known for his faithfulness to his friend Phintias.
Darius name of a Persian king, but of unknown meaning.
Darnell surname/place name; 'hidden nook'.
Darrell surname, indicating a man who came from a village in France called Airel.
Demetrius Greek; 'of Demeter, the Earth mother'.
Deon also **Dion.** Probably pet forms of *Dionysos* (*Denis*), name of the god of wine.
Derrick a modern spelling of *Derek*, 'ruler of the people'.
Deshawn apparently a new name based on *Shawn*, ie *John*.
Dion see *Deon*.
Dorian Greek; 'from the Dorian region', possibly indicating a Spartan. A male form of the name *Doris*.
Earl English; 'nobleman'.
Ernest Germanic; 'earnestness, vigour'.
Floyd surname; a variant of *Lloyd*.
Herman Old German; 'army man'.
Isaac biblical; Hebrew; 'God may laugh'.
Jamal Arabic; 'handsome'.
Jermaine possibly from a surname meaning 'German'.
Kelvin possibly a variant of *Calvin*.
Lamar probably from the surname, but the American writer Ashton Lamar was really Harry Sayler. The actress Barbara La Marr was born Reatha Watson, and Hedy Lamarr was formerly Hedwig Kiesler. There is a real French surname Lamare, indicating someone who lived near a pond.
Lamont surname, form of **Lamond;** Norse; 'lawyer'.
Leon Latin; 'lion'.
Marcus a Roman name connected with Mars, the god of war.
Marlon possibly from a French surname, ultimately meaning a 'blackbird', from a nickname given to one who liked to sing.
Marvin surname; from a Welsh name of unknown meaning.
Maurice saint; Latin; 'a Moor'.
Melvin surname; a form of Melville, a Norman place name.
Milton surname; English; 'settlement near a mill'.
Myron the name of a famous Greek sculptor
Omar Arabic; 'most high', or 'first son', or 'follower of the Prophet'.
Quentin saint; Latin; 'fifth'.
Roosevelt surname; Dutch; 'rose field'.
Terrance a variant of *Terence*.
Tommie a diminutive of *Thomas*, 'twin'.
Tyrone from an Irish place name, 'Eoghan's land'.
Winston surname/place name; English; 'Wine's village'.

Some Irish first names for boys

Aidan Gaelic 'fire'.
Cathal Irish 'battle mighty'.
Ciarán Irish 'black'.
Colm Irish 'dove'.
Connor Irish 'high desire'.
Cormac Irish 'charioteer'.
Cornelius Latin 'horn', a Roman clan name.
Declan an Irish saint's name of unknown meaning.
Dermot Irish 'envy free'.
Diarmuid same as *Dermot*.
Donal Gaelic 'world mighty'.
Eamonn Irish form of *Edmond*, Old English 'rich protector'.
Enda Irish 'bird'.
Eoghan Irish form of *Eugene*, Greek 'well born'.
Eoin Irish form of *John*.
Fergal Irish 'man of strength'.
Flannan Irish 'of ruddy complexion'.
Garrett Irish form of *Gerard*, Germanic 'firm spear'.
Niall Irish form of *Neil*.
Padraig Irish form of *Patrick*, Latin 'nobleman'.
Ronan Irish 'little seal'.
Seamus Irish form of *James*, itself a Latin form of Hebrew *Jacob* 'heel'.
Sean an Irish form of *John*.

Some Scottish first names for boys

Adair Scottish form of *Edgar*, Old English 'prosperity-spear'.
Alasdair a Scottish form of *Alexander*, Greek 'defending men'.
Alpin Gaelic 'white'.
Angus Gaelic 'unique choice'.
Arran Scottish place name.
Athol Scottish place name and family name.
Aulay Gaelic form of *Olave*, Old Norse 'forefather, ancestor'.
Blair Scottish place name and family name.
Broderick probably 'brother'.
Bruce Scottish family name, from Norman place name.
Calum Gaelic form of *Columba*, Latin 'dove' or pet form of *Malcolm*.
Campbell Scottish clan and family name 'crooked mouth'.
Clyde Scottish river name.
Cosmo Greek 'order'.
Crawford Scottish place name and family name 'ford where crows gather'.
Denholm Scottish place name and family name.
Diarmid Gaelic 'envy free'.
Drummond Scottish family name.
Dugald Scottish form of Irish *Dougal* 'black stranger'.
Erskine Scottish place name and family name 'green ascent'.
Ewan Form of Greek *Eugene* 'well born'.
Farquhar Gaelic 'very dear one'.
Fergus Gaelic 'supreme choice'.
Finlay Scottish family name 'fair hero'.
Forbes Scottish place name and family name 'field, district'.
Fraser Scottish family name from French place name.
Gilchrist Gaelic 'servant of Christ'.
Hamish phonetic form of *Seumas*, Gaelic form of *James*.
Keir Gaelic 'swarthy'.
Lachlan Gaelic 'fjord-land'.
Ludovic Latin form of German *Ludwig* 'famous in battle'.
Magnus Latin 'great'.
Maxwell Scottish place name and family name.
Mungo Gaelic 'amiable'.
Murdoch Gaelic 'mariner, sea warrior'.
Murray Scottish place name and family name 'from Moray'.
Ramsay Place name and family name.
Rowan Gaelic 'red'.
Torquil Old Norse name of unknown meaning.
Wallace Scottish family name 'Celt, Welshman'.

Some Welsh first names for boys

Aled Welsh river name.
Alun Welsh form of *Alan*, a Celtic name of unknown origin.
Arwel an ancient Welsh name of unknown meaning.
Arwyn Welsh 'muse'.
Awen a variant of *Arwyn*.
Bleddyn Welsh 'wolf'.
Bryn Welsh 'hill, mound'.
Brynmor Welsh 'great hill'.
Carwyn Welsh 'blessed love'.
Cemlyn Welsh place name 'bent lake'.
Ceri Welsh 'love'.
Cledwyn Welsh river name.
Dafydd Welsh form of *David*, Hebrew 'friend'.
Deinol Welsh 'attractive, charming'.
Dewi Welsh form of *David*, Hebrew 'friend'.
Dyfan Welsh 'ruler of a tribe'.
Dylan name of a Welsh sea god, perhaps 'son of the waves'.
Edryd Welsh 'restoration'.
Eifion Welsh place name.
Eilir Welsh 'butterfly'.
Elfed Welsh 'autumn'.
Elgan Welsh 'bright circle'.
Elis Welsh form of *Elias*, Hebrew *Elijah* 'my god is Jehovah'.
Elwyn Welsh 'white brow'.
Emrys Welsh form of *Ambrose*, Greek 'immortal'.
Emyr Welsh form of *Honorius* 'honour'.
Eryl Welsh 'watcher'.
Eurig Welsh 'gold'.
Euros variant of *Eurig*.
Geraint Welsh form of Latin name meaning 'old'.
Gerlad Welsh name of unknown meaning.
Gerwyn Welsh name of unknown meaning.
Gethin Welsh 'dusky'.
Glyndwr Welsh family name.
Gruffydd Welsh 'powerful chief'.
Gwilym Welsh form of *William* Germanic 'will-helmet'.
Gwyn Welsh 'fair, blessed'.
Gwynfor Welsh 'fair lord'.
Hefin Welsh 'summery'.
Huw Welsh form of *Hugh*, Germanic 'mind'.
Iestyn Welsh form of Latin *Justin* 'just'.
Ieuan Welsh form of *John*.
Ifan variant of *Ieuan*.
Iolo Welsh 'lord value'.
Iwan variant of *Ieuan*.
Llyr form of *Lear*, name of an ancient sea god.
Melfyn Welsh 'from Carmarthen'.
Morgan Welsh 'great and bright'.
Owain Welsh form of Greek *Eugene* 'well born'.
Rhodri Welsh 'circle-ruler'.
Rhys Welsh 'ardour'.
Wyn Welsh 'white, pure'.

Some biblical first names for boys

Unless otherwise stated these names are of Hebrew origin.

Abel 'vapour, smoke, ie vanity' or Accadian 'son'.
Abiel 'my Father is God'.
Abner 'the Father is the lamp'.
Abraham 'the Father loves'.
Absalom 'my Father is peace'.
Adlai 'my ornament'.
Ahab 'brother of the Father'.
Alvah 'height'.
Amon 'faithful'.
Amos 'strong'.
Ariel 'lion of God' or 'hearth of God'.
Asa 'myrtle' or 'healer'.
Asher 'what happiness!'.
Azariah 'Yah has helped'.
Azaziah 'Yah shows himself to be strong'.
Azel 'noble'.
Balaam Greek form of a Hebrew name probably meaning 'glutton'.
Barabbas 'son of the Father'.
Barak 'lightning flash'.
Bartholomew Aramaic 'son of Tolmai'.
Baruch 'blessed'.
Barzillai 'of iron'.
Becher 'young camel'.
Bela 'swallowed up'.
Boaz 'in him is strength'.
Cain 'blacksmith', though in Genesis explained as 'I have acquired'.
Caleb 'dog'.
Cephas 'rock'. (Aramaic).
Cyrus 'shepherd'.
Darius Greek 'one who upholds the good'.
Dodo 'His beloved'.
Ebenezer 'stone of help'.
Elhanan 'God shows favour'.
Eli 'Yah is raised up'.
Eliakim 'God sets upright'.
Eliezer 'my God is help'.
Elijah 'my God is Yah'.
Elisha 'God has helped'.
Elkanah 'God has created'.
Elnathan 'God has given'.
Enoch 'inauguration, dedication'.
Enos 'man'.
Ephraim 'fertile'.
Er 'vigilant'.
Erastus Greek 'lovable'.
Esau 'shaggy, hairy'.
Ethan 'constant, permanent'.
Ezekiel 'may God make strong'.
Ezer 'help'.
Ezra 'God is helper'.
Gabriel 'man of God' or 'God is strong'.
Gad 'fortune, luck'.
Gershom 'an alien there'.
Gideon 'swordfish', or 'cutter'.
Goliath 'mighty warrior'.
Haggai 'born on a festival day'.
Ham of unknown meaning.
Hanan 'Yah has shown favour'.
Hananiah 'Yah has shown favour'. *Ananias* is another form of this name.
Heman 'faithful'.
Herod Greek 'noble'.
Hezekiah 'my strength is Yah'.
Hiram 'my brother is on high'.
Hod 'majesty'.
Hodiah 'Yah is majesty'.
Ichabod 'where is the glory?'.
Immanuel 'with us is God'.
Ira 'ass'.
Ishmael 'God hears'.
Jabal 'lead, guide'.
Japheth 'may he extend'.
Jared 'servant'.
Jedaiah 'Yah knows'.
Jehudi 'Jewish'. This name is sometimes written *Yehudi*.
Jeroboam 'may the people increase'.
Jethro 'superabundance'.
Joab 'Yah is Father'.
Job of disputed origin.
Jonah 'dove'.
Josiah 'Yah supports'.
Judah 'praised'. Also found as *Judas, Jude*.
Kish 'gift'.
Korah 'baldness'.
Laban 'the white'.
Lazarus 'God has given help'.
Lemuel 'who belongs to God'.
Levi 'united to'.
Malachi 'my messenger'.
Malchiah 'my king is Yah'.
Malluch 'king'.
Manasseh 'to forget'.
Melech 'king'.
Mesha 'God saves'.
Micah 'who is like Yah?'.
Mordecai 'of *Marduk*' (name of a Babylonian god).
Moses traditionally explained as 'drawn from the water'.
Moza 'issue, source'.
Nabal 'brute, fool'.
Nahor 'snorer'.
Nahum 'consoled'.
Naphtali 'I have fought'.
Nebuchadnezzar '*Nabu*, protect the son!' (Nabu was a god of writing and wisdom).
Nehemiah 'Yah consoles'.
Noah 'rest, console'.
Obadiah 'servant of Yah'.
Obed 'servant'.
Oren 'laurel'.
Pedaiah 'Yah ransoms, delivers'.
Ram 'height'.
Raphael 'God has healed'.
Rosh 'head'.
Rufus Latin 'red'.
Samson 'sun'.
Saul 'asked for'.
Seraiah 'Yah struggles'.
Seth 'God has raised up'.
Shelah 'request'.
Shelemiah 'Yah has completed'.
Shem 'name, renown'.
Shemaiah 'Yah has heard'.
Shephatiah 'Yah has judged'.
Solomon 'the peaceful'.
Tob 'good'.
Tobias 'Yah is good'.
Uri 'my light'.
Uriah 'Yah is my light'.
Uriel 'God is my light'.
Uzziah 'Yah is my strength'.
Uzziel 'God is my strength'.
Zabad 'He has given a gift'.
Zabdiel 'gift of God'.
Zadok 'justice'.
Zebadiah 'gift of Yah'.
Zebedee Greek form of *Zebadiah*.
Zechariah 'Yah remembers'.
Zedekiah 'Yah is my justice'.
Zephaniah 'Yah protects'.
Zuriel 'God is my rock'.

The central stock of girls' names

Abigail biblical; Hebrew; 'father rejoiced'.
Adèle Norman; Germanic; 'noble'.
Aimée modern; French; 'loved'.
Alexandra royal; Greek; feminine form of *Alexander*, 'defending men'.
Alexis saint; Greek; 'defender'. Formerly a male name.
Alice literary; Old German; 'nobility'. A contraction of *Adalheidis* = **Adelaide.**
Alicia Latin form of *Alice*.
Alison, Allison literary; French; diminutive of *Alice*.
Amanda literary; Latin; 'lovable'.
Amber literary; Arabic; used in sense 'precious thing'.
Amelia historical; Germanic; of unknown origin.
Amy historical; Old French; 'loved'.
Andrea feminine form of *Andrew*, 'manly'.
Angela saint; Greek; 'messenger'.
Anika Slavonic diminutive of *Ann*.
Anita Spanish diminutive of *Ann*.
Ann biblical; Hebrew; form of *Hannah*, 'God has favoured me'. French form **Anne,** Latin **Anna.**
Annabel, Annabelle possibly a re-formation of Latin **Amabel,** 'lovable'.
Annemarie this blended name is also found as *Ann-Marie, Annmarie, Anne-Marie*, etc.
Annette French diminutive of *Anne*.
April the name of the month, also used in its French form **Avril.**
Audrey historical; Old English; 'noble strength'. A contraction of Etheldreda.
Autumn the name of the season. Usage still confined to USA.
Barbara saint; Greek; 'foreign'.
Becky diminutive of *Rebecca*.
Belinda literary; Old German; origin uncertain.
Beth pet form of *Elizabeth, Bethany*, etc.
Bethany biblical; Aramaic; 'house of poverty'. A place name in the Bible.
Beverley, Beverly modern; probably borrowed from Beverly Hills, in California. Originally 'beaver meadow'.
Bianca Italian; 'white'. Now replacing French **Blanche,** Latin **Candida.**
Bonnie literary; connected with French *bonne*, 'good'. Used to mean 'looking well, healthy, cheerful'.
Brenda historical; Old Norse; 'sword'.
Bridget saint; Celtic; 'the high one'.
Brook(e) a modern use of the word as a name. Perhaps from a surname. Also used for boys.
Bryony the name of the flower, perhaps used to link with *Brian/Bryan*.
Camilla literary; Etruscan; origin uncertain.
Candace, Candice biblical; Royal title in Ethiopia but meaning uncertain.
Cara Italian; 'dear one'.
Carissa a diminutive of *Cara*.
Carla feminine form of *Carl*.
Carly a variant of *Carla*. **Carley** and **Carlie** occur.
Carol(e) feminine form of *Charles*.
Caroline royal; Latin adjective formed on *Charles*, giving **Carolina.** Caroline is then the French form.
Carolyn(n) a modern variant of *Caroline*.
Carrie diminutive of *Caroline, Carol*, etc.
Cassandra literary; Greek; 'defending men'.
Catherine saint; Greek; 'pure'. This is the French form of *Katharine*.
Ceri from Welsh *caru* 'to love'.
Chantal saint; the French saint was Jeanne de Chantal, the name ultimately meaning 'stony place'. **Chantel, Chantelle,** etc, are found in English-speaking countries (not in France).
Charlene modern feminine form of *Charles*. Also **Charleen, Charline,** etc.
Charlotte royal; French feminine form of *Charles*.
Charmaine apparently from a 1920s song. Perhaps a form of **Charmian,** Greek: 'joy', though this is pronounced Karmian. Charmaine looks French but is not used in France.
Chérie the French word for 'darling' used as a name.
Cherry the name of the fruit or a form of *Chérie*. Formerly a pet form of **Charity.**
Cheryl a modern diminutive of *Cherry*.
Chloë biblical; Greek; 'a young green shoot'.
Christa diminutive of *Christine*.
Christina Old English; 'christian'. **Christine** is the French form.
Christy diminutive of *Christina, Christine*.
Cindy diminutive of *Lucinda, Cinderella, Cynthia*, etc.
Claire saint; Latin; 'bright, clear'. Claire is the French form, **Clare** the Latin form (properly **Clara**). **Clair** occurs, though this is masculine in French.
Colleen the Irish word for 'girl' used as a name.
Colette diminutive of *Nicolette*, from feminine form of *Nicholas*. **Collette** occurs in English-speaking countries.
Coral Greek; used in the sense 'precious substance'.
Corinne French diminutive of Greek *cora* 'maiden'.
Courtney a use of the surname, which derives from the French place name.
Crystal originally a Scottish diminutive of *Christopher*, then a surname. Perhaps also a 'jewel' name.
Cynthia Greek mythology; goddess of the moon.
Danielle French feminine form of *Daniel*.
Dawn the word used as a name.
Deanna modern variant of *Diana*.
Debbie pet form of *Deborah*.
Deborah biblical; Hebrew; 'a bee'. **Debra** now occurs.
Denise French feminine form of *Denis*.
Desirée French; 'desired'.
Diana mythological; name of the moon goddess. **Diane** is the French form. **Dianne** now occurs.
Donna Italian; 'lady'.
Dorothy Greek; 'gift of God'. Originally the elements of the name

were in reverse order, giving **Theodora.**

Elaine literary; French form of *Helen.*

Eleanor royal; another form of *Helen.* **Elinor** is found.

Elena Italian/Spanish form of *Helen.*

Elizabeth biblical; Hebrew; 'oath or fullness of God'. **Elisabeth** occurs.

Ellen English form of *Helen.*

Emily historical; Latin; the name of a noble Roman family of uncertain meaning. **Emilie** is found.

Emma royal; Old German; 'whole, universal'.

Erica Latin; scientific name for 'heather'. Used as a feminine form of *Eric.* **Erika** is common.

Erin poetic name for Ireland used as a first name.

Estelle literary; probably connected with Latin *stella* 'star'.

Esther biblical; Persian; 'star' or 'myrtle'.

Eve biblical; Hebrew; 'lively, living'.

Evelyn historical; Old German; of uncertain meaning.

Fay perhaps a use of the obsolete word meaning 'faith' as a name. Fay is also a form of *fey*, 'fairy'. **Faye** occurs.

Felicity Latin; 'happiness'.

Fiona literary; Gaelic; 'fair, white'.

Frances feminine form of *Francis*, 'Frenchman'. **Francesca,** the Italian form, is now popular.

Gail a pet form of *Abigail.* **Gayle** is now found.

Gaynor historical; a form of *Guinevere.*

Gemma Italian; 'gem'. **Jemma** is now frequent.

Georgina feminine form of *George.*

Geraldine feminine form of *Gerald.*

Gillian English form of *Juliana*, feminine of *Julian.*

Gina a pet form of *Georgina.*

Hannah biblical; Hebrew; 'God has favoured me'.

Harriet feminine form of *Harry* or *Henry.*

Hayley from a surname/place name, possibly meaning 'high clearing'.

Hazel the botanical name used as a first name.

Heather from the plant name.

Heidi a Germanic pet form of *Adelheid*, or *Adelaide.* See *Alice.*

Helen saint; Greek; 'the bright one'. **Helena** is frequent.

Hilary saint; Latin; 'cheerful'. **Hillary** occurs.

Holly the plant name used as a first name. **Hollie** is a modern variant.

Hope the word used as a name.

Ingrid old Norse; the name of a god Ingvi and a word of uncertain meaning.

Isabel Spanish form of *Elizabeth.* **Isabelle, Isabella, Isobel,** etc, are also used.

Jacqueline French feminine form of *Jacques*, or *Jacob.*

Jaime Spanish form of *James*, now used with **Jamie** (also male until recent times) as a girl's name.

Jane Feminine form of *John.* **Jayne** occurs. **Janet, Janice** and **Janine** are diminutives of Jane.

Jeanette diminutive of *Jean*, itself a form of *John.* **Jeannette** is found.

Jemma see *Gemma.*

Jennifer a Cornish form of *Guinevere*, which may have meant 'white-cheeked'. The pet forms **Jennie** and **Jenny** are popular as independent names.

Jessica biblical; Hebrew; 'God beholds'.

Jill pet form of **Jillian,** a variant of *Gillian.*

Joanna, Joanne feminine forms of *John.*

Jocelyn Old German, of uncertain meaning.

Jodi(e), Jody modern pet forms of *Judith* or *Judy.*

Josephine feminine form of *Joseph.*

Joy the word used as a name.

Joyce saint; Celtic; origin uncertain. Formerly a male name.

Judith Hebrew; 'a Jewess'. **Judy,** the pet form is found as an independent name.

Julia, Julie feminine forms of *Julian* 'downy beard'. **Juliet** is the diminutive.

Justine French feminine form of *Justin*, 'just'.

Karen Danish form of *Katharine.* **Karin** is the Swedish form. **Karina** is now found.

Karla feminine form of *Karl.*

Kate pet form of *Katharine, Katherine* used independently.

Katharine, Katherine saint; Greek; 'pure'. *Catherine* is the French form. The pet forms **Katie** and **Katy** occur often as names in their own right.

Kathleen Originally an Irish form of *Katharine.*

Kathryn a modern form of *Katharine.*

Katrina a modern variant of *Kathrina*, itself a short form of Germanic *Katharina*, or *Katharine.*

Kay(e) originally a pet form of names beginning with 'K'.

Keeley from an Irish surname, one meaning of which is 'graceful'. **Keelie** and **Keely** are also used.

Kelly from the Irish surname. The meaning 'strife' has been suggested. **Kellie** and **Kelli** are now found.

Kerry apparently a use of the Irish place name. In some instances a phonetic variant of *Carrie.* **Kerrie, Kerri, Keri** are found.

Kimberley a surname/place name used as a first name. The association of Kimberley in South Africa with diamonds may have influenced usage. **Kim,** the diminutive, occurs frequently as a name in its own right.

Kirsty Scottish pet form of *Christine.*

Kylie a native Australian word for a 'throwing stick'.

Lara Slavonic form of *Laura.*

Laura feminine form of *Laurence*, 'person from the town of Laurentium'. **Lauren** is a diminutive.

Leah biblical; Hebrew; 'cow', a symbol of domestic virtue. **Lea** occurs.

Leanne possibly a blend of *Leigh* and *Anne.* Possibly a variant of *Lianne*, which appears to be a pet form of names such as *Julianne*, Italian *Giuliana.*

Leigh a place name element meaning 'meadow'. Also a surname. This form also used for boys, though *Lee* is more commonly the male name.

Lena pet form of names like *Helena.*

Lesley feminine form (in Britain) of *Leslie.*

Lianne see *Leanne.*

Linda pet form of names like *Belinda.* **Lynda** is found.

Lindsay, Lindsey an English or Norman place name, then a surname and clan name in Scotland. Formerly used as a boy's first name, now mainly a girl's name. Much confusion as to its spelling. Forms include **Linsay, Linsey, Lyndsay, Lyndsey,**

Lynsay, Lynsey.

Lisa pet form of *Elizabeth.* **Liza** is also used.

Lori apparently a modern variant of *Laura.*

Lorna literary; from the title of the Marquesses of Lorne.

Lorraine apparently from Jeanne de Lorraine, another name for St Joan of Arc, or from Mary, Queen of Scots who was also Mary of Lorraine. In either case the origin is the French place name.

Louisa, Louise feminine forms of *Louis.*

Lucy saint; Latin; of uncertain origin.

Lynne diminutive of Linda. **Lyn** and **Lynn** occur.

Lynette literary; possibly a variant of linnet, the song-bird.

Madeleine biblical; Hebrew; 'woman of Magdala'. **Madeline** is found.

Mandy pet form of *Miranda, Amanda.*

Marcia regarded as a feminine form of *Mark* or *Marc.*

Margaret saint; Greek; 'pearl'. **Marguerite** occurs.

Maria, Marie Spanish/Italian and French forms of *Mary.*

Marianne a modern blend of *Maria* and *Anne.*

Martha biblical; Aramaic; feminine of *mar* 'lord'.

Martina, Martine feminine forms of *Martin.*

Mary biblical; Hebrew; 'lady or seeress'. **Miriam** is another form of the name.

Maureen an Irish diminutive of *Mary.*

Maxine a shortening of *Maximilian,* converted to female use.

Megan Welsh diminutive from *Margaret.* **Meghan** is found.

Melanie saint; Greek; 'black'.

Melissa literary; Greek; 'a bee'.

Melody the word used as a name.

Meredith Welsh; originally a male name. Based on a word meaning 'greatness'.

Michaela feminine form of *Michael.*

Michelle, Michele French feminine forms of *Michael* (*Michel*).

Monica saint; of unknown origin.

Nadine a diminutive of **Nadia,** Russian 'hope'.

Nancy originally a pet form of *Ann(e).*

Naomi biblical; Hebrew; 'pleasant one'.

Natalie saint; Latin; 'Christmas Day'.

Natasha Russian pet form of *Natalie.*

Nicola Italian (male) form of *Nicholas* used (in Britain only) as a girl's name. In the US the French feminine **Nicole** is usual. Pet forms such as **Nicky, Nikki** are used independently.

Nina Russian diminutive of *Ann(e).*

Olivia saint; Latin; 'olive'.

Pamela literary; Greek; 'all sweetness'.

Patricia feminine form of *Patrick.*

Paula Latin; feminine form of *Paul.* **Pauline** is a variant.

Penelope literary; Greek; of uncertain origin. The pet form **Penny** occurs independently.

Philippa feminine form of *Philip.*

Rachael, Rachel biblical; Hebrew; 'ewe'.

Rebecca biblical; Hebrew; see *Leah.*

Regina Latin; 'queen'.

Renée French; 're-born'.

Robin originally a male name based on *Robert,* now identified with the bird. **Robyn** occurs.

Rochelle French 'little rock'. Unknown as a first name in France. The pet form is said to be *Shelley.*

Rose the flower name used as a first name.

Rosemary a flower name, associated with 'remembrance'.

Roxanne historical; apparently Persian, but of unknown meaning. Name of the Persian wife of Alexander the Great, (**Roxana**).

Ruth biblical; Hebrew; origin uncertain.

Sabrina literary; legendary river goddess.

Sadie pet form of *Sarah.*

Sally pet form of *Sarah,* but long used independently. **Sallie** occurs.

Samantha possibly Aramaic, meaning 'listener'.

Sandra pet form of *Alexandra.* **Sandy** and **Sandie** also occur.

Sara(h) biblical; Hebrew; 'princess'.

Selina probably from French **Celine,** a saint's name ultimately connected with the Latin word for 'heaven'. **Selena** occurs.

Serena Latin; 'serene'.

Shannon apparently a use of the river/place name.

Sharlene a modern variant of *Charlene.*

Sharon biblical; Hebrew; 'plain' in its place-name sense. This is a place name in the Bible, not a personal name.

Sheena a phonetic rendering of Gaelic **Sine** or *Jean.*

Shelley this looks like a transferred use of the surname, but it is more likely to be a pet form of names like *Michelle, Rochelle,* etc, given a new spelling. **Shelly** also occurs.

Sheri a phonetic variant of *Chérie.*

Shirley surname/place name; Old English; 'bright clearing'. *Shelley* is also used as a pet form of this name.

Simone French feminine form of *Simon.*

Siobhan Irish form of *Joan.* **Sian** also occurs.

Sonia literary; Greek; Russian diminutive of *Sophia.* **Sonja** and **Sonya** also occur.

Sophia, Sophie royal; Greek; 'wisdom'.

Stacey pet form of **Anastasia. Staci, Stacie, Stacy** also occur.

Stephanie French feminine form of *Stephen.*

Summer the word used as a first name. Usage confined to USA for the moment.

Susan biblical; Hebrew; 'lily'. The full name is **Susannah. Susanne** and **Suzanne** are popular variants.

Sylvia literary; Latin; 'wood'.

Tamara Russian form of a Hebrew name meaning 'palm tree'.

Tammy pet form of **Tamsin,** itself from **Thomasin,** a Cornish feminine form of *Thomas.* **Tammie** is found.

Tania diminutive of *Tatiana,* name of a Russian saint. **Tanya** also occurs.

Tara use of a place name which occurs in Moore's *Irish Melodies* and the novel *Gone With the Wind.*

Teresa, Theresa saint; Greek; 'reaper'. **Terri, Terrie, Terry** occur as pet forms.

Tina pet form of names such as *Christina,* used independently.

Toni pet form of *Antonia,* feminine of *Antony.*

Tracey, Tracy formerly a pet name from *Teresa.* Later from the surname, which in turn derives from a French place name.

Vanessa literary; invented by Jonathan Swift, using parts of the

names Esther Vanhomrigh.
Verity Latin; 'truth'.
Veronica saint; Latin; 'true image'.
Victoria royal; Latin; 'victory'. **Vicki, Vicky, Vikki,** etc, now occur as names in their own right.
Virginia a Roman name, but associated with Elizabeth I, the Virgin Queen.
Vivienne literary, of uncertain origin.
Wendy literary; used by J M Barrie in *Peter Pan* and said to be taken from the phrase 'friendy-wendy'.
Yvonne French feminine form of **Yves,** 'yew tree'. **Yvette** is also used.
Zara an Arabic royal name of uncertain origin.
Zoe saint; Greek; 'life'.

Girls' names used by black American families

Aisha probably meant for **Ayesha,** favourite wife of the Prophet Mohammad.
Ayanna, Ayana of unknown origin.
Camille French form of *Camilla*, which is of unknown origin.
Carmen Spanish form of Hebrew *Carmel*, 'garden'.
Chandra the god of the moon in Hindu mythology.
Dionne probably meant for *Dione*, name of the mother of Venus.
Ebony the word used as a name.
Felicia a variant of *Felicity*, Latin 'happiness'.
Gloria Latin 'glory'.
Gwendolyn a Welsh name based on a word meaning 'white, fair'.
India the name of the country used as a first name.
Katina one of the *Katharine* group of names, based on Greek 'pure'.
Keisha of unknown origin.
Kenya the name of the country used as a first name.
Kenyatta the surname of the African political leader, Jomo Kenyatta, used as a first name. **Kenyetta** also occurs.
Kizzy Alex Haley claims an African origin for this name in *Roots*, which brought it back into use, but all the evidence suggests that it is a pet form of **Keziah**, a Biblical name, Hebrew 'cassia'. **Kizzie** also occurs.
Lakeisha the popular prefix La- attached to a second element. Also well-used are **Lashawn, Latanya, Latonya, Latasha, Latisha, Latoya** and **Latrice,** most of which are probably blends of La- and a name (or pet name) that can also be used independently. Some writers draw attention to the Roman version of *Leto*'s name, *Latona*—the mother of Artemis and Apollo by Zeus, but the resemblance to this name and Latonya is probably a coincidence.
Marlena a Germanic blend of *Maria* and *Lena*.
Mildred saint; Old English; 'mild power'.
Monique the French form of *Monica*.
Nakia of unknown origin.
Nakita this appears to be a diminutive of *Nakia*.
Patrice French form of *Patricia*.
Rasheda, Rashida of unkown origin.
Raven the name of the bird used as a first name.
Renita perhaps a variant of *Renata*, Latin 're-born'.
Shayla possibly a phonetic variant of *Sheila*.
Tamike, Tameke, Tomika, etc none of the books which purport to deal with black American names even admits to the existence of this very popular name, which occurs in a dozen or so spellings. If it is based on *Tam-* or *Tom-*, it would link ultimately with *Thomas*.
Tanisha possibly linked to a Hausa (African) day name which indicates birth on a Monday.
Tasha a pet form of *Natasha*.
Tawanna, Tawana of unknown origin.
Tenville of unknown origin.
Tiffany a form of *Theophania*, Greek 'manifestation of God'.
Toya 'toy' with a feminine ending?
Wanda a Slavic name of unknown meaning.
Yolanda a variant of *Viola*.

Some Irish first names for girls

Aileen variant of *Eileen*.
Áine an ancient Irish name now linked with *Anna*.
Aisling Irish 'dream, vision'.
Aoife Irish form of *Eva, Eve*.
Bernadette feminine form of *Bernard*.
Bridget Irish 'the high one'.
Ciara probably feminine form of *Ciaran* 'black'.
Deirdre Irish 'fear' or 'one who rages'.
Eileen English form of Irish *Eibhlin*, itself a form of *Evelyn* or *Helen*.
Ethna Irish 'little fire'.
Fidelma blend of *Fidel* 'faithful' and *Mary*.
Gráinne Irish 'love'.
Ita Irish 'thirst'.
Mairead Irish form of *Margaret*.
Majella a reference to *St Gerard Majella*.
Maura a variant of *Mary*.
Muirne Gaelic 'beloved'.
Niamh Irish 'bright'.
Nuala pet form of *Fionnuala* 'white shoulder'.
Orla Irish 'golden lady'.
Róisín Irish form of *Rose*.
Sheila a form of *Celia* or *Cecelia*, ultimately from a Roman clan name.
Sineád Irish form of *Janet*.
Siobhán Irish form of *Joan*.
Sorcha Irish 'bright'.
Una usually linked with Latin 'one'.

Some Scottish first names for girls

Ailsa from the name of the island rock, *Ailsa Craig*.
Alana feminine form of *Alan*.
Alexina feminine form of *Alexander*.
Antonia Latin feminine form of *Antony*.
Beathag Gaelic 'life'.
Catriona Gaelic form of *Catherine*.
Christy pet form of *Christina*, *Christine*.
Edwina feminine form of *Edwin*.
Eilidh Gaelic form of *Helen*.
Elspeth Scottish pet form of *Elizabeth*.
Esmé French 'esteemed'.
Fenella form of *Fionnghal*, Gaelic 'white shoulder'.
Ina pet form of *Georgina*, *Clementina*, etc.
Innes Gaelic 'island'.
Iona Scottish island name.
Isla Scottish river name.
Ismay Scottish family name.
Jessie pet form of *Jessica*, *Janet*.
Katrine Scottish loch name.
Kirstie Scottish pet form of *Christine*.
Mairi Gaelic form of *Mary*.
Malvina Gaelic 'smooth brow'.
Morag Gaelic 'great'.
Morna Gaelic 'beloved'.
Morven Gaelic 'big mountain peak'.
Rhona Scottish place name 'rough isle'.
Senga back-spelling of *Agnes*.
Shona English form of Gaelic *Seonaid*, feminine form of *John*.
Thora Scandinavian 'Thor battle'.

Some Welsh first names for girls

Angharad Welsh 'much loved'.
Anwen Welsh 'very beautiful'.
Arwenna Welsh 'muse'.
Bethan pet form of *Elizabeth-Ann*.
Bronwen Welsh 'white breast'.
Carys Welsh 'love'.
Catrin Welsh form of *Catherine*.
Ceinwen Welsh 'beautiful and blessed'.
Cerian diminutive of *Ceri*, 'love'.
Cerys Welsh 'love'.
Delyth Welsh 'pretty'.
Eirlys Welsh 'snowdrop'.
Elen Welsh 'nymph, angel'.
Eleri Welsh river name.
Elin pet form of *Elinor* or variant of *Helen*.
Eluned Welsh 'idol, icon'.
Enfys Welsh 'rainbow'.
Ffion Welsh 'foxglove'.
Heulwen Welsh 'sunshine'.
Llinos Welsh 'linnet'.
Lona pet form of *Maelona* 'princess'.
Lora variant of *Laura*.
Lowri Welsh form of *Laura*.
Mai Welsh form of *May*.
Mair Welsh form of *Mary*.
Meironwen Welsh 'white dairymaid'.
Meriel variant of *Muriel*.
Mererid Welsh form of *Margaret*.
Myfanwy Welsh 'my fine one'.
Nerys Welsh feminine of 'lord'.
Nesta Welsh pet form of *Agnes*.
Nia legendary name of unknown meaning.
Olwen Welsh 'white footprint'.
Rhiain Welsh 'maiden'.
Rhiannon Welsh 'nymph, goddess'.
Sian Welsh form of *Jane*.
Sioned Welsh form of *Janet*.

Some biblical first names for girls

Unless otherwise stated these names are of Hebrew origin.

Adah 'ornament'.
Atarah 'crown, diadem'.
Athaliah '*Yah* is exalted'.
Azubah 'abandoned'.
Bathsheba 'daughter of opulence'.
Bernice Greek 'bringer of victory'.
Bithiah Egyptian 'queen'.
Carmel 'orchard'. A place name.
Cassia English form of *Keziah*.
Cozbi 'luxuriant'.
Damaris possibly Greek 'calf'.
Delilah Old Arabic 'coquette, flirt'.
Dinah 'lawsuit'.
Dorcas Greek 'gazelle'.
Drusilla of unknown meaning.
Edna 'delight, pleasure'.
Eunice Greek 'fine victory'.
Evodia Greek 'good journey'.
Huldah possibly 'weasel' or 'mole'.
Jael 'antelope'.
Jemimah 'turtle dove'.
Jezebel 'control, domination'.
Kerenhappuch 'mascara'.
Keturah 'incense'.
Keziah 'cassia'.
Lilith Acadian, name of a devil.
Lois Greek, of unknown meaning.
Lydia Greek, 'woman from Lydia' (a place in Asia Minor).
Magdalene 'tower', a place name.
Marisa 'summit', a place name.
Martha Aramaic 'mistress'.
Milcah 'queen'.
Naamah 'loved, pretty'.
Rhoda Greek 'rose'.
Salome 'safe and sound, peace'.
Sheba 'seven, fullness or oath'.
Tabitha Aramaic 'gazelle'.
Tamar 'palm tree'.
Tirzah 'pleasure'.
Zilpah Arabic 'with a little nose'.
Zipporah 'bird'.

3 Fashionable names

Several distinct first-name periods have occurred during the last thousand or so years. Before the Norman Conquest, for instance, the single personal names in use were mainly composed of Old English elements. Some of those names live on today in slightly altered form: **Alfred, Alwin, Edgar, Edith, Edmund, Edward, Herbert, Mervin, Norman.** Others survive mainly as family names. Examples are: **Algar, Coleman, Derman, Gladwin, Godman, Godwin, Harding, Osmund, Sperling, Watman, Wulmar, Wumond.** A fuller list of such names is to be found on page 70, together with their meanings.

Since the Anglo-Saxons constantly formed new names by blending a series of traditional name elements, there was not at any time a central stock of names, only a stock of name parts which could be permutated. The names that were formed were meant to individualise their bearers, and duplication was avoided. This was partly because a name was felt to contain a person's spirit, and using his name for a new-born child might have drained that spirit from him. It was also partly because each person bore only one name, not a first name, middle name and last name, and that name was correspondingly more important for identification purposes.

Norman names

When the Normans conquered Britain in 1066 they brought with them a stock of new names and different ideas about naming. They were beginning to use the first name and last name system, which allowed the same first names to be borne by many different people at the same time. The names had also acquired a fixed form, they were not broken down and re-assembled for each new generation. Popular with the Normans were names like **Alan, Bernard, Brian, Denis, Everard, Geoffrey, Gerald, Gervase, Henry, Hugh, Louis, Maurice, Oliver, Piers, Ralph, Richard, Robert, Roger, Roland, Walter** and **Warren. William** was an outstanding favourite. As for the Norman ladies, they were often **Adela, Alice, Amice, Avis, Constance, Emma, Jocelyn, Laura, Marjorie, Maud, Oriel, Rosamond** and **Yvonne.**

In the centuries that followed their arrival on British shores, it was the Normans and their descendants who formed the aristocracy. As has always been the case, those who were lower in the social scale aped the habits and customs of their superiors. This led to the steady disappearance of the Old English names and their replacement by the names the Normans had introduced. These names in their turn ceased to be 'new' and were thought by succeeding generations to be thoroughly English.

Christian names

The next naming period introduced Christian names in the true sense, for the Church encouraged parents to use names of Christian significance. In the 16th century the split between Roman Catholics and Protestants was reflected in name usage. The Protestants turned away from Catholic names such as **Mary,** and from the names of saints such as **Augustine** and **Benedict, Barbara** and **Agnes.** They preferred to use the Bible as a principal source of names, especially the Old Testament. It was now that Hebrew names such as **Aaron, Abraham, Adam, Benjamin, Daniel, David, Jacob, Jonathan, Joseph, Joshua, Michael, Nathan, Noah, Samuel, Saul, Seth** and **Solomon** were brought into use for boys, while the girls became **Abigail, Beulah, Deborah, Dinah, Esther, Eve, Hannah, Keziah, Leah, Miriam, Naomi, Rachel,**

Rebekah, Ruth, Sarah and **Tamar.** These names were later to become especially associated with the USA, when religious persecution forced the Protestant groups to emigrate.

Not all the Old Testament names, incidentally, were as familiar and pleasant as those mentioned above. At this time children also received biblical names such as **Amaziah, Belteshazzar, Habakkuk, Jehoshaphat, Nebuchadnezzar** and **Onesiphorous** (boys); **Aholibamah, Eglah, Abishag** and **Maachah** (girls).

It was also in the 16th and 17th centuries that the religious extremists known as Puritans appeared on the scene. For some of them, even the names that had biblical sanction were not pure enough. They gave their children slogan names, such as **Be-Courteous, Faint-not, Fight-the-good-fight-of-faith, Fly-fornication, Make-peace, Safe-deliverance, Stand-fast-on-high, The-Lord-is-near.** Such names were much laughed at by the general public, of course, and sanity re-asserted itself. The more sensible Puritans had in the meantime managed to display their religious beliefs in less eccentric ways, creating a group of names which have survived to the present day. This naming layer featured the 'virtues', and it includes such names as **Amity, Charity, Faith, Felicity, Grace, Honour, Hope, Joy, Mercy, Patience, Prudence** and **Verity.**

The 18th century was marked by the emergence of diminutives as names in their own right. Until this time, women who might be known as **Bess, Beth, Betty, Eliza, Elsie, Liz** or **Liza** were all formally baptised as **Elizabeth.** Now the pet names began to appear in parish registers as official names. The names had perhaps been created centuries previously; they simply achieved official recognition from 1750 onwards.

Flower names

The end of the 19th century brought flower names into fashion. **Rose** and **Lily** were amongst the earliest of such names to be used if one discounts names in other languages, such as **Susanna,** which happens to mean 'lily' in Hebrew. **Hazel** quickly became popular in the USA, while **Ivy, Olive, Violet** and **Daisy** appealed to British parents.

Once the idea of using flower names had established itself, more exotic names were used. A **Bluebell** Smith was named in 1902, an **Eglantine** Smith in 1890. When searching through birth records of the period it is not difficult to find examples of **Blossom, Bryony, Cherry, Daffodil, Daphne, Fern, Heather, Holly, Iris, Laurel, Myrtle, Pansy, Poppy, Primrose, Snowdrop** and **Viola.** An English clergyman who made a rail journey in 1890 commented on 'a perfect nosegay of children, all members of one family' that he met. Their names were Daisy, May, Lily, Violet and Olive. The same clergyman commented on a superstition that arose at the time—that children who bore flower names were supposed, like the flowers themselves, to live only a short time.

Other groups of names

Soon after the flowers came the jewel names. The main ones to be used were **Pearl, Ruby, Beryl, Opal, Crystal, Amber, Coral, Amethyst, Jet, Onyx,**

Our oldest son was named George, after his uncle, who left us ten thousand pounds. I intended to call (my daughter) after Aunt Grissel, but my wife, who had been reading romances, insisted upon her being called Olivia. In less than another year we had another daughter, and now I was determined that Grissel should be her name; but a rich relation taking a fancy to stand godmother, the girl was, by her directions, called Sophia, so that we had two romantic names in the family, but I solemnly protest I had no hand in it.

Oliver Goldsmith *The Vicar of Wakefield*

'He will be christened Paul, of course. His father's name, Mrs Dombey, and his grandfather's'.

Charles Dickens *Dombey and Son*

Most of us are fairly certain to meet during our lifetime someone who bears the same first name as ourselves. From time to time I receive letters, however, from those who consider themselves to be nominally unique. A typical example of such a correspondent is **Harrianne** Mills, who writes from Gambier, Ohio. Miss Mills has borne her name since 1952. She explains the 'Harrianne' by saying simply: 'I was supposed to be a boy . . .' Not that all that many boys are called Harrianne, of course. I am compiling a list of these unique names, and would be glad to hear from those who bear them.

Jade and **Diamond. Margaret** actually belongs in this group, since it also means 'pearl'.

Another distinctive layer of names began to appear in the 1930s. We might call this the 'fanciful spelling' period, for it has led to dozens of modern names like **Vikki, Mandi, Lynda, Jayne, Carolyn, Kristine, Debra**. It will be noticed that these examples are all girls' names. The attitude still persists that one may be frivolous or experimental in naming a girl, but tradition must rule when a boy is named.

Other groups of first names can be identified quite easily but it is not always possible to assign them to a period of time. We have the classical names, for instance, such as **Diana, Cassandra, Venus, Cynthia, Delia, Corinna, Sylvia, Anthea.** We must not forget **Alexander,** the most famous Greek name of all and the most popular name of this type to be taken into our own name stock. These names began to be used before the 17th century, since William Camden mentioned several of them in his *Remains*, published in 1605, but there was never a period of thirty years or so when they suddenly appeared in great numbers.

Similar groups of names, which do not link with a particular period, are animal names (**Leo, Leonard, Lionel**—lion; **Orson, Ursula**—bear; **Deborah, Melissa**—bee; **Jemimah, Jonah, Malcolm**—dove; **Rachel**—ewe; **Arnold**—eagle), and colour names (**Candida, Blanche, Bianca**—white; **Roy, Russell, Ginger**—red; **Electra, Amber**—amber; **Boyd, Flavia**—yellow; **Duncan, Dugald, Dougal**—brown; **Aurelia**—gold; **Melanie**—black; **Douglas**—blue). One cannot say of such groups that they suddenly became fashionable in the way that flower names obviously did.

The present stock of names contains examples from each layer, and the personal preference of each set of parents determines which kind of name is used. Nevertheless, as name-counts of all kinds clearly show, certain names become far more popular than others at a particular moment. One can only speculate as to the reasons.

It is not enough to say that a name becomes popular because a famous person bears it. Queen Victoria was certainly famous enough during her reign, yet **Victoria** was very rarely used during the 19th century. **Winston** Churchill was likewise famous in 1945, yet few boys were given his name at that time. **Elvis** Presley and **Errol** Flynn failed to have a significant impact on naming in spite of their fame and popularity.

A famous person may make a name known, but it has to have something about it which makes a general appeal. Its sound may be important, for instance. It is noticeable that **Karen, Darren, Sharon**—and to a lesser extent, **Aaron,** became more fashionable at the same time, a phenomenon repeated in the case of **Vicky, Nicky** and **Ricky; Kerry, Terry, Sherri.** Then the name must have been little used for at least a generation. The name will be used at first by those who wish to get away from fashionable trends, but if they have chosen well, others will follow their lead. One can safely say that any name which is at the height of fashion at a given moment will go out of fashion within fifteen years, but it is impossible to predict which name will take its place. It does seem, however, that given time, every name will eventually have its day.

The top fifty first names* for boys, England and Wales

1700	1800	1850	1875	1900
1 John	1 William	1 William	1 William	1 William
2 William	2 John	2 John	2 John	2 John
3 Thomas	3 Thomas	3 George	3 George	3 George
4 Richard	4 James	Thomas	4 Thomas	4 Thomas
5 James	5 George	5 James	5 James	5 Charles
6 Robert	6 Joseph	6 Henry	6 Henry	6 Frederick
7 Joseph	7 Richard	7 Charles	7 Charles	7 Arthur
8 Edward	8 Henry	8 Joseph	8 Frederick	8 James
9 Henry	9 Robert	9 Robert	9 Arthur	9 Albert
10 George	10 Charles	10 Samuel	10 Joseph	10 Ernest
11 Samuel	11 Samuel	11 Edward	11 Albert	11 Robert
12 Francis	12 Edward	12 Frederick	12 Alfred	12 Henry
13 Charles	13 Benjamin	13 Alfred	13 Walter	13 Alfred
14 Daniel	14 Isaac	14 Richard	14 Harry	14 Sidney
15 Benjamin	15 Peter	15 Walter	15 Edward	15 Joseph
16 Edmund	16 Daniel	16 Arthur	16 Robert	16 Harold
17 Matthew	17 David	17 Benjamin	17 Ernest	Harry
18 Peter	18 Francis	18 David	18 Herbert	18 Frank
19 Nicholas	19 Stephen	19 Edwin	19 Sidney	19 Walter
20 Isaac	20 Jonathan	20 Albert	20 Samuel	20 Herbert
21 Christopher	21 Christopher	21 Francis	21 Frank	21 Edward
22 Abraham	22 Matthew	22 Daniel	22 Richard	22 Percy
23 Stephen	23 Edmund	Sidney	23 Fred	23 Richard
24 Jonathan	24 Philip	24 Harry	24 Francis	24 Samuel
25 Philip	25 Abraham	Philip	25 David	25 Leonard
26 Michael	26 Mark	26 Isaac	26 Percy	26 Stanley
27 Hugh	27 Michael	27 Herbert	27 Edwin	27 Reginald
28 Joshua	28 Ralph	Peter	28 Alexander	28 Francis
29 Anthony	29 Jacob	29 Alexander	29 Peter	29 Fred
30 Ralph	30 Andrew	Frank	Tom	30 Cecil
31 Andrew	31 Moses	Matthew	31 Benjamin	31 Wilfred
32 David	32 Nicholas	32 Stephen	Harold	32 Horace
33 Simon	33 Anthony	Tom	33 Daniel	33 Cyril
34 Roger	34 Luke	34 Abraham	Isaac	34 David
35 Alexander	35 Simon	Elijah	35 Edgar	Norman
36 Jacob	36 Josiah	36 Jacob	Matthew	36 Eric
37 Laurence	37 Timothy	Jonathan	Philip	37 Victor
38 Moses	38 Martin	Joshua	38 Stephen	38 Edgar
39 Nathaniel	39 Nathaniel	39 Edmund	39 Andrew	39 Leslie
40 Walter	40 Roger	Hugh	Sam	40 Bertie
41 Aaron	41 Walter	Josiah	41 Abraham	Edwin
42 Jeremy	42 Aaron	Reuben	Christopher	42 Donald
43 Owen	43 Jeremy	43 Amos	Oliver	43 Benjamin
44 Mark	44 Joshua	Christopher	Willie	Hector
45 Timothy	45 Alexander	Eli	45 Alan	Jack
46 Adam	46 Adam	Ralph	Bertram	Percival
47 Martin	47 Hugh	47 Andrew	Horace	47 Clifford
48 Josiah	48 Laurence	Horace	Leonard	48 Alexander
49 Luke	49 Owen	Israel	Ralph	Baden
50 Harry	50 Harry	Jesse	50 Reginald	50 Bernard
		Moses	Wilfred	Redvers
		Seth		

*Names with variant spellings are listed by their most frequent form

1925	1950	1965	1975	1985	1988
1 John	1 David	1 Paul	1 Stephen	1 Christopher	1 Daniel
2 William	2 John	2 David	2 Mark	2 Matthew	2 Christopher
3 George	3 Peter	3 Andrew	3 Paul	3 David	3 Michael
4 James	4 Michael	4 Stephen	4 Andrew	4 James	4 James
5 Ronald	5 Alan	5 Mark	5 David	5 Daniel	5 Matthew
6 Robert	6 Robert	6 Michael	6 Richard	6 Andrew	6 Andrew
7 Kenneth	7 Stephen	7 Ian	7 Matthew	7 Steven	7 Adam
8 Frederick	8 Paul	8 Gary	8 Daniel	8 Michael	8 Thomas
9 Thomas	9 Brian	9 Robert	9 Christopher	9 Mark	9 David
10 Albert	10 Graham	10 Richard	10 Darren	10 Paul	10 Richard
11 Eric	11 Philip	11 Peter	11 Michael	11 Richard	11 Robert
12 Edward	12 Anthony	12 John	12 James	12 Adam	12 Steven
13 Arthur	13 Colin	13 Anthony	13 Robert	13 Robert	13 Mark
14 Charles	14 Christopher	14 Christopher	14 Simon	14 Lee	14 Lee
15 Leslie	15 Geoffrey	15 Darren	15 Jason	15 Craig	15 Paul
16 Sidney	16 William	16 Kevin	16 Stuart	16 Benjamin	16 Benjamin
17 Frank	17 James	17 Martin	17 Neil	Thomas	17 Martin
18 Peter	18 Keith	18 Simon	18 Lee	18 Peter	18 Craig
19 Dennis	Terence	19 Philip	19 Jonathan	19 Anthony	19 Nicholas
20 Joseph	20 Barry	20 Graham	20 Ian	20 Shaun	20 Jamie
21 Alan	Malcolm	21 Colin	Nicholas	21 Gary	21 Anthony
22 Stanley	Richard	22 Adrian	22 Gary	22 Stuart	22 Carl
23 Ernest	23 Ian	23 Nigel	23 Craig	23 Jonathan	23 Jonathan
24 Harold	24 Derek	24 Alan	24 Martin	Simon	24 Peter
25 Norman	25 Roger	25 Neil	25 John	25 Philip	25 Alexander
26 Raymond	26 Raymond	26 Shaun	26 Carl	26 Darren	26 Luke
27 Leonard	27 Kenneth	27 Jonathan	27 Philip	27 Carl	27 Ashley
28 Alfred	28 Andrew	28 Nicholas	28 Kevin	28 Martin	28 Joseph
Harry	29 Trevor	29 Stuart	29 Benjamin	Nicholas	29 Shaun
30 Donald	30 Martin	30 Timothy	30 Peter	30 John	30 Aaron
Reginald	31 Kevin	31 Wayne	31 Wayne	31 Luke	31 Jason
32 Roy	32 Ronald	32 Brian	32 Adam	32 Neil	32 Ryan
33 Derek	33 Leslie	33 James	33 Anthony	33 Jason	33 Scott
34 Henry	34 Charles	34 Carl	34 Alan	34 Alexander	34 Gary
35 Geoffrey	George	35 Jeffrey	35 Graham	Kevin	35 Darren
36 David	36 Thomas	36 Barry	36 Adrian	36 Dean	36 Liam
Gordon	37 Nigel	37 Dean	37 Colin	37 Ian	37 Oliver
Herbert	Stuart	38 Matthew	Scott	Jamie	38 Simon
Walter	39 Edward	39 William	39 Timothy	39 Ryan	39 John
40 Cyril	40 Gordon	40 Keith	40 Barry	40 Stacey	40 Kyle
41 Jack	41 Roy	41 Julian	41 William	Timothy	41 Philip
42 Richard	42 Dennis	42 Trevor	42 Dean	Wayne	42 Gareth
43 Douglas	43 Neil	43 Roger	Jamie	43 Alan	43 Kevin
44 Maurice	44 Laurence	Russell	44 Nathan	Graham	44 Wayne
45 Bernard	45 Clive	45 Derek	45 Justin	Oliver	45 Nathan
Gerald	Eric	Lee	46 Damian	46 William	Timothy
47 Brian	47 Frederick	47 Clive	Thomas	47 Joseph	47 Ian
48 Victor	Patrick	Jeremy	48 Joseph	48 Gavin	William
Wilfred	Robin	49 Patrick	49 Alexander	Nathan	49 Gregory
50 Francis	50 Donald	50 Daniel	Alistair	50 Ben	Kieran
	Joseph	Kenneth	Nigel	Edward	
		Raymond	Shaun	Gareth	

The top fifty first names for boys, USA

1875	1900	1925	1940
1 William	1 John	1 Robert	1 Robert
2 John	2 William	2 John	2 James
3 Charles	3 Charles	3 William	3 John
4 Harry	4 Robert	4 James	4 William
5 James	5 Joseph	5 Charles	5 Richard
6 George	6 James	6 Richard	6 Thomas
7 Frank	7 George	7 George	7 David
8 Robert	8 Samuel	8 Donald	8 Ronald
9 Joseph	9 Thomas	9 Joseph	9 Donald
10 Thomas	10 Arthur	10 Edward	10 Michael
11 Walter	11 Harry	11 Thomas	11 Charles
12 Edward	12 Edward	12 David	12 Joseph
13 Samuel	13 Henry	13 Frank	13 Gerald
14 Henry	14 Walter	14 Harold	14 Kenneth
15 Arthur	15 Louis	15 Arthur	15 Lawrence
16 Albert	16 Paul	16 Jack	16 Edward
17 Louis	17 Ralph	17 Paul	17 George
18 David	18 Carl	18 Kenneth	18 Paul
Frederick	19 Frank	19 Walter	19 Dennis
20 Clarence	20 Raymond	20 Raymond	20 Gary
21 Alexander	21 Francis	21 Carl	21 Raymond
22 Fred	22 Frederick	22 Albert	22 Daniel
Howard	23 Albert	23 Henry	23 Frank
24 Alfred	Benjamin	24 Harry	24 Larry
Edwin	25 David	25 Francis	25 Carl
Paul	26 Harold	26 Ralph	26 Frederick
27 Ernest	27 Howard	27 Eugene	27 Allen
Jacob	28 Fred	28 Howard	28 Walter
29 Ralph	Richard	29 Lawrence	29 Anthony
30 Leon	30 Clarence	30 Louis	30 Ralph
Oscar	Herbert	31 Alan	31 Philip
32 Andrew	32 Jacob	32 Norman	32 Leonard
Carl	33 Ernest	33 Gerald	33 Harold
Francis	Jack	34 Herbert	34 Stephen
Harold	35 Herman	35 Fred	35 Roger
36 Allen	Philip	36 Earl	36 Norman
Herman	Stanley	Philip	37 Arthur
Warren	38 Donald	Stanley	38 Jack
39 Benjamin	Earl	39 Daniel	Peter
Eugene	Elmer	40 Leonard	40 Henry
Herbert	41 Leon	Marvin	Jerome
Lewis	Nathan	42 Frederick	42 Douglas
Maurice	43 Eugene	43 Anthony	Patrick
Richard	Floyd	Samuel	44 Eugene
45 Clifford	Ray	45 Bernard	45 Jerry
46 Earl(e)	Roy	Edwin	46 Louis
Edgar	Sydney	47 Alfred	47 Harry
Elmer	48 Abraham	48 Russell	48 Francis
Guy	Edwin	Warren	Howard
Isaac	Lawrence	50 Ernest	50 Bruce
Leroy	Leonard		Theodore
Stanley	Norman		Timothy
	Russell		

1950	1960	1970	1988 *Whites*	1988 *Non-whites*
1 Robert	1 Michael	1 Michael	1 Michael	1 Michael
2 Michael	2 David	2 Robert	2 Matthew	2 Christopher
3 James	3 Robert	3 David	3 Christopher	3 Brandon
4 John	4 James	4 James	4 Joshua	4 Anthony
5 David	5 John	5 John	5 Andrew	5 James
6 William	6 Mark	6 Jeffrey	6 Justin	6 Joshua
7 Thomas	7 Steven	7 Steven	7 Daniel	7 Steven
8 Richard	8 Thomas	8 Christopher	8 Ryan	8 Charles
9 Gary	9 William	9 Brian	9 James	9 Darryl
10 Charles	10 Joseph	10 Mark	10 David	10 Brian
11 Ronald	11 Kevin	11 William	11 Nicholas	Kevin
12 Dennis	12 Richard	12 Eric	12 Kyle	Robert
13 Steven	13 Kenneth	13 Kevin	13 Joseph	William
14 Kenneth	14 Jeffrey	14 Scott	14 John	14 Eric
15 Joseph	15 Timothy	15 Joseph	15 Brian	15 Jeremy
16 Mark	16 Daniel	16 Daniel	16 Robert	16 Justin
17 Daniel	17 Brian	17 Thomas	17 Steven	17 Derrick
18 Paul	18 Paul	18 Anthony	18 Jacob	18 David
19 Donald	19 Ronald	19 Richard	19 Brandon	19 Aaron
20 Gregory	20 Gregory	20 Charles	20 Eric	Andrew
21 Larry	21 Anthony	21 Kenneth	21 Jonathan	Marcus
22 Lawrence	22 Donald	22 Matthew	22 William	22 John
23 Timothy	23 Charles	23 Jason	23 Adam	23 Kenneth
24 Alan	24 Christopher	24 Paul	24 Timothy	24 Matthew
25 Edward	25 Keith	25 Timothy	25 Zachary	25 Antonio
26 Gerald	26 Edward	26 Sean	26 Jeffrey	Shawn
27 Douglas	27 Dennis	27 Gregory	27 Jason	27 Jonathan
28 George	28 Gary	28 Ronald	28 Benjamin	28 Ryan
29 Frank	29 Lawrence	29 Todd	29 Tyler	29 Mark
30 Patrick	30 Patrick	30 Edward	30 Sean	Phillip
31 Anthony	31 Scott	31 Derrick	31 Kevin	31 Corey
32 Philip	32 Darryl	32 Keith	32 Dustin	Terrance
33 Raymond	33 Gerald	33 Patrick	33 Cody	33 Keith
34 Bruce	34 Craig	34 Darryl	34 Thomas	Richard
35 Jeffrey	35 Douglas	35 Dennis	35 Aaron	35 Antoine
36 Brian	36 Alan	36 Andrew	36 Cory	Jason
37 Peter	37 George	37 Donald	37 Anthony	37 Darren
38 Frederick	38 Dwayne	38 Gary	38 Derek	Gregory
39 Roger	39 Peter	39 Allen	39 Jeremy	39 Daniel
40 Carl	40 Matthew	40 Douglas	40 Mark	40 Andre
41 Dale	41 Philip	41 George	41 Nathan	Terrell
Walter	42 Andrew	42 Marcus	42 Travis	42 DeAndre
43 Christopher	43 Bruce	43 Raymond	43 Bradley	Reginald
44 Martin	44 Frank	44 Peter	44 Richard	44 Carl
45 Craig	45 Raymond	45 Gerald	45 Charles	45 Edward
46 Arthur	46 Eric	46 Frank	46 Jared	Joseph
47 Andrew	47 Carl	Jonathan	47 Patrick	Larry
48 Jerome	48 Randall	Lawrence	48 Jesse	48 Jeffrey
49 Leonard	49 Martin	49 Aaron	49 Scott	49 Jared
50 Henry	50 Larry	Philip	50 Samuel	Timothy

The top fifty first names* for girls, England and Wales

1700	1800	1850	1875	1900
1 Mary	1 Mary	1 Mary	1 Mary	1 Florence
2 Elizabeth	2 Ann	2 Elizabeth	2 Elizabeth	2 Mary
3 Ann	3 Elizabeth	3 Sarah	3 Sarah	3 Alice
4 Sarah	4 Sarah	4 Ann	4 Annie	4 Annie
5 Jane	5 Jane	5 Eliza	5 Alice	5 Elsie
6 Margaret	6 Hannah	6 Jane	6 Florence	6 Edith
7 Susan	7 Susan	7 Emma	7 Emily	7 Elizabeth
8 Martha	8 Martha	8 Hannah	8 Edith	8 Doris
9 Hannah	9 Margaret	9 Ellen	9 Ellen	9 Dorothy
10 Catherine	10 Charlotte	10 Martha	10 Ada	Ethel
11 Alice	11 Harriet	11 Emily	11 Margaret	11 Gladys
12 Frances	12 Betty	12 Harriet	12 Ann	12 Lilian
13 Eleanor	13 Maria	13 Alice	13 Emma	13 Hilda
14 Dorothy	14 Catherine	14 Margaret	14 Jane	14 Margaret
Rebecca	15 Frances	15 Maria	15 Eliza	15 Winifred
16 Isabel	16 Mary Ann	16 Louisa	16 Louisa	16 Lily
17 Grace	17 Nancy	17 Fanny	17 Clara	17 Ellen
18 Joan	18 Rebecca	18 Caroline	18 Martha	18 Ada
19 Rachel	19 Alice	19 Charlotte	19 Harriet	19 Emily
20 Agnes	20 Ellen	20 Susannah	20 Hannah	20 Violet
21 Ellen	21 Sophia	21 Frances	21 Kate	21 Rose
22 Maria	22 Lucy	22 Catherine	22 Frances	Sarah
23 Lydia	23 Isabel	23 Amelia	23 Charlotte	23 Nellie
24 Ruth	24 Eleanor	24 Lucy	24 Lilly	24 May
25 Deborah	25 Esther	25 Clara	25 Ethel	25 Beatrice
Judith	26 Fanny	Esther	26 Lucy	26 Gertrude
27 Esther	27 Eliza	27 Betsy	Rose	Ivy
Joanna	Grace	Isabella	28 Agnes	28 Mabel
29 Amy	Sally	29 Eleanor	29 Minnie	29 Jessie
Marjorie	30 Rachel	Matilda	30 Fanny	30 Maud
Phoebe	31 Lydia	Sophia	31 Caroline	31 Eva
32 Jenny	32 Caroline	Susan	32 Amy	32 Agnes
33 Barbara	33 Dorothy	33 Rebecca	Jessie	Jane
Bridget	34 Peggy	34 Anna	34 Eleanor	34 Evelyn
35 Fanny	35 Ruth	35 Agnes	35 Catherine	35 Frances
36 Lucy	36 Kitty	Rachel	Maria	Kathleen
37 Betty	37 Jenny	37 Julia	37 Gertrude	37 Clara
Eliza	38 Phoebe	Rose	38 Isabella	38 Olive
Nancy	39 Agnes	39 Selina	39 Maud	39 Amy
40 Emma	Emma	40 Kate	40 Laura	40 Catherine
41 Charlotte	41 Amy	Nancy	Lilian	41 Grace
42 Dinah	Jemima	Phoebe	42 Amelia	42 Emma
Sally	43 Dinah	43 Annie	Esther	43 Nora
44 Harriet	44 Barbara	Lydia	44 Beatrice	44 Louisa
Jemima	45 Joan	Ruth	45 Bertha	Minnie
Kitty	46 Joanna	46 Priscilla	46 Susannah	46 Lucy
Mary Ann	47 Deborah	Rosanna	47 Lizzie	47 Daisy
48 Caroline	Judith	48 Jessie	48 Henrietta	Eliza
Peggy	49 Bridget	49 Amy	Nelly	49 Phyllis
Sophia	Marjorie	Grace	Rebecca	Ann
		Helen		
		Henrietta		
		Jemima		

*Names with variant spellings are listed by their most frequent form

1925	1950	1965	1975	1985	1988
1 Joan	1 Susan	1 Trac(e)y	1 Claire	1 Sarah	1 Rebecca
2 Mary	2 Linda	2 Deborah	2 Sarah	2 Claire	2 Sarah
3 Joyce	3 Christine	3 Julie	3 Nicola	3 Emma	3 Emma
4 Margaret	4 Margaret	4 Karen	4 Emma	4 Laura	4 Laura
5 Dorothy	5 Carol	5 Susan	5 Joanne	5 Rebecca	5 Rachel
6 Doris	6 Jennifer	6 Alison	6 Helen	6 Gemma	6 Samantha
7 Kathleen	7 Janet	7 Jacqueline	7 Rachel	7 Rachel	7 Charlotte
8 Irene	8 Patricia	8 Helen	8 Lisa	8 Kelly	8 Kirsty
9 Betty	9 Barbara	9 Amanda	9 Rebecca	9 Victoria	9 Nicola
10 Eileen	10 Ann	10 Sharon	10 Karen	10 Katharine	10 Amy
11 Doreen	11 Sandra	11 Sarah	Michelle	11 Katie	11 Gemma
12 Lilian	12 Pamela	12 Joanne	12 Victoria	Nicola	12 Claire
Vera	Pauline	13 Jane	13 Catherine	13 Jennifer	13 Victoria
14 Jean	14 Jean	14 Catherine	14 Amanda	Natalie	14 Catherine
15 Marjorie	15 Jacqueline	15 Angela	15 Trac(e)y	15 Hayley	15 Katie
16 Barbara	16 Kathleen	16 Linda	16 Samantha	Michelle	16 Kelly
17 Edna	17 Sheila	17 Carol	17 Kelly	17 Amy	17 Kayleigh
18 Gladys	18 Valerie	18 Diane	18 Deborah	Lisa	18 Stacey
19 Audrey	19 Maureen	19 Wendy	19 Julie	19 Lindsay	19 Lucy
20 Elsie	20 Gillian	20 Beverley	Louise	20 Samantha	20 Louise
21 Florence	21 Marilyn	21 Caroline	21 Sharon	21 Joanne	21 Jennifer
Hilda	Mary	22 Dawn	22 Donna	22 Louise	22 Leanne
Winifred	23 Elizabeth	23 Nicola	23 Kerry	23 Leanne	23 Danielle
24 Olive	24 Lesley	24 Michelle	24 Zoe	24 Helen	24 Lisa
25 Violet	25 Catherine	Sally	25 Melanie	25 Joanna	25 Jessica
26 Elizabeth	26 Brenda	26 Claire	26 Alison	26 Hannah	26 Natalie
27 Edith	27 Wendy	27 Sandra	27 Caroline	27 Jodie	27 Hayley
28 Ivy	28 Angela	28 Lorraine	28 Lynsey	28 Charlotte	28 Stephanie
29 Peggy	29 Rosemary	29 Janet	29 Jennifer	29 Kirsty	29 Lauren
Phyllis	30 Shirley	30 Gillian	30 Angela	30 Lucy	30 Emily
31 Evelyn	31 Diane	31 Elizabeth	31 Susan	31 Caroline	Joanne
32 Iris	Joan	32 Paula	32 Hayley	32 Elizabeth	32 Michelle
33 Annie	33 Jane	33 Donna	33 Dawn	33 Ashley	Tracy
Rose	Lynne	Jennifer	Joanna	Stephanie	34 Elizabeth
35 Beryl	35 Irene	Lesley	Lucy	35 Jessica	35 Kimberley
Lily	36 Janice	Louise	36 Natalie	36 Emily	36 Sophie
Muriel	37 Elaine	37 Ann	37 Charlotte	37 Kerry	37 Carly
Sheila	Heather	38 Andrea	38 Andrea	Tracey	Helen
39 Ethel	Marion	39 Mandy	Laura	39 Charlene	Jenna
40 Alice	40 June	40 Elaine	40 Paula	Danielle	40 Natasha
41 Constance	41 Eileen	41 Denise	41 Marie	Zoe	41 Amanda
Ellen	42 Denise	42 Christine	42 Teresa	42 Kate	42 Donna
43 Gwendoline	Doreen	Teresa	43 Elizabeth	Lauren	43 Holly
Patricia	Judith	44 Maria	Suzanne	44 Amanda	Jade
45 Sylvia	Sylvia	Melanie	45 Kirsty	45 Alison	Kerry
46 Nora	46 Helen	46 Julia	Sally	Anna	46 Alexandra
Pamela	Yvonne	Lisa	Tina	Carla	47 Zoe
48 Grace	48 Hilary	48 Tina	48 Jane	Carly	48 Kate
49 Jessie	49 Dorothy	49 Margaret	49 Ann(e)	Marie	Terri
50 Mabel	Joyce	50 Lynn	Jacqueline	50 Alexandra	50 Jenny
	Julia			Melissa	Melissa
	Teresa				

The top fifty first names for girls, USA

1875

1 Mary
2 Anna
3 Elizabeth
4 Emma
5 Alice
6 Edith
Florence
8 May
9 Helen
10 Katherine
11 Grace
12 Sarah
13 Ella
14 Clara
15 Mabel
16 Margaret
17 Ida
18 Jennie
Lillian
20 Annie
Edna
Gertrude
23 Bertha
24 Laura
25 Minnie
26 Blanche
27 Bessie
Elsie
29 Emily
Martha
Nellie
32 Marie
33 Lillie
34 Ethel
Lulu
36 Carrie
37 Amelia
38 Agnes
Frances
Harriet
Louisa
Maud
43 Ada
Lucy
Rose
Stella
47 Pauline
Rebecca
49 Alma, Belle
Charlotte, Dora
Eleanor, Esther
Eva, Fanny
Ruth, Sophia

1900

1 Mary
2 Ruth
3 Helen
4 Margaret
5 Elizabeth
6 Dorothy
7 Catherine
8 Mildred
9 Frances
10 Alice
Marion
12 Anna
13 Sarah
14 Gladys
15 Grace
Lillian
17 Florence
Virginia
19 Edith
Lucy
21 Clara
Doris
23 Marjorie
24 Annie
25 Louise
Martha
27 Ann(e)
Blanche
Eleanor
Emma
Hazel
32 Esther
Ethel
Laura
Marie
36 Julia
37 Beatrice
Gertrude
39 Alma
Mabel
Minnie
Pauline
Rose
44 Fanny
45 Agnes
Carrie
Edna
Evelyn
Harriet
Ida
Irene
Miriam

1925

1 Mary
2 Barbara
3 Dorothy
4 Betty
5 Ruth
6 Margaret
7 Helen
8 Elizabeth
9 Jean
10 Ann(e)
11 Patricia
12 Shirley
13 Virginia
14 Nancy
15 Joan
16 Martha
17 Marion
18 Doris
19 Frances
Marjorie
21 Marilyn
22 Alice
23 Eleanor
Catherine
25 Lois
26 Jane
27 Phyllis
28 Florence
Mildred
30 Carol(e)
31 Carolyn
Marie
Norma
34 Anna
Louise
36 Beverly
Janet
38 Sarah
39 Evelyn
40 Edith
Jacqueline
Lorraine
43 Grace
44 Ethel
Gloria
Laura
47 Audrey
Esther
Joanne
Sally

1940

1 Mary
2 Patricia
3 Barbara
4 Judith
5 Carol(e)
6 Sharon
7 Nancy
8 Joan
9 Sandra
10 Margaret
11 Beverly
12 Shirley
13 Linda
14 Diane
15 Janet
Joanne
17 Joyce
18 Marilyn
19 Catherine
20 Kathleen
21 Carolyn
22 Ann(e)
23 Dorothy
Elizabeth
25 Geraldine
26 Donna
27 Susan
28 Gloria
29 Karen
30 Betty
31 Dolores
32 Elaine
33 Virginia
34 Helen
35 Phyllis
36 Rose
37 Jacqueline
38 Suzanne
39 Brenda
40 Frances
41 Ruth
42 Alice
43 Janice
Marlene
45 Arlene
46 Sally
47 Christine
48 Gail
Jean
Marie

1950	1960	1970	1988 *Whites*	1988 *Non-whites*
1 Linda	1 Mary	1 Michelle	1 Ashley	1 Ashley
2 Mary	2 Deborah	2 Jennifer	2 Jessica	2 Brittany
3 Patricia	3 Karen	3 Kimberly	3 Amanda	3 Jessica
4 Susan	4 Susan	4 Lisa	4 Sarah	4 Sierra
5 Deborah	5 Linda	5 Tracy	5 Megan	5 Danielle
6 Kathleen	6 Patricia	6 Kelly	6 Jennifer	6 Tiffany
7 Barbara	7 Kimberly	7 Nicole	7 Katherine	7 Erica
8 Nancy	8 Catherine	8 Angela	8 Rachel	8 Crystal
9 Sharon	9 Cynthia	9 Pamela	9 Stephanie	9 Jasmine
10 Karen	10 Lori	10 Christine	10 Heather	10 Tanisha
11 Carol(e)	11 Kathleen	11 Dawn	11 Brittany	11 Candice
12 Sandra	12 Sandra	12 Amy	12 Nicole	12 Ebony
13 Diane	13 Nancy	13 Deborah	13 Amber	13 Latoya
14 Catherine	14 Cheryl	14 Karen	14 Emily	Whitney
15 Christine	15 Denise	15 Julie	15 Elizabeth	15 Michelle
16 Cynthia	16 Pamela	Mary	16 Lindsey	16 Stephanie
17 Donna	17 Donna	17 Laura	17 Samantha	17 Alicia
18 Judith	18 Carol(e)	18 Stacey	18 Lauren	Amber
19 Margaret	19 Lisa	19 Catherine	19 Melissa	Jennifer
20 Janice	20 Michelle	20 Lori	20 Danielle	Lakeisha
21 Janet	21 Diane	21 Tammy	21 Amy	21 Nicole
22 Pamela	22 Sharon	22 Elizabeth	22 Kelly	22 Angela
23 Gail	23 Barbara	Shannon	23 Rebecca	23 Tierra
24 Cheryl	24 Laura	24 Stephanie	24 Kristen	24 Dominique
25 Suzanne	25 Theresa	25 Kristin	25 Christina	Keisha
26 Marilyn	26 Julie	26 Heather	26 Jamie	26 Brandi
27 Brenda	27 Elizabeth	Susan	27 Kayla	Ciara
28 Beverly	28 Janet	28 Sandra	28 Crystal	28 Christina
Carolyn	29 Lynn(e)	29 Denise	29 Laura	Kimberly
30 Ann(e)	30 Margaret	30 Theresa	30 Tiffany	30 Andrea
31 Shirley	31 Christine	31 Christina	31 Michelle	Melissa
32 Jacqueline	32 Brenda	Tina	32 Whitney	32 Tiara
33 Joanne	33 Ann(e)	33 Cynthia	33 Katie	33 Amanda
34 Lynn(e)	34 Suzanne	Melissa	34 Casey	34 Natasha
Marcia	Angela	Patricia	35 Kimberly	35 Aisha
36 Denise	Renee	36 Renee	36 Allison	Kendra
37 Gloria	37 Sherry	37 Cheryl	37 Caitlin	Kierra
38 Joyce	38 Jacqueline	38 Sherry	38 Andrea	Latasha
39 Kathy	39 Sheila	39 Donna	39 Courtney	39 Jamie
40 Elizabeth	40 Judith	40 Erica	40 Erin	Kelly
41 Laura	41 Carolyn	41 Rachel	41 Angela	Keyonna
42 Darlene	42 Darlene	Sharon	42 Chelsea	Rachel
43 Theresa	Marie	43 Linda	43 Mary	Robin
44 Joan	44 Robin	44 Barbara	44 Erica	44 Courtney
45 Elaine	45 Beverly	Jacqueline	45 Stacey	Lauren
46 Michelle	46 Andrea	Rhonda	46 Brandy	Shannon
47 Judy	Colleen	47 Andrea	47 Anna	Stacey
48 Diana	48 Anne Marie	48 Rebecca	48 Hannah	48 Elizabeth
49 Frances	49 Kathy	Wendy	49 Alicia	Sade
Maureen	Kim	50 Maria	50 Kelsey	Tamika
Phyllis	Maureen			
Ruth				

The top fifty first names in Australia

BOYS

1950

1 John
2 Peter
3 Michael
4 David
5 Robert
6 Stephen
7 Paul
8 Philip
9 Christopher
10 Ian
11 Gregory
12 Richard
13 Anthony
William
15 Geoffrey
16 Mark
17 James
18 Graham
19 Andrew
20 Gary
21 Colin
22 Alan
23 Bruce
24 George
25 Ronald
26 Keith
27 Terence
28 Thomas
29 Neil
30 Patrick
Stuart
32 Barry
Brian
34 Dennis
Raymond
36 Arthur
Joseph
Ross
39 Kenneth
40 Douglas
41 Trevor
42 Edward
43 Adrian
Bernard
Donald
Francis
Malcolm
48 Alexander
Frank
Russell
Wayne

1975

1 Matthew
2 Andrew
3 David
4 Michael
5 Paul
6 Adam
7 Christopher
8 Daniel
9 Mark
10 Scott
11 Steven
12 Simon
13 Jason
14 Benjamin
15 Bradley
16 Craig
17 Brett
18 Shane
19 Anthony
20 Timothy
Glenn
22 Alan
23 Cameron
24 Damian
25 Ronald
26 Justin
27 Dean
28 Travis
29 James
Peter
31 Luke
Stuart
Nicholas
34 Leigh
Shaun
36 Adrian
37 Brendan
Troy
39 Richard
40 Gregory
41 Ashley
42 John
43 Christian
44 Nathan
45 Aaron
46 Jeffrey
47 Gavin
48 Dale
49 Wayne
50 Kane

1988

1 Matthew
2 Daniel
3 Michael
4 Benjamin
5 Thomas
6 Andrew
7 Christopher
8 James
9 Nicholas
10 David
11 Samuel
12 Ryan
13 Adam
14 Scott
15 Joshua
16 Luke
17 Mark
18 Steven
19 Timothy
20 Alexander
21 Jason
22 Bradley
23 Peter
24 Aaron
Nathan
26 Jarrad
27 Shaun
28 Simon
29 William
30 Shane
31 Brett
Jonathon
33 Anthony
34 Cameron
35 Craig
Todd
Tyson
38 Paul
39 Ashley
Robert
41 Dylan
42 Patrick
43 John
Rhys
45 Lachlan
Phillip
47 Jake
Joel
49 Jordan
Stuart

GIRLS

1950

1 Susan
2 Margaret
3 Ann(e)
4 Elizabeth
5 Christine
6 Jennifer
7 Judith
8 Patricia
9 Catherine
10 Helen
11 Kerry
12 Deborah
Lynette
14 Linda
15 Pamela
Robyn
17 Mary
18 Dianne
19 Sandra
20 Janet
21 Julie
Suzanne
23 Carol(e)
24 Barbara
25 Jane
Janice
27 Kathleen
Marilyn
Wendy
30 Jillian
31 Lynn(e)
32 Cheryl
Heather
Maria
35 Frances
Jill
Marion
Maureen
Roslyn
40 Gail
41 Joan
Lesley
Rosemary
Virginia
45 Michelle
46 Beverley
Lorraine
Penelope
49 Amanda
Kay

1975

1 Michelle
2 Catherine
3 Kylie
4 Nicole
5 Rebecca
6 Melissa
7 Lisa
8 Belinda
9 Rachel
10 Sarah
11 Kellie
12 Jodie
13 Emma
14 Melanie
15 Megan
16 Fiona
17 Sally
18 Amanda
19 Kate
20 Natalie
21 Danielle
22 Tania
23 Tracey
24 Joanne
25 Karen
26 Kim
27 Samantha
Jennifer
29 Narelle
30 Renee
31 Leanne
32 Claire
33 Elizabeth
Jacqueline
35 Jane
36 Simone
Julie
Alison
39 Sharon
40 Melinda
41 Carly
42 Deborah
43 Kristy
44 Kerrie
Susan
46 Donna
47 Christine
48 Vanessa
49 Angela
50 Andrea
Caroline
Naomi

1988

1 Jessica
2 Sarah
3 Amy
4 Lauren
5 Emma
Rebecca
7 Melissa
8 Kate
9 Amanda
10 Ashleigh
11 Samantha
12 Katherine
Nicole
14 Alicia
Rachel
16 Megan
17 Laura
18 Stephanie
19 Lisa
20 Danielle
21 Hannah
Kylie
23 Courtney
24 Emily
25 Alexandra
26 Kelly
27 Elise
28 Kimberley
29 Chloe
30 Hayley
31 Sophie
32 Carly
Jenna
34 Renee
35 Alice
Stacey
37 Elizabeth
Leah
39 Lucy
40 Alison
Tara
42 Erin
43 Crystal
Melanie
Natalie
46 Natasha
47 Chelsea
Gemma
Jade
Tegan

4 Naming the baby

In the last fifteen years I have received several hundred letters from parents in all English-speaking countries, explaining why they chose the names they did for their children. The reasons they mentioned can be arranged under a number of headings.

Fashion

A great many parents began with the question of which names they believed to be currently fashionable, for this had affected their choice of names one way or the other. Parents who had chosen **Philippa** for their daughter, for instance, said that they had 'a major desire to avoid modern excesses of vulgarity and trend following'. It was perhaps an accident that 'vulgarity' occurred in such close context with 'trend following', but it should be emphasised that the two are not connected. Vulgarity presumably refers to a name's respectability, which I shall be discussing later. As for trend following, it is doubtful whether the majority of parents are really aware of what the trend is until several years after it has begun. When it becomes generally known which names are being used a great deal, there is ample evidence to show that most people hastily move away from them. This is true, at least, of names that have not had a high following for several generations. There is a fear that such names will not stand the test of time and that they will therefore 'date' a child.

Jason has been a typical example of such a name in recent years. It came in for a great many negative comments from my correspondents, many of whom said things like: 'I shall scream if I hear of another Jason.' There was a general feeling that the name was working class, a word which some writers equated with 'vulgar'. Others scoffed at it because of its associations with characters on television.

I believe there are working-class names, just as there are middle-class names, but Jason is *not* marked in this way. It clearly appealed to a wide range of social levels. I also believe that some names are 'vulgar', but by my definition these are names which are totally unsuitable for use as first names which are given by publicity-seeking parents. Jason clearly does not fall into this class, either.

Nevertheless, the feelings reflected by my correspondents in the last few years have been equally well reflected in the popularity charts. Use of Jason has been declining rapidly, and it may be destined to return to obscurity.

A less dramatic swing of fashion than that which affected Jason can have a positive influence on a name, however. As one parent wrote about **Matthew:** 'Probably a few years ago I would never have dreamt of using this name, but simply for the fact that it has become popular one gets used to the sound of it and eventually likes it.'

This comment hints at another parental fear—that they will choose a name which is completely out of fashion. The majority of parents probably make a conscious attempt to steer between the two extremes. 'It isn't very common,' wrote a mother who had chosen **Timothy** during 1972, 'but it is not too unusual.' Other parents chose **Jessica** because it was 'not particularly fashionable, so wouldn't date her'. The parents of **John** considered the name 'not gimmicky, not easily dated'.

But if this conscious motivation is admirable in itself, how effectively do most parents achieve their aim? They tend to base their ideas about which names are popular and which names are not on their own social circle, which is a shaky base indeed. John, which seems to be a name that could not possibly be accused of dating a child, may well do so by the end of the century. It has suffered such an amazing decline on all sides that it is likely to become a rare name for future generations. Even

The practice of romantic names among persons, even of the lowest orders of society, has become a very general evil: and doubtless many unfortunate beauties, of the names of Clarissa and Eloisa, might have escaped under the less dangerous appellatives of Elizabeth or Deborah.

Isaac Disraeli *Influence of a Name*

now a John who is beginning school is likely to be the only boy of that name in the class—something which would have been out of the question a few years ago.

Social class associations

This is not the place to discuss the subtleties of what makes people 'working class' or 'middle class', or whether the labels can still be used meaningfully. Most of my correspondents clearly felt that there are still recognisable social strata and that the classes of people have different tastes in most things, including names.

Parents can certainly be influenced when choosing a name by their assessment of a name's social standing. Of **Benjamin** one parent wrote: 'It also appealed to the snob in me, seeming to be a name Hampstead-type people used.' On **Louise** another writer commented: 'it sounds very sophisticated', and a third parent said of **Alexandra:** 'I like regal names', which I take to be another indirect reference to social class.

Not all names, needless to say, suggest one social class rather than another. When the associations are there, they can change drastically with the passing of time. **Abigail** went out of fashion completely because it had become almost a synonym for a lady's maid. It now seems to be coming back into fashion at the other end of the social scale. If it follows a normal course it will make its way slowly down the social grades until it fades away again, waiting for the whole mysterious process to bring it back to the top.

Euphony

The sound of a first name when placed alongside the surname is a common factor considered by parents. **Paul, Mark, Joanne** and **Tracey** may be popular generally, but as the birth registers reveal very clearly, there is an avoidance of such combinations as **Paul Hall, Mark Clarke, Mark Martin, Joanne Jones** and **Tracey Thomas. Jason** has never caught on with the **Jackson** family, for similar reasons.

Sometimes parents fall in love with the sound of an individual name. One parent commented on **Bronia** that 'it has an interesting sound', and another said of **Bryony**: 'short musical sound and the combination of an abrupt start and a subtle ending'. The reference by one mother to 'the beautiful name **Berengaria**' was presumably another comment on euphony.

Initials

The parents of Colin Cowdrey, an English cricketer of some renown, made sure when they named him that his full initials would be M.C.C. Amongst cricket lovers throughout the world these initials are famous as being those of the Marylebone Cricket Club. Colin Cowdrey was thus dedicated to cricket from the moment of his baptism.

Elsdon C. Smith has said that black Americans consider it lucky to create a set of initials for a child which make a meaningful word. Most parents

Are we naming our daughters too fancifully? I am inclined to sympathise with the feeling that makes poor parents who have perforce to live in some soulless slum, seek for something sweet and wholesome, even if it be only a name, and I have given up moralising when I hear such a one called Doris or Ivy. It is ever so much better than condemning them to the hackneyed Mary Ann which seems to rob them of all chance. I like the flowers and the gems, but I do not care about the mythological names such as Diana, Psyche, and the like—they seem too heathenish.

Anonymous article on the Woman's Page, in *Great Eastern Railway Magazine*, November, 1912.

'What about Dawn?' she said. 'I like the sound of Dawn. Then Mary for a second name. Dawn Mary Parker, it sounds sweet'.

'Dawn! That's not a Christian name,' he said. Then he told her, 'Just as you please, dear'.

Muriel Spark *The Black Madonna*

would say that it rather depends what the word is. Amongst those who would seem to have begun life at a disadvantage in this respect are W. C. Fields and Sir Arthur Sullivan, of Gilbert and Sullivan fame. The latter gentleman began life as Arthur Seymour Sullivan.

Charles Dickens, who somewhere in his novels comments on every conceivable aspect of names and naming, was well aware of initial possibilities. In his *Pickwick Papers* he creates Peter Magnus, a man who thinks extremely highly of his own name. There is also the 'curious circumstance about those initials. You will observe—P. M.—post meridian. In hasty notes to intimate acquaintance, I sometimes sign myself "Afternoon". It amuses my friends very much, Mr Pickwick'. 'It is calculated to offer them the highest gratification, I should conceive,' is Mr Pickwick's reply.

Other surname influences

As we shall see when we come to discuss surnames in detail, there is a central surname stock just as there is a central first name stock. Some parents try to balance first names with surnames, the usual with the unusual or vice versa. In choosing **Guinevere,** for example, the **Day** family had in mind that this was 'a name to complement her surname', and **Jemima** was chosen as 'a fairly unusual name to go with **Brown**'. Another correspondent began by saying that they had had to find 'something unusual, because her surname is **Smith**'. This seems to be sensible thinking in principle, but all the evidence is that the majority of people with common surnames choose equally common first names.

Another factor that concerns the surname is the latter's meaning, or potential meaning when placed beside a first name. One comes across occasional instances of **Ann Teak, Handsome Mann, Orange Lemon** and the like, but one can safely say that the majority of parents are careful to avoid such combinations. Some may come about later by marriage. There is a recorded instance of a **Rose** family who named their daughter **Wild,** thinking that they had hit on a beautiful combination. She later married a gentleman called **Bull.**

Respectability

This is felt to be conferred on a name when it has been in existence for some centuries, though parents who are concerned with such a point often use euphemistic expressions such as 'traditional' or 'old-fashioned' rather than 'respectable'. We are not necessarily talking about the use of a name by one social class rather than another here. We are talking about the choice of **Sarah,** say, rather than **Trac(e)y**—both of them immensely popular over a wide social range—simply because Sarah has been in use as an English first name for centuries whereas Trac(e)y has not.

Whether for practical considerations, such as the difficulties that can be caused for the bearer of a relatively unfamiliar name, for historical nicety, or simply for the usual reasons of snobbishness, one detects in many letters from middle-class parents a strong reaction against modern first names such as **Craig, Darren, Scott, Shane, Warren** and **Wayne** for the boys, **Beverl(e)y, Cheryl, Gaynor, Hayley, Kelly, Kerrie, Lorraine, Mandy** and **Trac(e)y** for the girls. **Lee/Leigh** should also be included in both lists.

Originality

As we have seen, black American families value individuality in names rather more than white families. They are therefore more ready to invent new names, convert words into names or transfer them from other sources. Some white parents feel equally strongly that they should invent a name for their child. Their thinking appears to be that they have created the child concerned, so they should also create the child's name.

The arguments for original names are that they avoid associations with other people who have borne the name and really do identify an individual. But very great care must be taken by parents who tread this dangerous path. Several studies by psychologists have shown that people who have names that are considered to be decidedly unusual or odd by those around them can experience great difficulties in their normal social relationships. This can apply to well-established, but very outmoded names as well as invented ones, for Harvard students classed **Ivy, Rosebud, Hope, Patience, Cuthbert, Reginald** and **Egbert** as 'odd' a few years ago. Another age-group in another place would naturally compile quite a different list of odd names and perhaps accept most of these as perfectly normal.

It is certain that there are misunderstandings between the black and white communities because of their different ideas about naming. It would help if white people bore in mind that black parents use different criteria and have their own sound reasons for doing what they do. On the other hand, black parents who know that their children will have to make their way in a multi-racial society should perhaps be extra cautious about the names they give. Their task is to retain originality while avoiding at all costs what might be called oddity.

Sexual characteristics

Parents frequently mention that certain names are particularly masculine or feminine and that this has affected their choice. Most of our first names give clear indications of a child's sex, and it is obviously felt to be important to preserve this situation. **Leslie** and **Lesley** are both fading away rapidly in the popularity charts, perhaps because of this sexual confusion. I would expect both **Lee** and **Leigh** to drop away if more boys as well as girls are given the name.

I also detect in many letters the belief that a strong, masculine name will make a boy into a 'real man', while a soft, feminine name will somehow produce a 'lovely lady'. I emphasise that these are letters being written by young parents of today. Ideas about the sexual roles clearly do not change overnight.

Religion

The parents' religious beliefs often influence the choice of first names. There are plenty of Christian first names available, so parents have a wide choice. The recent upsurge of **Christian** itself as a first name presumably reflects religious motivation, but with first names one can take nothing for granted.

Use of the name **Mary** has undoubtedly declined a great deal in the last twenty years or so, its very popularity having at last brought about its own downfall. Those parents who do continue to use it are probably keenly aware of its religious significance and regard it as a name of great potency. Earlier attitudes to it were well displayed in Montaigne's *Essays*, first published in John Florio's translation in 1603:

> 'A licentious young man had one night gotten a wench to lie with him, who so soone as she came to bed, he demanded her name, who answered Marie: The young man hearing that name, was suddenly so strucken with a motive of religion, and an awfull respect unto that sacred name of the Virgin Marie, the blessed mother of our Saviour and Redeemer, that he did not onely presently put her away from him, but reformed all the remainder of his succeeding life.'

Personal associations

A name's associations with other people provide one of the most important reasons for choosing it or not choosing it. There can be both private and public associations.

Specific commemorative use of names, as we have seen, was normal for the naming of boys until the present century, with members of the family

---

She was named after Saint Therese of Lisieux, affectionately known as the Little Flower, a Carmelite nun who had died at the age of twenty-four in 1897 having apparently distinguished herself only by housework and obedience. But her autobiography found and published after her death, proved a document sweet, almost sickly, in its childlike influence. It became a runaway best-seller in the Catholic world and had been a favourite book in O'Halloran's boyhood home.

Bamber Gascoigne *Murgatreud's Empire*

Being known on her own authority as Miss Abbey Potterson, some water-side heads, which (like the water) were none of the clearest, harboured muddled notions that she was named after, or in some sort related to, the Abbey of Westminster. But Abbey was only short for Abigail . . .

Charles Dickens *Our Mutual Friend*

My father had combined diplomacy with the study of Anglo-Saxon history and, of course, with my mother's consent, he gave me the name of Alfred, one of his heroes (I believe she had boggled at Aelfred). This Christian name, for some inexplicable reason, had become corrupted in the eyes of our middle-class world; it belonged exclusively now to the working class and was usually abbreviated to Alf.

Graham Greene *Doctor Fischer of Geneva*

rather than public figures being honoured. A very large number of first names are still chosen in honour of friends and relations, particularly, it would seem, among the 'upper' classes. Such names are sometimes what Ian Hay once called 'sprats to catch testamentary whales'. But private or public associations of a name can just as frequently act against it. We all know of parents who reject names because they have known somebody unpleasant who bore it. A public taboo also operates against names like **Adolf,** not that this particular name was popular *before* the 1930s in the English-speaking world.

Origins

A few parents take account of a first name's origin when choosing a name for their child, but this tends to be a confirmatory rather than a deciding factor. If parents already have an inclination towards a certain name for other reasons, they are pleased to discover that it originally meant something favourable, as most of our first names did. But the parents of at least one boy who wrote to me were primarily influenced by the origin of the name they chose. Of **Selwyn** they wrote: 'an old English name meaning "house friend" . . . we liked its meaning'.

Fictional associations

Novels still continue to inspire parents when they are looking for names, though if a novel is made into a film it is obviously difficult to say which was the main source. *Gone With the Wind*, as both novel and film, was a major influence from 1939 onwards. **Melanie, Ashley** and **Bonnie** derived from that source, and other names which occurred in the story, such as **Scarlett** and **Careen,** have received some attention.

High Society, released in 1956, had Grace Kelly playing the part of Tracy Samantha Lord. **Tracy, Samantha** and **Kelly,** transferred to first name use, appeared almost from that moment. *High Society* was actually a re-make, with music, of *The Philadelphia Story*, released in 1939 and considered by many critics to be by far the better film. This version of the film, however, failed to influence parents-to-be.

A more recent film that had considerable impact on name usage was *The Graduate*, in which Dustin Hoffman played the part of **Benjamin.** That name has enjoyed a run of popularity ever since. It is interesting to note that it was the names of the fictional characters portrayed by Grace Kelly and Dustin Hoffman which became popular, not their own first names, as had been the case with **Shirley** Temple, **Leslie** Howard and the like in the 1930s.

Television series naturally have an effect on naming, in that they bring names to the public's attention. Probably the most outstanding television 'success' of recent times is that of **Emma,** re-introduced in *The Avengers* by Diana Rigg. Other names of this kind, used by parents because they admire the fictional characters bearing the names, are **Jason, Joshua, Fleur** and **Ricky.**

One final name that deserves a mention in this section is **Jennifer,** which was decidedly unusual in North America—though it had been popular in Britain—until Erich Segal published *Love Story*. The film version of this, released in 1970, caused

Jennifer to begin a swift ascent to the number one position amongst American girls' names. The film also showed that the real names of actors or actresses *could* still be noticed and copied, for **Ryan** O'Neal's name was also taken over.

Associated characteristics

Many people believe that everyone who bears a particular name will grow up to have the same characteristics. Laurence Sterne made superb fun of this idea in his 18th-century novel *Tristram Shandy*, expounding a 'philosophy of nomenclature' which was seized upon later by R. L. Stevenson in an essay of that name. More recently

I really can't see why you should object to the name of Algernon. It is not at all a bad name. In fact, it is rather an aristocratic name. Half of the chaps who go into the Bankruptcy Court are called Algernon.

Oscar Wilde *The Importance of Being Earnest*

'Annie' is boisterous, where 'Anne' has style and dignity.

G. B. Stern *A Name to Conjure With*

Archibald Jones had probably no rival. His Christian name helped him; it was a luscious, resounding mouthful for admirers.

Arnold Bennett *The Old Wives' Tale*

Roger Price and Leonard Stern had made suitable fun of the whole idea in their booklet *How Dare You Call Me That!* In the Introduction they say: 'Once you give a baby a name society begins to treat it as if it has the type of personality the name implies, and the child, being sensitive, responds consciously or unconsciously and grows up to fit the name.' The authors go on to give their own ideas about the public associations of a large number of names. A sample: '**Angus** is a giant who smiles a lot and looks as if he might have been at Bannockburn. Be careful shaking hands with Angus. He'll dislocate all bones up to the elbow.'

There is a modicum of truth in this name-

'I christened her Maria del Sol, because she was my first child and I dedicated her to the glorious sun of Castile; but her mother calls her Sally, and her brother Pudding-face.'

Somerset Maugham *Of Human Bondage*

characteristics theory. If a large number of people from the same social group were asked to describe a **Cuthbert** or an **Agnes**, a **Fred** or a **Rita**, they might well show some kind of agreement in what they said. They would be drawing upon information stored in their minds about the social class, age and profession of people they had met who bore these names. It is also partly true that when two girls who both started life as **Elizabeth** or whatever have become **Liz** in one case and remained Elizabeth in the other by the time they reach their twenties, the two forms of the name may reflect to some extent their different personalities.

Some names, then, do have generally accepted associated characteristics, and these can influence parents' choices. It is hard to say where associated characteristics end and personal associations begin on occasions. Did Jerry Lewis choose **Wilbur** as the name for a silly person because of characteristics that he felt were already associated with it, or is the name now associated with Lewis's portrayals?

In our own society it is of course impossible to pin down seriously these 'meanings' of names, which can be positive or negative, which can vary from person to person, region to region, and which are constantly mutating with the passing of time and the arrival of new social influences.

In some other societies, however, far more specific beliefs exist and the effect of those beliefs can to a certain extent be measured. G. Jahoda, for

People always grow up like their names. It took me thirty years to work off the effects of being called Eric. If I wanted a girl to grow up beautiful I'd call her Elizabeth, and if I wanted her to be a good cook I'd choose something like Mary or Jane.

George Orwell (Eric Blair) *Letters*

example, has made an interesting study of Ashanti day names (whereby children are named according to the day on which they are born), and the characteristics associated with each name. He discovered that a child born on a 'bad' day was more likely to end up in the juvenile court than a child whose name advertised the fact that he had been born on a 'good' day. The bad day name would cause others to act towards its bearer in a certain way, and this would affect his personality.

Verbal associations

Many of the names that have been common in the past have come to have verbal associations. Everyone is familiar with expressions like: 'every **Tom, Dick** or **Harry**', 'simple **Simon**', 'a **Jack** of all trades'. Simon seems to have overcome its unpleasant associations recently, but the first name popularity tables indicate that some names are

---

Now I wonder what would please her,
Charlotte, Julia or Louisa?
Ann and Mary, they're too common;
Joan's too formal for a woman;
Jane's a prettier name beside;
But we had a Jane that died.
They would say, if 'twas Rebecca,
That she was a little Quaker,
Edith's pretty, but that looks
Better in old English books.
Ellen's left off long ago:
Blanche is out of fashion now.

None that I have named as yet
Are so good as Margaret.
Emily is neat and fine.
What do you think of Caroline?
How I'm puzzled and perplexed
What to choose or think of next!
I am in a little fever
Lest the name that I shall give her
Should disgrace her or defame her.
I will leave Papa to name her.

Charles Lamb *Naming the Baby* (1809)

---

hampered by such idioms. The American use of 'the john' for the lavatory can hardly have helped the name **John,** and may have contributed to its recent spectacular downfall. Wise parents remind themselves of any verbal associations that may exist by checking a potential name in a good dictionary before finally deciding on it.

Other associations

Place names such as **Florence** and **Kent** have been used as first names because of a wish to commemorate the place of birth. American twins were given the names **Okla** and **Homa** for a similar reason. **Tulip** was chosen by the singer Tiny Tim to remind him of the song that made his fortune: 'Tip-toe through the tulips.' A more general transfer from a song in recent times is seen with **Michelle,** which the Beatles undoubtedly set on its way. It is also possible that the affectionate regard in the public's mind for the late Maurice Chevalier extended to his song 'Louise', and that the popularity of that name stems in part from the song. On the other hand one family wrote to explain that they had called their daughter **Louise** because 'this is the name of one of our cats, whom we love very much'.

Laura is another name which has been rising in popularity since the 1940s, when a song of that name made a big impact.

Nationality

Parents often want to proclaim their child's nationality in its name. Scottish, Welsh and Irish parents are especially fond of doing this—and I am speaking here of those who choose to do so. If one lives in Scotland, Wales or Ireland one is naturally exposed to a rather different central stock of first names and may pick a name from it without thinking of its national markings.

Various dictionaries of names which reflect different nationalities are listed in the Bibliography. My own special studies in this area bore fruit in 1978 when I published *Scottish Christian Names.*

Diminutive forms

The variant forms of a name are usually considered by parents, since it is accepted that many names are rarely used in their full forms by a child's friends. If parents do not like the usual diminutives and short forms they may well avoid a name altogether.

The first name **Kylie** has been particularly well-used in modern times in Australia. It may well be the inspiration for **Kayleigh, Kayley,** etc, which is rapidly gaining popularity in Britain, and **Kyla,** which is popular in the US. Kayleigh has no doubt been influenced by **Hayley** and **Kelly.** Kylie itself was first given as a nickname to Kathleen Tennant (1912–88), the distinguished Australian novelist, who wrote as Kylie Tennant. It is an Aboriginal word and means 'boomerang'.

I have already commented on the difference between these formalised nicknames and names like **Jim** or **Bob** when the latter are bestowed as the legal names. With the development of the latter, it is possible that at some time in the future someone bearing a name like **Richard** will always remain Richard, since **Dick** will be looked upon as a completely separate name and not a diminutive.

Incidents at birth

Incidents that occur at or close to a child's birth often influence the name that is given to it. One little girl was called **Caroline** because 'she was born in the middle of a power cut, and as the power came on "Sweet Caroline" was being played on the radio'. A boy likewise became **James** because of 'a song, "St James' Infirmary" which my husband was playing just before I went to hospital'. I have also been told of a girl who was called **Sirene** because she was born during an air-raid and the siren was heard soon afterwards.

Perhaps one should include here the mother who 'had a dream two weeks before she was born that I had a baby girl and that we had named her **Jessica**.' This dream name was duly given to the daughter. Names that relate to the time of birth are also incident names in their way. **Noël, Avril, April, June** and **Natalie** are well established for this purpose. One parent wrote to say that **Octavia** was chosen partly because of an October birth, an interesting example of an incidental link name.

There is also a kind of verbal incident name. In *The Forsyte Saga* is a well-known example, when Annette looks down at her newly born daughter:

'*Ma petite fleur!*' Annette said softly.

'*Fleur,*' repeated Soames: '**Fleur!** We'll call her that.'

Less poetic is the story reported in an American newspaper in 1975, to the effect that a baby boy had just been named **Bill** 'because he came on the last day of the month'.

Perhaps one should also set up a category called 'Incidents at conception,' though none of my correspondents have mentioned such events. But Professor R. N. Ashley reported in an American Name Society *Bulletin* that **Margot** Hemingway received her first name because her parents thought she was conceived after they drank a vintage Château Margeaux. Nancy Mitford also has a character called **Northey** in her novel *Don't Tell Alfred*. It is explained that 'she was conceived in the Great Northern Hotel—hence her curious name'.

Description

A **Serena** received her name, according to a correspondent, because a friend of the family described her as 'so serene'. A **Daniel** received his name 'because he looked like a judge'. The choice of a first name for descriptive reasons is rare, however. The majority of names are decided on before birth, and it is recognised that a baby's appearance is hardly likely to remain that way for long.

Pride lives with all; strange names our rustics give
To helpless infants, that their own may live;
Pleased to be known, they'll some attention claim,
And find some by-way to the house of fame.
Some idle deed, some child's preposterous name,
Shall make him known, and give his folly fame.

George Crabbe *The Parish Register* (1807)

Sibling influence

It should not be forgotten that a particular child may not be given a name because a brother or sister already bears it. Nevertheless, some families have been known to give all their sons the same name, and others like all the names of their children to begin with the same letter. Many parents consider whether a name they are thinking about for a later child will 'match' the names already in use in the family.

'Another flowery name!'

'What?' cried Jo. 'Come off it; I won't have no Carnations and such like in my family—and a boy, too!'

'He's William!' shouted Rosie 'Sweet William, and he is sweet.'

Eve Garnett *The Family From One End Street*

Spelling and pronunciation

The rarer names may cause pronunciation problems. Looking through the birth registers for instance, I wonder myself how I would pronounce **Annarenia, Deion, Gyda** and the like. Parents sometimes try a name out on friends to see whether the pronunciation causes difficulty.

The spelling situation is far worse. Even very common names appear in strange forms, such as **Henery, Jonothon, Katheryne, Markk, Neal, Trever, Osker, Daved, Freada.** If these names, which should be familiar, cause problems, then one can be quite sure that anyone given a really unusual name will go through life constantly having to spell it out. Even then that person will have the irritating experience of seeing the name mis-spelled on countless occasions.

Family tradition

At one time it was common for families to have what were virtually hereditary first names which they passed on from generation to generation. A few of my correspondents still refer to family traditions, but these are tending to disappear along with the custom of naming children after their parents and grandparents.

Some conclusions

As the above notes are meant to illustrate, naming a baby can be a complicated affair. For parents who have yet to make a choice I have tried to provide help in the flow chart following this section. The golden rule that should always be observed was hinted at by Charles Lamb in the poem quoted earlier about choosing a name. 'I wonder what would please *her*,' he said. It was the right thing to wonder. When you choose a name for a baby you are acting on the child's behalf and doing something that is of great importance for its future. You are not simply satisfying a personal whim.

The responsibility is rather frightening, and it is all too clear that a minority of parents are not capable of exercising that responsibility properly. One can sometimes see the arguments in favour of an official bureau that would vet and advise on the choice of first names, a function which the more enlightened registrars unofficially perform already. In view of the undoubted psychological damage that can be caused to children by the bestowal of absurd names, such a bureau would have to have powers of veto. Naturally there would be no question of all names needing approval, but doubtful cases could be submitted by registrars.

'What is his name?'

'An old-fashioned name, I thought. For such a modern couple. Tobias.'

'That's not the cat?'

'Cotton is the cat. Tobias was Ken's grandfather.'

John Updike *Couples*

But let us not end this brief survey of the first name situation on a sour note. First names are usually little volumes of social history in themselves as well as evocations of friends and loved ones. They provide a fascinating study, and if your appetite has been aroused, you will find suggestions for continuing the investigation in the Bibliography at the end of this book. We shall not be putting first names entirely to one side, but it is time now to look at their normal companions—surnames.

Naming the Baby

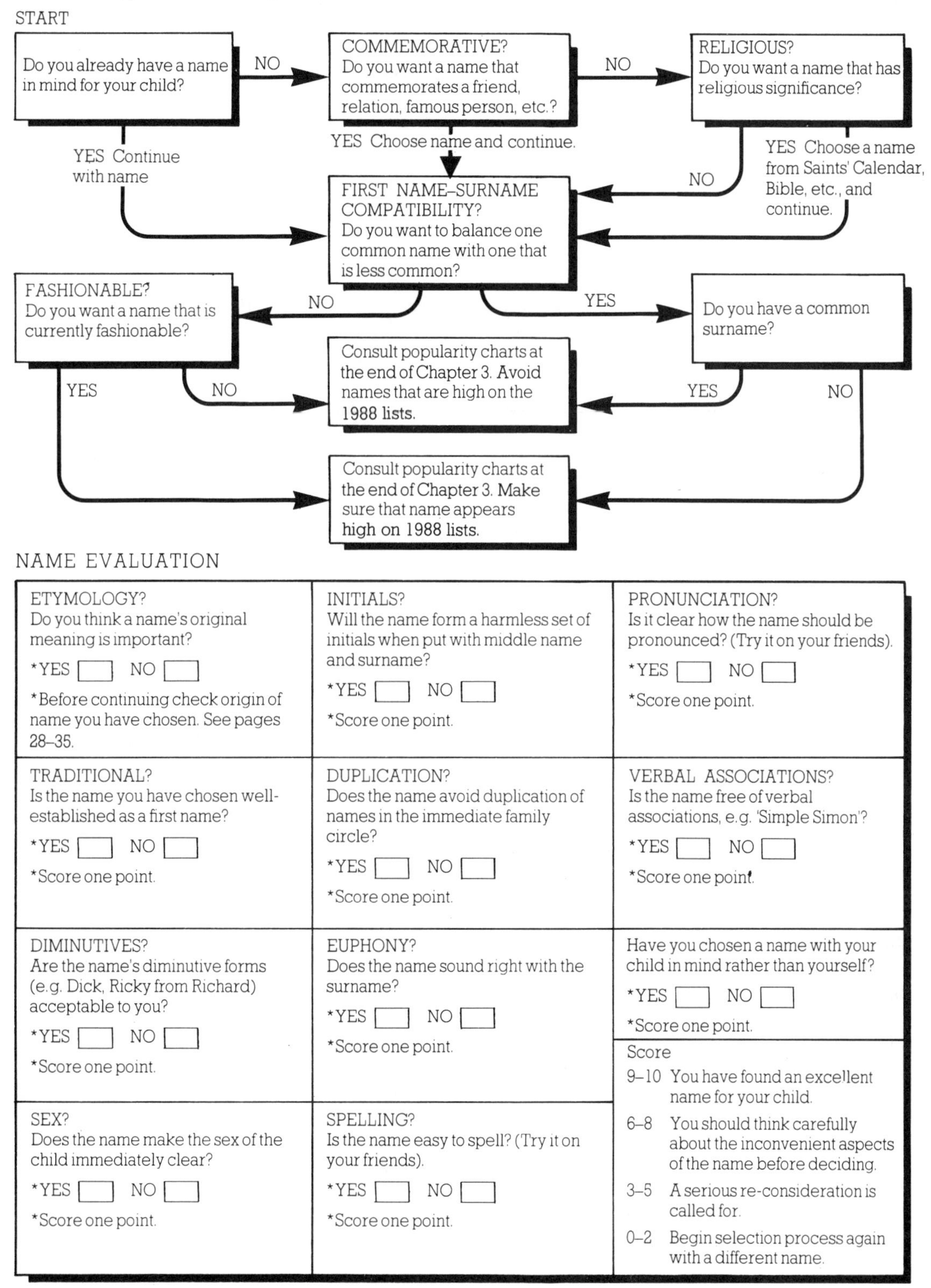

START
Do you already have a name in mind for your child?
NO
COMMEMORATIVE?
Do you want a name that commemorates a friend, relation, famous person, etc.?
NO
RELIGIOUS?
Do you want a name that has religious significance?
YES Continue with name
YES Choose name and continue.
YES Choose a name from Saints' Calendar, Bible, etc., and continue.
NO
FIRST NAME–SURNAME COMPATIBILITY?
Do you want to balance one common name with one that is less common?
FASHIONABLE?
Do you want a name that is currently fashionable?
NO
YES
Do you have a common surname?
Consult popularity charts at the end of Chapter 3. Avoid names that are high on the 1988 lists.
YES
NO
YES
NO
Consult popularity charts at the end of Chapter 3. Make sure that name appears high on 1988 lists.
NAME EVALUATION
ETYMOLOGY?
Do you think a name's original meaning is important?
*YES NO
*Before continuing check origin of name you have chosen. See pages 28–35.
INITIALS?
Will the name form a harmless set of initials when put with middle name and surname?
*YES NO
*Score one point.
PRONUNCIATION?
Is it clear how the name should be pronounced? (Try it on your friends).
*YES NO
*Score one point.
TRADITIONAL?
Is the name you have chosen well-established as a first name?
*YES NO
*Score one point.
DUPLICATION?
Does the name avoid duplication of names in the immediate family circle?
*YES NO
*Score one point.
VERBAL ASSOCIATIONS?
Is the name free of verbal associations, e.g. 'Simple Simon'?
*YES NO
*Score one point.
DIMINUTIVES?
Are the name's diminutive forms (e.g. Dick, Ricky from Richard) acceptable to you?
*YES NO
*Score one point.
EUPHONY?
Does the name sound right with the surname?
*YES NO
*Score one point.
Have you chosen a name with your child in mind rather than yourself?
*YES NO
*Score one point.
SEX?
Does the name make the sex of the child immediately clear?
*YES NO
*Score one point.
SPELLING?
Is the name easy to spell? (Try it on your friends).
*YES NO
*Score one point.
Score
9–10 You have found an excellent name for your child.
6–8 You should think carefully about the inconvenient aspects of the name before deciding.
3–5 A serious re-consideration is called for.
0–2 Begin selection process again with a different name.

Superlative first names

SHORTEST NAMES Many families have used single-letter first names, such as **A.** The best-known example is the middle **S** of President Harry S Truman's name.

LONGEST NAMES The longest 'normal' first name is probably **Alexanderina,** which is mainly found in Scotland. In 1861 a **Tilgathpilneser** Smith was named in England. The parents, or the registrar, were presumably not quite able to cope with the name of King **Tiglathpileser,** founder of the Assyrian Empire, who is several times mentioned in the Bible. Some of the extreme Puritans in the late 16th-century were given, or adopted, 'slogan' first names. Two well-known examples were **Jesus-Christ-came-into-the-world-to-save** Barebone and his brother, **If-Christ-had-not-died-for-thee-thou-hadst-been-damned** Barebone. The latter, 'whose morals were not of the best' according to one commentator, was known to most people as Damned Barebone.

ODDEST FIRST NAME Probably the Norwegian name **Odd.** It is more familiar in its German form, **Otto.**

FUNNIEST FIRST NAME May well be **Joke,** a feminine Dutch name, ultimately a form of **John.**

UNLUCKIEST NAMES According to the 18th-century writer Laurence Sterne, **Tristram** was the worst name that could be given to a child. It would be sure to bring misfortune. The antiquarian William Camden had earlier reported that some names were generally considered to be 'unfortunate to princes'. He mentioned '**John** in France, England and Scotland; and **Henry** lately in France'.

MOST RACIALLY MARKED NAMES Black and white Americans theoretically make use of the same stock of first names, but some names are favoured by one group and virtually ignored by the other. Thus, young Americans who are called **Amy, Laura, Julie; Matthew, Scott, Todd** are almost certain to be white. Names used almost exclusively by black Americans include **Tamika, Kenya, Latonya; Jermaine, Reginald, Willie.**

MOST POPULAR 'INSECT' NAME There are more 'bees' buzzing around in the English-speaking world than ever before, due to the popularity in recent times of **Deborah** and **Melissa,** both of which mean 'bee'.

MOST USED 'PLACE' NAME The Italian city of **Florence** has probably lent its name to more people in the English-speaking world than any other place, thanks to Florence Nightingale, who was born there.

RUDEST NAME Perhaps the rudest first name is **Tacy,** which derives from Latin *tace*, 'be silent'. Every time a Tacy (**Tacey**) announces her name to someone she is saying 'Shut up!'

MOST VALUABLE FIRST NAME Every American **Bill** knows that he is worth a hundred **Bucks. Richards** are often thought of as being **Rich.**

MOST MYSTERIOUS NAME According to Charles Dickens, who made use of it to name several characters, the most mysterious name for a girl was **Sophronia.**

MOST POPULAR 'ANIMAL' NAMES Bears, lions and wolves are all very well represented in first names. The 'bear' is present in **Arthur, Bernard, Ursula, Orson, Björn.** The 'lions' include **Leo, Leonard** and **Lionel.** A 'wolf' occurs in names like **Adolph, Ralph, Randolph, Phelan.**

FASTEST FIRST NAMES Perhaps those borne by **Jaguar Ferrari** Tonniges, of Nebraska, whose father is a car-freak.

FRUITIEST FIRST NAMES The most used are **Cherry,** originally a form of **Charity,** and **Berry,** often from **Berenice,** or **Bernice.**

HIGHEST NUMERICAL NAME Professor Weekley suggested that **Vicesimus** Knox, whose first name meant 'twentieth', was probably the record-holder in this area, leaving behind competitors such as **Septimus** ('seventh'), **Octavia** ('eighth'), **Decimus** ('tenth'). I have come across a lady whose name was **Mille,** which appears to be 'thousand' in French, but she was probably meant to be a **Millie.**

LOWEST NUMERICAL NAME **Zero** Mostel made his nickname well-known by his many screen appearances. He said his name was given to him as a result of poor performances at school. The father of the South African athlete **Zola** Budd was determined to give his child a name beginning with Z, and in one interview said that had she been a boy, the name would have been Zero.

MOST SURPRISING NAME A British family named their daughter **Surprise** a few years ago. They had confidently expected a son.

MOST MUSICAL NAMES A music-loving family in Honolulu named their children **Dodo, Rere, Mimi, Fafa, Soso, Lala, Sisi** and **Octavia.**

MOST COLOURFUL NAME Welsh parents are now using **Enfys** (rainbow) to name their daughters. **Rainbow** itself is occasionally used by English-speaking parents. My own day is occasionally brightened by a letter from Barbara Rainbow Fletcher, of Seattle, author of **Don't Blame the Stork** and avid collector of unusual personal names.

MOST POPULAR 'MONTH' NAME **April** is the most popular month-name, thanks to the use of its French form **Avril** alongside April itself. **June** and **May** are runners-up.

MOST POPULAR 'TIME OF DAY' NAMES A birth at dawn or when stars are shining seems to be most likely to attract a special name. 'Dawn' names include **Dawn** itself, **Aurora, Oriana, Roxana;** 'star' names are **Estelle, Stella, Astra, Esther.**

MOST ODOROUS NAME Black American parents, especially, are now making good use of **Chanel,** which they sometimes spell **Channel, Shanel, Shanell, Shannell.** Madame Gabrielle Bonheur Chanel would no doubt have been pleased at the compliment. She herself was known to her intimates as **Coco.**

MOST FLOWERY NAMES A very large number of flower names were used to name girls at the end of the 19th-century. Perhaps the most flowery of all was **Carmel,** which means 'garden'.

MOST PROLIFIC NAMER Several cases are known of parents who have given large numbers of names to an individual child, such as one beginning with each letter of the alphabet. The Reverend Ralph William Lionel Tollemache, born in 1826, married twice and had twelve children. Each was given a string of names, so that eventually 100 different names were distributed amongst them.

SEXIEST NAMES There have been several surveys designed to reveal the sex-appeal rating of different first names. In 1975 a British survey discovered that young men favoured **Susan, Samantha, Carol, Linda, Jennifer, Catherine, Amanda, Kerry, Claire** and **Natalie.** Girls would have willingly gone on a blind date with a **David, Stephen, Paul, Mark, Adam, Robert, Richard, Michael, Christopher** or **Philip.** Some ten years later a survey of *Daily Mirror* readers put **Samantha** as the sexiest girl's name, followed by a host of names with a French flavour—**Gabrielle, Dominique, Cerise, Nadine, Genevieve, Simone, Leonie. Michael** was voted sexiest male name, followed by **James, Stephen, David** and **Clint.** A reader who was able to sign herself I. A. M. Bliss rightly claimed that her name must rank highly in sex appeal. In the early 1980s a survey in the US asked young men to rate girls' names by sexiness. **Christine** emerged as the clear winner, followed by **Cheryl, Melanie, Dawn, Heather, Jennifer, Marilyn, Michelle** and **Susan.**

LEAST SEXY NAMES The biggest 'turn-offs', according to the American respondents, were **Ethel, Alma, Florence, Mildred, Zelda, Myrtle, Silvana, Edna** and **Elvira.** *Daily Mirror* readers mentioned **Agnes, Gertrude, Agatha, Bessie, Enid, May, Nora, Maud, Freda, Ida, Edda** and **Margaret** in this category. They also condemned **Ivor, Basil, Cyril, Cuthbert, Willie, Horace, Norman, Alfred, Rupert, Percival, Cecil, Archibald, Herbert, Harold, Bernard, Sidney** and **Herman.**

MOST STERTOROUS NAME Borne by an ancestor of Abraham and also by Abraham's brother, **Nahor,** which means 'snorer', was perhaps a reference to a baby which snuffled.

TASTIEST NAME R. A. Bullen writes from Reading, Berks., about the man he knew who was named **Delicious. Delicia** has also been used as a feminine name.

MOST RIOTOUS NAME Born of British parents who were living at the time in Ceylon, and during a period of martial law when riots were taking place almost daily, **Rioty** M. Winter was given a name to commemorate the circumstances. His parents no doubt read the Riot Act to him when he misbehaved.

MOST UNEXPECTED NAME According to journalistic report, a boy was named **Onyx,** after the precious stone, because he was onyx-pected.

MOST ORIGINAL NAME The name **Original** was given in the early 16th century to the eldest son and heir of certain well-to-do families. Original Bellamy, for instance, who was buried at Stainton in 1619, aged eighty, had a son of the same name and a grandson Original, born in 1606. The name was no doubt meant to suggest that the boy concerned was carrying on the original stock. It did not come into general use because most people assumed that it referred to original sin.

MOST COMMON ANANYM An ananym is a word or name formed by spelling another word or name backwards. The most commonly-used first name of this type is **Senga,** found fairly frequently in Scotland, especially in former times when **Agnes** was being well used there. **Adnil** and **Azile** are other names of this type which occur in the records. Some Russian parents in the 1920s and 30s named their sons **Ninel.**

MOST HESITANT NAME There are three different men mentioned in the Bible whose name is **Er,** which actually means 'vigilant'. According to Luke (3:28) one of these Ers was an ancestor of Jesus.

MOST FREQUENT BIBLICAL NAME In one sense the most frequently-used biblical name is **Yahweh,** Hebrew *Yahveh*, the proper name of the God of Israel. In one form or another, eg as **Yah** in expressions like Alleluia, Hebrew *hallelu-Yah* 'praise Yah!' it occurs over 6000 times and is the most frequently-used word (as well as name) in the Bible. Traditionally, to prevent the sacred name of God from being uttered during the reading of the Scripture, the artificial form **Jehovah** was used. Of the names used for people, **David** is the most frequently-occurring in the Bible, with 1150 mentions. However, all these mentions refer to the same man, whereas thirty *different* men bear the name **Zechariah.** There are some twenty-five **Johns** (or **Johanans**), twenty **Hananaiahs** (or **Ananiases**), eighteen **Simeons** (or **Simons**), sixteen **Joshuas** (or **Jesuses**), thirteen **Josephs,** ten **Michaels** and eight **Philips.** The name **Eve** is mentioned only five times. **Mary,** mother of Jesus, is mentioned by name only nineteen times, but there are references to seven other women who bear that name (or its alternative form **Miriam**). **Esther** occurs fifty-nine times, **Sarah** fifty-eight times.

ANGRIEST NAME **Paddy** has come to mean 'a show of anger or temper', reflecting the frequency with which Irishmen named **Patrick** displayed such symptoms. In the Bible a man named **Maaz** 'anger' is mentioned. There are also three different men named **Ahimaaz** 'my brother is angry'. That might rank as the most puzzling name—why should my brother be angry?

WINDIEST NAME **Gale** is probably the windiest name in common use, though it is probably meant to be **Gail,** the pet form of **Abigail.** **Storm** Jameson, the novelist, has made her name well-known, but it has not been copied. **Tempest** is occasionally found in 19th-century records.

SWEETEST NAME Most people would probably vote for **Candy** as the sweetest name in use, though it came into being as a pet form of **Candace. Dulcie** is based on Latin *dulcis* 'sweet'. There are several names in use which contain a reference to 'honey', Greek *meli*, *melitos*, Latin *mel*, *mellis*. They include **Melita, Melinda, Melissa** and **Pamela,** the last of these meaning 'all honey'.

MOST ALCOHOLIC NAME There is **Carling** Bassett, the tennis player, but the name most frequently used in modern times is **Brandy** (**Brandi, Brandee,** etc). There also plenty of girls called **Sherry,** though this name probably began as *chérie*, French 'darling'.

MOST POPULAR 'DAY' NAME It is the child born on Christmas Day who is most likely to be given a name to commemorate the fact. **Noël, Noëlle, Natalie** and **Natasha** all mean 'Christmas Day'. In the 19th century parents might well have used **Christmas** itself as a first name. **Carol** is not a Christmassy name by origin, but is understandably popular at that time of year.

5 The family name

"Tell me - are you one of the Somerset Spratts?"

There was a time when no one had a hereditary surname. The Norman Conquest of 1066 is a convenient point at which we can note the appearance of the first family names, but the Normans certainly did not have a fully developed surname system. It was not yet their conscious policy to identify a family by one name, but the idea was soon to occur to them. There is every sign that it would also have occurred spontaneously to the people they conquered, but the Norman example no doubt helped speed things along.

Before we turn to modern surnames, let us look at the situation that existed before the 11th century. Our remote ancestors had single *personal names* which were quite enough to distinguish them in the small communities in which they lived. Personal names were either well-established name elements, or permutations of such elements. These in turn usually referred to abstract qualities such as 'nobility' and 'fame'. A new single-element name, or a new permutation, was given to every child, so that everyone in the community had a truly personal name. Natural duplication must have caused the same name to come into being simultaneously in different communities, but names were not deliberately re-used.

Some of the Anglo-Saxon personal names later made the change to become first names such as **Alfred, Audrey, Cuthbert, Edgar, Edmund, Edward, Harold** and **Oswald.** Many more of them survived long enough to form the basis of modern surnames. **Allwright,** for example, was once a personal name composed of *aethel* and *ric*, or 'noble' and 'ruler'. **Darwin** was *deor wine*, 'dear friend', and **Wyman** was *wig mund*, 'war protection'.

Scandinavian names

When the Danes and later the Norwegians invaded England and settled in large numbers, they naturally took their own names with them. Still more important, they retained their own ideas about naming. The Scandinavian personal names sometimes resembled those of the Anglo-Saxons, so that both Old Norse *Harivald* and Old English *Hereweald* could lead to **Harold,** while similar pairs led to **Oswald** and **Randolph.** Many truly Scandinavian names survive today in surnames though not usually in an easily recognisable form.

But it was the Scandinavian method of naming, rather than the names themselves, that eventually had the biggest effect on the English naming system. Among the Anglo-Saxons, personal names that had been made famous by distinguished ancestors had always been honoured by *not* using them for descendants. The Scandinavians, however, readily duplicated their personal names in different generations of the same family. It was also their common practice to name a son after a famous chief or a personal friend. They believed, as Sir Frank Stenton has explained, that 'the soul of an individual was represented or symbolised by his name, and that the bestowal of a name was a means of calling up the spirit of the man who had borne it into the spirit of the child to whom it was given'.

The natural result of consciously re-using the same personal names, apart from creating a far smaller central stock of names, was to make those names far less effective as identifiers of individuals. When exact identification was particularly necessary it became essential to add a second name which gave extra information about the person concerned. This did not lead to the immediate creation of surnames, but it was certainly a step in that direction.

Bynames

The new second names that came into existence at this period, at first among the Scandinavian settlers, were temporary surnames, similar to nicknames in many ways. It is useful to distinguish them as a historical phenomenon, however, from surnames or nicknames as we know them today. For this purpose they have often been referred to as 'bynames'. Bynames were meant to be added to someone's personal name to help identification, but sometimes they simply replaced it completely. As substitute personal names they were probably not always to their bearers' liking. Many men must have begun life with flattering traditional names, only to become at a later date **Drunkard, Clod, Idler, Short Leg, Shameless, Squinter, Clumsy** or **Miser**. These are all direct translations of names which occur in medieval records. When these bynames were common enough to be used frequently they sometimes became true surnames at a later date. Of those mentioned above, for instance, the first three subsequently became family names, though their meanings would fortunately not now be recognised. In a modern directory they might appear as **Gipp, Clack** and **Sling.**

The need for a supplementary name, then, had made itself felt in England before the Normans arrived, but the Normans, even more than the Scandinavians, believed in using the same personal names over and over again. They also needed second names to identify them properly, especially in legal documents. In the Domesday Book of 1086 almost all the Norman landowners have such names. An earlier version of this survey also gives bynames for many of the former English landowners, and those Englishmen who managed to retain their lands under the new régime also have them. The Norman bynames were frequently the names of the villages from which they came or were the personal names of their fathers, but some described occupations and others personal characteristics. Many of the elements of modern surnames were thus present.

A major difference between bynames and surnames is that the former were not passed on from one generation to the next. They were meaningful names that were meant to apply to the individuals who bore them. The retention of a particular name as a family identifier may have been deliberate, but it could just as easily have happened accidentally at first. One way in which it could occur, for instance, was by the inheritance of property. If the father was known as 'of' followed by the name of his estate, the eldest son might logically take over both the estate and the name.

However it began, one can imagine how this passing of a name from one generation to the next was noted as an aspect of aristocratic behaviour—for it would certainly have begun at baronial level—and duly imitated.

'I wish, my dear, you would cultivate your acquaintance with Towneley, and ask him to pay us a visit. The name has an aristocratic sound.'

Samuel Butler *The Way of all Flesh*

The officials who dealt with wills and the like must also have found what soon became a fashion of great convenience to them, and no doubt they encouraged the habit. Slowly bynames were turned into hereditary family names, a process which spread downwards through society until even the humblest person had one. It was to be 300 years, however, before that happened. At the end of that period, the concept of the single personal name had gone for ever. Bynames introduced a great many place names into the personal name system, but transfer of names between people and places

'Gabriel what?'

'Oh, Lord kens that; we dinna mind folk's after-names muckle here, they run sae muckle into clans. The folks hereabout are a' Armstrongs and Elliots, and so the lairds and farmers have the names of the places that they live at . . . and then the inferior sort o' people, ye'll observe, are kend by sorts o' bynames, as Glaiket Christie, and the Deuke's Davie, or Tod Gabbie, or Hunter Gabbie.'

Sir Walter Scott *Guy Mannering*

had always seemed natural. This type of byname was probably readily accepted, as were the patronymic link names. The latter simply described someone as '**John**'s son' or '**William**'s son', so that the new names contained an obvious personal name element. It was the descriptive names that must have had a harder time of it. One would expect it to take longer for phrases like 'the carpenter' or 'the short one' to convert to the names **Carpenter** and **Short.** Where some activity names were concerned, two factors would help the process. One of these would be the following of the same occupation by a succession of fathers and sons, thus enabling the same byname to remain in a family for a long period and appear to be a hereditary name.

A second factor that would have helped this group would be natural duplication. During the period we are considering, which is between 1066 and 1400, each community had its important and easily recognisable craftsmen, tradesmen, officials and other workers. It would have been natural for every village to have someone who was a smith, another who was a baker, and so on. All these medieval occupations are seen in modern surnames as we see on pages 75–6. We must not forget, however, that with each of these names there had to come a point when their status as names was finally accepted. When it was considered quite usual for a **John Carpenter** to be a baker or follow some other trade, 'carpenter' had in one sense lost its meaning. It had acquired, however, a new kind of referential meaning and had passed through the byname stage to become a surname.

Patronyms also had to get by this hurdle, though with names of the John **Andrews** type it is very easy to see how new generations could inherit it, with those around them slightly adjusting its meaning. At first they would have said to themselves that he was the son of **Andrew,** later, that he was the grandson, later still, that he was a descendant of someone called Andrew. Eventually this type of name, like the others, would no longer be interpreted at all in a literal sense, but as showing a connection with the Andrews family.

Locative bynames were easily inherited, too. A family that lived by the village green, on the hill, near the ford, or wherever, was likely to remain there for several generations. As for place names, when these indicated provenance rather than inherited property one can see how they were passed on. Even today a village community will remember for several generations that a family came from some other place.

But if one can understand how a great many bynames of different types developed into hereditary surnames, those which described an individual's physical or moral attributes are surprising. A father may rightly have been described as a drunkard, but surely this was not a suitable name for his descendants? Such names may have been another kind of patronymic to begin with, indicating 'son of the drunkard'. If they were bestowed as bynames late in the 14th century, by which time the majority of people had surnames, they may have been mistaken for surnames. Nevertheless, one would expect this kind of name to have survived less frequently as a surname and all the evidence points quite clearly to this being the case. The early bearers of such surnames must have occupied a very lowly social position and had no say in the matter. Later descendants who have been of higher standing have frequently rid themselves of such embarrassing family reminders.

We shall never know the exact details of how bynames became surnames, but from the beginning of the 15th century nearly all English people inherited a surname at birth and the word 'surname' was used with the meaning we give it today. It had been borrowed from the French *surnom*, deriving in turn from Latin *super-* or *supranomen*, and was used at first to mean simply 'an extra name', 'a nickname'. Modern French retains that meaning and translates 'surname' as *nom de famille*.

Spelling and pronunciation

Most of our surnames have, therefore, been in the family for 500 years or more, but that is not to say that the one name among many by which our ancestors finally came to be known is exactly the same as the name we bear today. The names came into existence, but they had no fixed forms. Our ancestors—and this probably includes any who were of the upper classes—were for centuries mostly illiterate. Their names were occasionally recorded by a parson or clerk when there was a birth, marriage or death in the family, and he wrote down what he heard using his own ideas about the spelling. He was obliged to do this, for though the spelling of ordinary words very slowly became standardised after the 15th century, there were no agreed forms for names. It was the printed books

Mr P. S. Clark of Sutton Coldfield writes to point out that he probably has a uniquely chemical name. It appears in correct sequence in the Periodic Table, where Elements with the atomic numbers 15–19 inclusive are respectively P (phosphorus), S (sulphur), Cl (chlorine), Ar (argon) and K (potassium).

which helped to fix the words, but only a tiny proportion of names ever appeared in print.

The same name could be written down in many different ways by different clerks, and even, as the parish registers clearly show, by the same clerk at different times. A further complication was provided by regional dialects. A sound which in the personal name period could be represented by 'y', for example, became 'i' in the North and East Midlands, 'e' in the South East and 'u' in the Central Midlands and other southern counties. These changes had occurred by the beginning of the surname period.

The influence of the French officials who later came to write down English names has also been felt in our surnames. They, too, spoke different dialects and had varying orthographic systems. All in all it is hardly surprising that what was once the same name can appear in a wide variety of modern forms. We normally refer to Sir Walter **Raleigh,** for instance, but **Rawley** probably captured the name's pronunciation more accurately. Other forms include **Ralegh, Raughley, Rauly, Rawleigh, Rawleleygh** and **Rayley.**

Almost every modern surname has its variant forms. Even the short man we referred to earlier whose byname lived on as a surname has become **Shortt** in some instances, acquiring a superfluous letter somewhere along the line. As a word this would long ago have been regularised; as a name it now remains fossilised in the form it accidentally took on.

Many names have acquired extra letters, but we should note that the initial 'ff' preserved by some families is rather different. This was a medieval scribal alternative for an 'F' and should always be written, therefore, as two small letters. P. G. Wodehouse, in *A Slice of Life*, made marvellous fun of such names:

'Sir Jasper Finch-Farrowmere?' said Wilfred.

'ffinch-ffarowmere,' corrected the visitor, his sensitive ear detecting the capital letters.

In some cases the spelling of a name has remained artificially fixed while its pronunciation has changed. One finds the same lack of relationship between spelling and pronunciation in many place names. Well-known surname examples include **Cholmondeley,** 'Chumley', **Mainwaring,** 'Mannering', **Marjoribanks,** 'Marchbanks', **Beauchamp,** 'Beecham', **Featherstonehaugh,** 'Fanshaw'. With these names as with many others the pronunciation normally used by one family may differ from that preferred by another.

Irish names

As in England, bynames preceded surnames in Ireland. The earliest kind mentioned the name of the father, preceded by 'Mac', or that of a grandfather or earlier ancestor, in which case 'O' preceded the name. Later, names were formed by adding these prefixes to the father's byname, which could be of any of the kinds seen in England. The 'Mac' (or 'Mc', which means exactly the same) and 'O' prefixes were dropped during the period of English rule, but the 'O' especially has now been resumed by many families.

Other influences on Irish surnames include translation from Gaelic to English, abbreviation and absorption of rare names into common ones. By translation, which in many cases was demanded by the English authorities, families such as the **McGowans** correctly became **Smiths**, but many mistranslations were made.

'There's some devilish queer names, like that army doctor in the war that was called Major Marchbanks although to read it you would have said it was Marjory Banks.'

'A very queer name altogether, that,' Tom agreed. 'Major Marjory Banks, as if it was a lassie that was in it.'

Compton Mackenzie *Whisky Galore*

The Norman invasion of Ireland in the 12th century naturally carried many of their personal names and bynames there. Some of these, in the form of surnames such as **Burke, Cruise** and **Dillon,** are now thought of as essentially Irish, and with good reason. Later English settlement in Ireland also caused many English surnames to become well established.

Scottish names

In the Scottish Lowlands surnames developed along the same lines as in England, though at a slightly later date. In the Highlands the development of hereditary surnames was held back by the clan system. Many families voluntarily allied themselves to a powerful clan or were forced to do so, and in either case they assumed the clan name as their new surname.

The power of the clan names in their day is seen in the action taken by James VI against the **McGregors**. By an Act of Council he proscribed and abolished the name altogether, because 'the bare and simple name of McGregor made that whole clan to presume of their power, force and strength, and did encourage them, without reverence of the law or fear of punishment, to go forward in their iniquities'. The proscription against the name was not finally removed until 1774.

Gaelic names from the Highlands began to spread south in the 18th century, and later throughout the English-speaking world. Mrs Cecily Dynes, who keeps records of the names used by parents in New South Wales, noted in 1972 'a sudden upsurge of "Mac" or "Mc" middle names'. Other typically Highland names, such as **Cameron,** are already being used as first names.

Welsh names

The many Welshmen who came into England in the byname period were treated like Englishmen as far as their names were concerned. A few Welsh personal names, such as **Morgan, Owen, Meredith,** thus became established as surnames centuries before hereditary surnames were normal in Wales itself. The usual custom there was for a man to be something like **Madog Ap Gryffyd Ap Jorweth,** with 'ap' meaning 'son of'. As late as 1853 the Registrar-General was able to say—using expressions that no one would dare use today—that 'among the lower classes in the wilder districts ... the Christian name of the father still frequently becomes the patronymic of the son'.

Traces of the 'ap' system survive in names like **Price,** formerly **Ap Rhys,** and many of the original Welsh personal names have managed to live on, but the well-known preponderance in modern Wales of names like **Jones, Davies, Williams, Thomas, James, Phillips, Edwards, Roberts, Richards** and **Hughes** show all too clearly that the **John, David** and **William** type of first name became thoroughly established there. When formal surnames were eventually used, the traditional method of naming after the father was remembered but it was the new names that formed their base.

Other American family names

British surnames, as we have seen, are not without their complications. When those surnames have been taken to other countries and mixed with

---

'My name is not spoken. More than a hundred years it has not gone upon men's tongues, save for a blink. I am nameless like the Folk of Peace. Catriona Drummond is the one I use.'

Now indeed I knew where I was standing. In all broad Scotland there was but the one name proscribed, and that was the name of the McGregors.

R. L. Stevenson *Catriona*

'Ay, Macintosh is my name,' said the traveller . . .

Mr Brown felt inclined to say that it was a very good name to have on such a morning (it was pouring with rain), but having heard that the Celts lacked humour he decided to refrain.

Compton Mackenzie *Whisky Galore*

'Tickler is a rather unusual name,' he said.

I made what has necessarily become a set speech.

'It's an Americanization of Tichelar,' I said, spelling it out. 'Tichel is the Dutch word for brick, tichelaar for tile-worker or bricklayer . . . . I might as well have been sea-changed into Jimmy Bricklayer—or James Mason—as Jimmy Tickler, which is simply a phonetic spelling of the way the name has always been pronounced here in this country anyway.'

Peter de Vries *The Glory of the Hummingbird*

surnames from all over the world, the situation becomes almost impossible to cope with. A glance at a list of common surnames in America, for instance, shows that there are as many **Jorgensens** as **Cliffords,** as many people called **Lombardo** as **Dickens.** It is not that these common names cause difficulty, for a 'son of **George**' is not particularly difficult to recognise even in his Danish disguise, and a 'man from Lombardy' is not concealed by that final '-o', but for every common name there are a dozen unusual ones brought from the same country.

Elsdon C. Smith has made a heroic attempt to cope with the difficulties in his *American Surnames* and other works, in all of which he has collated information from a vast range of sources. His work has an added interest in that it compares surname development and types of modern surname in many countries. Not unnaturally he expands on **Smith,** which has its equivalent in many countries. Apart from the German **Schmidt** and French **Lefevre,** Gaelic **Gowan** and Latin **Faber,** it occurs as the Syrian **Haddad,** Finnish **Seppanen,** Hungarian **Kovacs,** Russian **Kuznetsov,** Ukrainian **Kowalsky,** Lithuanian **Kalvaitis,** and so on. One can see why Mark Lower, a highly entertaining writer on names in the 19th century, suggested that there should be a science called *Smithology* to deal properly with all aspects of this family name.

Many surnames in America have retained the form they had in other countries, but others were consciously adapted by immigrants so that English-speakers would find them easier to spell and pronounce. The Dutch name **Van Rosevelt,** 'of the rose field', became **Roosevelt;** German **Huber,** 'tenant of a hide of land', became **Hoover,** while German **Roggenfelder,** 'rye field', became **Rockefeller.** The Finnish name **Kirkkomäki** was changed to **Churchill.**

Some such names, according to Elsdon C. Smith, have become particularly American 'because their bearers made such significant contributions to American life and history'. His full list of distinguished names is as follows: **Audubon, Barnum, Baruch, Carnegie, Edison, Eisenhower, Emerson, Franklin, Hancock, Hawthorne, Jefferson, Knickerbocker, La Fayette, Lincoln, Longfellow, McCormick, Penn, Pershing, Pullman, Rockefeller, Roosevelt, Thoreau, Wanamaker** and **Washington.** By origin, these names derive from many different national sources, but as Smith says, who can doubt that they are truly American?

In Spain, a married woman keeps her maiden name, but tacks on her husband's after a 'de'. Thus, on marrying Wifredo Las Rocas, our Majorcan friend Rosa, born an Espinosa, became Rosa Espinosa de Las Rocas—a very happy combination. It means 'Lady Thorny Rose from the Rocks'. Rosa was luckier than her maternal cousin Dolores Fuertes, who thoughtlessly married a lawyer named Tomás Barriga, and is now Dolores Fuertes de Barriga, or 'Violent Pains of the Stomach'.

Robert Graves *A Toast to Ava Gardner*

Family names that link with first names

The following surnames mostly began by meaning 'son of' (later 'descendant of') or 'employee of' the person named.

Adam Adams, Adamson, Adcock, Addison, Addy, Adkins, Aitken, Aitkins, Atkin, Atkins, Atkinson.
Agatha Aggass, Tag.
Agnes Annis, Annison, Anson.
Alan Alcock, Allan, Allanson, Allen, Alleyn, Allinson.
Alexander Sanders, Sanderson, Saunders, Saunderson.
Amice Ames, Amies, Amis, Amison, Aymes.
Andrew Anderson, Andrews, Dandy.
Augustine Austen, Austin.
Bartholomew Bartle, Bartlet(t), Bate, Bateman, Bates, Bateson, Batkin, Batt, Batten, Batty, Tolley.
Beatrice Beaton, Beatty, Beet, Beeton.
Benedict Benn, Bennett, Benson.
Cassandra Case, Cash, Cass, Casson.
Cecily Sisley, Sisson.
Christian Christie, Christison, Christy.
Christopher Kitson, Kitt, Kitts.
Clement Clements, Clementson, Clemms, Clempson, Clemson.
Constance Cuss, Cussans, Cust, Custance.
Daniel Daniels, Dannet, Dannson.
David Dakins, Davidge, Davidson, Davies, Davis, Davison, Davitt, Dawe, Dawes, Dawkins, Dawson, Day, Dowson.
Denis Dennett, Dennis(s), Dennison, Denny, Dyson, Tennyson.
Donald Donald, Donaldson.
Durand Durant, Durrance, Durrant.
Edith Eade, Eady, Eddis, Eddison, Edis, Edison.
Edmund Edmond, Edmonds, Edmondson, Edmons, Edmund, Edmunds.
Edward Edwardes, Edwards.
Eleanor Ellen, Ellinor, Elson.
Elias Eliot, Elliot(t), Ellis, Ellison.
Elizabeth Bethell.
Emery Amery, Emerson.
Emma Emmett, Empson.
Evan Evans, Bevan, Bevin.
Geoffrey Jeeves, Jefferies, Jefferson, Jeffrey, Jephson, Jepp, Jepson.
Gerald Garrard, Garratt, Garrett, Garrod, Gerard, Jarrett, Jerrold.
Gervais Gervas, Gervis, Jarvie, Jarvis.
Gilbert Gibb, Gibbin, Gibbons, Gibbs, Gibson, Gilbart, Gilbertson, Gilbey, Gilpin, Gilson, Gipps.
Gregory Greer, Gregson, Greig, Grierson, Grigg, Grigson.
Hamo Hamblin, Hamlet, Hamley, Hamlyn, Hammett, Hammond, Hamnet, Hampson, Hamson.
Harvey Harvie, Hervey.
Henry Harriman, Harris, Harrison, Hawke, Hawkins, Henderson, Hendry, Henryson, Heriot, Parry, Perry.
Herman Armand, Arment, Harman, Harmon.
Howel Howell, Poel, Powell.
Hubert Hobart, Hubbard.
Hugh Hewes, Hewett, Hewitson, Hewlet, Hewson, Howkins, Howson, Hudson, Huggett, Huggins, Hughes, Hullett, Hullis, Hutchings, Hutchins, Hutchinson, Pugh.
Humphrey Boumphrey, Humphreys, Humphries, Pumphrey.
Isabel Bibby, Ibbotson, Ibson, Libby, Nibbs, Nibson, Tibbs.
Jacob Jacobs, Jacobson.
James Gemson, Gimson, Jamieson, Jimpson.
John Hancock, Hankin, Hanson, Jackson, Jaggs, Jenkins, Jennings, Jennison, Johns, Johnson, Jones, Littlejohn.
Juliana Gill, Gillett, Gillott, Gilson, Jewett, Jolyan, Jowett, Julian, Julien, Julyan.
Katharine Catlin, Caton, Cattling, Kitson.
Laurence Larkin(s), Laurie, Law, Lawrence, Lawrie, Lawson, Lowry.
Lewis Llewellyn, Louis, Lowis.
Luke Lucas, Luck, Luckett, Luckin, Lukin.
Mabel Mabbot, Mabbs, Mapp, Mappin, Mapson, Mobbs.
Magdalen Maddison, Maudling.
Margaret Maggs, Magson, Margerison, Margetson, Margretts, Meggeson, Meggs, Mogg, Moggs, Moxon, Pegson, Poggs.
Martin Martell, Martens, Martinet, Martinson.
Mary Malleson, Mallett, Marion, Marriott, Marrison, Marryat, Maryat, Mollison.
Matilda Madison, Maudson, Mault, Mawson, Mold, Mould, Moulson, Moult, Tillett, Tilley, Tillison, Tillotson.
Matthew Machin, Makins, Makinson, Matheson, Mathieson, Matson,, Matterson, Matthews, Mattin, Maycock, Mayhew, Maykin.
Maurice Morcock, Morrice, Morris, Morrison, Morse, Morson.
Michael Michell, Michieson, Mitchell, Mitchelson, Mitchison.
Nicholas Cole, Collett, Colley, Collins, Collinson, Collis, Coulson, Nicholson, Nickells, Nicks, Nickson, Nicolson, Nixon.
Nigel Neal, Neilson, Nelson.
Pagan Paine, Pannel, Payne.
Patrick Paterson, Paton, Patterson, Pattinson, Pattison.
Peter Parkin, Parkinson, Parks, Parr, Parrot, Pears, Pearse, Pearson, Perkins, Perrin, Perrot, Person, Peters, Peterson, Pierce.
Petronella Parnell, Purnell.
Philip Filkins, Phelps, Phillips, Phillipson, Philpot, Phipps, Potts.
Ralph Rawkins, Rawle, Rawlings, Rawlins, Rawlinson, Rawlison, Rawson.
Randal Randall, Randolph, Rand(s), Rankin, Ransome.
Reynald Rennell, Rennie, Rennison, Reynolds, Reynoldson.
Rhys Rice, Reece, Price, Preece.
Richard Dickens, Dickinson, Dickson, Dix, Dixon, Hickie, Hicks, Hickson, Higgins, Higgs, Hitchens, Prickett, Pritchard, Pritchett, Richards, Richardson, Ricketts, Rix.
Robert Dabbs, Dobbie, Dobbs, Dobie, Dobson, Hobart, Hobbs, Hobson, Hopkins, Hopkinson, Nobbs, Probert, Probyn, Robbie, Robbins, Robens, Roberts, Robertson, Robey, Robinson, Robson.

Roger Dodd, Dodge, Dodgson, Dodson, Hodges, Hodgkinson, Hodgkiss, Hodgson, Hodson, Hotchkiss, Rogers, Rogerson.
Simon Simms, Simmonds, Simpkins, Simpson, Sims, Symonds.
Stephen Stenson, Stephens, Stephenson, Stevens, Stevenson.
Thomas Tamblin, Tamlin, Tampling, Thomason, Thompson, Tombs, Tomlinson, Tompkins, Tomsett, Tonkins, Tonks.
Walter Walters, Waterson, Watkins, Watkinson, Watson, Watts.
William Gilham, Gillam, Gilliam, Mott, Wilcock, Wilcox, Wilkie, Wilkins, Wilkinson, Williams, Williamson, Willis, Wills, Wilson.

Family names from Old English personal names

Some Old English personal names have survived as surnames. The meaning of these names is rather special. *Edrich*, for example, contained the elements *ead* and *ric*, the first meaning something like 'prosperity' or 'happiness', the second indicating 'power' or 'rule'. This is not to say that the name therefore means 'prosperous rule'. It may well have come about because the mother's name contained *ead* (in a name like *Edith*) and the father's name *ric* (in a name like *Kenrick*). Such names must often have been blended simply in order to show parentage. This accounts for the names where the elements seem to contradict each other. In their modern forms, many elements have more than one possible origin. *Al-* and *El-* could derive from 'elf' or 'noble', for instance. Alternative possibilities are indicated below.

Adlard noble—hard.
Alflatt elf/noble—beauty.
Allnatt noble—daring.
Alvar elf—army.
Alwin noble/old/elf—friend.
Averay elf—counsel.
Aylmer noble—famous.
Aylwin noble—friend.
Badrick battle—famous.
Baldey bold—combat.
Balman bold—man.
Balston bold—stone.
Bedloe command—love.
Brightmore fair—famous.
Brunger brown—spear.
Brunwin brown—friend.
Burchard fortress—hard.
Burrage fortress—powerful.
Burward fortress—guard.
Cobbald famous—bold.
Cutteridge famous—ruler.
Darwin dear—friend.
Eastman grace—protection.
Eddols prosperity—wolf.
Eddy prosperity—war.
Ellwood elf—ruler.
Elphee elf—war.
Elsegood temple—god.
Elsey elf—victory.
Elvey elf—war.
Erwin boar—friend.
Frewin free—friend.
Frewer free—shelter.
Gladwin glad—friend.
Godwin good—friend.
Goldbard gold—bright/beard.
Goldburg gold—fortress.
Goldhawk gold—hawk.
Goldwin gold—friend.
Goodliffe good/God—dear.
Goodrich good/God—ruler.
Goodwin good—friend.
Gummer good/battle—famous.
Hulbert gracious—bright.
Kenward bold/royal—guardian.
Kenway bold/royal—war.
Kerrich family—ruler.
Lambrick land—bright.
Leavey beloved—warrior.
Leavold beloved—power/ruler.
Lemmer people/dear—famous.
Lewin beloved—friend.
Lilleyman little—man.
Litwin bright—friend.
Lovegod beloved—god.
Loveguard beloved—spear.
Milborrow mild—fortress.
Ordway spear—warrior.
Orrick spear—powerful.
Osmer god—fame.
Oswin god—friend.
Outridge dawn—powerful.
Quenell woman—war.
Redway counsel—warrior.
Seavers sea—passage.
Siggers victory—spear.
Stidolph hard—wolf.
Trumble strong—bold.
Wennell joy—war.
Whatman brave—man.
Whittard elf—brave.
Wilmer will—famous.
Winbolt friend—bold.
Winbow friend—bold.
Winmer friend—famous.
Winney joy—battle.
Woolgar wolf—spear.
Wyman war—protection.
Yonwin young—friend.
Youngmay young—servant.

Some additional American family names

A selection of family names frequently found in America deriving from various European languages.

Alvarez son of **Alvaro** 'the prudent one'.
Bauer farmer.
Berg dweller on or near a hill or mountain.
Berger shepherd.
Brandt farmer on land cleared by burning.
Camero dweller in or worker at a hall.
Carlson son of *Carl*.
Carson dweller near a marsh.
Castillo dweller near a castle, or a castle servant.
Castro see *Castillo*.
Chavez descendant of **Jaime,** or *James*.
Christensen descendant of *Christian*.
Cohen the priest.
Cruz dweller near a cross.
Diaz descendant of **Diego,** or *Jacob*.
Fernandez descendant of **Fernando,** 'the adventurer'.
Figueroa maker of statuettes.
Fischer fisherman or fish-trader.
Flores dweller in flowery place.
Friedman descendant of the peaceful man.
Garcia descendant of Garcia, or *Gerald*.
Garza dweller at the sign of the heron or dove.
Goldberg family from Goldberg 'gold mountain', name of various places in Germany.
Goldstein descendant of a goldsmith.
Gomez descendant of **Gomo,** or **Gomesano.**
Gonzales descendant of **Gonzalo** 'battle', name of an early saint.
Gora dweller on, or near, a hill or mountain.
Gross descendant of the large or fat man.
Gutierrez descendant of Gutierre, or *Walter*.
Haas dweller at the sign of the hare, or one who could run as swiftly as the hare.
Hahn dweller at the sign of the cock, or one who had the characteristics of the cock.
Hansen descendant of Hans, or *John*.
Hanson see *Hansen*.
Hartman descendant of the strong man.
Herman descendant of Herman 'army man'.
Hernandez descendant of **Hernando** 'the adventurer'.
Hess(e) family from Hesse 'hooded people' in Germany.
Hoffman farmer or farm-worker.
Hoover tenant of a hide of land, about 120 acres.
Jensen descendant of Jen, or *John*.
Katz descendant of a priest.
Kaufman descendant of a merchant or tradesman.
Keller worker in a wine-cellar.
Klein descendant of the small man.
Kline see *Klein*.
Koch descendant of a cook.
Kramer descendant of an itinerant tradesman.
Krause descendant of the curly-headed man.
Kruger descendant of an inn-keeper.
Lang descendant of the tall man.
Larsen son of Lars, or *Laurence*.
Larson see *Larsen*.
Levine descendant of the wine-dealer.
Levy descendant of **Levi** 'united'.
Lopez descendant of **Lope** or **Lupe** 'the wolf-like man'.
Maldonado descendant of *Donald*.
Mann descendant of a servant.
Marks dweller near the mark or boundary, or descendant of Mark, or family from Marck in France.
Martinez descendant of *Martin*.
Mayer descendant of the head-servant or farmer.
Medina dweller near the market, or worker in a market.
Meyer see *Mayer*.
Morales descendant of Moral, or family from Morales 'mulberry tree', the name of two places in Spain.
Moreno descendant of the dark-complexioned man.
Mueller descendant of a miller.
Mullen descendant of Maolan 'bald man'.
Myers see *Mayer*.
Nielsen descendant of *Niel* 'champion'.
Novak descendant of the stranger or newcomer.
Olsen descendant of Olaf 'ancestor'.
Olson see *Olsen*.
Ortiz descendant of Ordono, 'fortunate one'.
Perez descendant of Pedro, or *Peter*.
Ramirez descendant of **Ramon** 'wise protector'.
Ramos descendant of Ramos 'palms'.
Reyes descendant of one of the king's household, or family from Reyes, name of places in Spain.
Rivera dweller near a brook or river.
Rodriguez descendant of **Rodrigo,** or *Roderick*.
Romero descendant of a pilgrim to Rome.
Rosenberg family from Rosenberg 'rose mountain', name of several places in Germany.
Ruiz descendant of **Ruy,** or *Rodrigo* (*Roderick*).
Sanchez descendant of **Sancho** 'sanctified'.
Santiago family from Santiago 'St James' in Spain.
Schaefer descendant of a shepherd.
Schneider descendant of the tailor or cutter.
Schoen descendant of the beautiful or handsome person.
Schroeder descendant of the tailor.
Schultz descendant of the magistrate or sheriff or steward.
Schwartz descendant of the swarthy man.
Silva dweller in or near a wood.
Snyder see *Schneider*.
Stein dweller near a significant stone or rock.
Torres dweller at or near a tower or spire.
Vandermeer dweller at or near a lake.
Vazquez a Basque family or descendant of a shepherd.
Wagner descendant of a wagon-driver or wagon-maker.
Weber descendant of a cloth weaver.
Weiss descendant of a man with white hair or skin.
Werner descendant of Werner 'protection-army'.
Zimmerman descendant of a carpenter.

Some Celtic names

The surnames of Scotland, Wales, Ireland, Cornwall and the Isle of Man have distinct characteristics, deriving as they do from Celtic languages such as Gaelic and old Welsh. Separate dictionaries exist which deal with them in detail (see the Bibliography). Some examples of common and well-known names are given below.

Agnew 'action'.
Aherne 'steed lord'.
Bane 'white'.
Bardon 'bard'.
Begley 'little hero'.
Behan 'bee'.
Berryman 'man from St Buryan'.
Bevan son of Evan (*John*).
Bosanquet 'dwelling of Angawd', a Cornish place name.
Boyd 'yellow-haired'.
Boyle 'pledge'.
Brennan 'sorrow/raven'.
Bruce from a Norman place name.
Burke probably from Burgh, a place name.
Burns 'dweller by the stream'.
Cameron 'crooked nose'.
Campbell 'crooked mouth'.
Cardew 'dark fort'.
Carrick 'rock mass'.
Craig 'dweller by rocks'.
Cunningham from Scottish place name, or descendant of Con (Ireland).
Daly 'assembly'.
Docherty 'the stern one'.
Douglas from place name, 'dark stream'.
Doyle 'dark stranger'.
Duncan 'brown warrior'.
Dyer 'thatcher' (Cornwall).
Farrell 'man of valour'.
Ferguson son of 'man choice'.
Findlay 'fair hero'.
Forbes from the place name, 'field'.
Freethy 'eager, alert'.
Furphy 'perfect'.
Galbraith 'British stranger'.
Gale 'stranger'.
Gallacher 'foreign help'.
Gough 'red-faced or red-haired'.
Guinness son of *Angus*, 'one choice'.
Hamilton from place name.
Innes 'dweller on an island'.
Jago son of *James*.
Jory son of *George*.
Kelly son of Ceallach, 'war'.
Kennedy 'ugly head'.
Kermode son of Diarmaid, 'freeman'.
Kerr 'dweller by the marsh'.
Lloyd 'grey'.
McFarlane son of *Bartholomew*.
McGregor son of *Gregory*, 'to be watchful'.
McIntosh son of the 'chieftain'.
McIntyre son of the 'carpenter'.
McKay son of Aodh, 'fire'.
McKenzie son of Coinneach, 'fair one'.
McLean son of the devotee of St John.
McLeod son of Ljotr, 'the ugly one'.
McMillan son of Mhaolain, 'the tonsured man', a religious servant.
McPherson son of the 'parson'.
Mundy 'dweller in the mine house'. (Cornwall).
Munro from a place name, 'mouth of the River Roe'.
Murphy descendant of the 'sea warrior'.
Murray from the place name, 'sea settlement'.
Nance 'dweller in the valley'.
Negus 'dweller by the nut grove'.
Nolan descendant of the 'noble one'.
O'Brien descendant of *Brian*, from King Brian Boru.
O'Byrne descendant of the 'bear' or 'raven'.
O'Connor descendant of Connor, 'high will'.
O'Neill descendant of the 'champion'.
Opie descendant of **Osbert.**
O'Reilly descendant of the 'prosperous or valiant one'.
Pascoe 'Easter child'.
Pengelly 'dweller by the top of the copse'.
Penrose 'dweller at the top of the heath'.
Quiggin son of Uige, 'skill'.
Quirk son of Corc, 'heart'.
Rafferty 'prosperity wielder'.
Rafter 'decree'.
Ratigan 'decree'.
Reagh 'grey'.
Reavey 'grey'.
Reilly 'prosperity'.
Renehan 'sharp pointed'.
Ring 'spear'.
Ritchie son of *Richard*.
Ross from the place name.
Ryan descendant of Rian.
Sinclair from places called Saint-Clair in Normandy.
Stewart 'the steward'.
Sullivan part of the name means 'eye'. The other part could mean 'black', 'one', 'hawk', etc.
Sutherland from the place name, 'south land'.
Trease 'dweller in the homestead by a ford'.
Tremaine 'dweller in the stone homestead'.
Trevean 'dweller in the little homestead'.
Trevor from the place name, 'big village'.
Trewen 'dweller in the white homestead'.
Vaughan 'the little man'.
Vessy 'son of life'.
Weeney 'wealthy'.
Weir 'steward'.
Whearty 'noisy'.
Whelan 'wolf'.
Wogan 'frown'.
Wynn 'fair'.

Tracing the origin of a family name

I give below the typical procedure for investigating the origin of a family name, using Dunkling as an example.

1 Is the modern spelling of the name reliable? The only way to find out is to check your family history to see how the name was recorded in earlier times. Such a check quickly revealed that before 1900 Dunkling had no final '-g'. My grandfather was illiterate, and the officials who recorded his name no doubt thought that when he said 'Dunklin' he was mispronouncing 'Dunkling'. They therefore 'corrected' the name.

2 To which language does the name belong? Again, a check into one's family history probably offers the best clue. My direct ancestors were settled in Buckinghamshire, England, by 1726. Dunklin also shows no obvious signs of being Gaelic, French, Dutch, etc. For both positive and negative reasons it is likely to be an English name.

3 Given that Dunklin represents fairly reliably the form of the name that probably became attached to the family in the surname-formation period (1066-1400), and that it is English, into which class of name does it fall? Does it
   a describe an ancestor's trade or profession?
   b describe his physical appearance or moral character?
   c describe his relationship to another named person?
   d describe where he came from?

4 The names of medieval trades were normal words, and as such were fairly well documented. Names of this kind are certainly amongst those which have been most convincingly explained and listed by scholars, and explanations can be found in either good surname dictionaries or the *Oxford English Dictionary*. A check of such reference works shows that Dunklin is not such a name.

5 English nicknames used in the Middle Ages were again normal words and have been thoroughly investigated by etymologists. A check on dictionaries shows that Dunklin could not have been a nickname.

6 Family names which link with other personal names have also been well studied. There appears to be no known personal name which could have led to Dunklin, meaning 'descendant of someone called Dunk, Dunkl or Dunklin'.

7 Family names of place name origin do in fact form the largest class, so there is every likelihood of Dunklin being a place name by origin. A check in reference works on place names for any name vaguely resembling the *sound* of Dunklin bears fruit in *The Place-Names of Worcestershire*, by A. Mawer and F. M. Stenton. The entry for Dunclent Farm, near the village of Stone, reveals that on Saxton's map of the county of Worcestershire, published in 1577, the farm-name was given as Dunklyn. Again, in Ogilby's *Itinerarium Angliae*, of 1699, it is mentioned as Dunklin. This is an indication of how pronunciation of the name had changed locally, and clear evidence that the family name Dunklin is the same as the place name Dunclent. The farm, which I visited in 1981, is a few miles from the Clent Hills. The 'dun' of the name means 'down', and the place name means 'settlement at the foot of the Clent Hills'. The family name simply means that the original Dunklins came from that place, since there appear to be no other places of a similar name in England.

8 A search for the origin of a family name should begin, then, with consultation of the main reference works (place name dictionaries as well as surname dictionaries). See the Bibliography for details. Research into one's own family history will always make the conclusions about the name more reliable.

Surnames that put a man in his place

A very large number of surnames originally indicated where a man lived, where he came from or where he worked. These names began as phrasal descriptions, often mentioning a specific place name. When a surname is the same as an English place name, this kind of origin is always possible. Other surnames made use of a topographical feature, such as a *Ford*, or a building, such as a *Hall*, to indicate residence or working place. The surnames below are among the most frequent of this kind.

Alston, Barton, Benton, Bolton, Burton, Carlton, Clayton, Clifton, Compton, Cotton, Dalton, Denton, Dutton, Eaton, Fenton, Hampton, Hilton, Hinton, Horton, Houston, Hutton, Melton, Milton, Morton, Newton, Norton, Pendleton, Preston, Shelton, Skelton, Stanton, Stapleton, Stratton, Sutton, Thornton, Thurston, Tipton, Walton, Washington, Winston, Worthington, Wotton.

Alford, Ashby, Bentley, Blackwell, Bradford, Bradley, Bradshaw, Brandon, Buckley, Caldwell, Churchill, Clifford, Conway, Crawford, Crosby, Davenport, Dudley, Durham, Farley, Hartley, Hastings, Hatfield, Holbrook, Holloway, Kirby, Langford, Langley, Lincoln, Mayfield, Moseley, Norwood, Oakley, Prescott, Ramsey, Rowland, Shipley, Stafford, Stanford, Stanley, Stokes, Ware, Warren, Wells, Wesley, Westbrook, Whitaker, Willoughby, York.

Banks, Bridges, Brooks, Castle, Downs, Fields, Green, Grove, Hayes 'enclosure', **Heath, Hill, Holmes** 'island', **Holt** 'thicket', **House** 'religious house', **Knapp** 'hilltop', **Knowles** 'hilltop', **Lake, Lane, Lee** 'glade', **Meadows, Mills, Shaw** 'small wood', **Townsend, Woods, Yates** 'gate'.

Another way of assigning a man to his place was to describe his nationality. Some of the following names have more than one possible origin, but all could have indicated the nationality of the man who was so named.

Brittany
Breton, Brett, Britt, Britten, Britton.

Cornwall
Cornell, Cornish, Cornwall, Cornwallis, Cornwell.

Denmark
Dence, Dench, Dennis, Denns.

England
England, English, Inglis.

Flanders
Flament, Flanders, Fleeming, Flement, Fleming, Flinders.

France
France, Frances, Francis, Frankish, French, Gascoigne, Gascoyne, Gaskain, Gaskin, Loaring, Loring, Lorraine.

Germany
Germaine, German, Germing, Jarman, Jermyn.

Ireland
Ireland, Irish.

Italy
Romain, Romayne, Rome, Room, Roome.

Netherlands
Dutch, Dutchman.

Norway
Norman, Normand (but also Norman French).

Portugal
Pettengale, Pettingale, Pettingell, Portugal, Puttergill.

Scotland
Scollan, Scotland, Scott, Scutts.

Spain
Spain, Spanier.

Wales
Walch, Wallace, Walles, Wallis, Walsh, Walsman, Welch, Wellish, Wellsman, Welsh.

Surnames reflecting medieval life

The surnames given below are examples of the traditional 'occupational' group. Taken together they provide us with a wide-ranging picture of medieval life and activities.

Archer a professional archer, or perhaps a champion.
Arrowsmith responsible for making arrow-heads.
Bacchus a worker in the bakehouse.
Backer a baker.
Bacon he would have sold or prepared bacon.
Bailey a bailiff, a word that described (high) officials of several kinds.
Baker the bread-maker.
Barber he trimmed beards, cut hair, pulled out teeth and performed minor operations.
Barker he worked with bark for the leather trade.
Bayliss usually the son of a *Bailey*.
Baxter a female baker.
Bowman like *Archer*.
Brasher a brazier, brass-founder.
Brewer occasionally from a place name, but usually what it says.
Brewster a female brewer.
Butcher as now, though once a dealer in buck's (goat's) flesh.
Butler chief servant who supervised the bottles.
Campion a professional fighter, a champion.
Carpenter as now.
Carter driver, perhaps maker, of carts.
Cartwright maker and repairer of carts.
Carver a sculptor.
Castle(man) man employed at the castle.
Catchpole sheriff's official who seized poultry in lieu of debts.
Cater purveyor of goods to a large household.
Century belt-maker.
Chafer worker at a lime-kiln.
Chaffer merchant.
Chalker white-washer.
Challender seller of blankets.
Challinor as *Challender*.
Chalmers as *Chambers*.
Chamberlain once a nobleman's personal servant, but became a general factotum in an inn.
Chambers as *Chamberlain*.
Champion see *Campion*.
Chandler he made or sold candles.
Chaplin a chaplain.
Chapman at first a merchant, later a pedlar.
Chaundler as *Chandler*.
Clark(e) a minor cleric.
Coke a cook.
Collier he sold charcoal.
Cook(e) a professional cook. The extra *-e* acquired accidentally in such names or an attempt to disguise the name's meaning.
Cooper concerned with wooden casks, buckets, etc.
Cowper as *Cooper*.
Day often a worker in a dairy.
Draper maker and seller of woollen cloth.
Dyer a cloth-dyer. Dye was deliberately changed from die to avoid confusion.
Falconer in charge of the falcons, used for hunting.
Falkner, Faulkner etc., as *Falconer*.
Farmer, the modern meaning came after the surname. He was a tax-collector before that, 'farm' once meaning 'firm or fixed payment'.
Farrar a smith or farrier.
Fearon an ironmonger or smith.
Feather a dealer in feathers.
Fisher a fisherman.
Fletcher he made and sold arrows.
Forester a gamekeeper.
Forster sometimes a cutler, scissors-maker, or as *Forester*.
Fowler a hunter of wild birds.
Frobisher he polished swords, armour and the like.
Fuller he 'fulled' cloth, cleansing it.
Gardner, Gardiner, etc, a gardener.
Glover a maker and seller of gloves.
Goldsmith often a banker as well as a goldsmith.
Grave a steward.
Grieve manager of property, a bailiff.
Harper maker or player of harps.
Hayward literally a 'hedgeguard'. In charge of fences and enclosures.
Herd a herdsman.
Hooper he fitted hoops on casks and barrels.
Hunt, Hunter both 'huntsman'.
Kellogg literally 'kill hog', a slaughterer.
Kemp as *Campion*.
Knight in the surname period the meaning was 'a military servant'.
Lander a launderer.
Lavender a launderer.
Leach a doctor.
Leadbeater, Leadbetter, Leadbitter, etc, worker in lead.
Leech a doctor.
Lister a dyer of cloth.
Lorimer a spur-maker.
Machin a mason, stoneworker.
Marchant a merchant.
Marshall a marshal, originally in charge of horses, rising to be a high official.
Mason a skilled stoneworker.
Mercer a dealer in silks and such-like fabrics.
Merchant a dealer, especially wholesale imports/exports.
Mills a miller.
Miller a corn-miller.
Milner as *Miller*
Mulliner as *Miller*.
Naylor a maker and seller of nails.
Page a minor male servant.
Paget a little *Page*.
Paige as *Page*.
Parker keeper of a private park.
Parson a parson, rector.
Parsons servant or son of the *Parson*.
Pepper a dealer in pepper and other spices.
Piper a pipe-player, but may include the name *Pepper*.
Plummer a plumber, lead-worker.
Potter a maker and seller of earthenware.
Proctor a 'procurator', a steward, agent, tithe-farmer.
Redman sometimes from 'reed-man', a thatcher.
Reeve a high-ranking official, a bailiff, a steward.

Saddler a saddle-maker.
Salter a salt-worker, or seller of salt.
Sargent a domestic, legal, or military servant.
Sawyer a sawer of wood.
Shepherd, Sheppard, etc., a shepherd.
Singer a professional singer.
Skinner a preparer of skins, a tanner.
Slater a slate-layer.
Slatter as *Slater.*
Smith a metal-worker, maker of all-important weapons and implements.
Smithers son of *Smith.*
Smythe as *Smith.*
Spencer a dispenser of provisions, a steward or butler.
Spicer a seller of spices.
Spooner a spoon-maker, or roofing-shingle maker.
Squire a knight's attendant, usually a young man of good birth.
Steele a steel-worker.
Stringer a maker of strings for bows.
Tanner a tanner of hides.
Taylor a maker of clothes, though the Normans could also 'tailor' other materials, such as stone.
Thatcher 'thatch' is linked with the Roman 'toga' and means 'to cover'.
Thrower a potter.
Tiller farmer.
Tillman tile-maker or farmer.
Todd foxhunter.
Toddman officially appointed foxhunter.
Toller toll-collector.
Trainer trapper.
Tranter waggoner.
Trapp trapper.
Travers tollbridge-keeper.
Trinder wheelmaker.
Trotter messenger.
Tucker a cloth-worker.
Turner a wood-worker, but possibly a turnspit-operator, a translator, competitor in tournaments, etc.
Tyler maker and layer of tiles.
Vickers son or servant of a vicar.
Wainwright a waggon-maker and repairer.
Walker a cloth-worker, who trod cloth in order to cleanse it.
Waller sometimes a builder of walls, but other origins possible.
Ward a watchman, guard.
Weaver, Webb, Webber, Webster all mean weaver.
Wheeler a maker of wheels.
Woodward a forester.
Wright a workman who made a variety of articles.

Some family names which are not what they seem

Allbones a form of *Alban's.*
Anguish descendant of *Angus.*
Ball descendant of *Baldwin.*
Batty descendant of *Bartholomew.*
Billion descendant of *William.*
Blackbird one with a black beard.
Blanket one with a white skin.
Body descendant of *Baldwin.*
Bone a good person.
Boosey dweller near a cow stall.
Bowell form of *ap Howell*, or *Powell.*
Brolly dweller near a wood or thicket.
Budd descendant of *Baldwin.*
Chessman seller of cheese.
Coffin a bald man.
Collie descendant of *Nicholas.*
Custard a round-headed man.
Deadman one from *Debenham*, Norfolk.
Devil French *de ville* 'of the town'.
Duck descendant of *Duke*, ie *Marmaduke.*
Eels descendant of *Elias.*
Earthy descendant of *Arthur.*
Eye dweller on an island.
Fear a proud man or a companion.
Foal a fool, jester.
Forty dweller on an island near a ford.
Fullman a foal man.
Gosling descendant of *Jocelyn.*
Gumboil descendant of *Gumbold.*
Ham dweller near a river meadow.
Handshaker one from *Handsacre*, Staffs.
Hogg descendant of *Roger.*
Hollyman a holy man.
Human servant of Hugh.
Jelly descendant of *Jilly (Juliana).*
Killer lime kiln worker.
Kisser maker of cuisses (armour).
Lush an usher.
Maggot descendant of Margaret.
Money one from *Monaye*, France.
Moneypenny 'many penny', a rich man.
Moody courageous man.
Pate descendant of *Patrick.*
Quail = *MacPhail*, son of Paul.
Salmon descendant of *Solomon.*
Shufflebottom dweller in a sheep valley.
Smellie dweller near a small enclosure.
Smoker maker of smocks.
Spittle worker at a hospital.
Swindle one from Swindale.
Tombs servant of *Tom.*
Tortoiseshell man from *Tattershall.*
Trollope a strolling man.
Whisky dweller near the river *Wiske.*
Woof descendant of *Wulf.*

Some descriptive surnames

Arlott young fellow, rogue.
Armstrong as *Strongitharm.*
Ballard a bald man.
Bass a short man.
Bassett diminutive of *Bass.*
Beard a man who was bearded when beards were not fashionable.
Belcher a man who belched or had a 'pretty face'.
Bell (sometimes) the handsome man.
Bellamy handsome friend.
Best a man who was beast-like.
Biggs son of a big man.
Black with black hair, or darkish skin.
Blackbird with a black beard.
Blake usually as *Black.*
Blundell a blond man.
Blunt as *Blundell.*
Bossey a hunch-backed man.
Bragg a brisk man, or a proud one.
Brennan (English) a man whose job was to 'burn the hand' of a criminal, or a man whose hand was branded.
Brent (sometimes) a branded man.
Brown with brown hair.
Burnett with dark brown hair, or wearer/seller of cloth of that colour. Other meanings are also possible.
Carless free from care.
Cave (usually) a bald man.
Crippen with curly hair.
Cripps as *Crippen.* Also **Crisp** and **Crispin.**
Cronk a vigorous man.
Cruikshank with crooked legs.
Crump crooked, stooping.
Cuckow a cuckoo-like person, silly.
Curtis courteous/educated, or a wearer of short hose.
Doggett 'dog head'.
Dunn a swarthy man.
Dwelly a foolish man.
Fairchild a handsome young man.
Fairfax with beautiful hair.
Fortescue a strong shield.
Fry(e) free, generous.
Gay a cheerful man.
Giddy a madman.
Goodfellow a good companion, a **Goodman.**
Goolden with yellow hair.
Grant a tall man.
Gray or **Grey,** a grey-haired man.
Gulliver a glutton.
Hardy a tough man, courageous.
Hendy a courteous man.
Hoare a grey-haired man.
Jolliffe as **Jolly,** a cheerful man.
Keen a brave man.
Lang a tall man.
Lemon a lover.
Long a tall man.
Lovelace (sometimes) a man who loved the lasses.
Mallory an unlucky or unfortunate man.
Moody a bold man.
Moore (sometimes) swarthy as a Moor.
Noble of noble character.
Parfitt a man who was **Perfect.**
Pettit a small man.
Pratt a cunning man.
Prettyman as *Pratt.*
Proudfoot a man with a haughty walk.
Prowse a valiant man.
Puddifoot a man with a big paunch.
Pullen a frisky or lascivious person.
Quartermaine a man with 'four hands', wearing mailed gloves.
Rank a strong or proud man.
Read (usually) a man with red hair.
Reed as *Read.*
Russell as *Read.*
Savage a savage man. *Best* is the same type of name.
Shakespeare a shaker or brandisher of a lance or spear, a soldier.
Sharp a quick-thinking man.
Short a small man.
Shorthouse a wearer of short hose.
Simple an honest man.
Skegg a bearded man.
Small a thin or small man.
Smart as *Sharp.*
Smollett a man with a small head.
Snell a bold man.
Snow a white-haired man.
Sorrell with reddish-brown hair.
Strang a **Strong** man.
Swift a swift man.
Tait a cheerful man.
Thoroughgood a thoroughly good man.
Turnbull a strong man, able to turn a bull.
Wagstaffe similar to *Shakespeare.*
Whitbread (sometimes) a man with a white beard.
Whitehouse (sometimes) a man with a white neck.
Wild a man who behaved wildly.
Wise a wise man.
Worledge and **Woollage,** a distinguished man.
Wrenn a wren-like person, small or shrewd.
Yapp a deceitful or smart man.

. . . much of its greatness it owes to the Browns. For centuries, in their quiet, dogged, homespun way, they have been subduing the earth in most English counties, and leaving their mark in American forests and Australian uplands. Talbots and Stanleys, St Maurs, and such like folk, have led armies and made laws, time out of mind; but those noble families would be somewhat astounded, if the accounts ever came to be fairly taken, to find how small their work for England has been by the side of that of the Browns.

Thomas Hughes *Tom Brown's Schooldays*

Henry Guppy's 'Peculiar' Names

In 1890 Henry Brougham Guppy published his *Homes of Family Names in Great Britain*. Guppy had made a particular study of the names of farmers, whom he described as 'the most stay-at-home class of the country', and discovered that in each county their surnames fell into various groups:

a) General—names found all over the country
b) Common—names found in 20–29 counties
c) Regional—names found in 10–19 counties
d) District—names found in 4–9 counties
e) County—names found in 2–3 counties
f) Peculiar—names found mainly in one county only.

I list below the names he considered to be peculiar to one county. They provide strong clues for those interested in their family history as to where further investigations should be made. I have retained the former county names, though many of these have now changed for administrative purposes.

Bedfordshire
Battams, Breary, Brightman, Buckmaster, Claridge, Cranfield, Darrington, Dillamore, Duncombe, Fensom, Foll, Hallworth, Harradine, Hartop, Inskip, Kempson, Malden, Mossman, Negus, Quenby, Scrivener, Scroggs, Stanbridge, Stanton, Timberlake, Whinnett.

Berkshire
Adnams, Benning, Buckeridge, Bunce, Corderoy, Corderey, Crockford, Dormer, Fairthorne, Freebody, Frogley, Froome, Halfacre, Headington, Izzard, Keep, Kimber, Lanfear, Lay, Lonsley, Lyford, Maslen, Napper, Pither, Poyey, Shackel, Tame, Tyrrell, Wilder.

Buckinghamshire
Belgrove, Boughton, Brazier, Dancer, Darvell, Darvill, Dover, Dwight, Edmans, Fountain, Fountaine, Ginger, Gomm, Holdom, Horwood, Ing, Kingham, Plaistowe, Purssell, Roads, Sare, Sear, Slocock, Stratford, Syratt, Syrett, Sirett, Tapping, Tattam, Tofield, Tomes, Tompkins, Varney, Viccars, Warr, Willison, Wilmer, Wooster.

Cambridgeshire
Bays, Chivers, Clear, Collen, Coxall, Dimmock, Dimock, Doggett, Elbourn, Frohock, Fullard, Fyson, Ground, Grounds, Haggar, Hagger, Hurry, Ivatt, Jonas, Maxwell, Murfitt, Mustill, Purkis, Ruston, Sallis, Shepperson, Skeels, Stockdale, Thoday, Vawser, Wayman, Yarrow.

Cheshire
Acton, Adshead, Allman, Ankers, Ardern, Astbury, Aston, Basford, Baskerville, Basnett, Bebbington, Birtles, Blackshaw, Boffey, Bolshaw, Bracegirdle, Braddock, Broadhurst, Broster, Callwood, Cash, Chesters, Done, Dooley, Dutton, Eden, Erlam, Etchells, Furber, Gallimore, Gleave, Goddier, Goodier, Gresty, Hankey, Hassall, Hassell, Henshall, Hickson, Hockenhall, Hockenhull, Hocknell, Hollinshead, Hooley, Hopley, Houlbrook, Huxley, Jeffs, Jepson, Kennerley, Kinsey, Leah, Leather, Littler, Major, Marsland, Minshall, Minshull, Mottershead, Mounfield, Mountfield, Mullock, Newall, Noden, Norbury, Oakes, Okel, Oulton, Pimlott, Pownall, Priestner, Rathbone, Ravenscroft, Rowlingson, Ruscoe, Sandbach, Scragg, Sheen, Shone, Shore, Siddorn, Snelson, Sproston, Stelfox, Stockton, Summerfield, Swinton, Tapley, Thompstone, Thornhill, Tickle, Timperley, Trickett, Trueman, Urmston, Wheelton, Whitelegg, Whitlow, Witter, Woodall, Woollam, Woollams, Wych, Yarwood.

Cornwall
Benny, Berriman, Berryman, Bice, Biddick, Blamey, Boaden, Boase, Bolitho, Borlase, Brendon, Brenton, Budge, Bullmore, Bunt, Burnard, Cardell, Carlyon, Carne, Carveth, Cawrse, Chenoweth, Clemow, Clyma, Clymo, Coad, Cobbledick, Cobeldick, Congdon, Couch, Cowling, Crago, Cragoe, Craze, Crowle, Cundy, Curnow, Dingle, Dunstan, Dunstone, Eddy, Eva, Freethy, Galtey, Geach, Geake, Gerry, Gillbard, Glasson, Goldsworthy, Grigg, Grose, Gynn, Hambly, Hawke, Hawken, Hawkey, Hayne, Hearle, Henwood, Higman, Hodge, Hollow, Hotten, Ivey, Jane, Jasper, Jelbart, Jelbert, Jenkin, Jose, Julian, Julyan, Keast, Kerkin, Kestle, Kevern, Kitto, Kittow, Kneebone, Laity, Lander, Lanyon, Lawry, Lean, Liddicoat, Littlejohn, Lobb, Lory, Lugg, Lyle, Mably, Maddaford, Maddiver, Magor, Mayne, Morcom, Morkam, Moyle, Mutton, Nance, Oates, Oats, Odger, Odgers, Old, Olver, Opie, Oppy, Pascoe, Paynter, Pearn, Pedlar, Pedler, Pender, Pengelly, Pengilly, Penna, Penrose, Peter, Pethick, Philp, Pinch, Polkinghorne, Prisk, Raddall, Raddle, Rapson, Retallack, Retallick, Rickard, Rodda, Roose, Roseveare, Rosewarne, Roskelly, Roskelly, Roskilly, Rouse, Rowse, Rundle, Runnalls, Sandercock, Sandry, Scantlebury, Seccombe, Skewes, Spargo, Tamblyn, Tinney, Tippett, Toll, Tom, Tonkin, Trebilcock, Tregear, Tregellas, Tregelles, Tregoning, Treleaven,

Treloar, Tremain, Tremayne, Trembath, Trerise, Tresidder, Trethewey, Trevail, Treweeke, Trewhella, Trewin, Tripcony, Trounson, Trudgen, Trudgeon, Trudgian, Truscott, Tyack, Tyacke, Uren, Vellenoweth, Venning, Verran, Vivian, Vosper, Wearne, Wellington, Whetter, Wickett, Woodley, Woolcock, Yelland.

Cumberland and Westmorland
Beattie, Beaty, Burns, Carruthers, Dalzell, Dalziel, Donald, Faulder, Fearon, Fleming, Johnston, Martindale, Mossop, Mounsey, Pattinson, Routledge, Sim, Simm, Spotterswood, Thomlinson, Topping.

Derbyshire
Alton, Bark, Barnsley, Beardsley, Biggin, Boam, Bowmer, Briddon, Brocksopp, Broomhead, Burdikin, Byard, Chadfield, Clewes, Clews, Copestake, Crookes, Cupit, Cutts, Drabble, Dronfield, Eley, Else, Fearn, Fitchett, Foulke, Fowke, Fretwell, Gent, Gratton, Gyte, Hadfield, Handford, Hartle, Hawley, Henstock, Housley, Hulland, Jerram, Joule, Knifton, Knott, Limb, Litchfield, Longden, Ludlam, Lynam, Mallinder, Marchington, Marples, Maskery, Maskrey, Mortin, Murfin, Nadin, Oakden, Outram, Peat, Plackett, Pursglove, Purslove, Rains, Renshaw, Revell, Revill, Rowarth, Saint, Seal, Shacklock, Sherwin, Shirt, Sidebottom, Skidmore, Smedley, Spalton, Staley, Staniforth, Stoppard, Storer, Tagg, Towndrow, Townrow, Townroe, Turton, Tym, Tymm, Udall, Wager, Wallwin, Waterfall, Waterhouse, Wetton, Wheatcroft, Whittingham, Wibberley, Wigley, Winson, Wragg.

Devonshire
Addems, Alford, Amery, Anning, Arscott, Babbage, Balkwill, Balman, Balsdon, Bastin, Bater, Beedell, Beer, Besley, Bickle, Blatchford, Blowey, Bloye, Bolt, Boundy, Bovey, Bradridge, Bragg, Braund, Brayley, Breayley, Bridgman, Brimacombe, Broom, Bucknell, Burgoin, Burgoyne, Burrough, Burrow, Cawsey, Chaffe, Chamings, Chammings, Channin, Channing, Chave, Cheriton, Chowen, Chown, Chubb, Chugg, Cleverdon, Coaker, Cockram, Cockeram, Colwill, Coneybeare, Conybear, Connibeer, Coombe, Copp, Courtice, Crang, Crimp, Crocombe, Cuming, Dallyn, Damerell, Darch, Dare, Dart, Dayment, Densem, Densham, Dicker, Dimond, Dymond, Doble, Doidge, Dommett, Dufty, Earl, Earle, Easterbrook, Estabrook, Eggins, Ellacott, Ellicott, Elston, Elworthy, Endacott, Eveleigh, Evely, Fairchild, Fewings, Foale, Foss, Friend, Furneaux, Furse, Furze, Gammon, German, Gidley, Gillard, Gloyn, Gorwyn, Grendon, Halse, Hamlyn, Hannaford, Hartnell, Hartnoll, Hayman, Headon, Health, Heaman, Heard, Heddon, Heggadon, Helmer, Hext, Heyward, Heywood, Hillson, Hilson, Hockridge, Honniball, Hookway, Hurrell, Huxham, Huxtable, Irish, Isaacs, Jackman, Kerslake, Kingwell, Knapman, Lambshead, Lang, Langman, Langworthy, Lear, Lerwill, Lethbridge, Letheren, Ley, Lidstone, Littlejohns, Loosemoor, Loosmoor, Lovering, Luscombe, Luxton, Madge, Manley, Maunder, Melhuish, Melluish, Metherall, Metherell, Mildon, Mill, Millman, Milman, Mogford, Mugford, Mortimore, Mudge, Nancekivell, Nancekeville, Nankevil, Netherway, Newcombe, Norrish, Northam, Northmore, Nosworthy, Oldreave, Oldreive, Paddon, Palfrey, Palk, Parkhouse, Pavey, Pearcey, Penwarden, Perkin, Perrin, Petherbridge, Petherick, Pinhay, Pinhey, Powlesland, Prettejohn, Prettyjohn, Pring, Pugsley, Pym, Quance, Rabjohns, Raymont, Raymount, Reddaway, Reddicliffe, Retter, Rew, Ridd, Routley, Seldon, Sellek, Sercombe, Seward, Shapland, Sharland, Shorland, Sherrill, Sherwill, Shopland, Slader, Slee, Sluggett, Smale, Smallbridge, Smallridge, Smaridge, Smerdon, Smyth, Soby, Soper, Spurrell, Spurle, Squance, Stanbury, Stidston, Stoneman, Tancock, Taverner, Toms, Tope, Tozer, Tremlett, Trick, Trott, Trude, Tuckett, Tully, Underhay, Underhill, Vallance, Vanstone, Venner, Voaden, Vodden, Vooght, Wadland, Wakeham, Ware, Waycott, Were, Westacott, Westaway, Westcott, Western, Westren, Wheaton, Whiteaway, Whiteway, Widdicombe, Willing, Withecombe, Witheycombe, Witheridge, Wonnacott, Woolland, Wotton, Wrayford, Wreford, Wroth.

Dorsetshire
Antell, Ballam, Bastable, Besent, Bowditch, Brickell, Brine, Bugg, Bugler, Caines, Cake, Chilcott, Cluett, Dominy, Dorey, Dunford, Durden, Ensor, Fifett, Fooks, Foot, Gatehouse, Genge, Gillingham, Guppy, Hames, Hann, Hansford, Hayter, Homer, Honeyfield, Hounsell, Jesty, Kellaway, Keynes, Kingman, Larcombe, Legg, Lodder, Loder, Mayo, Meaden, Meatyard, Meech, Milledge, Munckton, Peach, Pomeroy, Rabbetts, Ridout, Ross, Rossiter, Samways, Scutt, Shute, Spicer, Sprake, Studley, Swaffield, Symes, Topp, Trowbridge, Tuffin, Wakely, Walden, Walden, Wareham, Wrixon.

Durham
Applegarth, Beadle, Bruce, Bullman, Bulman, Burdon, Callender, Coatsworth, Eggleston, Greenwell, Heppell, Hepple, Hewitson, Hopps, Jameson, Jamieson, Kirkup, Kirton, MacLaren, Makepeace, Mallam, Pallister, Pease, Proud, Quelch, Shotton, Surtees, Tarn, Tinkler, Walburn, Wearmouth.

Essex
Basham, Beddall, Belcham, Bentall, Byford, Cant, Caton, Challis, Christy, Dowsett, Eve, Fairhead, Felgate, Fenner, Folkard, Gowlett, Halls, Hasler, Hockley, Housden, Hutley, Kemsley, Ketley, Kettley,

Lagden, Littlechild, Lucking, Marriage, Maskell, Matthams, Meeson, Metson, Milbank, Millbank, Mott, Muggleston, Nottage, Pannell, Parish, Parrish, Patmore, Pegrum, Pilgrim, Pledger, Quilter, Raven, Rickett, Root, Ruffle, Savill, Scruby, Shave, Sorrell, Spurgeon, Staines, Stock, Strutt, Sweeting, Taber, Tabor, Thorington, Tilbrook, Tofts, Tween, Wenden, Wendon, Whitlock.

Gloucestershire

Arkell, Ballinger, Biddle, Blandford, Browning, Bubb, Cadle, Clutterbuck, Comely, Cornock, Croome, Cullimore, Dobbs, Dowdeswell, Fawkes, Flook, Fluck, Flux, Garne, Gazard, Goulding, Goulter, Hanks, Hatherell, Hewer, Hignell, Holder, Iles, Kilminster, Kilmister, Limbrick, Lusty, Minchin, Minett, New, Niblett, Organ, Parslow, Pegler, Penson, Priday, Radway, Ricketts, Righton, Rugman, Rymer, Selwyn, Shields, Shipp, Shipway, Staite, Stinchcombe, Theyer, Till, Trotman, Tuffley, Vick, Vimpany, Wadley, Werrett, Wintle, Wintour, Witchell, Yeend.

Hampshire

Abbinett, Amey, Attrill, Ayles, Barfoot, Blackman, Broomfield, Budd, Clift, Cobden, Drewitt, Drudge, Edney, Fay, Fitt, Jolliffe, Lavington, Light, Mew, Poore, Portsmouth, Potticary, Rumbold, Seaward, Southwell, Stares, Stride, Turvill, Twitchin, Whitcher, Witt.

Herefordshire

Allcott, Apperley, Banfield, Berrow, Bodenham, Bounds, Bromage, Callow, Eckley, Embrey, Godsall, Godsell, Hancorn, Hobby, Hoddell, Maddy, Mailes, Mainwaring, Marfell, Meadmore, Monnington, Ockey, Orgee, Paniers, Panniers, Pantall, Scudamore, Sirrell, Skerrett, Skyrme, South, Tudge, Vale, Welson, Went.

Hertfordshire

Acres, Ashwell, Bonfield, Campkin, Chalkley, Chennells, Clinton, Hankin, Ivory, Kingsley, Kitchener, Mardell, Orchard, Overell, Parkins, Patten, Sears, Tittmuss, Vyse, Walby, Woollatt.

Huntingdonshire

Achurch, Bletsoe, Cheney, Corney, Ekins, Humbley, Jellis, Ladds, Lenton, Looker, Mash, Speechley, Spriggs.

Kent

Ballard, Barling, Belsey, Benstead, Bensted, Bing, Boorman, Boulden, Brenchley, Brice, Broadley, Buss, Chantler, Clinch, Coultrip, Coveney, Crowhurst, Curling, Dark, Dilnot, Dungey, Fagg, File, Filmer, Finn, Fremlin, Godden, Goodhew, Gower, Hambrook, Harden, Hartridge, Hickmott, Hogben, Hogbin, Holness, Honess, Hollamby, Hollands, Inge, Jarrett, Kingsnorth, Langridge, Larkin, Larking, Laslett, Leney, Love, Luck, Manwaring, Matcham, Maylam, Maxted, Millen, Milne, Minter, Miskin, Missing, Morphett, Murton, Neame, Offen, Orpen, Orpin, Oyler, Pidduck, Pittock, Pilcher, Prebble, Quested, Rigden, Scoones, Seath, Shorter, Solley, Solomon, Southon, Stace, Stickles, Stunt, Stuppies, Swaffer, Tassell, Thirkell, Tickner, Tomkin, Tompsett, Tuff, Usherwood, Unicume, Vinson, Wacher, Waterman, Whitebread, Wiles, Wyles, Witherden.

Lancashire

Alker, Almond, Alty, Aspinall, Aspinwall, Atherton, Bamber, Battersby, Bent, Bibby, Bleasdale, Bleazard, Blezard, Blezzard, Bonney, Bretherton, Brindle, Bulcock, Butterworth, Caldwell, Cardwell, Cartmell, Catlow, Catterall, Caunce, Charnley, Charnock, Collinge, Coward, Critchley, Crompton, Cropper, Culshaw, Cunliffe, Dagger, Dearden, Dewhurst, Drinkall, Duckworth, Dunderdale, Duxbury, Eastham, Eaves, Eccles, Entwisle, Entwistle, Fairclough, Fazakerley, Fish, Forrest, Forshaw, Gornall, Gorst, Greenhalgh, Gregson, Grimshaw, Hacking, Hakin, Halliwell, Halsall, Hardman, Haworth, Haydock, Hayhurst, Haythornthwaite, Hesketh, Hesmondhalgh, Higson, Hindle, Horrocks, Huddleston, Ibison, Iddon, Kellett, Kenyon, Kilshaw, Lawrenson, Leaver, Lever, Livesey, Livesley, Longton, Longworth, Lonsdale, Lyon, Lythgoe, Lithgoe, Maden, Margerison, Margerson, Marginson, Margison, Martland, Mashiter, Maudsley, Mawdsley, Mayor, Molyneux, Newby, Nutter, Ollerton, Pemberton, Pendlebury, Pickup, Pilkington, Pilling, Pimblett, Pollitt, Pomfret, Postlethwaite, Rainford, Ramsbottom, Rawcliffe, Rawlinson, Riding, Ryding, Rimmer, Rogerson, Rosbotham, Rosbottom, Rosebotham, Rossall, Rossell, Rothwell, Sagar, Segar, Salthouse, Scholes, Seddon, Sefton, Sephton, Shacklady, Shakelady, Sharples, Sharrock, Shorrock, Silcock, Singleton, Stanworth, Starkie, Stuart, Swarbrick, Tattersall, Threlfall, Topping, Townson, Tyrer, Unworth, Wallbank, Walmsley, Walsh, Wareing, Waring, Whipp, Whiteside, Winder, Winstanley, Worsley.

Leicestershire and Rutlandshire

Beeby, Berridge, Branson, Burnaby, Cobley, Dalby, Darnell, Dawkins, Dexter, Dowell, Drackley, Draycott, Eayrs, Eayres, Forryan, Frearson, Freestone, Geary, Gimson, Hack, Henson, Hollier, Jarrom, Jesson, Keetley, Keightley, Kirkman, Lacey, Leadbeater, Leadbetter, Loseby, Macaulay, Mackley, Matts, Musson, Oldacres, Orson, Paget, Pochin, Pretty, Royce, Scotton, Sheffield, Shipman, Toon, Toone, Wilford, Wormleighton.

Lincolnshire
Anyan, Bemrose, Bett, Blades, Blankley, Border, Borman, Bowser, Brackenbury, Bristow, Broughton, Brownlow, Brumby, Burkill, Burkitt, Butters, Cade, Cammack, Capes, Casswell, Chatterton, Codd, Collishaw, Coney, Cooling, Cottingham, Coupland, Cranidge, Cropley, Cutforth, Cuthbert, Dannatt, Daubney, Desforges, Dook, Dows, Dowse, Drakes, Drewery, Drewry, Dring, Drury, Dudding, Elmitt, Elvidge, Epton, Evison, Forman, Frisby, Frow, Gaunt, Gilliart, Gilliatt, Gillyatt, Goodyear, Goose, Grummitt, Hay, Herring, Hewson, Hides, Hildred, Hoyes, Hoyles, Hutton, Ingall, Ingle, Laming, Lamming, Leggett, Leggott, Lill, Lilley, Lynn, Mackinder, Maidens, Marfleet, Markham, Mastin, Maw, Mawer, Merrikin, Minta, Mowbray, Odling, Overton, Palethorpe, Patchett, Pick, Pickwell, Pocklington, Ranby, Reeson, Rhoades, Riggall, Rippon, Sardeson, Sargisson, Scarborough, Scholey, Scoley, Scrimshaw, Scrimshire, Searson, Sergeant, Sharpley, Sneath, Stamp, Storr, Stowe, Strawson, Stuble, Temple, Thurlby, Trafford, Ullyatt, Vinter, Waddingham, Wadsley, Wass, Westerby, Westoby, Whitsed, Willey, Willows, Winn, Wroot.

Middlesex
Ewer, Woodland

Norfolk
Abbs, Amies, Amis, Arthurton, Atthow, Attoe, Banham, Batterham, Beales, Beanes, Beck, Bettinson, Boddy, Brasnett, Bunn, Cannell, Case, Claxton, Copeman, Cossey, Cubitt, Culley, Curson, Duffield, Dyball, Dye, Eglinton, Failes, Flatt, Gamble, Gapp, Gayford, Gaze, Gedge, Gooch, Goulder, Greenacre, Heading, Howes, Huggins, Ingram, Kerrison, Lain, Land, Larwood, Leeder, Leeds, Lewell, Mack, Mallett, Milk, Minns, Mullinger, Nurse, Plumbly, Poll, Purdy, Ringer, Rising, Rivett, Rix, Roofe, Sands, Savory, Scales, Sheringham, Shreeve, Slipper, Soame, Spink, Spinks, Starling, Stimpson, Thrower, Tooley, Utting, Warnes, Whalebelly, Whittleton, Woolston, Wortley.

Northamptonshire
Aris, Barford, Bazeley, Bazley, Bellairs, Bellars, Borton, Brafield, Britten, Bromwich, Buswell, Butlin, Chew, Dainty, Drage, Dunkley, Gibbard, Goff, Golby, Goode, Gulliver, Hales, Heygate, Holton, Hornsby, Judkins, Kingston, Linnell, Mackaness, Main, Mawle, Measures, Montgomery, Newitt, Panther, Roddis, Scriven, Siddons, Spokes, Stops, Turnell, Vergette, Warwick, Westley, Whitton, Whitney, Woolhouse, Wrighton, Wyman, York.

Northumberland
Alder, Allan, Annett, Arkle, Aynsley, Bewick, Bolam, Borthwick, Bothwick, Brewis, Brodie, Bushby, Cairns, Carmichael, Cockburn, Common, Cowan, Cowen, Cowing, Craig, Dand, Dinning, Embleton, Fairbairn, Gallon, Gilhespy, Glendinning, Harle, Herdman, Hindmarsh, Hogg, Howey, Howie, Jobling, Laidler, Lumsden, Middlemas, Middlemiss, Morrison, Nevin, Nevins, Ormston, Phillipson, Pringle, Renton, Renwick, Roddam, Shanks, Shield, Stewart, Stobart, Stobert, Straughan, Telfer, Telford, Usher, Wanlace, Wanless, Weddell, Weddle, Younger.

Nottinghamshire
Annable, Barrowcliff, Bartram, Beardall, Beecroft, Billyard, Binge, Bingley, Blatherwick, Broadberry, Buttery, Byron, Carver, Challand, Cheshire, Chettle, Collingham, Corringham, Cumberland, Darwin, Derry, Doncaster, Duckmanton, Eddison, Esam, Farnsworth, Fenton, Footitt, Footit, Gagg, Gelsthorpe, Gunn, Hardstaff, Harpham, Hempsall, Herrick, Herrod, Hickton, Holbrook, Howett, Howitt, Hurt, Huskinson, Keyworth, Leavers, Leivers, Lindley, Merrills, Millington, Norwood, Ogle, Oliphant, Olivant, Paling, Payling, Paulson, Peatfield, Pell, Pickin, Plumtree, Quibell, Radley, Redgate, Roadley, Selby, Staples, Stendall, Straw, Stubbins, Templeman, Truswell, Weightman, Wombwell, Woombill.

Oxfordshire
Akers, Aldworth, Arnatt, Batts, Blencowe, Breakspear, Buller, Calcutt, Chaundy, Clapton, Clare, Coggins, Deeley, Edginton, Filbee, Florey, Hatt, Hutt, Hobley, Hone, Honour, Loosley, Louch, Lovegrove, Luckett, Midwinter, Neighbour, Nevell, Padbury, Paxman, Paxton, Pether, Pettipher, Rowles, Sabin, Savin, Shrimpton, Spurrett, Stanbra, Turrill, Tustain, Widdows, Wilsdon, Witney, Woolgrove.

Shropshire
Ashley, Back, Bather, Batho, Beddoes, Benbow, Blakemore, Boughey, Bowdler, Breakwell, Brisbourne, Broughall, Cadwallader, Cleeton, Corfield, Cureton, Duce, Eddowes, Everall, Felton, Fowles, Growcott, Gwilt, Heatley, Heighway, Hinton, Home, Hotchkiss, Inions, Instone, Jacks, Kynaston, Lawley, Madeley, Mansell, Mellings, Millichamp, Minton, Munslow, Nock, Onions, Paddock, Pinches, Pitchford, Podmore, Ravenshaw, Rodenhurst, Sankey, Shuker, Tipton, Titley, Warder, Wellings.

Somerset
Amesbury, Aplin, Ashman, Arney, Baber, Badman, Bagg, Banwell, Barnstable, Barrington, Batt, Bicknell, Binning, Bisdee, Board, Bowering, Brimble, Burch, Burston, Carey, Cary, Chard, Churches, Clapp, Clothier, Coate, Cogan, Coggan, Corner, Corp, Cosh, Counsell, Croom, Crossman, Dampier, Denman, Denning, Derrick, Dibble, Dicks, Diment, Dyment, Durston, Evered, Farthing, Fear, Floyd,

Gare, Giblett, Greed, Haggett, Hatch, Hebditch, Hembrow, Hockey, Horsey, Hurd, Hurley, Isgar, Keedwell, Keel, Keirl, Kidner, Look, Loveybond, Lovibond, Loxton, Lutley, Mapstone, Meaker, Oram, Padfield, Perham, Phippen, Pople, Pottenger, Pow, Puddy, Rawle, Reakes, Rood, Rugg, Say, Sealey, Sealy, Singer, Speed, Sperring, Spratt, Stallard, Steeds, Stuckey, Sully, Summerhayes, Swanton, Sweet, Tarr, Tatchell, Tazewell, Teek, Tilley, Toogood, Treasure, Tyley, Vigar, Vigors, Vowles, Walrond, Wescott, Winslade, Winstone, Withey, Withy, Wookey, Yeandle.

Staffordshire

Ash, Averill, Bagnall, Bakewell, Baskeyfield, Batkin, Beardmore, Bickford, Boden, Boon, Bott, Bould, Boulton, Bowers, Brindley, Brunt, Cantrell, Cantrill, Chell, Clewlow, Clulow, Clowes, Colclough, Corbishley, Cumberledge, Deakin, Durose, Eardley, Elsmore, Fallows, Farrall, Fern, Forrester, Goldstraw, Hambleton, Hammersley, Heler, Hodgkins, Hollingsworth, Hollins, Howson, Jeavons, Jevons, Keeling, Kidd, Lakin, Leese, Leighton, Lindop, Lovatt, Loverock, Lymer, Limer, Malkin, Marson, Mayer, Mottram, Myatt, Orpe, Parton, Pyatt, Sharratt, Sherratt, Shelley, Shemilt, Shenton, Shirley, Shoebotham, Shoebottom, Stoddard, Swetnam, Tomkinson, Torr, Tunnicliff, Turnock, Warrilow, Whitehurst, Wilshaw, Wint, Wooddisse, Woodings.

Suffolk

Aldous, Alston, Aves, Baldry, Bendall, Blowers, Borrett, Button, Calver, Catling, Cattermole, Cobbold, Colson, Cracknell, Cutting, Debenham, Deck, Feaveryear, Feaviour, Finbow, Fincham, Fisk, Fiske, Flatman, Fulcher, Garnham, Gooderham, Grimsey, Grimwood, Hadingham, Haward, Hitchcock, Hurren, Ingate, Jillings, Juby, Keeble, Kemball, Kerridge, Kerry, Kersey, Last, Meen, Nesling, Newson, Pendell, Pendle, Sawyer, Sheldrake, Sheldrick, Southgate, Squirrell, Stannard, Steggall, Sturgeon, Thurman, Tricker, Whitmore, Wolton, Woollard.

Surrey

Caesar, Charlwood, Chuter, Gosden, Puttock, Smithers, Tice, Wenham.

Sussex

Akehurst, Allcorn, Ayling, Aylwin, Barham, Bodle, Boniface, Botting, Bourner, Challen, Chitty, Churchman, Coppard, Corke, Cornford, Diplock, Dumbrell, Dumbrill, Etheridge, Evershed, Fogden, Funnell, Gander, Gates, Goacher, Gorringe, Haffenden, Head, Heaver, Hide, Hoadley, Hoath, Hobden, Hobgen, Honeysett, Hook, Isted, Joyes, Killick, Leppard, Longley, Mannington, Message, Newington, Packham, Pankhurst, Penfold, Pennifold, Rapley, Sayers, Sinden, Sparkes, Stay, Sturt, Suter, Tester, Tobitt, Towes, Towse, Tribe, Verrall, Wakeford, Walder, Wickens, Woodhams, Wren, Wrenn.

Warwickshire

Arch, Boddington, Burbidge, Chattaway, Crofts, Currall, Edkins, Elkington, Fitter, Grimes, Hands, Hicken, Hickin, Hollick, Ibbotson, Jeffcoate, Jephcott, Keyte, Knibb, Ledbrook, Moxon, Murcott, Rainbow, Tibbetts, Tidy, Trippas, Truelove, Warden, Weetman, Wilday, Willday.

Wiltshire

Awdry, Beak, Bracher, Breach, Compton, Cottle, Cuss, Cusse, Doel, Eatwell, Frankcombe, Frankcome, Freegard, Freeth, Garlick, Ghey, Greenaway, Greenhill, Grist, Hathway, Henley, Howse, Hulbert, Jupe, Keevil, Kemble, Kinch, Knapp, Manners, Maundrell, Melsome, Milsom, Mintey, Minty, Morse, Newth, Ody, Parham, Pickett, Pinchin, Puckeridge, Ruddle, Rumming, Russ, Sidford, Sloper, Taunton, Titcombe, Whatley.

Worcestershire

Albutt, Allbutt, Allington, Amphlett, Blakeway, Boucher, Boulter, Byrd, Careless, Cartridge, Doolittle, Essex, Firkins, Follows, Gabb, Ganderton, Granger, Grove, Guilding, Hadley, Halford, Harber, Hemus, Hingley, Hollington, Holtom, Huband, Hyde, Merrell, Moule, Munn, Mytton, Newey, Nickless, Penrice, Purser, Quinney, Quinny, Smithin, Spiers, Stinton, Tandy, Tipping, Tolley, Tongue, Willets, Willetts, Winnall, Winwood, Workman, Wormington, Yarnold.

Yorkshire, North and East Ridings

Agar, Blenkin, Blenkiron, Bosomworth, Botterill, Bowes, Brigham, Bulmer, Codling, Coverdale, Creaser, Danby, Dinsdale, Duck, Duggleby, Elgey, Elgie, Ellerby, Foxton, Galloway, Garbutt, Goodwill, Grainger, Harker, Harland, Hawking, Hebron, Heseltine, Hick, Holliday, Holyday, Horsley, Hugill, Iveson, Jacques, Jordison, Judson, Kendrew, Kettlewell, Kilvington, Kipling, Knaggs, Lamplough, Lamplugh, Laverack, Laverick, Leak, Leake, Leaper, Leckenby, Matson, Matterson, Mattison, Medforth, Megginson, Meggison, Megson, Monkman, Nornabell, Nottingham, Outhwaite, Parnaby, Petch, Pickersgill, Plews, Porrett, Porritt, Precious, Prodham, Prudom, Pybus, Raw, Readman, Rennison, Rider, Rodmell, Rounthwaite, Routhwaite, Rowntree, Scarth, Sedman, Sellars, Sellers, Severs, Spenceley, Spensley, Stainthorpe, Stavely, Stockhill, Stockill, Stokell, Stonehouse, Sturdy, Suddaby, Suggett, Suggitt, Sunter, Tennison, Tweedy, Tyerman, Tyreman, Ventress, Ventris, Weighell, Weighill,

Welburn, Wellburn, Welford, Whitwell, Wilberforce, Wilberfoss, Witty, Wray, Wrightson.

Yorkshire, West Riding

Addy, Ambler, Appleyard, Armitage, Balmforth, Bamforth, Barraclough, Batty, Battye, Beever, Beevers, Beevors, Bentham, Binns, Blakey, Bottomley, Bramall, Brear, Brears, Broadbent, Broadhead, Butterfield, Capstick, Clapham, Clough, Cockshott, Crapper, Crawshaw, Demain, Demaine, Denby, Denison, Dibb, Dyson, Earnshaw, Emmott, Feather, Firth, Garside, Geldard, Gelder, Gledhill, Gott, Haigh, Hainsworth, Haley, Hampshire, Hanson, Hardcastle, Helliwell, Hepworth, Hey, Hinchcliff, Hinchcliffe, Hirst, Hobson, Holdsworth, Houldsworth, Holroyd, Horsfall, Houseman, Ingleby, Jagger, Jowett, Jubb, Kenworthy, Laycock, Lodge, Longbottom, Lumb, Mallinson, Mawson, Midgley, Moorhouse, Murgatroyd, Myers, Newsholme, Newsome, Noble, Peel, Popplewell, Poskitt, Ramsden, Redmayne, Rishworth, Rushworth, Robertshaw, Roebuck, Sedgwick, Shackleton, Sheard, Stansfield, Sugden, Sunderland, Tatham, Teal, Teale, Thackery, Thackray, Thackwray, Thornber, Thwaites, Tinker, Townend, Umpleby, Uttley, Varley, Verity, Wadsworth, Watkinson, Weatherhead, Whiteley, Whitley, Widdop, Widdup, Woodhead, Wrathall.

North Wales

Bebb, Bellis, Colley, Foulkes, Ryder, Tudor.

South Wales

Beynon, Duggan, Harry, Matthias, Mordecai, Ormond.

Monmouthshire.

Crowles, Duckham, Ellaway, Gwynne, Jeremiah, Moses, Rosser.

A substantial and authoritative source of information about British and European surnames became available in November, 1988, with the publication of *A Dictionary of Surnames*, by Patrick Hanks and Flavia Hodges, published by Oxford University Press. The books deals with some 70 000 surnames, and includes a full treatment of Jewish names by David L. Gold. Biographical information is added where appropriate.

---

6 Making a name for yourself

A great many people have a burning ambition to make a name for themselves. Although 'name' here is used for 'reputation', the name itself remains of great importance. If it is to be widely used and remembered, other people must be able to say it and spell it easily, and it must not suggest anything undesirable or silly. At the same time, a slight dash of the unusual is welcome to provide the necessary individuality. Many of our surnames, casually bestowed centuries ago and badly treated since, do not fulfil these criteria. Bearers of such names are left with little alternative but to change them if they really are set on a public life. They must begin quite literally by making a name for themselves.

Stage names

The world of entertainment naturally comes immediately to mind. Stage names are an accepted part of the profession. Among those who have adapted their real surnames to some purpose are Dirk **Bogarde,** otherwise Derek Gentron Gaspart Ulric van den **Bogaerde;** Fred **Astaire**—Frederick **Austerlitz;** Danny **Kaye**—David Daniel **Kaminsky;** Jerry **Lewis**—Joseph **Levitch;** Greta **Garbo**—Greta **Gustafsson.** The smallest possible change was made by Warren **Beatty,** formerly **Beaty.** His sister, Shirley Maclean Beaty, emerged as Shirley **Maclaine. Liberace** is one who retained his real surname but dropped the **Wladziu Valentino** that preceded it. Others have preferred to take more drastic action and forget the old surname completely. Well-known examples include Diana **Dors,** formerly Diana **Fluck;** Judy **Garland**—Frances **Gumm;** Kirk **Douglas**—Issur Danielovitch **Demsky;** Engelbert **Humperdinck**—Arnold **Dorsey.**

'Alan Bolt? Nothing. Let's get a name for him, somebody. A long one. That one is too short. It's over before you know it. I like long names. They look bigger on the billing. People think they're getting more for their money. Like Rudolph Valentino, now there's a good name'.

Garson Kanin *Moviola*

Politicians can hardly be described as entertainers, but they also need names that the public can cope with. Spiro **Agnew** understandably adapted his Greek family name, **Anagnostopoulos,** for this reason. Such changes differ from the adoption of political pseudonyms, which have been used in countries such as Russia. **Stalin,** 'steel', was chosen by **I. V. Dzhugashvili,** whose real name derived from a word meaning 'dross'. **Lenin**'s name was meant to be a reminder of political disturbances on the River **Lena,** in Siberia, though it exists as a real name, derived from **Alexander.** Lenin's real name was **Ulyanov.**

Mention of Russian names brings us back to stage names, for in certain circles, such as the ballet, they have great prestige. Those not as fortunate as Rudolf **Nureyev,** who is able to use his real name, have sometimes adopted one that has a suitably Russian-sounding flavour. Alice **Marks** became Alicia **Markova,** while Patrick **Healey-Kay** changed to Anton **Dolin.** The dignity and romanticism of such names contrasts interestingly with the names of some other dancers, who appear in the Parisian Crazy Horse Cabaret. The latter appear under such evocative names (and little else) as Pamela **Boum-Boum.** Polly **Underground** and Rita **Cadillac.**

Pen names

Writers' pseudonyms have been used far longer than stage names and often for different reasons. The desire is not necessarily to escape from an unfortunate name, but genuinely to conceal the writer's true identity. In the past it was sometimes thought that readers would be prejudiced against women writers, so many of them wrote as men or tried to conceal their sex in non-committal names, such as those used by the Brontë sisters, **Currer, Ellis** and **Acton Bell.** Other authors have been ashamed of their works for one reason or another and have not wished anyone to know their true identities. In modern times there are authors who would flood the market if they used their own name all the time, and a string of pseudonyms becomes necessary. A single pen name can, on the other hand, conceal the fact that several different authors are writing the stories concerned. Finally, if an author has made himself something of an authority in one area, he may feel that another name is required when he turns to pastures new.

About this time, to her more familiar correspondents, Charlotte Brontë occasionally calls herself 'Charles Thunder', making a kind of pseudonym for herself out of her Christian name, and the meaning of her Greek surname.

Elizabeth Gaskell *The Life of Charlotte Brontë*

(In fact Brontë was a form of Prunty or Pronty, Irish Proinntigh, 'bestower, generous person', the change to Brontë having been made by Charlotte's father. He was probably more influenced by the fact that Lord Nelson had been made Duke of Brontë, a place in Sicily, in 1799, than by *bronte*, Greek for 'thunder').

One would expect authors to choose pen names that have linguistic point to them. **Lewis Carroll** has a suitably etymological connection with **Charles Lutwidge Dodgson,** its inventor. Lutwidge is a form of **Ludwig,** which can be directly translated as Lewis. Charles is **Carolus** in Latin, and Carroll simply adapts it slightly. The 19th-century writer **Ouida** looks as if she transferred her name from the city of that name in Morocco, but she herself

Her real name wasn't Lois Angeles, it was Linda Peabody, which struck him as a damn good reason for changing it to almost anything else you could think of.

L. J. Davis *Walking Small*

explained it as a natural linguistic development. It represented her own attempt as a child to pronounce her middle name, **Louise.**

Aliases

These last examples once again retain a definite link with the real name, which many people who adopt a new name consider to be necessary. Traces of name magic are revealed here, for this hints at a deep-rooted belief that one's real name is somehow part of one's real self, and that complete abandonment of it will have evil consequences. Criminal records support this contention strongly, for an analysis of aliases that have been used shows that the adopted surnames normally have the same initial, number of syllables and basic sound as the originals. What appears to be a totally new name is more often drawn from the namer's immediate onomastic environment. It will be the mother's maiden name or the surname of a close friend, or a name transferred from a street or place that has strong personal associations. The link with the real past is maintained.

As we have seen, immigration into an English-speaking country can be another reason for name change and here again an attempt is often made to link with the original name. The Ukrainian Vasyl **Mykula** who became William **McCulla** showed one way of doing it. Other Russian-English pairs are **Prishchipenko—Price, Chernyshev—Chester, Grushko—Grey.** Direct translation, eg of German **Müller,** French **Meunier,** Hungarian **Molnar,** Dutch **Mulder** into English **Miller** achieves a similar result.

'Under what name did you make your appearance here?'
'I used my own.'
'I would have preferred Polkinghorne or Gooch or Withers,' said the Bishop pensively. 'They sound more legal.'

P. G. Wodehouse *Cats Will Be Cats*

Maiden names

'I offer you my name and hand, Laetitia!'

George Meredith *The Egoist*

Mr Alfred Cortez married her and gave her his name and the two foundations of her family, Alfredo and Ernie. Mr Cortez gave her that name gladly. He was only using it temporarily anyway. His name, before he came to Monterey and after he left, was Guggliemo.

John Steinbeck *Tortilla Flat*

Nancy kept her own name for all purposes, refusing to be called 'Mrs Graves' in any circumstances. She explained that as 'Mrs Graves' she had no personal validity.

Robert Graves *Goodbye to all That*

'I sometimes think of marrying old Maltravers,' said Mrs Beste-Chetwynde, 'only "Margot Maltravers" does sound a little too much, don't you think?'

Evelyn Waugh *Decline and Fall*

But by far the commonest reason for a surname change is marriage. Here, of course, there is no question of a woman consciously choosing a new name; she is simply re-exposed to the complex of accidental factors that gave her a surname in the first place. As for the name that has been so much a part of her life for many years, she finds that it becomes a mere maiden name. It is instantly reduced to at best middle-name status, and perhaps even less.

The implications of this marital name change have been much commented on, but although one reads at regular intervals of women who insist on using their maiden names after marriage, no general protest seems to be made. Suggestions that both husband and wife should take on a new name at marriage—perhaps blending parts of their surnames—are not taken very seriously. The blocking up of both surnames with hyphens between them has unfortunate connotations of pretentiousness, apart from leading to some very unwieldy combinations. Perhaps the problem will only be solved if we finally abolish hereditary surnames altogether. They are already superfluous in many ways. If we were allocated an individual number name at birth and used that for all official purposes, we could probably get by very well with one other personal name.

Other surname changes

Meanwhile, however, a large number of ordinary people who are not seeking public fame or trying to conceal their identities, change their surnames every year. They make use of a very simple legal process to rid themselves of a name which for one reason or another is an embarrassment to them. Who can possibly blame the Mr **Bugg** who became a **Howard,** or the gentlemen called **Bub, Holdwater, Poopy, Piddle, Honeybum, Leakey, Rumpe** and **Teate** who quietly dropped these surnames a century ago? Curiously enough, they *were* criticised at the time, though the criticisms were directed at the names they adopted, thought to be too high and mighty for ordinary citizens.

Personally, I can only wonder why more people do not follow the sensible example set by these name-changes. Why on earth do *I*, for example, put up with **Dunkling,** which is frequently converted into **Dumpling** by the hard-of-hearing or malicious? I have had its replacement standing by for years, an easy-to-spell, easy-to-say, pleasant-sounding name with the most respectable literary and other associations, and not, to my knowledge, at present attached to any other family. If I do not adopt it, is it because—not being an actor by nature—I would not be able to live out my life behind an onomastic disguise? Or am I conceited enough to think that I can overcome the natural disadvantages of my name and win through anyway?

You have a name and one thing after another happens to you, and you behave in various ways and do things, so that soon the name begins to have a meaning. Things have accumulated around the name. If it is bad and you have a bad reputation, then you can't jump out of your name and escape like that. And if it is good and you have a good reputation, then you should be content and satisfied.

Carson McCullers
The Member of the Wedding

Ideas about what is unusual also change with the passing of time. At one time somebody named **Petard,** which derives from a word meaning 'to break wind', would presumably have wanted to change it: today his friends might simply associate him vaguely with a passage in *Hamlet* and he would not feel under attack. A **Belcher,** on the other hand, was quite happy when others interpreted his name as *bel chiere*, 'pretty face'. The forgetting of this early meaning has left him sadly exposed.

If you ever have occasion to write to me, would you mind sticking a P at the beginning of my name? P-s-m-i-t-h. See? There are too many Smiths, and I don't care for Smythe. I've decided to strike out a fresh line. In conversation you may address me as Rupert (though I hope you won't), or simply Smith, the P not being sounded.

P. G. Wodehouse *Mike*

Other men are quite happy with their names until they reach adulthood and take up a profession. They then fall victim to the inevitable comments about their being **Berriman** the undertaker, or **D. Kaye,** the dentist. Partnership names such as **Reid** and **Wright** for Belfast printers, and **Doolittle** and **Dally** for estate agents are also much commented on, though they do have the advantage of attracting publicity.

If you are seriously thinking of changing your surname you would do well, for your descendants' sake, to begin it with a letter near the front of the alphabet. The custom when groups of people are gathered together for any purpose of working through them in alphabetical order has had a serious effect on people named **Young** and the like, psychologists tell us. They are constantly made to feel insignificant because they are dealt with last.

Psychological effects of surnames

If you are *not* thinking about a surname change, perhaps you should be. At the very least you should make an honest evaluation of your surname to see whether it is a definite hindrance to you, or whether it will be so for your children. As an adult you may be well aware that your surname is totally irrelevant in any evaluation of your total worth as a human being, but your children will spend many important years in a group where there is no such awareness. Studies such as that made by Christopher Bagley and Louise Evan-Wong ('Psychiatric Disorder and Adult and Peer Group Rejection of the Child's Name') prove beyond all reasonable doubt that children who consider a surname derisive will transfer their feelings about the name to the person who bears it. The attitude of his class-mates is likely to reinforce a child's negative opinion of himself, which will have been influenced by his own assessment of his name.

I ought to explain that it was not the peculiarity of Mr Loggerhead's name that produced the odd effect. Loggerheads is a local term for a harmless plant called the knapweed, and it is also the appellation of a place and of quite excellent people, and no-one regards it as even the least bit odd.

Arnold Bennett *Why the Clock Stopped*

A point not pursued in the above-mentioned article is that if children evaluate unusual names, they presumably evaluate *all* names. How does a **Smith** child react, one wonders, when he realises

Richard Vlk, of Pittsburgh, had often thought of changing his surname, which is of Czech origin and means 'wolf'. Most people had no idea how to pronounce it ('Velk'), and spelled it wrongly. Many simply laughed at it.

In 1983 Mr Vlk and his wife Kathy had the last laugh when they won over twenty thousand dollars in a contest run by the Pepsi-Cola Bottling Co. of Pittsburgh. They collected flip tops with letters on them that spelled their name. Consonants were easy to come by, vowels were hard to get. The Vlks suddenly found that a short, vowel-less name was just the thing to have.

---

that he has a very common name? It could conceivably lead him to think that he must be a very ordinary person. And what effect does it have on a child who discovers that he happens to possess a rather distinguished name? I can personally recall, as a child, envying a boy in the class *because of his name*, which happened to be **Nelson.** Surely I am not the only one to have known such feelings? And was the young Nelson so self-confident and assured partly because of his name?

I am not advocating a change of surname as a way of adjusting a person's psychological balance, or as a way of instantly improving his self-image. It appears to be a belief of the Kabalarians, founded in 1926 by Alfred J. Parker and based in Vancouver, that the one will automatically lead to the other. An article in *The Province*, December 1972, gives several examples of name changes advised by this organisation. They include **Jennifer Lulham** to **Alannah Matthew, Dorothy Rayner** to **Dhorea Delain, Marian Birch** to **Natallia Hohn.**

The very existence of the Kabalarians, and their ability to attract adherents, proves that a belief in the association of name with character can be carried into adult life. The name-changers clearly believe that mystic qualities of the new name will rub off on to them. They speak in the newspaper article of immediate and beneficial results of taking on a new name, and in this one can readily believe. But one can believe, too, that it boosts a normal person's morale to be well groomed and dressed. The effects of the new name will last no longer than the effects of make-up if the underlying attitude is wrong.

The name-makers

Where should those who are considering changing their name turn for guidance? Should they begin, for instance, with the most practised and prolific name-makers in our society, the writers of fiction? Novelists as name-makers provide an interesting study. The writers still occasionally fall back on the literary convention of type-names, the **Shallow** of Shakespeare or the Mrs **Slipslop** of Fielding, but when they do so the characters concerned are usually personifications of abstract ideas rather than ordinary people. At their best, novelists have a feeling for a name's associated characteristics—for surnames have these just as first names do—and use a name that works below the conscious level to

---

'Quilp is my name. You might remember. It's not a long one—Daniel Quilp.'

Charles Dickens *The Old Curiosity Shop*

'I'm surprised and rather disappointed that you like Scarp. I know it simply means a steep descent, but as a name it suggests somebody small, hard and mean—perhaps a dwarf moneylender in a Victorian novel.'

J. B. Priestley *Out of Town*

---

achieve the desired result. Dickensian characters such as **Pickwick** and **Scrooge** seem to be perfectly named. One wonders whether Pickwick appealed to the author because it partly echoed his own name, or did he simply see the name somewhere and jot it in his notebook, as he frequently did with names. Scrooge seems to be a made-up name, based on the word 'screw' as in the sentence used by Thackeray: 'I must screw and save in order to pay off the money.'

But authors are not always objective in their naming. They often seem to have a liking for particular sounds, and they return to these again and again. Thackeray clearly fell in love with the

I always judge a young author by the names which he bestows upon his characters. If the names seem to be weak or to be unsuitable to the people who bear them, I put the author down as a man of little talent, and am no further interested in the book.

Emile Zola *Dr Pascal*

One of the subtler difficulties that confront an author's name-sense arises from the necessary re-naming of such characters who have been adapted from real life, and whose own names cling to them closely as a wet bathing-costume.

G. B. Stern *A Name to Conjure With*

surname **Crump,** which actually exists and originally meant 'stooping'. He used it for three different characters. He has another character named **Crampton.** Dickens, as it happens, has a **Crumpton** and a **Crupp.** Both Dickens and Thackeray made use of **Crawley** as a character name, and between them they cover a wide range of other names beginning with 'Cr-'. Those they omit are accounted for by Sir Walter Scott, George Eliot, Jane Austen, Thomas Hardy, John Galsworthy and Anthony Trollope, all of whom begin the surnames of more than one character with these letters. Perhaps they pay a subconscious tribute to the first fictional character in English literature, **Robinson Crusoe,** but they may be revealing what a linguist might call their 'phonaesthetic preference'.

An analysis of any writer would probably reveal quite quickly his particular likes in this respect. Graham Greene, for example, has characters called **Rank, Rolt** and **Rowe, Rennit, Rimmer** and **Robinson.** If we ourselves were faced with the problem of naming a series of characters in different books we, too, would no doubt fall into some kind of pattern. If we tried to make a name for ourselves we would make use again of our linguistic preferences. This would be something to beware of, for it would be subjective. There is no point, surely, in changing one's name unless one is totally objective about it. The name would be meant to appeal to other people, not oneself.

Namesakes

Which surnames *do* please people? There have been no studies made that I am aware of which could answer that question. The names of popular people presumably have a head start on others, but it would be an error for anyone to turn himself into a namesake. I can think of nothing more depressing than having to answer the constantly repeated question: 'Not *the* **James Stewart?**' (or whoever) with 'No', or a wan smile.

Some people evidently enjoy being namesakes. The Jim Smith Society was founded in 1969 and has annual gatherings in America. One object of the society, according to a letter from its founder, James H. Smith, Jr, of Camp Hill, Pennsylvania, is to seek 'background information about acts of heroism by Jim Smiths'. Such as founding a Jim Smith Society, perhaps. I gather that a lot of fun is had by all concerned at the annual meetings, and perhaps we shall see more societies of this type in the future.

Becoming a partial namesake of someone famous might be an answer to the name-change problem. A little glory will rub off, possibly, and one will avoid the jokes. Reflected glory of a kind has been turned to commercial advantage in recent years by the firms which supply coats of arms. What happens here is that a coat of arms which has been awarded to a family is treated as being attached to the surname rather than the family concerned. In fact, a coat of arms in its 'undifferenced' form can be used only by the head of the family to which it was granted. Other members of the family use it too, but incorporate cadency marks. A man cannot sell his

'Tis but thy name that is my enemy;
Thou art thyself, though, not a Montague.
What's Montague? It is nor hand, nor foot,
Nor arm, nor face, nor any other part
Belonging to a man. O, be some other name.

William Shakespeare *Romeo and Juliet*

coat of arms or give someone else permission to use it, so there is absolutely no question of another family, which happens to have the same name, having the right to use it. This does not deter a great many people from displaying in their homes someone else's coat of arms with the shared family name written beneath it. There is little doubt that many people confuse coats of arms with clan tartans as far as usage is concerned, though the firms concerned usually explain the situation fairly clearly in the small print of their advertisements.

Perhaps no harm is done, other than to the occasional outraged head of a family who sees his personal property being trampled on, as it were. He might console himself with the thought that those meaningless little plaques are exerting a little name magic, enabling some anonymous people to feel somehow more dignified and content with the names they bear. If name magic is to continue having an influence, even in our apparently civilised society, it might as well have some positive effects as well as negative.

I have talked at some length about changing names, but my main object has been to stimulate a few thoughts about the meaning in modern times of the surnames that we inherit. Changing one's name is easy from a legal point of view, but it is understandable that many people are reluctant to do it. Those of us who put up with what we have must console ourselves with the thought that a change might not bring about the desired result in any case. Our bright new name might be brushed aside in favour of a nickname, and nicknames are not always complimentary as we shall see in the next chapter. Or perhaps our new names would simply fail to convince. Mr A. A. Willis makes this point in a story he passed on to me about a gentleman named **Brown** who applied to change his name to **Smith.** He was asked why he wanted to make this change, as he had changed his name only six months previously from **Gorfinckel** to **Brown.** His reply was: 'Becos ven pipple say to me: "Vot vas your name before it was Smith?" I vant to be able to say: "It was Brown—so there."'

A name—if the party had a voice
What mortal would be a Bugg by choice,
As a Hogg, a Grubb or a Chubb rejoice,
Or any such nauseous blazon?
Not to mention many a vulgar name
That would make a doorplate blush for
shame
If doorplates were not so brazen.

Thomas Hood

Some famous real names

Paul Anka
Gene Autry
Tallulah Bankhead
Harry Belafonte
Candice Bergen
Ingrid Bergman
Humphrey Bogart
Clara Bow
Marlon Brando
Pearl Buck
Hoagy Carmichael
Primo Carnera
Johnny Cash
Charlie Chaplin
Noel Coward
Olivia de Havilland
Neil Diamond
Bradford Dillman
Clint Eastwood
Nelson Eddy
Marianne Faithfull
Errol Flynn
Jane Fonda
Clark Gable
Art Garfunkel
Greer Garson
Bobbie Gentry
Dizzy Gillespie
Zane Grey
Rider Haggard
Susan Hampshire
Russell Harty
Goldie Hawn
Will Hay
Thora Hird
Alfred Hitchcock
Dustin Hoffman
Celeste Holm
Jimmy Jewell
Yootha Joyce
Gene Kelly
Eartha Kitt
Kris Kristofferson
Jack U. Lemmon
Gina Lollobrigida
Mercedes McCambridge
Steve McQueen
Lee Majors
Barry Manilow
Melina Mercouri
Spike Milligan
Roger Moore
Derek Nimmo
Walter Pidgeon
Cole Porter
Tyrone Power
Elvis Presley
Suzi Quatro
Anthony Quinn
Burt Reynolds
Cesar Romero
Damon Runyon
Telly Savalas
Frank Sinatra
Freddie Starr
Rod Steiger
Rod Stewart
Barbra Streisand
Mel Torme
Spencer Tracy
Ben Turpin
Gore Vidal
King Vidor
Orson Welles
Mae West
Frank Zappa

Some people who made a name for themselves

Anouk Aimée Françoise Sorya.
Woody Allen Allen Stewart Konigsberg.
Julie Andrews Julia Elizabeth Wells.
Pier Angeli Anna Maria Pierangeli.
Mary Astor Lucille Langehanke.
Lauren Bacall Betty Joan Perske.
Brigitte Bardot Camille Javal.
Eva Bartok Eva Sjöke.
Jack Benny Benjamin Kubelsky.
Irving Berlin Israel Baline.
Sarah Bernhardt Rosine Bernard.
Scott Brady Gerald Tierney.
Dora Bryan Dora May Broadbent.
Richard Burton Richard Walter Jenkins.
Michael Caine Maurice Joseph Micklewhite.
Rory Calhoun Francis Timothy Durgin.
Phyllis Calvert Phyllis Bickle.
Eddie Cantor Edward Israel Iskowitz.
Jeannie Carson Jean Shufflebottom.
Jeff Chandler Ira Grossel.
Lee J. Cobb Lee Jacoby.
Claudette Colbert Lily Claudette Chauchoin.
Gary Cooper Frank J. Cooper.
Lou Costello Louis Cristillo.
Constance Cummings Constance Halverstadt.
Tony Curtis Bernard Schwartz.
Vic Damone Vito Farinola.
Bebe Daniels Virginia Daniels.
Bobby Darin Walden Robert Cassotto.
Doris Day Doris Kappelhoff.
Yvonne de Carlo Peggy Yvonne Middleton.
Marlene Dietrich Marie Magdalene Dietrich von Losch.
Douglas Fairbanks Julius Ullman.
José Ferrer José Vincente Ferrer Otero y Cintrón.
Gracie Fields Grace Stansfield.
W. C. Fields William Claude Dukinfield.
Bud Flanagan Chaim Reuben Weintrop.
Mitzi Gaynor Francesca Mitzi Marlene de Charmey von Gerber.
Sam Goldwyn Samuel Goldfish.
Cary Grant Alexander Archibald Leach.
Nadia Gray Nadia Kujnir-Herescu.
Kathryn Grayson Zelma Hedrick.
Jean Harlow Harlean Carpenter.
Rex Harrison Reginald Carey Harrison.
Laurence Harvey Larushka Mischa Skikne.
Susan Hayward Edythe Marriner.
Hy Hazell Hyacinth Hazel O'Higgins.
Audrey Hepburn Edda Hepburn van Heemstra.
William Holden William Franklin Beedle.
Judy Holliday Judith Tuvim.
Leslie Howard Leslie Stainer.
Rock Hudson Roy Harold Fitzgerald.
Tab Hunter Arthur Andrew Gelien.
Burl Ives Burl Icle Ivanhoe.
Elton John Reginald Kenneth Dwight.
Al Jolson Asa Yoelson.
Boris Karloff William Henry Pratt.
Buster Keaton Joseph Francis Keaton.
Veronica Lake Constance Ockleman.
Hedy Lamarr Hedwig Kiesler.
Dorothy Lamour Dorothy Kaumeyer.
Mario Lanza Alfredo Arnold Cocozza.
Wilfrid Lawson Wilfrid Worsnop.
Gypsy Rose Lee Rose Louise Hovick.
Peggy Lee Norma Dolores Egstrom.
Vivien Leigh Vivian Mary Hartley.
Herbert Lom Herbert Charles Angelo Kuchacevich ze Schluderpacheru.
Sophia Loren Sofia Scicolone.
Dean Martin Dino Crocetti.
Tony Martin Alvin Morris.
Virginia Mayo Virginia May Jones.
Ethel Merman Ethel Zimmerman.
Ray Milland Reginald Truscott-Jones.
Carmen Miranda Maria de Carmo Mirando de Cunha.
Marilyn Monroe Norma Jean Baker.
Anna Neagle Marjorie Robertson.
Kim Novak Marilyn Novak.
Ivor Novello David Ivor Davies.
Merle Oberon Estelle Merle O'Brien Thompson.
Maureen O'Hara Maureen Fitzsimmons.
Jack Palance Walter Palanuik.
Cecil Parker Cecil Schwabe.
Jean Parker Mae Green.
Mary Pickford Gladys Mary Smith.
Jane Powell Suzanne Burce.
Chips Rafferty John William Goffage.
Ted Ray Charles Olden.
Debbie Reynolds Mary Frances Reynolds.
Cliff Richard Harold Roger Webb.
George Robey George Edward Wade.
Ginger Rogers Virginia Katharine McMath.
Roy Rogers Leonard Slye.
Mickey Rooney Joe Yule.
Romy Schneider Rosemarie Albach-Retty.
Randolph Scott Randolph Crane.
Mack Sennett Michael Sinott.
Moira Shearer Moira Shearer King.
Tommy Steele Thomas Hicks.
Connie Stevens Concetta Ann Ingolia.
Gale Storm Josephine Cottle.
Jacques Tati Jacques Tatisceff.
Robert Taylor Spangler Arlington Brough.
Terry-Thomas Thomas Terry Hoar-Stevens.
Mike Todd Avrom Hirsch Goldbogen.
Sophie Tucker Sophia Abuza.
Lana Turner Julia Turner.
Twiggy Lesley Hornby.
Rudy Vallee Hubert Prior Vallee.
Odile Versois Militza de Polakoff-Baidarov.
Erich von Stroheim Hans Erich Maria Stroheim von Nordenwall.
Anton Walbrook Adolf Wohlbrück.
Jean Wallace Jean Wallasek.
Jack Warner Jack Waters.
John Wayne Marion Michael Morrison.
Clifton Webb Webb Parmelee Hollenbeck.
Shelley Winters Shirley Schrift.
Jane Wyman Sarah Jane Fulks.

Signs of the times

A person's signature is thought to reveal far more than the name of the person concerned. Psychologists seem to agree that the larger the signature, the greater the person's self-esteem. Studies have shown that men normally have larger signatures than women, reflecting the greater status they have traditionally enjoyed. Individuals are also likely to increase the size of their signature if they happen to be feeling satisfied with themselves because of something they have just achieved, or because their status has been advanced by long-term achievement. Richard L. Zweigenhaft, for instance, in an article published in *Social Behaviour and Personality*, 1977, shows how one man's signature steadily became larger as he advanced from being a student to a member of the faculty. Zweigenhaft also reports on students who were asked to sign their names as themselves, then while imagining themselves to be President of the United States. The imaginary status was enough to cause an increase in signature size. Self-esteem, however, is not necessarily linked to real status. Conceited people are found at all levels of society.

The style of signature is also thought to be revealing. The average person, who has a first name, middle name and last name, has to choose between six possible styles:

a) *J. Smith* Use of the initial suggests an unwillingness to disclose oneself to others, and hints at emotional, possibly sexual, repression.

b) *John Smith* The style of a conventional conformist, but one who is easily approachable. Tends to be informal and frank, and of liberal views.

c) *J. D. Smith* An insecure person who wishes to present a mature image to the world. Possibly repressed emotionally or sexually. Has a strong preference for traditional ways of behaviour.

d) *John D. Smith* Very conventional, likely to have right wing views. Believes in strict rules and punishments. Inclined to be religiously dogmatic.

e) *J. David Smith* A narcissistic person, obsessed with his own image. Considers himself highly individualistic and is determined that others should think so too.

f) *John David Smith* The sign of an exhibitionist who likes to publicise himself. Certainly does not suffer from low self-esteem.

The above comments are based on a newspaper interview with a Canadian psychologist, Dr Elizabeth Willett.

Individuals will, of course, change their signature according to circumstances. To test your friends, give them a blank sheet of paper and ask them to sign their names in the way they prefer.

'I have signed my name,' said Louis, 'already twenty times. I, and again I, and again I. Clear, firm, unequivocal, there it stands, my name . . . all the furled and close-packed leaves of my many folded life are now summed in my name.'

Virginia Woolf *The Waves*

---

7 Eking out names

With his first name, middle name and surname it might seem that the average person was adequately identified, but far from it. We are all given additional names for official purposes—mostly number names or code names—and most of us acquire an unofficial extra name as well. We use the term 'nickname' to describe the latter, which is usually friendly. The word 'sobriquet', which we borrowed centuries ago from the French, is also useful. It describes a name which is decidedly unfriendly, meant to cut a person down to size. The etymology of the word seems to hint at a 'taming', for the original meaning was 'a chuck under the chin', as when a horse is reined in.

'Nickname' itself simply means 'an additional name', with no bias towards a good or bad name and no indication as to whether a person, place or thing is involved. The word derives from the expression 'an eke name', which later became 'a nekename'. This is the 'eke' we use when we say that we must 'eke out our supplies'. Traced back far enough it probably links up with the Latin word *augere*, which is the root of words such as 'augment'.

This explanation of 'nickname' is fairly modern, by the way. Dr Johnson thought it must derive from the French *nique*, which means a gesture (but not a name) of mockery. Harry Long, a 19th-century writer on names, appears to have connected it with the German *nicken*, which means 'to nod', for he explains it as 'a name given with a contemptuous nick of the head'. Long also explained 'sobriquet' wrongly, but he can perhaps be forgiven because of his fine comment that nicknames and sobriquets are 'biographies crowded into a word'.

To-names

We have already separated out bynames as a special kind of nickname, acting as a temporary surname. There is another special kind of personal nickname which is sometimes called a *to-name*. This is an extra name that becomes necessary for identification purposes in communities where many people bear the same surname. John McPhee, for example, in his book about the Scottish island of Colonsay (*The Crofter and the Laird*) describes the substitute surnames taken on by the McNeills and McAllisters. Many of them are

---

'Swidge' is the appellation by which they speak of Mrs William in general, among themselves, I'm told; but that's what I say, sir. Better be called ever so far out of your name, if it's done in real liking, than have it made ever so much of, and not cared about! What's a name for? To know a person by. If Mrs William is known by something better than her name—I allude to Mrs William's qualities and disposition—never mind her name, though it is Swidger, by rights. Let 'em call her Swidge, Widge, Bridge—Lord! London Bridge, Blackfriars, Chelsea, Putney, Waterloo or Hammersmith Suspension—if they like!

Charles Dickens *The Haunted Man*

---

known by place names, of which there is an ample supply. Only 138 people lived on the island when McPhee was there, but there were 1600 recorded place names—with the most minor landmarks being counted as places.

. . . four inhabitants called Andrew, or Dandie, Oliver. They were distinguished as Dandie Eassil-gate, Dandie Wassil-gate, Dandie Thumbie and Dandie Dumbie. The two first had their names from living eastward and westward in the street of the village; the third from something peculiar in the conformation of his thumb; the fourth from his taciturn habits.

Sir Walter Scott *Guy Mannering*

Another system is for a husband and his wife to borrow each other's first names. **Peter McAllister** is known as **Peter Bella,** his wife as **Bella Peter.** Such a system might be very useful at an ordinary social gathering, such as a cocktail-party, and it would certainly add a touch of charm. The more usual kind of patronymic nickname is seen in **Mary Calum Coll,** Calum being the lady's father, Coll her grandfather. **Donald Gibbie** is the son of Gilbert, but his cousin is **Angus the Post.**

Welsh nicknames

This last example naturally reminds us of Wales, where the commonness of **Jones** traditionally necessitated nicknames. An article in the London *Times* (December 1970) by Trevor Fishlock, however, claimed that names like **Jones the Meat, Flat Nose Jones, Jones King's Arms, Jones Popbottle** and **Jones the Bread** were fast disappearing. In modern times people know fewer of their neighbours than they did in the older communities, and there is less need to distinguish between individuals. One hopes that the folk-wit displayed in the names will be recorded before it is too late. **Dai Piano,** for instance, was not the musician his nickname might suggest. He was for ever cadging cigarettes and saying that he had left his own at home on the piano. **Amen Jones** and **Jones Hallelujah** were men who responded over-enthusiastically in chapel.

Sartorial as well as verbal habits could provide nicknames, as in **Jones Spats** and **Harry Greensuit.** A favourite food or drink could lead to names like **Jones Caerphilly** and **Dai Brown Ale.** The phrasal equivalents of activity surnames—**Jones the Milk, Eddie Click-Click** (for a photographer)—were found everywhere, as were locative names—**Jones Cwmglo, Jones Craig-Ddu** (from farms), **Will Plough, Huw Railway Inn** (from public houses).

In any community where surnames failed to distinguish individuals, nicknames were formerly added or substituted. In the 19th century the shopkeepers in towns like Peterhead would write down the 'fee-names' of their customers. Their account-books reveal names like **Buckie, Beauty, Bam, Biggelugs, The Smack, Snuffers, Toothie, Doodle, Carrot** and **Nap.** The novelist Henry Treece has described Black Country nicknames that were applied to the many **Fosters** and **Wilkes.** A character in *The Rebels*, himself nicknamed **Bacca Chops** because of his habit of chewing plug tobacco, remarks on **Ode Mouldyhead,** whose hair grew in patches, **Ode Foxy, Gentleman, Whackey, Dragon, Bullet, Brick End** and **Soft Water Jack.**

In the case of royal nicknames, a similarity of first names may be one of the reasons that brings them into being. The kings took on a sequential surname, **The First, The Second,** etc, but their subjects usually replaced this with a descriptive nickname. **Richard Lionheart** was more fortunate than **Richard the Coxcomb** and **Richard the Boar.**

Jubilee town was the name of the settlement; and when the schoolmaster announced his own, David King, the title struck the imitative minds of the scholars, and turning it round, they made 'King David' of it, and kept it so.

Constance Fenimore Woolson *King David*

King James' real name was James King; but the people reversed it because it seemed to fit him better, and also because it seemed to please his majesty.

O. Henry *The Last of the Troubadors*

The Georges likewise varied from **The Turnip-Hoer** and **Farmer George** to **Augustus** and **George the Greater.** In France the eighteen kings called

Louis naturally attracted nicknames. **Baboon, The Foolish, The Universal Spider, The Fat** and **The Indolent** were among the less complimentary, but one or two were rather better favoured. The last Louis had a nickname which is impossible to translate, punning on his liking for oysters (*des huîtres*) and his sequential surname, 18 (*dix-huit*).

Other reasons for nicknames

It would be foolish, however, to imply that personal nicknames are always to-names, given because they are genuinely needed for identification purposes. They arise for a number of other reasons, reflecting such human habits as ornamenting what is plain, being clever, showing dislike or affection, being funny, being secretive, showing group membership. Most of these reasons could be applied to the use of slang, with which nicknames have a great deal in common.

Tommy's real name was Tommy Flynn, but he was younger than any of them so that neither he nor they were ever quite sure that he ought to belong to the gang at all. To show it they called him all sorts of nick-names, like Inch because he was so small; Fatty because he was so puppy-fat; Pigeon because he had a chest like a woman; Gong Gong because after long bouts of silence he had a way of suddenly spraying them with wild bursts of talk like a fire alarm attached to a garden sprinkler.

Sean O'Faolain *The Talking Trees*

Family members naturally share a special knowledge of one another, and this may well extend to nicknames. They are frequently bestowed on children by the parents, though more often by the father than the mother, it would seem. A teacher friend discovered recently that his ten-year-olds were known at home as **Crunchy, Boo, Squitface, Popsy Dinkums, Woo, Moonbeam, Muff** (girls), and **Dilly, Dump, Hug, Longlegs, Luscious Legs, Bigpants** (boys). It is much rarer for children to have a nickname for either parent, but Angus Wilson, in his *Anglo-Saxon Attitudes*, may be reflecting a real-life situation known to him when he makes **Thingy** the mother's nickname.

Other nicknames connected with children are those that arise at school. Children invariably seem to nickname one another and their teachers, sometimes following intricate paths to arrive at the final name. The point is illustrated in a letter from Mr James B. Fryer, commenting on **Whiskers Bowles.** He writes: 'Bowles became "bowels". The Latin for "bowels" is *viscera*. Pronouncing the "v" in Latin as "w" we get *wiscera*, whence the easy transfer to "whiskers".' One can compare the French headmaster who became **The Doe** (*La Biche*). Trying to maintain his dignity as he crossed the playground he stuck his chest out and looked rather haughty. A pupil remarked quietly that he was 'as proud as Artaban', a normal French simile that refers to a character in a play. **Artaban** became his nickname, but was soon changed to the more agreeable sounding **Artabiche.** This was finally shortened to **Biche.**

If anything like these complications led to the formation of medieval bynames, the philologists clearly have an impossible task before them where the elucidation of some surnames is concerned. Some of the bynames, one would think, must have been inspired in some way by whatever personal

'Flopsy's a lovely name. It comes from the Flopsy Bunnies in Peter Rabbit.*'*

'It does not,' said Hamish, entering the room. 'It is taken from the immortal English surrealist Edward Lear and his Mopsikon-Flopsikon bear.

Angus Wilson *Crazy Crowd*

The baby's flat face, together with its peculiar body, caused it automatically to be called Tularecito, Little Frog.

John Steinbeck *The Pastures of Heaven*

A most exemplary gentleman (called Old Foxey by his friends from his extreme sagacity).

Charles Dickens *The Old Curiosity Shop*

'Why is he called Sunny?' I asked.
'Because his Christian name is Sunderland,' said Peter.
Anthony Powell *A Question of Upbringing*

He was known by intimates and strangers as Ace. The original name, like a scar, he reopened each morning, while shaving. 'I am Eustace,' he would mumble into the mirror.
James Purdy *Eustace Chisholm and the Works*

name an individual already had. Nicknames of this type are certainly very frequent. Mr **Fryer,** for instance, remarks that he himself became **Tuck,** which one might call an *associated transfer.* A colleague whose surname is **Snow** is known as **Fairy** because of the soap powder *Fairy Snow.* Dr T. Keough has also told me of a friend in his Canadian home-town who was **Twenty Below** because his name was **Ozero.** His sister was called **Scratch Below** for a slightly different reason.

Abel Sampson, commonly called, from his occupation as a pedagogue, Dominie Sampson.
Sir Walter Scott *Guy Mannering*

He called her Dreary sometimes instead of Deirdre and it seemed to make her a little cross.
Penelope Gilliatt *A State of Change*

Dubby was the ordinary name by which, among friends and foes, Mr Daubeny was known.
Anthony Trollope *Phineas Finn*

Link nicknames are even more common. Those based on first names we usually refer to as 'diminutives' or 'pet names', but **Maggie** from **Margaret** is just as much a nickname as **The Barrow Boy** from **Nabarro.** A newspaper correspondent, commenting on the nicknames of her classmates, reveals that her own is **Ballbag,** based on her surname **Ball.** I am sometimes obliged to answer to **Dunkers,** and my son tells me he is **Dunks** to his friends.

Miss Ball goes on to say that her girl-friends have such nicknames as **Bun, Bondy, Snuff, Crunk, Melon, Twiggy** and **Spindle,** while the boys in the class are known by such names as **Primrose, Flapper, Squelch, Haggis, Leggy, Reverend, Fizz** and **Ribs,** all of which reveal a cheerful friendliness. Some of these are clearly descriptive, others might be further examples of surname links. With names like **Crunk** one suspects a verbal incident, perhaps a slip of the tongue one day when another word was intended.

Incident nicknames

Verbal incidents are well represented in nicknames, in the adult world as well as at school level. **Azzerwuz, Juicy, Banjo** and **Rabbit** have come into being in this way, from the favourite expressions 'As I was saying' and 'D'you see?'; because of a constantly repeated remark about being 'highly strung', and because of a teacher's remark about a certain family breeding 'like rabbits'. A comment by the head of a typing-pool: 'Let's have no bloomers today, girls', immediately earned her the nickname **Naughty-Naughty,** and a favourite remark, 'Leave it to me', was the reason for **The Pawnbroker.**

G. B. Stern, in her book *A Name To Conjure With,* tells of the house-party she attended at which all the guests adopted nicknames for the week-end. H. G. Wells was already **Jaguar,** but Miss Stern was unnamed. She remarked that she would like to be something between a tigress and a sphinx, whereupon he dubbed her **Tynx.**

A few pages later Miss Stern describes an incident name of another kind, perhaps what one might call an 'internal incident'. Her eight-year-old friend, Naomi,

> 'swallowed a penny and was seriously ill and away from school for several months. When she returned . . . she was greeted callously and a little cruelly by Upper and Lower School with "Hello, **Moneybox!**", while reeling from our own wit, we

Laura: He used to call me Blue Roses.

Amanda: Why did he call you such a name as that?

Laura: When I had that attack of pleurosis—he asked me what was the matter when I came back. I said pleurosis—he thought I said Blue Roses!

Tennessee Williams *The Glass Menagerie*

'It ain't going too far to say he is a pudd'n-head.'

Mr Wilson stood elected. The incident was told all over the town. Within a week he had lost his first name. Pudd'n-head took its place. In time he came to be liked, and well liked too; but by that time the nickname had got well stuck on, and it stayed.

Mark Twain *Pudd'n-head Wilson*

would beg her to cough up a penny to buy a bun, and keep the halfpenny change.'

Children *would* reel with their own wit, of course. They love playing with words and names and are delighted with names like **Woolly Wog, Ruby Nose** and **Lumber Bonce** for their sound alone. Where meanings are concerned, they have little time for euphemism, preferring to be simple and direct. Those who are named usually take no offence. Another of my own nicknames, **Pug,** was hardly complimentary, but I distinctly recall sharing the joke when it was proposed. There is a degree of pleasure gained *in being named* which offsets the thought of insult, and if one accepts the nickname it tends to lose its force in any case.

Descriptive nicknames

In a classroom situation, one or two of the brighter children will probably be throwing suggestions for nicknames into the continuous flow of group conversation. There will be instant acceptance, or counter-suggestion, or rejection. If the whole class is present and can see the steps that have led to the name, it will have point to the whole group. A larger community, such as a village, may have to use simpler names, based on characteristics that will be obvious to all. Many of these will be visual names, for just as locative names began by being a person's address, so these names are often verbal portraits. A summary of their origins was given in 1682 by Sir Henry Piers, writing about the Irish:

'They take much liberty, and seem to do it with delight, in giving of nicknames; and if a man have any imperfection or evil habit, he shall be sure to hear of it in the nickname. Thus if he be blind, lame, squint-eyed, gray-eyed, be a stammerer in speech, be left-handed, to be sure he shall have one of these added to his name, so also from the colour of his hair, as black, red, yellow, brown, etc, and from his age, as young, old, or from what he addicts himself to, or much delights in, as in draining, building, fencing or the like; so that no man whatever can escape a nickname, who lives amongst them.'

At Sandy Bar in 1854 most men were christened anew. Sometimes these appellations were derived from some distinctiveness of dress, as in the case of 'Dungaree Jack'; or from some peculiarity of habit, as shown in 'Saleratus Bill', so-called from an undue proportion of that chemical in his daily bread; or from some unlucky slip, as exhibited in 'Iron Pirate', a mild, inoffensive man, who earned that baleful title by his unfortunate mispronunciation of the term 'iron pyrites'. Perhaps this may have been the beginning of a rude heraldry; but I am constrained to think that it was because a man's real name in that day rested solely upon his own unsupported statement.

Bret Harte *Tennessee's Partner*

Traditional nicknames

Nicknames *ought* to be tailor-made and meaningful, but there are some which are hand-me-downs, others which come as almost meaningless accessories with one's surname. The former arise partly because there are a number of human features which are always commented on, and a limited number of ways in which the allusions can be made. Baldness, for example, begins by attracting a name like **Baldy** or **Patch,** or is immediately contradicted with a name like **Curly.** Metaphorical descriptions then begin to apply, such as **Dutchy** (because of the appearance of some Dutch cheeses) and **Skating Rink,** shortened to **Skates.** There is a tendency to pass on such names, particularly in the Services, to each new generation of bald-headed men. There is still room for wit, of course, and not every bald-headed man needs to be dubbed with a cliché. A former teacher of mine was, I hope, grateful for his own **Cue-Ball,** bestowed by some unknown wag.

'How are things, Lightning?' He got his nickname ironically of course, but not because of the speed with which he yields a hammer, but because he never strikes twice in the same place.

Peter de Vries *Let Me Count the Ways*

There were the nicknames of her friends: Poody and Pip and Pebble, Shrimp and Brute and Tug, Squeck, Bumpo, Baba— it sounded, I said, as though she had gone to Vassar with Donald Duck's nephews.

Philip Roth *Portnoy's Complaint*

A list of nicknames used by school-children, collected by Iona and Peter Opie and published in *The Lore and Language of Schoolchildren*, shows how these avid nicknamers deal with a number of features. A fat person may be **Balloon, Barrel, Barrel-Belly, Billy Bunter, Buster, Chubby, Chunky, Diddle-Diddle Dumpling, Falstaff, Fat Belly, Fatty Harbuckle, Football, Guts, Piggy, Podge, Porky, Steam-Roller, Tank, Tubby** or **Two Ton Tessy** among others. But wide as this selection may appear to be, there is a great deal of duplication, for probably every class in every school has at least one person whose obesity calls for comment. The Opies make the interesting point that when children use names like Fatty Harbuckle (as they spell it) they are usually unaware that they are commemorating a real person, Roscoe **Arbuckle,** a star of the silent screen until his career ended in a scandal. It is unlikely, too, that many of them have actually read the Bunter stories or know of the original Two-Ton Tessie. Such evidence clearly shows the traditional nature of these nicknames.

Clan nicknames

But though traditional and formalised, such names are at least still meaningful, telling other people something about the person named. Another class of personal nicknames, which have sometimes been described as 'inseparables', have almost no meaning at all. They are treated as if they were clan nicknames, applicable to anyone bearing a certain surname. The system leads to men called **Martin** automatically being nicknamed **Pincher** when they join the Royal Navy. Originally the nickname applied to Admiral Sir William F. Martin, a disciplinarian who had ratings put under arrest ('pinched') for the smallest offence. His name is still so well known in naval circles that associated transfer of his nickname follows.

Criminal nicknames

Tradition dictates the use of clan nicknames, but a more practical reason for the use of nicknames is to conceal one's identity, especially from officials such as the police. It is very noticeable that criminals, both great and small, are very fond of nicknames. Their great ambition seems to be to achieve the fame, or notoriety as we would call it, of such figures as **Scarface Al Capone** or **Jack the Ripper.** The public accepts the right of criminals to have nicknames, and is quick to bestow one on someone whose identity is unknown. A **Charlie Chopper** was terrorising New York in the early 1970s, the name apparently having been coined by local children. Most people remember **The Boston Strangler,** who will probably go down in criminal history under that nickname rather than under his real name, Albert De Salvo.

'Your name isn't Skip,' Pomeroy had replied.
'It's my nickname.'
'No, it isn't. People don't give themselves nicknames, Lieberman. They inspire them in others. Whatever you are now, Lieberman, or ever hope to be, you are not now and never will be a Skip.'

Joseph Heller *Good as Gold*

Elsdon C. Smith reports that the FBI has a Nickname File containing at least 150 000 entries as part of its background material, and presumably police forces everywhere are obliged to make similar collections. The New York file contains examples like **Gold Tooth Frenchy, Clothesline Slim, Wild Cat Alma** and **Iron Foot Florence. Fire Alarm Brown** was so named from his habit of raising a fire alarm, then picking pockets among the crowd that gathered. **Step Ladder Lewis** would pretend to be a painter and enter houses through upper windows.

Names like Wild Cat Alma for the women bring to mind the nicknames used by their sisters in what have been called 'houses of horizontal refreshment'. Bill Carmichael has listed many of them in his *Incredible Collectors*, and they are best left to speak for themselves: **The Roaring Gimlet, Sweet Fanny, Glass-Eyed Nellie, Tin Pot Annie, Rotary Rosie, The Galloping Cow, Smooth Bore, Madam Moustache, Madam Butterfly.** This last name was given a totally new meaning, of course, by Puccini but it was a genuine non-Japanese nickname for a prostitute before he made use of it.

Political nicknames

At such a level nicknames are simply amusing, but one should not forget that they can have more serious significance. Nicknames can help make public figures seem friendly and accessible, however remote they remain in reality. **Dizzy** and **Old Hickory** performed this function for Benjamin Disraeli and Andrew Jackson. Gladstone, Disraeli's rival, was never given an affectionate nickname, which reflects his different kind of reputation. Some modern politicians consciously try to become known by a nickname in order to make an emotional appeal to the public.

Just what can happen to a politician's name is exemplified by Sir Robert Peel, British Home Secretary in the early 19th century. He acquired several nicknames, including the inevitable **Orange Peel** when he displayed anti-Catholic tendencies. He later became **The Runaway Spartan** when he changed his mind and worked in favour of the Irish Emancipation Bill. His surname was also adapted to **Peeler** and applied as a generic nickname for a policeman when he founded the Metropolitan Police in 1829. An alternative form, **Bobby,** was derived from his first name. This has lasted longer and has gone on to become a word.

When we remember that bynames are a kind of nickname, and that surnames are all derived from bynames, we can well understand Ernest Weekley's comment that 'every family name is ety-

Brevity is the soul of wit; and of all eloquence a nickname is the most concise, of all arguments the most unanswerable. It is a word and a blow.
A nickname is the heaviest stone that the devil can throw at a man.

William Hazlitt *On Nicknames*

I should explain that Maria Spaghetti-maker had never made any spaghetti; it was her great-grandmother who plied the trade, but the nickname persisted in the female line. Similarly, Sentiá Dog-beadle inherited his nickname from an ancestor whose task had been to keep stray dogs from taking sanctuary on hot days in the cool of Palma Cathedral. Sentiá is short for Sebastian.

Robert Graves
The Viscountess and the Short-Haired Girl

I had heard his mother tell my mother that when he was a dear little fellow, just learning to talk, his best version of his name, Percy Boyd, was Pidgy Boy-Boy, and she still called him that in moments of unbuttoned affection. I knew that I had but once to call him Pidgy Boy-Boy in the schoolyard and his goose would be cooked; probably suicide would be his only way out.

Robertson Davies *Fifth Business*

mologically a nickname'. In spite of this Weekley himself appears to have made no serious attempt to collect the nicknames of his time together with evidence about how the names had come into being. In his many books on names he stays well within his chosen philological area, rarely venturing past the Middle Ages. Other writers of equal eminence on surnames have dutifully nodded in the direction of modern nicknames, but once again none of them has made anything like a real attempt to get to grips with what is, in effect, the only living personal name system. There is an obvious need for a full-scale linguistic inquiry into personal nicknames and nicknaming today. The conclusions that would emerge from a thorough study could not fail to help the philologist in the interpretation of his data.

Previous works on nicknames

Julian Franklyn's *Dictionary of Nicknames* (1962) contains about 1500 entries, but the examples are all of the institutional type. They apply to anyone who has a certain surname or first name, fits a descriptive category or fills a particular role. We learn that **Trugs,** for instance, is a nickname given to a lazy man and that it is 'Scottish dialect'; that **Enzedder** is an Australian way of referring to a New Zealander, and so on. These are fossilised nicknames, generic names that border on being common names.

Within this rather restricted area Franklyn's work is valuable for reference purposes, an advance in many ways on studies such as Latham's *Dictionary of Names, Nicknames and Surnames* and Albert Frey's *Sobriquets and Nicknames*. Both of these do actually contain truly individual nicknames—those borne by major historical figures—but there are not enough of them. Latham also goes beyond personal nicknames to take in some of those attached to towns, states, battles, institutions, newspapers and anything else. But both writers restrict themselves to names that occur in polite literature and are careful not to descend to the level of everyday speech.

It is precisely that, of course, that is needed. It may only be of anecdotal interest to know that a nurse was nicknamed **Tonsils** because several doctors wanted to take her out, or that a young man was called **Yankee** because he doodled all day, but enough examples like this gathered together would soon reveal patterns of name formation, related to statistics, for worthwhile statements to be made about certain linguistic habits. The vast majority of names, obviously, would not be amusing puns, but they would have their own interest. Whoever does eventually take on the task will not find it a dull one. Nicknames comment, and always have done, on every conceivable aspect of human behaviour.

In facetious homage to the smallness of his talk, and the jerky nature of his manners, Fledgeby's familiars had agreed to confer upon him (behind his back) the honorary title of Fascination Fledgeby.

Charles Dickens *Our Mutual Friend*

Obsolete nicknames

One must not be misled by the relatively simple types of nickname that developed into our surnames. Our ancestors did not name everyone by the colour of his hair, his job, his father's name or where he lived. These are, it is true, the types of name that have mainly survived, but a great many others that are now obsolete are recorded in medieval Subsidy Rolls, Tax Returns and the like. The following examples were all solemnly written down, in their Middle English form, in documents of this kind in order to identify individuals. They allow us to gain some idea of the names that must

The real name of the little man was Harris, but it had gradually merged into the less euphonious one of Trotters, which, with its prefatory adjective Short, had been conferred upon him by reason of the small size of his legs. Short Trotters, however, being a compound name, inconvenient of use in friendly dialogue, the gentleman on whom it had been bestowed was known among his intimates either as 'Short', or 'Trotters,' and was seldom accosted at full length as Short Trotters, except in formal conversations and on occasions of ceremony.

Charles Dickens *The Old Curiosity Shop*

have been in colloquial use: William **Breakwomb,** William **Catchmaid,** Simon **Cutpurse,** Hugo **Lickbread,** Leofric **Lickdish,** Geoffrey **Lickfinger,** Robert **Eatwell,** John **Skipup,** John **Spillwater,** Emma **Spoilale,** Muchman **Wetbed,** John **Leavetoday,** Serle **Gotochurch,** Adam **Hangdog,** Adam **Fairarmfull,** Elias **Overandover,** Robert **Moonlight,** Arnold **Pokestrong.** Dozens more like this, including many that are rather too obscene to reproduce here, occur in the documents. Fuller lists of them are cited by Dr Reaney in his *Origin of English Surnames* and Professor Weekley in his *Surnames.*

Range of nicknames

Mention of Latham's *Dictionary* a moment ago serves to remind us that nicknames are not restricted to people. They can replace any proper names, ranging from those of football teams such as **Arsenal (The Gunners),** to regiments—**The 11th Hussars (The Cherry-pickers** or **Cherubims);** newspapers—**The Times (The Thunderer);** cities—**Portsmouth (Pompey);** States—**Pennsylvania (The Keystone State);** shops—**Marks and Spencer (Marks and Sparks);** periods of time—**The Silly Season;** musical works—**Haydn's Symphony No. 96 (The Miracle);** railways—**Somerset and Dorset (Slow and Dirty),** and many others.

Where there is not an obvious linguistic connection between name and nickname, there is usually an anecdote to be told. 'The Thunderer' was originally the personal nickname of Edward Sterling, a contributor to *The Times,* but was extended to the newspaper itself. 'The Miracle' was named at the first performance of the symphony, when the audience miraculously escaped injury from a falling chandelier. Nicknames of all kinds do as they claim; in other words—they eke out real names, augmenting them with wit, biographical detail or anecdote. They are a fascinating study, jewels in the great treasury of names, and we should be grateful for them.

Colonel Ford, known in the regiment as 'Scatter' (short for 'Scatter-cash' because, when he first joined, he had spent his allowance so lavishly).

Robert Graves *Goodbye to all That*

Clan nicknames

Some examples of nicknames that have become associated with particular surnames.

'Birdy' for **Sparrow, Wren,** etc.
'Blacky' **White.**
'Blanco' **White,** from the trade name of a whitener.
'Bodger' **Lees.**
'Bogey' **Harris.**
'Bricks(an)' **Morter.**
'Bronco' **Rider.**
'Buck' **Taylor,** from a member of Buffalo Bill's team.
'Bunny' **Warren.**
'Bushey' **Fox.**
'Butch(er)' **Lamb.**
'Captain' **Kettle** or **Kidd.**
'Chalky' **White.**
'Chippa' **Wood.**
'Chunka' **Wood.**
'Daisy' **Bell,** from the music hall song.
'Dick(y)' **Richards,** or **Bird.**
'Ding-Dong' **Bell.**
'Dodger' **Long.**
'Doughy' **Baker.**
'Drawers' **Chester.**
'Duck(y)' or 'Ducks' **Drake.**
'Dusty' **Miller,** or **Rhodes** (roads).
'Dutchy' **Holland.**
'Fanny' **Adams,** from the name of a murder victim originally.
'Fishy' **Pike, Chubb,** etc.
'Foxy' **Reynolds,** because of Reynard.
'Ginger' **Beer.**
'Happy' **Day.**
'Hopper' **Long.**
'Jelly' **Pearson.**
'Johnny' **Walker,** because of the whisky.
'Jumper' **Cross.**
'Knobby' **Coles.**
'Lefty' **Wright.**
'Muddy' **Waters,** or **Walters.**
'Ned' **Kelly.**
'Needle' **Cotton.**
'Nick' **Carter,** for a fictional detective.
'Nigger' **Brown.**
'Nobby' **Clark,** said to be because clerks had to look as if they were 'nobs' or gentlemen in spite of being poorly paid.
'Nocky' **Knight.**
'Norman' **Conquest.**
'Nosey' **Parker.**
'Nosmo' **King,** from 'No Smoking' signs.
'Nutty' **Cox.**
'Peeler' **Murphy,** probably from 'peel a spud'.
'Peggy' **Legg,** from Peg-Leg.
'Piggy' **May.**
'Poppy' **Tupper.**
'Powder' **Horne,** from a character in a strip cartoon.
'Rabbit' **Hutch, Hutchins** or **Hutchinson.**
'Rattler' **Morgan.**
'Reelo' **Cotton.**
'Rusty' **Steele.**
'Sandy' **Brown.**
'Schnozzle' **Durrant,** because of Schnozzle Durante.
'Sharky' **Ward,** possibly from a pirate so named.
'Shiner' **Bright,** thence to **Wright** and **White.** Also **Black** because a 'black-eye' is a 'shiner'. Also **Bryant** because of 'shine a light' being associated with Bryant and May on match-boxes.
'Shoey' **Smith.**
'Shorty' **Long** or **Little.**
'Shover' **Smith.**
'Slide' **Overett.**
'Slider' **Cross.**
'Slinger' **Wood(s).**
'Smitty' **Smith.**
'Smokey' **Holmes,** perhaps a reference to Sherlock Holmes's famous pipe.
'Smudger' **Smith.**
'Smutty' **Black.**
'Snip' **Taylor.** Also **Parsons,** from parsnip.
'Snowball, -drop, -flake' **Snow.**
'Snowy' **Baker,** referring to white flour.
'Soapy' **Hudson, Pears, Watson,** from names associated commercially with soap.
'Spider' **Webb.**
'Spike' **Sullivan,** possibly because itinerant potato-pickers gave the name Sullivan when working on the 'spike'. Or from a prize-fighter.
'Splinter' **Wood.**
'Spokey' **Wheeler.**
'Spongey' **Baker.**
'Spud' **Murphy,** both 'spud' and 'murphy' being slang terms for a potato.
'Swank' **Russell.**
'Sticker' **Leach.**
'Stitch' **Taylor.**
'Stormy' **Gale.**
'Sugar' **Cain** or **Kane.**
'Timber' **Wood(s).**
'Tod' **Hunter,** 'tod' being a fox.
'Topper' **Brown.**
'Topsy' **Turner,** a play on 'topsyturvey'.
'Tottie' **Bell.**
'Tubby' **Martin.**
'Tug' **Wilson.**
'Wheeler' **Johnson.**
'Wiggy' **Bennett.**
'Youngy' **Moore,** a joke based on *Old Moore's Almanack.*

Some famous nicknames

'The Admirable Crichton' a Scottish scholar who gained his Master of Arts degree at the age of fourteen.

'Beau' or 'Buck Brummel' patronised by George IV until Brummel's 'Who's your fat friend?' remark deliberately insulted him.

'Bloody Mary' Queen Mary, daughter of Henry VIII, who persecuted the Protestants.

'Blue Beard' Possibly meant to refer to Giles de Retz, Marquis of Laval.

'Boney' Napoleon Bonaparte.

'Bozzy' James Boswell.

'Capability (Launcelot) Brown' who always saw 'capabilities' in the gardens he looked at.

'Conversation (Richard) Sharpe' a critic.

'Crum-Hell' One of the nicknames of Oliver 'Cromwell', whose name was pronounced Crum-ell in his own time. Also known by names such as the 'Almighty Nose', 'King Oliver'.

'Dizzy' Benjamin Disraeli.

'Elocution (John) Walker', author of a pronouncing dictionary and teacher of elocution.

'Farmer George' George II, said to have the dress, manners and tastes of a farmer, and to have referred more to his farming problems than matters of State when opening Parliament.

'Goldy' Oliver Goldsmith.

'Hotspur' Henry Percy, son of the Earl of Northumberland, so named because of the fiery temper he could not control.

'Iron Duke' The Duke of Wellington. An iron steam-boat named after the Duke was known as the *Iron Duke*. The nickname was later jokingly applied to the Duke himself.

'Ironside' Edmund II, from his iron armour.

'King Coll' Colley Cibber.

'King of Bath' or 'Beau Nash,' who managed social events at Bath.

'Lionheart' Richard I, for his courage, though one writer tells of his plucking out the heart from a lion.

'Log-Cabin Harrison' an insulting reference to a log cabin was turned into a successful election slogan by President Harrison.

'Long Hair' General Custer's name among the Indians.

'Man in the Iron Mask' The great historical mystery man in France. Guessing his identity is as much a sport as deciding who wrote Shakespeare's plays for him. A summary of the theories appears in Frey's *Sobriquets and Nicknames*.

'Merry Andrew' Andrew Borde, Physician to Henry VIII.

'Merry Monarch' Charles II.

'Old Harry' and 'Old Nick' are the best-known nicknames of the devil, who is also known as 'Auld Clootie', 'Auld Hangie', 'Nickie-Ben', 'Old Scratch', etc.

'Old Hickory' Andrew Jackson, because he was as tough as old hickory.

'Old Rough and Ready' Zachary Taylor, twelfth President of the USA.

'Prince of Showmen' Phineas Barnum.

'Railway King' George Hudson of Yorkshire, but also applied to William Vanderbilt.

'Rob Roy' Robert Macgregor, later Campbell, the Robin Hood of Scotland.

'Sixteen-String Jack' John Rann, a highwayman renowned for his stylish dress, especially the eight tags on each side of his breeches which gave him his name. Hanged in 1774.

'Stonewall (Thomas) Jackson', so called after another general remarked that he was standing there in front of the enemy like a stone wall.

'Swedish Nightingale' Jenny Lind, later Jenny Goldschmidt, the singer.

'Tumbledown Dick' Richard Cromwell, son of Oliver.

'Turnip-Hoer' George I, who talked of planting turnips in St James's Park.

'The Unready' Ethelred II, who was without 'rede' or counsel.

'The Venerable Bede', ecclesiastical historian of the 8th century.

'Virgin Queen' Elizabeth I.

'Water Poet' John Taylor, who worked as a Thames waterman.

'The Witch-finder' Matthew Hopkins, who toured England in the 17th century finding witches. His own test—he floated in water—eventually proved him a wizard and he was executed.

Self-generated nicknames

In his booklet *Welsh Nicknames*, D. Leslie Chamberlain tells of the minister of a chapel in Rhos, near Wrexham, who told the deacons of his many degrees and theological works and added: 'But I want to be called Reverend, pure and simple.' Reverend Pure and Simple he immediately, and permanently, became.

Jones Balloon was likewise so-called because of his appeal to his workmen when an important visitor was about to visit the factory: 'Now don't let me down, boys.'

Literary nicknames

'Agony'
Mike ('Agony') Lammermoor, so nicknamed because of the suffering he went through with and over women.
Comfort Me with Apples Peter de Vries

'Bat'
Bat got his name at school, possibly from the whimsical, peering expression in his eyes.
Thomas H. B. Cresswell

'Beany'
'Now, Beany—for they called me by that name, having begun by calling me Beanpole, I always being spare-made, boy as well as man. . . .'
Night Rider Robert Penn Warren

'Black Peter'
He was known in the trade as Black Peter, and the name was given him, not only on account of his swarthy features and the colour of his huge beard, but for the humours which were the terror of all around him.
Black Peter A. Conan Doyle

'Chicken'
Chicken was a 'hobo'. He had a long nose like the bill of a fowl, an inordinate appetite for poultry, and a habit of gratifying it without expense, which accounts for the name given him by his fellow vagrants.
The Passing of Black Eagle O. Henry

'Demi'
His real name is John, but they call him Demi-John, because his father is John too.
Little Men Louisa M. Alcott

'Dinger'
The new master, Edwin Bell—already 'Dinger' to the whole school.
Darkness Visible William Golding

'Doodle-calf'
Everything came to pieces in his hands, and nothing would stop in his head. They nicknamed him Jacob Doodle-calf.
Tom Brown's Schooldays T. Hughes

'Duke'
James Mears, better known as 'Duke' Mears, because he was always smartly dressed in correct riding costume.
The Web and the Rock Thomas Wolfe

'Flap-Fanny'
His buttocks spread and jounced flabbily in the saddle. For this reason he was known to the soldiers as Captain Flap-Fanny.
Reflections in a Golden Eye Carson McCullers

'Flopper'
The legendary Flopper, so-called because of the inimitable manner in which he had once minded the nets for the Boston Bruins.
Joshua Then and Now Mordecai Richler

'Glory'
A rather sentimental headmaster once referred to his exploits as 'glorious', and from that arose his nickname.
Lost Horizon James Hilton

'Handy Andy'
Andy Rooney was a fellow who had the most singularly ingenious knack of doing everything the wrong way; disappointment waited on all affairs in which he bore a part, and destruction was at his fingers' ends: so the nickname the neighbours stuck upon him was Handy Andy.
Handy Andy Samuel Lover

'Honey'
Honey Wilkes, so called because she indiscriminately addressed everyone from her father to the field hands by that endearment.
Gone With the Wind Margaret Mitchell

'Hoofer'
Mr Prout, whose school name, derived from the size of his feet, was Hoofer. . . .
Stalky & Company Rudyard Kipling

'Jampot'
Old Jampot, the nurse (her name was Mrs Preston and her shape was Jampot). . . .
Jeremy Hugh Walpole

'Jules'
I invented the name for him on account of Vernon=Verne=Jules of *Round the World in Eighty Days.*
Absolute Beginners Colin MacInnes

'July'
She was called July by all, although she was named Ada. She had a slightly older sister named June.
The Children Sing Mackinlay Kantor

'Lousy'
Scripps had a daughter whom he playfully called Lousy O'Neil. Her real name was Lucy O'Neil.
The Torrents of Spring Ernest Hemingway

'Magnet'
A term of affection the sailor often used in allusion to his niece's personal attractions.
The Pathfinder James Fenimore Cooper

'Mop'
He had been nicknamed 'Mop' from this abundance of hair, which was long enough to rest upon his shoulders.
Life's Little Ironies Thomas Hardy

'Old Stut'
'Old Stut' stuttered. . . .
Lark Rise Flora Thompson

'Scud'
Scud was East's nickname, or Black, as we called it, gained by his fleetness of foot.
Tom Brown's School Days Thomas Hughes

'Smiler'
His name is Ronnie, but she calls him Smiler, because he has a sad, rejected face, like a dog pressed against a locked door on a cold night.
Kate & Emma Monica Dickens

'Stuffy'
His name is George, but we call him Stuffy 'cause he eats so much.
Little Men Louisa M. Alcott

'Trout'
'Trout' they used to call her, because her fair skin was speckled with freckles.
Joshua Then and Now Mordecai Richler

8 A local habitation and a name

So far we have talked mainly about the names of people—the names they inherit, are given or adopt. Men have obviously named one another from time immemorial. After themselves they named their gods, then they named the places in which they lived and the rivers, hills and natural features around them.

The earliest place names

The English-speaking countries in the modern world contain layers of place names which stretch back century by century into the remote past. The oldest names are those given by the earliest inhabitants of each country and which have managed to survive in one form or another. In Britain some names are thought to be pre-Celtic, which would take them back to before 500 BC. The name of the River **Wey,** for example, cannot be explained by Old English or Celtic scholars, and they assume it to be older than names in either of these languages. Other words were added much later to give place names such as **Weybridge** and **Weymouth.**

In America it is impossible to date accurately the Indian names that were taken over by settlers, but these are certainly the earliest names there. With nothing known at the time of Indian languages or customs, it was inevitable that such names should change their sound and form considerably. **Chicago** may well have been the Algonquian word 'stinking' originally, but if so one cannot be sure whether the reference was to wild onions, stagnant water or skunks.

Australia has its ancient names such as **Murrumbidgee** and **Woomera,** and here again there are often difficulties of interpretation. While these two names are normally translated as 'big water' and 'throwing stick', **Paramatta** might have meant anything from 'the dark forest' to 'the head of the river' or 'the place where eels lie down' when it was first given. The Aborigines had a great many languages which they did not write down, and even intelligent guesses are difficult to make in such circumstances.

In New Zealand the Maori names are relatively numerous and quite well preserved. As the New Zealand writer Mrs C. M. Matthews points out, in her *Place Names of the English-Speaking World*, there is only one Maori language. Then Captain Cook took with him from Tahiti a boy called Tupia, who discovered that the Maoris could understand his own Polynesian words. Cook was able to talk to the natives through Tupia and record their place names, while later missionaries learned Maori and interpreted them well. Sometimes the words seem simple, but the original meaning was a metaphorical one. **Rangi** means 'sky', and by extension 'light' or 'day', **Rangitoto** is therefore 'day of blood', not 'sky of blood', and is a reference to the wounding there of a folk-hero.

Maori place names often record historical or mythological incidents in complete sentences. This tends to make them rather long, though not all equal the length of Taumatawhakatangihangakoauauotamateaturipukakapikimaungahoronukupokaiwhenuakitanatahu. Known more usually as *Taumata*, the name of this hill in New Zealand means 'the place where Tamatea, the man with the big knee who slid, climbed and swallowed mountains, known as Traveller, played on his flute to his loved one'.

Maori names were more fortunate than native names elsewhere. European settlers from the 16th century on had a strong tendency to rename their colonies in Africa, North America and elsewhere by transferring familiar names to them or describing them as they themselves saw them. A respect for the original names only arose in the later 19th century, and they began to appear on maps as well as being heard in native speech. The new attitude affected the Victorian explorers of Central Africa, who mostly made an effort to record the names they found rather than impose new ones. Even then, patriotism revealed itself in **Lake Victoria** and the like.

In general we must remember that countries are usually settled or taken over by highly practical men rather than scholars. They are concerned with convenience and their own pride when they name places, and are not inclined to stand back and take an enlightened historical view. The Romans and Normans look like exceptions to this rule, for they made very few changes to the place names they found in Britain, but both groups lived as a separate, ruling class and had a rather different attitude from the normal settler.

Difficulties of place name studies

One way to examine place names is to take them layer by layer according to age, but it is best to stay within definite geographical boundaries when doing this. Names which may have come into being at roughly the same time, but in different parts of the world, are likely to have very little in common. The beliefs and attitudes of the namers are more important than the time of naming, and these—perhaps more so in the distant past than now—varied considerably from tribe to tribe, nation to nation. Since it is usually easier to assign a place name to its language, and therefore to the people who gave the name, rather than to an exact period, we will do well to follow familiar paths through the place name jungle.

The jungle, as it may justly be called, is primarily a linguistic one. In Britain the number of languages concerned is relatively small, with Celtic—or Primitive Welsh, Gaelic, Old English, Old Norse, Latin and Norman French being the more important. In America there are the many Indian tribal languages, which began to receive serious attention only in recent times. As one travels round the world, African, Polynesian and Aboriginal languages make their appearance. With each language one has to do also with the culture that lies behind it.

This linguistic jungle, however, has had its Spekes and Livingstones. England has been especially fortunate, for a determined army of scholars, mostly gathered together in The English Place Name Society, has been hacking away at the undergrowth for over fifty years. Names like Stenton, Mawer, Gover and Ekwall are mostly unknown to the general public, but these are a few of the men who first penetrated into really difficult areas. Other men and women now use the methods they established to explore new areas and refine our knowledge of the others, but the quantity and quality of work done by the pioneers was quite outstanding. In America George R. Stewart has also made a particularly noteworthy contribution to place name studies, though as a social historian rather than a philologist.

Paths, then, have been established and made familiar. A fuller list of the scholars who have helped lay them appears in the Bibliography of this book, but some may be overlooked. Scholars know that is the fate of road-builders to make travel easy for others and be forgotten themselves.

When the Anglo-Saxons invaded Britain it is clear that they took over many place names *as names*, without understanding their meaning. The evidence is to be found in names like Penhill, where Old English *hyll* was added unnecessarily to a word which represented Old Welsh *penn*, 'hill'. A Penhill in Lancashire developed into Pendle and was later expanded to Pendle Hill, a name which means 'hill-hill-hill'. England also has a Torpenhow Hill, or 'hill-hill-hill-hill'.

Celtic place names

Let us start out, then, along the first main path. It is as well to begin with British place names because, as with surnames, so many of them were later transferred to other countries. The first layer of names that have a known meaning are those left by the Celts, who came to Britain from central Europe from about 500 BC onwards. **London** is one of their many place names that remains in use today, but

One of the mysteries about *Loch Ness*, in Scotland, is the origin of its name, or the name of the river that flows into it, at least. Professor W. F. H. Nicolaisen has tentatively suggested that it might derive from Nessos/Nessa, earlier Nestos/Nesta, from Nedtos/Nedta, linking with an Indo-European word meaning 'to flood'. This would make it a pre-Celtic name.

As for the name of the monster which is said to lurk in the depths of the lake, Nessie is doubly suitable. Apart from the river name connection, Nessie was formerly the common abbreviation for Agnes, once a popular name in Scotland.

opinions differ as to its exact meaning. It is likely to have been 'the settlement of **Londinos**', a man (or god) whose name in turn meant 'the bold one'. **Carlisle** is another Celtic name, its modern form having been influenced by French-speaking clerks who adapted what they heard to fit their own spelling system. What they heard was **Cair Luel,** with *cair* being an earlier version of the Welsh *caer*, 'fort'. The Venerable Bede noted in the 8th century that Luel was how the Latin name **Luguvallium** was then being pronounced. The Latin version of the name indicates what the Romans had heard the natives saying centuries before, an original name which may have meant 'strong in Lugus', Lugus being a popular god. The links in this complex chain, from Carlisle back to Luguvallium, happen to exist in this case, but with many names there is no such help available.

Carmarthen contains the word 'fort' twice, for besides beginning with *caer* it ends with what was once *din*, which had the same meaning. The name was originally the 'fort near the sea', represented by the Romans as **Mari Dunum.** The Welsh made it **Myrddin.** Just as we might now talk of Carmarthen Castle, unaware that Carmarthen already twice refers to a castle, so by the 8th century it was forgotten that Myrddin contained the word. *Caer* was added, and **Caer Myrddin** was interpreted four centuries later by Geoffrey of Monmouth as 'the castle of Myrddin'. The non-existent Myrddin became *Merlinus* in Latin and has been part of the Arthurian legend ever since.

The Anglo-Saxons who invaded Britain from the 5th century onwards did not immediately occupy the whole of England, and a study of place names enables their progress across the country from the east to the west to be traced. They appear to have killed or driven away most of the people in the eastern area, for very few of the original Celtic names remain. As they slowly pushed west, leaving behind settlers, they took over or adapted more and more names. The adaptations often appear as *hybrids*, with elements of more than one language joined together. The density of Celtic names or elements increases all the time until one comes to Wales and Cornwall, where we have as much proof as we want that the Britons continued to live their own lives and speak their own language.

The Angles pushed north into Caledonia, but this area was later over-run by migrants from Ireland, called 'Scots'. The Scots gave their name to Scotland, and eventually displaced or absorbed the mysterious Picts, who lived in the Highlands. Gaelic, Old English and Pictish names are found in Scotland today, together with Scandinavian and Norman names that were introduced later. It is hardly surprising that many names remain unexplained. **Edinburgh,** for example, has a second element meaning 'fortress', but 'Eidyn', which is the first element, cannot be interpreted. All that can be said with any certainty is that Edinburgh does *not* mean 'Edwin's fortress' as is popularly supposed. The evidence for the refutation is best set out in *The Names of Towns and Cities in Britain*, by Nicolaisen, Gelling and Richards.

Ireland's place names derive mainly from Gaelic, but their forms have been much distorted by non-Gaelic-speaking officials. P. W. Joyce says in his *Irish Names of Places* that it was necessary to ask

In 1865 a couple named their son after the place where they had first met. The name later became world-famous when the man concerned won the Nobel Prize for Literature, yet no other parents seem to have been attracted to it. *Rudyard* Kipling is possibly the only man to have borne that Christian name. It derives from Rudyard Lake, in Staffordshire, and may have meant 'pond in which rudd were kept'. An alternative explanation is 'lake near a garden in which rue was grown'.

local people how they pronounced the names before the origins became at all clear. **Dublin** is well known to be *dubh linne*, an exact translation of which appears in the English name **Blackpool. Belfast** takes its name from its proximity to a natural sandbank formed near the mouth of a river by the opposing currents and able to be used as a *farset*, or 'ford'.

To return to England, one of the place name facts that most people know is that 'caster', 'chester' or 'cester' in a name indicates Roman connections. This is true, but it was not the Romans themselves who named places in this way. For them *castra* was a military camp, but they did not bother to add this word to the names of the camps. It was the Anglo-Saxons who did so, having taken the word into Old English as *ceaster.*

The Romans had actually withdrawn from England before the Anglo-Saxons invaded, but wherever the newcomers went they would have found the very distinctive signs of Roman occupation. One must assume that the Celts had taken *castra* into their language and were able to pass it on to the Anglo-Saxons. The latter made full use of it, sometimes attaching it to a Celtic name, as in **Gloucester,** where the first element meant 'bright'; sometimes adding another of their own words, as in **Chesterfield,** with 'field' originally meaning 'open land'. The Romans had frequently referred to camps by the names of nearby rivers, and this led to place names like **Doncaster, Lancaster** and **Exeter,** from the rivers **Don, Lune** and **Exe.** By no means every Roman settlement, however, had a *ceaster* added to it, and some names that were given it lost it again quickly. London was referred to as **Lundenceaster,** for instance, but this was clearly felt to be too unwieldy.

The Romans themselves had attempted to call London **Augusta,** but like most of their attempts at bestowing place names in Britain, this failed. To all intents and purposes, the Romans left behind them in Britain no place names of their own invention. What they did during their long stay of over three centuries was to record in Latin the Celtic names they heard, but it was not these written forms that were passed on to the Anglo-Saxons. The Celtic names the latter took over—mostly the names of larger settlements and rivers—would have been passed to them by word of mouth. Many others had to be given, and this the Anglo-Saxons proceeded to do.

Anglo-Saxon clan names

The earliest Anglo-Saxon names reflect the fact that they were moving across new territory. What was important to them at the time was their own identity as a group, which was the one thing that remained constant. They travelled as bands, each with a leader whose name they took. If the leader was Reada, then they were *Readingas*, his followers and dependants. Eventually, when they decided to settle, that place would be known as 'the Readingas' place', **Reading** as it is today. Some names of this kind also add a '-ham' or '-ton' to indicate a settlement.

Not every English place name that contains 'ing' can automatically be given this kind of meaning. The suffix '-ing' can also mean 'place' or 'river', and sometimes it refers to an Old Norse *eng*, 'meadow'. A '-ridding' is a 'clearing', a '-ling' often a 'bank' or 'ridge'. A place name student must have evidence that the '-ing' was once a plural before he can say that it refers to a clan name. In a few cases this plural has survived, as in **Hastings** and **Cannings.**

The clan names were in use at the end of the 5th century. Although at that time they described people and not places they changed their nature completely long before the byname period. Once they had permanently settled the small groups who had borne these names gradually joined together and formed larger kingdoms. The later place names of the Anglo-Saxons were obviously true place names from the beginning, but the existence of these early transferred names is a great help to

---

It has long been a popular pastime to invent explanations for place names. Thus it is said that *Purfleet* received its name on the day that Queen Elizabeth I stood by the river and saw her battered war-ships returning from the fight against the Spanish Armada. Seeing their battered condition, she is said to have exclaimed: 'My poor fleet'.

The name was in existence, however, at least three hundred years before the sea-battle took place. Its second element means 'stream', while the first part of the name probably contains an obscure personal name.

London has several botanical connections. *London pride*, for example, is another name for the Sweet William, perhaps because that flower was formerly much grown in the city's window boxes. Foxgloves have also been known as *London buttons*. After the Great Fire of London in 1666, a plant (*Sisymbrium irio*) sprang up abundantly amongst the ruins. It became known as *London rocket*.

London ivy, on the other hand, was once a slang name for the clinging London fog (also known as a London particular). But when Cockneys refer to a 'London fog' in their rhyming slang they mean a dog.

historians. Plotting them on a map helps to show not only where the Anglo-Saxons went but when they went there.

The clan names (sometimes called '-ing names' or 'folk names') often contain the personal name of the clan leader, but it is not only these names, transferred to places, that contain personal names. Thousands more link the name of an individual farmer or landowner with his property. These are not the great names of history, but the names of ordinary people. As we saw when we looked at the history of first names the typical Anglo-Saxon names—**Eanwulf, Helmheard, Cynewulf, Beornred** and the like—were later replaced by names of foreign origin, though many are known to us from coins and charters. Many others, however, live on only in place names such as **Hauxton, Hawkesbury** and **Hawksworth,** all of which mention a man called **Hafoc.**

There were other ways of describing in a place name the people who lived there without using a personal name. **Sussex** uses the tribal name, describing the 'South Saxons', and **Grantchester** the name of a river. The '-chester' here is a modern form of Old English *saete*, meaning 'dwellers', not the usual *-ceaster*, so the name meant 'dwellers on the River Granta'. The *-ingas* of the clan names can also occur attached to a generally descriptive word instead of a personal name. **Epping** was once the 'people of the upland', not the 'followers of Yppe'. **Norfolk** and **Suffolk** are other obvious descriptive names of people, dividing them into northern and southern groups.

Other Anglo-Saxon place names

The Anglo-Saxons appear to have done little conscious naming of the places in which they came to live. Most of the names clearly began as phrases in normal speech and gradually became fossilised. In the place names that arose during the Anglo-Saxon period there is therefore a true picture of England as it was, filled in with many fine details. Apart from the country itself, many names tell us about the people, their beliefs and customs. The Anglo-Saxons came to Britain as pagans, for instance, but were slowly converted to Christianity. We know this from other sources, but the change can be seen in the place names. Some early names contain references to heathen temples, as in **Harrow-on-the-Hill** and **Weedon,** or are theonymic links, as in **Tuesley** and **Wednesbury.** The latter names naturally remind us of the day names **Tuesday** and **Wednesday** in which the names of the gods **Tiw** and **Woden** again appear. Pagan customs such as sacrificing animals and burying the dead alongside their weapons and domestic items are probably hinted at in names like **Gateshead,** 'goat's head' and **Hounslow,** 'Hund's burial mound'.

Christian place names often mention a monastery or church, as in **Warminster** and **Cheriton,** 'minster on the River Were' and 'village with a church'. Saints' names also occur: **Felixstowe, Bridstow,** St Felix and St Bridget being linked with '-stow', which often meant 'holy place'. 'Holy' itself, Old English *hālig*, is seen in **Halliwell** and the like, while many other names refer to priests, canons, abbots, nuns, monks and bishops.

Lay society is also reflected in many place names. **Kingston, Queenborough, Aldermanbury** are self-explanatory, but modern Englishmen no longer refer to 'churls' in the sense of 'free peasants'. **Charlton** and **Chorlton** refer to farms held by such men. 'Knights' are still with us, but this word has been considerably upgraded. The Anglo-Saxons used it to refer to a youth, and **Knightsbridge** was therefore a bridge where young men met.

All this is very proper, but the Anglo-Saxons had their thieves and other criminals whom they dealt with in no uncertain manner. **Shackerley** was a 'robbers' wood, **Warnborough,** 'felon stream', a stream where they were drowned. The gallows are referred to in many local names, often the names of the fields where the executions took place. **Dethick** is thought to derive from a name given to a particular tree, 'the death oak', where no doubt Anglo-Saxon justice was frequently carried out.

Scandinavian names

The Anglo-Saxons settled and named their places, and the time of their coming receded into the past. In the 9th century it was the turn of new invaders, the Vikings, to establish a permanent foothold in Britain. By 886 King Alfred had signed a treaty with Guthrum, the Danish leader, and the Danelaw came into being. The newcomers responded exactly as the Anglo-Saxons had done before them to the place names they found—accepted them as they found them, adapted their pronunciation to suit their own language (usually called 'Old Norse'), added words of their own to existing names, thus creating new hybrids, or gave entirely new names. Naturally their own personal names, and those of their gods, were also linked to their place names, which are especially concentrated in Yorkshire and Lincolnshire.

Old Norse and Old English had far more in common with each other than with Celtic or Gaelic, but there were differences of vocabulary and usage. The distinctive word of the Danes was *by*, used instead of Old English *tun*. They also made frequent use of *thorp*, whereas the Anglo-Saxons were not fond of their equivalent *throp*, both of which meant an 'outlying farm'. Typical pronunciation preferences are reflected in **Keswick,** the Scandinavian way of saying **Chiswick** 'cheese farm'; **Skipton** and **Shipton,** 'sheep farm'. Once again, the plotting of Scandinavian place names on a map of Britain provides evidence of where they settled and in what numbers.

Norman influence

Invasion and settlement did not end with the Vikings, but place name scholars tend to talk of the Norman influence on English place names rather than French names. The Normans came to England 200 years after the Vikings, and by then place names were thick on the ground and well established. Not many Normans came and they did not settle in the same way as the Vikings and Anglo-Saxons. They became rulers, not farmers, and were concerned with the building of castles rather than cottages.

When they did give names they were frequently subjective descriptions rather than the down-to-earth factual descriptions of the past. **Bewley** is another form of **Beaulieu,** 'beautiful place'. **Merdegrave,** an Anglo-Saxon name probably referring to 'martens', they hastily changed to **Belgrave,** an interesting early example of whitewashing a name (*merde* in French meaning 'faeces'). Rather similar was their change of **Fulepet,** 'foul pit', to **Beaumont,** 'beautiful hill'.

The ordinary Englishman, as the Normans must have quickly realised, could not cope with French names, which had sounds and spellings totally strange to him. But the same was true of the Norman clerks who tried to write down English names. They wrote what they heard, but in their own spelling system. When English sounds did not exist in French they wrote the nearest thing. Often they turned the '-chester' ending into '-sester', spelling it '-cester', as in **Gloucester, Cirencester.**

There have been many other changes to place names in Britain since the Middle Ages, apart from changes in pronunciation. Names have been changed by folk-etymology, the process that turns the unfamiliar into the familiar. **Chartreuse,** for instance, was turned into **Charterhouse,** which seemed more meaningful to Englishmen. Names have been shortened over the centuries, but they have also been lengthened. **Ditton,** 'a farm by a dyke or ditch', split into **Thames Ditton** and **Long Ditton,** two more precise locations. They might have become North and South, Great and Little (*Magna* and *Parva*), High and Low. They could have taken the names of different landowners, as has frequently happened in English place names. Instead one took a simple adjective, the other became linked to one of the world's most famous river names.

The origin of **Thames,** incidentally, which was mentioned a moment ago, is not known. It is possibly a simple description, 'dark river', parallel to a tributary of the Ganges, **Tamasa.** The older river names are mostly of this type, many of them simply meaning 'water' or 'river', with no qualification of any kind. **Avon, Dore, Dover, Lent, Esk, Axe, Exe, Don, Ouse, Arrow** and others all have such an origin. I find it easy to understand this. Like everyone else who lives near a river I go down 'to the river' for a walk without ever specifying it more exactly. When Thames *is* used for any reason, the 'h' is not pronounced of course. The letter was artificially inserted centuries ago, as a 'b' was in words like 'doubt' and 'debt', but has never been pronounced.

What a natural, simple county, content to fix its boundaries by these tortuous island brooks, with their comfortable names—Trent, Mease, Dove, Tern, Dane, Mees, Stour, Tame, and even hasty Severn.

Arnold Bennett *The Old Wives' Tale*

The study of river names is a special aspect of place name studies. Eilert Ekwall spent several years looking for early forms of the names in unpublished medieval documents and travelled round England looking at the rivers themselves. The results of his researches are to be found in his *English River Names*, but this is primarily a book by a philologist for other philologists. (See page 115.)

Field names

Among the many other specialised aspects of place name studies may be mentioned that of field names. Town-dwellers rarely hear these names, and are perhaps unaware that they exist, but countless thousands of them are there. They were applied first to open stretches of country cleared of trees, for this was the earliest meaning of 'field'. Later they identified the furlongs of open fields and finally they were applied to the enclosed fields we think of today.

Just as street names usually contain a word that means some kind of street, so field names usually contain a substitute for 'field', such as 'bottom', 'erg', 'jack', 'slang'. The first of these is used for land in a valley, the second for pasture used only in summer. 'Jack' refers to common land while a 'slang' describes the narrowness of the field.

Accompanying the wide variety of 'field' words are descriptions of the land's size and shape, its distance or direction from the village, its soil or crop, its plants or animals, its buildings or natural features. The names of the owners are often linked to them, and there are transferred names such as **Bohemia** and **Zululand** as light-hearted references to remote fields. A humorous reaction to unproductive land leads to names like **Bare Arse, Muchado,** **Pinchgut, Cain's Ground** and the like. Names given after the 18th century may be arbitrary conversions, reflecting the whim of the namer but saying nothing about the fields themselves.

Some samples of English field names:

Bangland land on which beans were grown.
Botany Bay a distant field in which hard labour was needed.
Catsbrains a common name for a field with mixed clay and pebbles.
Cupid's close a corruption of 'coalpit's close', a field near a coalpit.
Gallantry bank a field in which there was once a gallows.
Greedy guts a field needing a lot of manure.
Hoppit a small enclosure.
Nackerty a field with many corners.
Pickpocket an unprofitable field.
Pudding acre a field with soft, sticky earth.
Shivery sham a field with an unstable surface.
The Wong an enclosed area in an open field.
Zidles 'side hills', a field with hilly land at the side.

One interesting aspect of field names is that there is scope for the amateur researcher. In many areas the names have not been collected yet, and a real contribution to a worthwhile study can be made. The names often fall within the bounds of local history rather than philology, though the interpretation of older names needs the help of an expert. Field names often repay in themselves the time that has been spent searching for them. I am rather fond, personally, of some Scottish names—**Knockmarumple, Glutty** and **Gruggle O' the Wud,** but English field names offer similar pleasures. Many examples are to be found in John Field's *English Field Names.*

The amateur can often interpret field names, but it must be said once again that the interpretation of place names must on the whole be left to the specialist. This has not prevented a great many mythological explanations being offered by sages of the past. H. G. Stokes quoted a favourite place name legend in his *English Place Names* concerning the village of **Kirkby Overblow,** where the second half of the name actually refers to early smelters. The locals tell the tale of a lovelorn maiden flinging herself from a nearby cliff in despair, but floating harmlessly down when her petticoats and skirts acted as a parachute. It is surprising that the legend does not extend to the invention of the parachute itself.

'Territorial names,' Oscar explained, gravely, 'have always a "cachet" of distinction; they fall on the ear full toned with secular dignity. That's how I get all the names of my personages, Frank. I take up a map of the English counties, and there they are. Our English villages have often exquisitely beautiful names. Windermere, for instance, or Hunstanton.'

Frank Harris *Oscar Wilde*

Pleasures of place names

Legends of this kind are one of the pleasures of place names if one is not too deadly serious about the whole subject. Another pleasure is to be found in many of the names themselves. Many people collect interesting place names that have a happy combination of sounds and hinted meanings. Stokes let his imagination run riot with **Bursteye** ('What an address for a film studio!') and delighted in names like **Bouncehorn, Rhude, Furtherfits, Badnocks, Shambelly, Undy, Snoring, Nobottle, Nicknocks, High Harpers.** A. A. Willis, another ardent collector, listed such names as **Shavington-cum-Gresty, Stank End, Dottery, Snoreham in Ruins, Maggots End, Great Fryup** and **Finish.** Surely we all recall, when we speak these names aloud, the time when language was new to us, when every word acquired was a linguistic toy waiting to be played with? The speaking aloud is important, for as our eyes run over the printed page we do not always translate into sound.

Poets, as we have seen, may respond to place names in a different way:

> Our maps are music and our northern titles
> Like wind among the grass and heather, grieve.

Ivor Brown begins his poem 'The Moorland Map' with those fine words. John Betjeman has played poetically with Dorset place names, and many other poets have sensed the poetry inherent in ancient names.

We are not all place name specialists, humorists or poets, but there is something in certain place names for us all. There are names which have for us that private meaning that we spoke of at the beginning of this book, a thousand and one personal associations. Some names spoken aloud will be like pebbles thrown into a pool of memory, recalling our childhood or other periods of our lives. One must never forget this quality of names, which may make them hardly meaningful to some people but very meaningful indeed to others.

When the Great Age of Discovery began in the 16th century, British place names already had these intense personal meanings for the explorers and colonists. It is hardly surprising that they frequently transferred those names to the new lands. Even without being attached to new places, many of the names would have spread round the world, for they had now become the names of the emigrants themselves. On the *Mayflower*, for example, were men named **Allerton, Billington, Bradford, Britteridge, Chilton, Crackston, Eaton, Holebeck, Howland, Leister, Rigdale, Standish, Tilley, Warren** and **Winslow,** all of which remain to this day in one form or another as English place names. There, too, among the names on the land are **Cromwell** and **Raleigh, Lincoln** and **Washington.** Our place names may have had humble beginnings, but they have sometimes become the proudest names of all.

County names

Present and former county names of the United Kingdom.

Aberdeenshire 'mouth of the Don' (formerly Devona, 'goddess').
Anglesey 'Angles' island'.
Angus (belonging to) 'Aeneas', brother of Kenneth II.
Antrim 'Aentrebh', name of a monastery in the 5th century.
Argyll 'boundary of the Gaels'.
Armagh (Queen) 'Macha's height'.
Ayrshire from the Ayr, 'running water'.
Banffshire 'young pig' (possibly alternative name for the Deveron). Or 'Banba/Banbha', a poetic name for Ireland used as a district name in Scotland. Animal names for rivers do occur, but the young pig reference might also be to totemism.
Bedfordshire 'Bieda's ford'.
Berkshire 'hilly'.
Berwickshire 'barley farm'.
Breconshire 'Brycean's territory'.
Buckinghamshire 'land belonging to Bucca's clan'.
Bute 'beacon' or 'hut, bothy'.
Caernarvonshire 'the fort in Arfon, opposite Mona (Anglesey)'.
Caithness 'ness of the Cataibh'.
Cambridgeshire 'bridge on the Granta'. (Grantabridge became Crantbridge, Cantbridge, Canbridge, Cambridge.)
Cardiganshire 'land of Ceredig'.
Carmarthenshire 'fort near the sea'.
Cheshire 'Roman camp'.
Clackmannanshire 'stone of Manau'.
Cornwall 'the Welsh (foreigners) in the land of the Cornovii tribe'.
Cumberland 'land of the Cumbrians (Britons)'.
Denbighshire 'little fort'.
Derbyshire 'village or farm near a deer park'.
Devon 'territory of the Dumnonii'.
Dorset 'dwellers in the Roman town of Durnovaria ('fist play'—with reference to a nearby amphitheatre).
Down 'fort'.
Dumfriesshire 'fort of the copses'.
Dunbarton 'fortress of the Britons'.
Durham 'island with a hill'.
East Lothian from a personal name.
Essex 'East Saxons'.
Fermanagh 'Monach's men'.
Fife presumably from a personal name.
Flintshire 'the flinty (rocky) place'.
Glamorgan 'Morgan's territory'.
Gloucestershire 'Roman town of Glevum (bright)'.
Hampshire 'estate on a promontory'.
Herefordshire 'army ford'
Hertfordshire 'hart ford', ie crossing-place for stags.
Huntingdon and Peterborough 'huntsman's hill' and St Peter's town'.
Inverness-shire 'mouth of the Ness'.
Isle of Wight possibly 'that which juts from the sea; an island'.
Kent 'coastal area'.
Kincardineshire 'at the head of a wood'.
Kinross-shire 'head of the promontory'.
Kircudbrightshire 'St Cuthbert's Church'.
Lanarkshire 'glade'.
Lancashire 'Roman fort on the Lune'.
Leicestershire 'Roman town of the Ligore tribe'.
Lincolnshire 'Roman settlement (*colonia*) by the lake'.
London, Greater based on 'Londinos', a personal name.
Londonderry 'London (because of a charter granted to the Livery Companies of the City of London) + oak wood'.
Merionethshire based on personal name 'Marion'.
Middlesex 'Middle Saxons'.
Midlothian probably based on a personal name.
Monmouthshire 'mouth of the Mynwy'.
Montgomeryshire after a castle built by Roger de Montgomery, a Norman.
Moray 'territory by the sea'.
Nairnshire 'the river'.
Norfolk 'northern people'.
Northamptonshire 'north settlement'.
Northumberland 'land north of the Humber'.
Nottinghamshire 'settlement of Snot's clan'.
Orkney 'whale islands'.
Oxfordshire 'oxen ford'.
Peebleshire 'shiels, huts'.
Pembrokeshire 'end land'.
Perthshire 'copse'.
Radnorshire possibly based on 'red' (referring to colour of land?).
Renfrewshire 'flowing brook'.
Ross and Cromarty 'moor' and 'crooked bay'.
Roxburghshire 'Hroc's fortress'.
Rutland 'Rota's land'.
Selkirkshire 'hall church'.
Shetland based on a personal name.
Shropshire 'fortified place of Scrobb's clan', or 'in the scrub land'.
Somerset 'dwellers at the summer village'.
Staffordshire 'ford by a landing-place'.
Stirlingshire no satisfactory explanation can be proposed.
Suffolk 'southern people'.
Surrey 'southern district'.
Sussex 'land of the southern Saxons'.
Sutherland 'the southern land'.
Tyrone 'Owen's territory'.
Warwickshire 'dwellings by the weir'.
West Lothian as *Midlothian*.
Westmorland "land of the people west of the (Yorkshire) moors'.
Wigtownshire 'dwelling-place'.
Wiltshire 'village on the Wylye'.
Worcestershire 'Roman settlement formerly inhabited by the Weogora tribe'.
Yorkshire 'estate of Eburos'. *Riding* is 'thridding', a 'third'.

The re-organisation of local government in England and Wales led to the adoption of the following 'new' county names. Most of the names are, in fact, restorations of ancient names or transferred river names.

Avon from the river name.
Cleveland 'the hilly district'.
Clwyd from the river name.
Cumbria the name of an ancient tribe.
Dyfed name of an ancient province.
Gwent name of an ancient province.
Gwynedd name of an ancient province.
Humberside based on a river name.
Manchester, Greater 'the Roman town *Mamucium*', of uncertain meaning.
Merseyside based on a river name.
Midlands, West descriptive.
Powys name of an ancient province.
Salop from *Salopesberia*, a Norman-French version of *Scrobesbyrig*, or *Shrewsbury*.
Tyne and Wear from two river names.

Place name elements

A selection of elements that occur in place names throughout Britain is given below. The elements were originally words in Celtic (Old Welsh), Gaelic, Old English and Old Norse. In their passage through the centuries they have undergone many changes, and what was once the same word may exist in many modern forms. It is never possible to explain the original meaning of a British place name on the basis of its modern form alone. Only by examining the earliest forms known to be recorded can a philologist give a judgment as to the intended meaning; even then he must always consider topographical information about the natural features as well as linguistic facts.

In the list an element that normally occurs as a prefix is shown thus: *Aber-*; *Ac-*; *Aird-*, etc. An element that is normally a suffix is shown thus: *-beck*; *-borne*; *-by*, etc. Elements that can occur as names in themselves, or as prefixes or suffixes, are shown thus: *Barrow*; *Firth*; *Haigh*, etc.

Aber- 'river mouth'.
Ac- 'oak'.
Aird. 'height'.
Ard- 'height'.
Auch(in)- 'field'.
Avon- 'water, river'.
Bally- 'farm, village'.
Bar- 'barley'.
Barrow 'hill, tumulus, grove'.
-beck 'stream'.
Ber- 'barley'.
-ber 'grove'.
-berry 'burial mound'.
Bold- 'building'.
-borne 'stream'.
-borough 'fortified place'; 'burial mound'
-bourne 'stream'.
Bryn- 'hill'.
Bur- 'fortified place'.
Burn- 'stream'.
-burgh 'fortified place'.
-bury 'fortified place'.
-by 'farm, village'.
Cam- 'crooked'.
Car- 'fortified place'.
Carl- 'churl'.
Carn- 'heap of stones'.
-caster 'Roman settlement'.
Charl- 'churl'.
Chat- 'wood'.
Chep- 'market'.
Chester 'Roman settlement'.
Chip- 'market'.
Coat- 'cottage'.
-combe 'deep valley'.
Comp- 'deep valley'.
-cot(e) 'cottage'.
Crick- 'small hill'.
Dal- 'dale; meadow by a stream'.
Darwen- 'oak tree'.
Dean- 'valley'.
Den- 'valley'; 'fortress'.
Din- 'fortress'.
-don 'hill'.
Down- 'hill'.
Drogh- 'bridge'.
Drum 'ridge'.
Dub- 'black'.
Dun- 'hill'; 'fortified place'.
Ea- 'water, river'; 'island'.
Eglo- 'church'.
Ey- 'island'.
-ey 'water, river'; 'island'.
-fell 'hill'.
Firth 'fiord'.
-ford 'ford'; 'fiord'.
Gal 'stranger'.
Garth 'enclosure'.
-gethly 'wood'.
-gill 'narrow ravine'.
Glais- 'stream'.
Glas- 'stream'; 'greeny blue'.
Graf- 'grove'.
-grave 'grove'.
-greave 'grove'.
-guard 'enclosure'.
Hag- 'hedge, enclosure'.
Haigh 'hedge, enclosure'.
Hal(e) 'corner'.
-hall 'corner'; 'hall'.
Ham 'homestead'; water-meadow'.
-haugh 'hedge, enclosure'.

Hayle- 'salt water'.
Hel- 'salt water'.
-hithe 'landing-place'.
Holme 'small island'.
Holt 'thicket'.
Hoo 'high land'.
Hop- 'valley'.
Hough 'high land'.
How(e) 'mound, hill'.
Hurst 'wooded hill'.
Hythe 'landing-place'.
Inch 'island'.
Innis 'island'.
Inver- 'river mouth'.
Kil- 'monastic cell, church'.
Killi- 'wood'.
Knock- 'small hill'.
Kyle 'strait'.
Lan- 'enclosure, church'.
-law 'mound, hill'.
Lee 'glade'.
Leigh 'glade'.
Lin 'lake, pool'.
Lis- 'court, hall'.
-low 'mound, hill'.
Lyn(n)- 'lake, pool'.
Magher- 'coastal plain'.
Mar- 'lake'.
Mal- 'hill'.
-mel 'sandbank'
Mel- 'hill'.
Mer 'lake'.
-mere 'lake'.
Mine- 'mountain'.
Mon- 'mountain'.
Mor- 'sea'.
Moy- 'coastal plain'.
Mynd 'mountain'.
-ness 'cape'.
-ock 'oak'.
Oke- 'oak'.
Or- 'bank'.
Pen- 'head'.
Pol- 'pool'.
Rath- 'fort, court'.
-rith 'ford'.
Ros(s) 'moorland'.
-rose 'moorland'.
Ru- 'slope'.
-ryn 'cape'.
-scar 'rock, reef'.
Sel- 'sallow (a tree)'.
-set 'hill pasture'.
Shaw 'small wood'.
Sher 'bright'.
Shir- 'bright'.
Sil- 'sallow (a tree)'.
Skerry 'rock, reef'.
Slieve 'range of hills'.
Stain- 'stone'.
Stan- 'stone'.
-stead 'place'.
-sted 'place'.
-ster 'place'.
Stock 'holy meeting-place'; 'tree-stump'.
Stoke 'holy meeting-place'.
Stow(e) 'place'.
Strat- 'Roman road'.
Strath- 'a wide valley'.
Stret- 'Roman road'.
Thorp(e) 'farm, village'.
Thwaite 'glade, clearing'.
-tire 'land'.
-ton 'farm. village'.
Tre- 'farm, village'.
-try 'shore, sands'.
Ty- 'house'.
Tyr- 'land'.
Usk 'water'.
Wal- 'foreigner, Briton'.
Wen- 'white'.
-wich 'dwelling, farm'.
Wick 'dwelling, farm'; 'sea inlet'.
Win- 'white'.
Worth(y) 'enclosure, farm'.
Wyke 'dwelling, farm'.

English river names

The names of rivers are often amongst the most ancient known to us. Interpreting them is exclusively a matter for the trained philologist, as a glance into *English River-Names*, by the Swedish scholar Eilert Ekwall, will clearly reveal. This book was first published in 1928 by the Oxford University Press and is still available. It is a remarkable labour of love and a model piece of research. Those interested in the meanings of English river names, as far as they can be ascertained, should consult the above-mentioned book, which also gives their precise locations. Below I list a selection of the names themselves.

Adur
Allen
Aller
Allow
Alwin
Amber
Anker
Ann
Ant
Anton
Ark
Arrow
Arun
Ash
Avon
Axe
Bain
Ball
Beal
Beam
Beane
Bedwyn
Belah
Bell
Biddle
Biss
Blackwater
Bleng
Blyth(e)
Borrow
Bourne
Boyd
Brain
Bray
Brent
Bride
Brock
Brue
Burn
Cad
Calder
Cam
Camel
Can
Cary
Char
Cherwell
Chess
Chet
Chew
Chid
Churn
Claw
Cocker
Cole
Colne
Connor
Coquet
Corve
Cover
Craddock
Crake
Crane
Crouch
Cunkel
Curry
Dacre
Dane
Dart
Dee
Deer
Dent
Derwent
Devon
Dewey
Don
Douglas
Dove
Duddon
Earn
Eden
Ellen
Erewash
Erme

Esk
Evenlode
Exe
Eye
Fal
Fleet
Flitt
Flyford
Font
Foss
Foulness
Freshwater
Frome
Gade
Gaunless
Gelt
Gilpin
Glem
Glen
Glendermackin
Glyme
Gowan
Granta
Greet
Greta
Gussage
Hail
Hamble
Hamps
Hannon
Hayle
Hel
Hems
Hipper
Hiz
Hodder
Hull
Humber
Hundred
Idle
Inny
Irk
Irthing
Irwell
Isis
Isle
Itchen
Ive
Keer
Kemp
Kenn
Kennet
Kensey
Kent
Kenwyn
Kex Beck
Key
Kyle
Kym
Lambourn
Lark
Laver
Lea
Leach
Leam
Leen
Lemon
Len
Lew
Lickle
Linnet
Liza
Loddon
Looe
Loose
Loud
Low
Lox
Lud
Lugg
Lune
Luney Stream
Lyd
Lyde
Lyme
Lyn
Mad Brook
Manifold
Marden
Mardle
Medina
Medway
Meon
Mere
Mersey
Mimram
Mint
Mite
Mole
Morda
Must
Nadder
Nanny
Nar
Nent
Nidd
Noe
O Brook
Ock
Onk
Onny
Ore
Orwell
Otter
Ottery
Ouse
Pang
Pant
Parret
Penk
Peover
Perry
Piddle
Pilling
Pipe
Plym
Pont
Pow
Quarme
Quinny
Rattle Brook
Ray
Rea
Rede
Rib
Ribble
Roach
Rom
Rother
Rye
Sark
Sem
Sence
Seph
Seven
Severn
Sheaf
Sheepwash
Shooter
Sid
Silk Stream
Silver
Skerne
Skippool
Skitter Beck
Slea
Smite
Soar
Sow
Sprint
Stiffkey
Stour
Swale
Sway
Swift
Tala Water
Tamar
Tame
Tavy
Taw
Team
Tees
Teign
Test
Thames
Thrushel
Tiddy
Till
Tone
Tory Brook
Trent
Trym
Turkdean
Tweed
Tyne
Ure
Valency
Ver
Wampool
Wandle
Wash
Waveney
Waver
Wear
Weaver
Welland
Went
Were
Wey
Wharfe
Whitsun Brook
Wiley
Wimborne
Windrush
Wiske
Wissey
Witham
Woburn
Wolf
Worf
Worm Brook
Wreak
Wye
Wyre
Yare
Yarrow
Yarty
Yealm
Yeo

Place name overtones

Humorists have managed to find ingenious new answers to the question: what's in a place name? It was the British writer Paul Jennings who first seems to have noticed that place names 'carry wonderful overtones—they seem to have been drawn from some huge, carelessly profuse stock of primal meaning'. Mr Jennings began to assign his own meanings to place names, as if they were normal words. Thus **Woking** became 'the present participle of the verb *to woke*, an obsolete word meaning 'to day-dream'.'

In 1983 Douglas Adams and John Lloyd came along with *The Meaning of Liff*, in which they also made use of some of the spare words 'doing nothing but loafing about on sign-posts'. They found place names useful to name 'experiences, feelings, situations and even objects which we all know and recognise, but for which no words exist'. **Farnham**, for example, became a noun meaning 'the feeling you get at about four o'clock in the afternoon when you haven't got enough done'.

Adams and Lloyd even tampered with one of the most literary of all place names, **Adlestrop**. They made it 'that part of a suitcase which is designed to get snarled up on conveyor belts at airports'. Commuters and other travellers might care to compile their own 'travel dictionaries', using the place names encountered *en route*.

9 Names take their places

The place names of the English-speaking countries other than Britain reflect the histories of those countries as clearly as British place names tell the story of the Celts, Gaels, Romans, Anglo-Saxons, Vikings and Normans. A historial approach to them has accordingly been made by writers such as George Stewart and Mrs C. M. Matthews, both of whom bring a literary elegance to name studies that is very refreshing. Details of their books, together with others on which this chapter is based, are given in the Bibliography.

My own approach will not be primarily historical, for when the Age of Discovery began in the 15th century it seems to me that we entered a new era of place naming that was quite unlike anything that had happened previously. Broadly speaking, place names that came into existence before the 10th century evolved naturally in the midst of descriptive speech. Place name transfers did not occur, and those place names that contained personal names were accidentally evolved links. People wanted to distinguish between one habitation and another and one natural way for them to do it was to link them to their owners' names. 'Ecga's homestead', say, and 'Ceabba's homestead' gradually became the accepted labels for those two places, surviving even after **Ecga** and **Ceabba** were forgotten. **Egham** and **Chobham** had taken the first step to becoming real place names. At no time had Ecga and Ceabba done the naming—it was their neighbours who made use of their names.

Signs of conscious naming appeared with the Normans, when the names they gave to their castles indicated an interest in the names themselves. **Beaurepaire,** later **Belper,** meant 'beautiful retreat', and was clearly never intended to be descriptive in a functional way. British place names would have changed in kind as well as language had the Normans done far more naming, but Britain had most of the names it needed by the time they came. There was, therefore, a gap of several centuries before the naming of places began again in earnest on the other side of the ocean, and this time the name giving was normally deliberate. Often the same names as those that had arisen in Britain were given to new places, but those names had changed in kind. Their origins had usually been forgotten, but they had acquired new 'meanings'.

Transfer of place names

It is easy to see why the principle of name transfer was taken for granted by the Europeans when they went to the New World. (We must obviously say Europeans rather than British, for many of the place names now in the English-speaking world were given by Spanish, Portuguese, French and Dutch explorers and settlers.) These men all had far more place names as part of their total vocabulary than had been the case with their ancestors. They knew their own countries more thoroughly, and knew more about one another's countries.

Secondly, they had all become used to name transfer in other nomenclatures. The development of first names and surnames had been roughly parallel throughout Europe, and both systems established a stock of names which was re-used as required. Finally, and perhaps most importantly, many place names had become usable almost as words because of their meanings. **Plymouth**, for example, must have meant almost the same as 'home' to a 17th-century Englishman when he was far from home himself. A settlement of that name could bring security and familiarity to a strange land. The name might no longer be relevant to the new place that bore it, in that it was not 'the mouth of the River **Plym**', but it was very meaningful to the namers.

The naming of America is well described by George R. Stewart in his *Names on the Globe*. The basic facts about the naming are:

a. Columbus missed his opportunity to name the new continent because he failed to realise that the continent *was* new.
b. It was left to the Florentine Amerigo Vespucci (whose name in its Latin form was Americus or Albericus Vesputius) to insist that the lands he, and earlier Columbus, had visited did in fact constitute a New World.
c. A German scholar called Waldseemüller, who in the fashion of the 16th century used a classical form of his name, Hylacomylus, then suggested that the new continent should be named Americus—or since Europe and Asia were named for women, and since countries were always feminine in Latin grammar, the name might take its feminine form and become America. He entered this name on a map published in 1507, applying it to the present-day South America.
d. When it was realised that two continents had been discovered, the second one became North America. Subsequently the name of the continent was applied to the country.

The USA is thus named for a man, but uses the feminine form of his name, which seems a fair compromise.

There seem to be no signs of this kind of place name transfer in the earlier naming period, though another kind of transfer had its faint beginnings with the Anglo-Saxons and Vikings. We have seen how they occasionally linked the names of their gods to places, as in **Grimsdyke** and **Grimsbury** (**Grim** being an alternative form of **Woden**). This linking *between nomenclatures* obviously increased as time passed and affected name transfers. By the 16th century the present-day situation, whereby names can be transferred with almost total freedom from one naming system to another, had been established. The great explorers of the period lived with a constant reminder of this fact, for the very ships in which they sailed often had transferred names.

Columbus and Columbia

Columbus made early use of the name of a flagship, the **Marie Galante,** by transferring it to an island which has kept the name to this day. He may have been the first to take a name from a ship and root it firmly on the land, but he was certainly not the last. Captain Cook, for example, named a strait and a river after his ship, the **Endeavour.** When America had at last discovered Columbus (as Professor Stewart brilliantly puts it) another ship was sailing round the American coast with Robert Gray as its master. This ship's name commemorated Columbus himself in the form **Columbia**, and when Gray found a new river, he transferred his ship's name to it.

Columbia almost became the name of the United States of America. Poets of the 18th century referred to the new country by this name, but the statesmen failed to ratify the choice. The opportunity was missed, for others were quick to seize on a name which was historically apt and pleasant in sound. It was given to a city and to the **District of Columbia** as well as the river. **British Columbia** and **Colombo** came into being subsequently, as did towns called **Columbus, Columbiana** and **Columbiaville.**

Long before all this Columbus was revealing his own deeply religious convictions by naming islands after churches, which had already been named after saints. **Santa Maria La Antigua De Sevilla** was one such name, though it was later shortened to **Antigua**, 'ancient'. This was as far from Columbus's original intention as **Rum Cay**, which he had named **Santa Maria De La Concepción**. British seamen were responsible for the renaming, which incorporates a local word meaning, 'sandy island'. They also changed **St Christopher,** which he named in honour of his patron saint, into its diminutive form, **St Kitt's.**

Royalty in place names

Columbus dutifully tried to bestow some names in honour of his royal patrons, but names must live in

The Puritans who named *Boston*, in Massachusetts, thought they were simply transferring the name from Boston in the English county of Lincolnshire. They were later disconcerted to discover that the meaning of the original name was 'St Botulf's stone', indicating a stone church or cross, or a boundary stone used by the saint as a meeting place. The 'saintly' connection was a great embarrassment.

Later developments of the place name, in which it came to mean a kind of card game, a dance and a type of cream cake, would certainly not have pleased them.

the mouths of men in order to survive, not just on charts and maps. Most of these early royal names disappeared, but during the 17th century new ones appeared in profusion, especially when **New England** was founded. Prince Charles, for instance, was invited by John Smith to strike out native names that had temporarily been inserted on the map and give more suitable names. The young Prince responded to the invitation with pleasure. **Cape Elizabeth, Cape Anna** and **Cape James** were immediately named after his sister, mother and father. Cape James did not survive, for local people had already been speaking of it as **Cape Cod** for a long time, and the fish were still there to make the name a suitable one.

Charles named the **Charles River** after himself and was later to honour himself yet again, in Latin, with **Carolina.** His wife's name was linked to **Maryland.** A glance at the map will show many other royal names that have been transferred or linked to places. **Georgia, Georgetown, Williamsburg, Annapolis, Frederick County, Fredericksburg, Augusta, Orangeburg, Cumberland** and **New York** represent a small selection. The last of these was after the Duke of York, later James II. **Victoria** naturally appeared everywhere during the 19th century. French royalty was similarly commemorated in names like **Louisiana,** and at least one American town called **Isabella** was named after the Spanish queen of that name.

Royalty established a naming fashion that was to be extensively imitated. Kings and queens might give their names to large areas of land, but there were a million smaller places to be named. The early explorers naturally put their own names on the maps, though many of them were extremely modest about it. **Cook, Tasman, Vancouver, Cabot, Cartier, Drake, Flinders** and the like are all attached to places which show where they travelled, but since all of them needed a great number of names to identify the places they came across, they made use of all the names they knew. They had a golden opportunity to please other people, such as their superior officers, shipmates, friends and relations, at no cost to themselves, and it was natural for them to do so.

Sometimes the people whose names found a permanent place on the maps had a real connection with the places they named. Captain Cook buried a seaman named **Sutherland** and gave the name to that area. It lives on as a suburb of Sydney. **Sydney** itself, however, was named after Lord Sydney, an English statesman. The city has made his name known throughout the world, but he himself was never to set eyes on Australia.

Names of people great and small have been transferred or linked to place names since the 16th century. In more recent times men have gone a long way from the relative dignity of royal first names or noble surnames. **Sniktaw**, in California, reverses the name of a local journalist; **Squeaky Creek** in Colorado incorporates the nickname of an earlier settler; **Ekalaka** in Montana comes from the name of the Sioux wife of a settler. Such names somehow seem to be quite at home in states that are rather more poetically named themselves.

But in spite of all the names of people in place names, still more are simple transfers from other places. **Plymouth** was mentioned earlier, a name that can be found today in twenty-five American states. Contrary to popular belief, the Pilgrim Fathers did not actually name their new settlement: it had already been done for them by Charles Stuart. When he ran out of family names that could be used for place names on John Smith's map, he inserted the names of some English towns. The *Mayflower* was thus able to sail from Plymouth to Plymouth. Later settlers arrived at the same port, then went inland to found new towns which needed naming. It was natural for many of them to turn to the name of the last town they had seen in the homeland and the first in the new.

The duplication of so many British names in America, Canada, Australia, New Zealand and

Some political commentators believe that John F. Kennedy lost Washington's electoral vote in 1960 because he referred in a speech to *Spoke-Ayne,* instead of *Spoke-Ann,* which is how people in Washington pronounce the name Spokane.

other countries has an odd result for present-day travellers. They are likely to find clusters of familiar place names strangely rearranged as if by a giant earthquake. The pronunciation of the same names can also differ from country to country. In Britain an old name will usually have an unstressed ending, so that **Chatham** becomes 'Chat-em'. Elsewhere it is likely to be pronounced as spelt, with the '-ham' given its full value.

Other names transferred to places

It should be stressed that there are many possible sources of transfer for place names. Saints' names were often bestowed because a place was first seen on their feast-days. **Garryowen** in Montana was named for the regimental tune of the 7th Cavalry; the Bible has supplied names like **Shiloh** and **Bethesda; Buccaneer Bay** in Canada was named after a race-horse; poetry led to **Hiawatha** and **Avoca; Kodak** was borrowed from the trade name for places in Kentucky and Tennessee. The endlessness of the possibilities is perhaps best exemplified by **Truth or Consequences** in New Mexico. The name was transferred in 1950 from a radio programme as a result of certain inducements to the citizens, who voted on the matter.

While few transferred or linked place names come into being because of such specific advantages, most of them at least do so for positive reasons. It is hard to imagine a hated name being bestowed on a place, but this happened in Canada. The towns of **Luther** and **Melancthon** were named by a Roman Catholic surveyor because 'as it was the meanest tract of land he had ever surveyed he would name the country after the meanest men he ever heard of'.

Charles II also had vindictive intentions when he insisted on William Penn's name being linked to the suggested **Sylvania.** He knew perfectly well that **Pennsylvania** would greatly distress the modest Quaker, making him seem proud before his followers. Penn made desperate attempts to get the name changed, but perhaps it is as well that he did not succeed. Time has made the name a fine memorial, with the original unpleasant motive forgotten.

Mention of Penn brings number names to mind (for reasons which will become clear when we deal with street names). There is a group of such place names, and they show that such names can be as evocative as any other names. **Seventy-Six,** for instance, is a place in Kentucky which reminds everyone of the year of Independence. **Fortynine Creek** links the place with 1849, when wagon-trains poured through it. **Forty Fort** is a reminder of the number of settlers who built the stockade. In West Virginia the name **Hundred** arose because Henry Church and his wife both lived to be over 105 years old. **One Hundred and Two River**, in Missouri, translates the French name **Cent Deux,** but this probably represented a mis-heard Indian word that meant 'upland forest'.

Another group of North American place names are not quite what they seem to be. **Battiest, Loving, Kilts, Breedlove, Schoolcraft** and **Buncombe** are all perfectly straightforward transferred surnames from early settlers and the like, whatever else they might suggest. Similarly, **Otter Point** in British Columbia contains the surname 'Otter' rather than a direct reference to the animal. When a very unusual surname becomes a place name, however, later residents may adapt it in an effort to make sense of it. **Swearing Creek** in North Carolina is from the Swearington family, while **Due West** in a neighbouring State shows what can happen to a name like **De Witt.**

Folk-etymology can accidentally conceal a transferred name, but there can also be deliberate concealment at the time of naming. **Subligna** in Georgia is an attempt to translate the surname 'Underwood' into Latin, while **Irvona** in Pennsylvania vaguely Latinises the name 'Irvin'. A place **Neola** in West Virginia owes its name to **Olean** in New York, but the namer preferred to mix up the letters. Back-spellings are even commoner in the USA than anagrams, **Remlap** and **Remlig** being examples from Alabama and Texas.

Link place names

Place names which are blends of other names are links rather than transfers, but once again they usually conceal their origins. Parts of names may

She had been christened Bethany, after the town in Connecticut her mother had come from.

Thomas Tryon *Harvest Home*

'Georgia?' his mother said. 'Why in the world would a mother want to give her daughter such an outlandish name?'

'Georgia's named for a whole state.'

'How'd thee like to be called Ohio?' his mother said.

'Thee was born there.'

Jessamyn West *Except for Me and Thee*

be used, or parts of names coupled with other elements. The results look like **Clemretta, Texhoma, Ethanac, Fluvanna, Cresbard** and **Ninaview.** The various paths leading to such names include putting together parts of two cow names, Clementine and Henrietta, for a place in Canada; blending the state names Texas and Oklahoma because a town borders on both; using parts of Ethan A. Chase, the name of an early landowner; putting part of the Latin *fluvius*, 'river', next to Anna (a similar name being **Rivanna**); joining parts of two surnames, Cressey and Baird; adding a common element to the name Nina.

Incident place names

Another way of arriving at names that was known to our remote ancestors was description or conversion arising out of an incident. In the place names of the English-speaking world there are many that recall incidents connected with the places concerned. One of the best known is **Cannibal Plateau** in Colorado, where a certain Alfred Packer kept alive through the winter by eating the five companions he had killed. Other place names refer to a **Murder, Suicide, Earthquake** or **Battle.** An island called **Naked** supposedly received its name from a crazed Indian woman who was found wandering there, but the name may originally have referred to the lack of vegetation. One of the problems with names of this type is sorting out the genuine explanations from the later myths.

The names just mentioned were almost certainly given by early settlers, who were a hardy breed. Their rawness is aptly reflected in many other names they gave, which are among the most genuine on the map. Genteel residents who come later, however, are apt to change such names. Both Cook and Flinders, when they were sailing round the coast of Australia, were much influenced by incidents when they were giving names. Cook, for example, changed his mind about **Stingray Harbour**, a name he had just decided on, when the botanists who were sailing with him, including the famous Joseph Banks, came back to the ship in high excitement. They had found a great number of previously unknown plants. Cook thought of Botanists' Bay, and finally decided on **Botany Bay.** Banks himself was remembered by **Cape Banks,** and he was later to give his name to the genus of flowers that so excited him.

Flinders named **Cape Catastrophe** and **Memory Cove** after the loss of a boat and its crew. A meeting with a French ship, which might have led to a battle, caused him to name **Encounter Bay.** One entry in his log reads: '**Anxious Bay,** from the night we passed in it.' Incident names are all of this type, in fact—sudden glimpses into the diaries of the namers. They are the least formal of place names, recalling the intimacy of some nicknames. They are the names on the map which stir even the dullest imagination with their suggestion of real-life drama.

Some of the place names in Hawaii commemorate mythological incidents. *Puuenuhe*, for instance, literally means 'caterpillar hill', but the local story is of a legendary caterpillar who married a girl when he assumed human form. He fed his wife on his own food, sweet potato greens, and she wasted away. The caterpillar husband was then cut into pieces by Kane. The pieces became the caterpillars of today, which Hawaiians are careful not to injure.

Invented place names are unlikely to have such an effect. **Tono,** in Washington, was first connected with a railway, but no one can be sure what was in the namer's mind when he gave the name. One suggestion is that it is taken from 'ton of coal'. If so, it is not a particularly attractive part-conversion. **Sob Lake** in Canada has done rather better, especially when one thinks that it began as the phrase 'son of a bitch', used to describe a trapper who had a cabin there.

Another kind of converted place name is far less arbitrary, for it represents a deliberate attempt to supply a name of good omen. **Accord, Concord, Optima, Utopia** and **Paradise** are all found in several English-speaking countries. Oklahoma has a place name **Fame** which was intended to bring just that. Florida has a **Niceville**. This seemingly French blend is all American, for 'ville' was extremely popular as a place name element in America from the end of the 18th century. Even the German immigrants who lived in Pennsylvania liked it, and were not averse to creating place names such as **Kleinville** and **Schwenkville.** The suffix '-ville' is the truly American equivalent of '-ton', a distinctive element in settlement names. As for being French, it is said that there are more places in America which end in '-ville' than there are in France.

Indian place names

Each of the English-speaking countries has its own special kind of place names which help to add interest to a world gazetteer. The other typical American names are naturally those taken over from the Indians, though they may have changed their form somewhat. **Suckabone,** for example, represents an Algonquian *suc-e-bouk*, which meant a place in which either potatoes or groundnuts grew. **Minnehaha** is a Siouan name, 'waterfalls', and in this case it is the meaning rather than the form of the name which has been changed in the popular imagination. The '-haha' was assumed to mean 'laughing' for obvious but unfounded reasons, and Longfellow took it over as 'laughing waters'.

Other tribal languages that have led to American names include Choctaw — **Seyoyah Creek;** Potawatomi — **Shabbona;** Ojibway — **Sha-Bosh-Kung Bay;** Aleut — **Einahnuhto Hills;** Muskogean — **Egoniaga**; Athapascan — **Mentasta;** Iroquoian — **Sacandaga.** The variety of languages and corruption of the names often makes their interpretation difficult or impossible, but most Indian place names appear to be topographical descriptions or incident conversions.

Canada also has its Indian names, such as the rivers **Illecillewaet**, which apparently means 'swift water', and **Incomappleux**, 'fish'. Its French names are both important and distinctive. **Montreal** captures 'royal mountain' in an early form of French, the mountain being the extinct volcano on whose slopes the city stands. **Frontenac** is a form of **Frontignac,** a place in France which gave its name to the Duke of Frontenac, Governor of New France for twenty-seven years. It is said that he asked to be sent to North America in order to escape his shrewish wife.

Australia's Aboriginal place names are a fine heritage, and the national accent also seems to come through in names like **Bargo Brush, Bong Bong, Blue's Point, Broken Hill, Cobbity, Diggers' Rest, Gippsland, Kissing Point, The Paroo, Pretty Sally's, Violet Town** and **Yackandandah.** New Zealand is rightfully proud of its Maori names, many of which can be accurately translated. **Waimakiriri** is beautiful either in that form or as 'snow-cold water'. **Taupo Nui A Tia,** 'the big cloak of Tia', names the country's largest lake by poetic metaphor.

Wherever one looks, the place names of a country manage to individualise it in spite of the vast number of duplicated British names. Countless languages have contributed to the great reservoir of names, from the Polynesian **Hawaii,** 'place of the gods', to English, German and French, as in **Applebachsville.** New names continue to appear, some disappear, others are consciously changed.

The changes may be regrettable from an onlooker's point of view, but they are understandable. **Skull Creek** in Colorado is now **Blue Mountain,** for instance. The former name conjures up a vivid picture of early reality, the present one suggests a reproduction painting for a popular market, but this is no criticism of the people who made the change. Just as we admitted the need to change some surnames because of the image they create, so we must admit that some place names, in the ordinary run of daily life, give a false impression of a place and its inhabitants. It is the inhabitants who matter. The name of the place in which they live is, in a sense, their collective name, and they have a right to adjust it.

Some name changes manage to satisfy everyday

Some places have known multiple name-changes. *Babcock's Grove* was named in 1833 after its first settlers, but by 1834 it had become *DuPage Center*. In 1835 it changed again to *Stacy's Corner*, but in 1849 it emerged as *Newton's Station*. Two years later it was re-named *Danby*, only to become *Prospect Park* in 1882. Since 1889 it has been *Glen Ellyn*. *Portland*, Maine, was formerly *Machigonne, Indigreat, Elbow, The Neck, Casco* and *Falmouth*.

interests and those of the scholar at the same time. These are the old names that are restored after being out of use for a long time. **San Salvador** is a name of this kind, for though it was one of the first names given by Columbus when he arrived in the West Indies (it means 'holy saviour') the name did not survive. It was restored fifty years ago after careful research had established which island had been so named. Other changes satisfy everyone by being pleasant jokes. Local residents can enjoy the collective impression they give of being wits. The best example is the community in West Virginia that made a **Mountain** out of a **Mole Hill**.

We shall be looking in a later chapter at the further possibilities offered by place names for light-hearted games. We have already seen how some place names can take on very special meanings and pass into the ordinary language. For the moment we must remember that 'places' are often towns and cities which have a complex internal structure of neighbourhoods and streets. Naturally, all these have names, and it is to these names within place names that we will now turn.

When the meaning can be made out at all, the native Alaskan names are most commonly simple descriptives. Like other primitive peoples, also, the various tribes labored under no sense of obscenity. Thus Anaktuvuk Pass on the Arctic watershed is a narrow gap which forces the migrating herds of caribou to concentrate thickly. The name means something to the effect of 'dung-all-around-every-where'.

George R. Stewart *Names on the Land*

Some national names

Algeria Arabic 'the islands'. The name of the country was transferred from the name of Algiers, the city.
Argentina Latin 'silvery'.
Australia Latin 'southern (land)'.
Austria Latin 'eastern (land)'.
Bahrain Arabic 'two seas'.
Belgium Celtic 'brave, warlike'.
Bolivia based on the name of Simon Bolivar.
Brazil Portuguese 'heat'.
Burma Sanskrit 'strong ones'.
Cameroon Portuguese 'prawns', which were seen in the River Cameroon.
Canada Iroquois 'cabin'.
Chile Araucanian 'cold, winter', but not connected with the English word 'chilly'.
China from the Ch'in dynasty.
Colombia for Christopher Columbus.
Denmark Germanic 'territory of the Dane tribe'.
Dominican Republic Spanish 'holy Sunday'.
Ecuador Spanish 'equator'.
El Salvador Spanish 'the saviour'.
England 'Angles' land'. The Angles came from Germany.
Ethiopia Greek 'people with sunburnt faces'.
Finland Swedish 'land of the Finn tribe'.
France Germanic 'Franks, freemen'.
Germany Latin form of tribal name, possibly meaning 'strong hands'.
Greece possibly 'venerable people'.
Haiti Native word for 'mountainous'.
Honduras Spanish 'depths', ie of sea off the coast.
Hungary 'tribe who lived by River Ugra'.
Iceland 'Land of ice'.
India from name of River Indus.
Indonesia *India*+ Greek word for 'island'.
Iran Sanskrit 'worthy'.
Iraq Arabic 'shore, lowland'.
Ireland Erse 'western' or 'green'.
Israel Hebrew 'god Isra'.
Italy 'land of Vitali tribe'.
Ivory Coast for the ivory-trading that occurred.
Jamaica Arawak 'island of springs'.
Japan Chinese 'land of rising sun'.
Jordan from River Jordan.
Kuwait Arabic 'the enclosed' or 'little port'.
Lebanon Hebrew 'white mountain'.
Liberia Latin 'free'.
Malawi Chichewa 'flames'.
Malta Phoenician 'shelter, refuge'.
Mauritania Greek 'black-(skinned people)'.
Mexico Aztec 'moon-water', name of a lake.
Monaco Greek 'monk'.
Mongolia native word meaning 'brave ones'.
Netherlands 'low-lying lands'.
New Zealand 'new Zeeland' (Dutch province).
Niger from River Niger, 'flowing water'.
Nigeria same as *Niger*.
Norway Norse 'northern (sea)-way'.
Pakistan an acronym/blend from the Moslem states Punjab, Afghanistan, Kashmir, Iran and Baluchistan.
Paraguay from river name meaning 'water'.
Peru from River Biru.
Philippines for Philip II of Spain.
Poland Slavonic 'plain dwellers'.
Portugal Latin 'warm harbour', formerly Roman name for what is now Oporto.
Romania 'people from Rome'.
San Marino 'Saint Marinus', a 4th century Italian.
Saudi Arabia from the name of King Ibn-Saud.
Scotland 'Scots' land', the Scots possibly being 'wanderers'.
Sierra Leone Spanish 'lion mountains'.
Singapore Sanskrit 'lion town'.
Spain Carthaginian 'rabbit' or Basque 'shore'.
Sudan Arabic 'country of the black people'.
Sweden Swedish 'Svea kingdom'.
Switzerland from the canton name Schwyz.
Tanzania a blend of Tanganyika and Zanzibar, which united to form it in 1964.
Thailand native words 'country of the free'.
Trinidad Spanish 'Trinity'. Perhaps named on Trinity Sunday, or with reference to three peaks which Columbus saw from the sea.
Venezuela Spanish 'little Venice'.
Vietnam Annamese 'land of the south'.
Wales 'foreigners'.
Yemen Arabic 'right', ie on the right as one faces Mecca.
Yugoslavia Slavonic 'southern Slavs'.
Zambia from River Zambezi.

Names and nicknames of the American states

Alabama An Indian tribal name of unknown meaning, its form influenced by Spaniards. Also: 'Heart of Dixie', 'Cotton State', Yellowhammer State'.

Alaska An Aleutian word for 'mainland'. Also: 'The Last Frontier', 'Land of the Midnight Sun'.

Arizona Papago for 'place of the small spring'. Also: 'Grand Canyon State', 'Apache State'.

Arkansas An Indian tribal name, pronounced Arkansaw. The 's' was erroneously added by the French to make a plural. Also: 'Land of Opportunity', 'Wonder State', 'Bear State'.

California An invented name for an imaginary island. Cortés is said to have transferred the name to the state. Also: 'Golden State'.

Colorado Spanish 'reddish,' for the colour of the Colorado river. Also: 'Centennial State', because it was admitted to the Union a hundred years after the Declaration of Independence.

Connecticut Algonquian 'long river'. The second 'c' has never been pronounced. Also: 'Constitution State', 'Nutmeg State'—because of the alleged manufacture there of wooden nutmegs for export.

Delaware For Thomas West, Lord de la Warr (1577–1618). Also: 'First State', 'Diamond State'—ie a rich state.

Florida Spanish 'flowered, flowery', but also suggesting Easter, when the name was given. 'Sunshine State', 'Peninsula State'.

Georgia For George II. Also: 'Empire State of the South,' 'Peach State.'

Hawaii 'Place of the Gods' with particular reference to the volcanoes. Also: 'Aloha State', from the local word for 'love', used as both greeting and farewell.

Idaho An Apache name of uncertain meaning. Also: 'Gem State', 'Gem of the Mountains'.

Illinois Algonquian 'men, warriors'. Also: 'Prairie State'.

Indiana Latinised name in honour of Indian tribes. Also: 'Hoosier State'. Many anecdotes purport to explain the nickname, eg local habit of saying 'Who's yere?' when someone knocks on the door. Other explanations are equally ingenious and unreliable.

Iowa An Indian tribal name of uncertain meaning. Also: 'Hawkeye State'—for an Indian chief of this name.

Kansas Based on the name of an Indian tribe. Also: 'Sunflower State', 'Jayhawk State'—from a fictitious bird according to some, others say a corruption of 'the gay Yorker', applied to Colonel Jennison of New York, then to his soldiers.

Kentucky Iroquois 'meadow land'. Also: 'Bluegrass State'.

Louisiana For Louis XIV of France. Also: 'Pelican State', because of the pelican in its coat of arms; 'Creole State', 'Sugar State', 'Bayou State'.

Maine The word 'mainland', later altered by the French to conform with the name of a French province. Also: 'Pine Tree State'.

Maryland For Henrietta Maria, wife of Charles I. Also: 'Old Line State', because of the Old Maryland line of troops; 'Free State'.

Massachusetts Algonquian 'at the big hills'. Also: 'Bay State', 'Old Colony State'.

Michigan Algonquian 'big lake' or 'forest clearing'. Also: 'Wolverine State' because of the prairie wolves.

Minnesota Sioux 'cloudy water'. Also: 'North Star State', 'Gopher State'.

Mississippi Algonquian 'big river'. Also: 'Magnolia State'.

Missouri From an Algonquian name for the river, possibly meaning 'muddy'. Also: 'Show Me State', because of the local insistence on proof.

Montana Spanish 'mountainous'. Also: 'Treasure State'.

Nebraska Sioux 'flat water', referring to the River Platte. Also: 'Cornhusker State', 'Beef State', 'Tree Planter's State'.

Nevada Spanish 'snowed upon, snowy', with reference to the Sierra Nevada mountains. Also: 'Sagebrush State', 'Silver State', 'Battle Born State'.

New Hampshire Named by a settler, John Mason, who came from the English county of Hampshire. Also: 'Granite State'.

New Jersey Named by Sir George Carteret, who came from the Channel Island Jersey. Also: 'Garden State'.

New Mexico Named in the hope that the territory would prove to be as rich as Mexico. Also: 'Land of Enchantment', 'Sunshine State'.

New York For the Duke of York, brother of Charles II. Also: 'Empire State'.

North Carolina For Charles IX of France, then Charles I and Charles II of England. (A Latin feminine form of 'Charles'.) Also: 'Tar Heel State', from the tar industry;' Old North State'.

North Dakota An Indian tribal name of unknown meaning. Also: 'Sioux State', 'Flickertail State', for its squirrels.

Ohio Iroquoian 'beautiful river'. Also: 'Buckeye State', from the trees that grow there.

Oklahoma Choctaw 'red people'. Also: 'Sooner State', for the settlers who anticipated the official opening.

Oregon Possibly from a mis-reading of the river name, Wisconsin, spelt Ouaricon-sint on an 18th century map, with the last four letters on the next line. Also: 'Beaver State'.

Pennsylvania For William Penn, plus a Latin word meaning 'woodland'. Also: 'Keystone State', because its name appeared on the keystone of the bridge between Washington and Georgetown.

Rhode Island Likened to the Greek island of Rhodes. Also: 'Little Rhody'.

South Carolina Derivation as for *North Carolina*. Also: 'Palmetto State' because of the palmetto tree in the seal of the Commonwealth.

South Dakota Derivation as for *North Dakota*. Also: 'Coyote State', 'Sunshine State'.

Tennessee From a Cherokee river

name of unknown meaning. Also: 'Volunteer State'.

Texas Possibly the name of an Indian tribe, or an incident name arising from a misunderstanding of a greeting, meaning 'good friend'. Also: 'Lone Star State' because of the star in the centre of its flag.

Utah An Indian tribal name of unknown meaning. Also: 'Beehive State'.

Vermont Based on French words meaning 'green mountain'. Also: 'Green Mountain State'.

Virginia For Elizabeth I, the Virgin Queen. Also: 'The Old Dominion', 'Cavalier State'.

Washington For George Washington, first President of the USA. Also: 'Evergreen State', 'Chinook State'.

West Virginia Derivation as for *Virginia*. Also: 'Mountain State', 'Panhandle State', because of its shape.

Wisconsin Algonquian 'long river'. Also: 'Badger State', because miners are said to have made homes for themselves by burrowing into the ground.

Wyoming Algonquian 'broad plains'. Also: 'Equality State', with reference to the early acceptance of women's suffrage.

A selection of world place names explained

Amsterdam (Netherlands) 'dam on the River Amstel'.

Athens (Greece) after Athene 'queen of heaven', patron goddess.

Baghdad (Iraq) 'God's gift'.

Bermudas (Atlantic islands) after Juan Bermudez, the discoverer.

Belgrade (Yugoslavia) 'white city'.

Bombay (India) earlier Bombain, after Mumbain=goddess Mumbadevi.

Bonn (West Germany) 'town'.

Brisbane (Australia) after Sir Thomas Brisbane, the founder.

Brussels (Belgium) 'buildings on a marsh'.

Buenos Aires (Argentina) 'good winds', part of a title for Our Lady.

Cairo (Egypt) 'victorious', part of full Arabic name 'Mars the victorious', Mars being visible when city was founded.

Chattanooga (USA) 'rock rising to a point'.

Cologne (West Germany) Roman 'colony' of Claudia Agrippina.

Copenhagen (Denmark) 'merchants' harbour'.

Denver (USA) after General James Denver, former Governor.

Des Moines (USA) 'of the monks', probably by folk-etymology from an original Indian name.

Dover (England) 'waters'.

Dresden (East Germany) 'forest-dwellers'.

Edmonton (Canada) transferred from Edmonton, London='Eadhelm's estate'.

El Paso (USA) 'crossing, ford'.

Glasgow (Scotland) 'green hollow'.

Helsinki (Finland) 'Helsingi' was the name of the tribe living here.

Istanbul (Turkey) possibly Turkish corruption of Constantinople= 'Constantine's city'.

Jamaica (Caribbean island) 'island of springs'.

Liverpool (England) 'pool with clotted water'.

Los Angeles (USA) 'the angels', part of a title for Our Lady.

Madrid (Spain) 'timber'.

Manitoba (Canada) 'great spirit' or 'prairie lake'.

Marseilles (France) for the Massili tribe.

Melbourne (Australia) for Lord Melbourne, British Prime Minister.

Memphis (USA) transferred from ancient Egyptian city.

Miami (USA) 'peninsula-dwellers'.

Minneapolis (USA) a blend of 'Minne-' from Minnesota+Greek *polis*, 'city'.

Moscow (USSR) from River Moskva.

Munich (West Germany) 'monk', because city founded on site of monastery.

Naples (Italy) 'new town'.

Ontario (Canada) 'beautiful (lake)'.

Oslo (Norway) 'mouth of River Lo' or 'forest clearing'.

Ottawa (Canada) 'big river' or 'traders'.

Peking (China) 'northern capital'.

Pittsburgh (USA) for William Pitt, the English statesman.

Quebec (Canada) 'place where the river narrows'.

Rome (Italy) from River Ruma.

Seville (Spain) 'lower land'.

Shanghai (China) 'on the sea'.

Sheffield (England) 'open land by the River Sheaf'.

Tokyo (Japan) 'eastern capital'.

Trinidad (West Indies) 'Trinity'.

Vienna (Austria) from River Vienna.

Wellington (New Zealand) after the Duke of Wellington.

Winnipeg (Canada), 'muddy water'.

Yukon (Canada) from River Yukon 'big river'.

10 Neighbourly names

The name of the street in which we live can take on a deep personal significance. It can evoke an area that we know in detail and a small community of people whom we know well. Another street name that we have known in the past might instantly recall our childhood and a thousand small incidents, reminding us of friends and neighbours and the passing years.

Street names can have this private meaning, but they are also felt to have a more public meaning. As with place names, street names reflect on the people who live in the streets concerned, particularly on their social status. Few people, therefore, care to live in **Thieves Lane,** say, or **Cowdung Street,** though such names almost certainly indicate that the street has been there since the Middle Ages. For that matter, few people, it seems, care to live in a street that is actually called a street.

'Street'

This curious fact has impressed itself on estate-developers everywhere. A few years ago an estate agent complained in a British newspaper: 'Streets have gone out of fashion and no one wants to live in one. You can call them roads, avenues, lanes, groves, drives, closes, places—anything but streets.' It was about this time that a builder was complaining of customers who were cancelling orders for new houses. They had learned that the street in which they stood was going to be referred to as a 'street' in its name.

As it happens, there are plenty of euphemisms available nowadays. They have a certain interest in themselves, and I have listed them as street name elements on pages 135–6. But this sensitivity to the generic word in a street name is a sure indication that residents will look very closely indeed at the element attached to it to see whether that reflects on their status. The result is a steady flow of applications to local councils asking to change existing names to something that 'sounds better'. Sometimes the local authority itself quietly 'loses' certain names in the cause of respectability.

What sort of name disappears? A few that have disappeared from London include **Foul Lane, Stinking Lane, Hog Lane, Bladder Street, Grub Street** and **Pudding Lane.** Of these, 'foul' and 'stinking' were accurate descriptions no doubt in medieval times, while hogs and bladders would have been sold in the streets concerned. 'Puddings' were the entrails of animals which were carried along Pudding Lane to be dumped in the Thames. Grub Street probably included the name of an early resident, though a reference to caterpillars or worms is just possible. The street may have been infested with them.

Grub Street is now **Milton Street,** which shows an especially interesting change. The original name had come to be associated with low-quality writing because of the hack-writers who lived there in the 17th century. In the 19th century the residents deliberately decided to use the name of the poet in an attempt to raise the street's status.

The loss of Foul Lane and the like for general purposes is inevitable, though such names are carefully examined by the historian. Like obsolete surnames and place names they can help to paint an accurate picture of medieval life. Non-historians are quite happy for the names to be in records of the past, but they do not want to see them displayed on the street corner. They are also not fond of names like **Foundry Street,** which blatantly implies that manual work goes on in the district.

A similar kind of reaction to street names is discernible in the United States. Estate agents know that a suburban house will be easier to sell if the street name contains an element suggestive of rural peace, such as 'Hayloft' or 'Corncrib'. Streets laid out in strict geometric patterns are no longer

Among the Liverpool docks occur the names of the King's and Queen's. At the time, they often reminded me of the two principal streets in the village I came from in America, which streets once rejoiced in the same royal appellations. But they had been christened previous to the Declaration of Independence; and some years after, in a fever of freedom, they were abolished, at an enthusiastic town-meeting, where King George and his lady were solemnly declared unworthy of being immortalised by the village of L-.

Herman Melville *Redburn*

popular, nor are the efficient number names that went with them. **Seventh Avenue** may be easier to find than **Rosemont Drive,** but there is actually prestige to be gained these days in being difficult to find.

Number names for streets

Such names, however, are thoroughly established both in the USA and Canada. They owe their existence, primarily, to William Penn, who was far from being the non-literary person such names might suggest. He was a classical scholar who used a Greek name for the city he founded in 1682—**Philadelphia,** 'brotherly love'. Had he wanted to he could certainly have suggested similar names for the streets.

When Penn came to Philadelphia many houses had already been built. People were referring to the existing streets by the name of the most important person living there. But Penn was founding a Quaker colony, and the last thing he could allow was a street name system that raised some people above others. Like all Quakers he objected strongly to any social custom that emphasised different ranks of people. He had deeply offended his father, for instance, by refusing to take off his hat in his presence.

The Quakers referred even to Sunday as **First Day,** thus removing the pagan reference, and this may have inspired Penn to use a similar system to identify the streets of his city. These were not the haphazard sprawl of a typical English town, but were laid out at right angles to one another at regular intervals. Penn began at the eastern boundary with **First Street** and continued with his simple sequential names from there. For the streets which crossed from north to south he decided on verbal names, but once again he was careful to avoid links with people. He turned to nature and 'the things that spontaneously grow in the country'. **Chestnut Street, Walnut Street, Spruce Street, Pine Street** and the like were created. For a road that faced the river Penn wrote of **Front Street,** and he allowed the use of such names as **Market Street.**

Whether there was a general appreciation of the high principles which had led to the Philadelphian street name system, or whether the practicality of at least having a system of some kind made its appeal, we shall never know, but other towns quickly followed suit. Not only were the number names transferred elsewhere—often the tree names were borrowed, too, regardless of whether the trees concerned grew in the area. Yet with all its apparent simplicity, the number name system posed problems for the towns that adopted it in Ohio, Kentucky, Louisiana, Virginia, Tennessee and elsewhere. Where was First Street to be, for example, and would it remain First Street?

The Quaker William *Penn* was strongly opposed to the practice of naming streets after people. The number names and nature names he used in Philadelphia were much copied by other cities, but the general fondness for commemorating people in street names remained. Perhaps the best proof of this is the fact that by the beginning of the 20th century, over a hundred streets and avenues in various US cities were named after Penn himself.

St Joseph had a **First Street, Second Street** and **Third Street** at one time, but the land caved into the river and left **Fourth Street** to begin the sequence. A more frequent occurrence was for towns to develop later beyond the original boundary, causing no problems at the open end of the number

The Street Directory of the Principal Cities of the United States (1908 edition, republished by Gale Research Co. in 1973) reveals the curious fact that there are many more *Second Avenues* in the US than there are *First Avenues*. It also shows that New York has more numbered streets than any other city, the system continuing to *262nd Street*.

Streets which were laid down after number names had already been allocated, caused many *½ streets* to come into being. Apart from the ½ Street in Washington, DC and Wabash, Indiana, many cities have *1½ Street, 2½ Street, 3½ Street*, etc. In Moline, Illinois, is *15¾ Street*.

sequence but considerable problems at the beginning. Number names were always interpreted as being sequential in space, not time, and an **Eighty-seventh Street** could not be placed out of order on the basis that it merely recorded that eighty-six streets had been built previously. The usual solution was for suburban streets to take on verbal names and remain outside the general system.

When Washington was laid out at the beginning of the 19th century the street names included the usual number names in one direction. Letter names were introduced, however, for the streets that crossed them, and important streets, called 'avenues' for the first time, were linked to the names of states. **A Street, B Street** and the like did not appeal to other city-planners, but some copied the idea of using the names of the states. What really caught on everywhere was the use of 'avenue', though even this may have been influenced as much by New York as Washington. A few years later, when New York was extended, the ultimate in street name systems was devised. The **First Street, Second Street,** etc, from Philadelphia were there, but crossing them were **First Avenue, Second Avenue** and so on. A few streets that lay outside the grid became **Avenue A, Avenue B, C** and **D**. There were also occasional survivals of established street names, such as the Dutch **De Bouwerij,** 'the farm', in its anglicised form **The Bowery,** and **Breede Wegh,** which easily became **Broadway.** These were mostly streets which ran diagonally and thus cut across the basic grid pattern.

New York's system would no doubt have been widely followed, but it came late in the day. One other city that influenced American street names because it gave an example from an early date was Boston. Here one cannot talk of a system unless one calls it the English non-system. All streets were named, either by description as in **Commercial Street,** by conversion, as in **Congress Street,** after national and local figures, or from the places the streets led to. Other towns followed Boston's example, or the English example as it may have been in many cases, if local usage established street names before the City Fathers turned their minds to the matter. Occasionally there must have been a deliberate rejection of number names, the reason for their use not being known or respected. There must also have been occasions when the people who were in a position to influence street names already had their own family names linked to them. In such cases they would obviously have been tempted to allow them to remain undisturbed.

Medieval street names

Britain had no William Penn who could start a national street name fashion with a single flash of original thinking, and there were not, of course, cities to be founded in the same way. Towns and cities had been growing naturally for centuries, and the streets within them acquired the same kind of naturally descriptive names as the places themselves had done. The principal street in medieval times was the **High Street** in Southern England, **High Gate** in the North. 'Street' had been borrowed from Latin in Anglo-Saxon times to describe the Roman roads which were far superior to anything previously known in Britain. The Northern 'gate' was not the kind of gate one opens and shuts but the Old Norse *gata*, 'street'. The ordinary 'gate' also occurred in medieval street names to indicate the entrance to a walled town or the presence of a water-gate.

The name 'High Street' was taken at first to the New World, but 'high' tended to be interpreted as 'elevated' rather than 'important'. In most cases **Main Street** came to replace it. 'Main' is also used in Britain, but usually in connection with a road rather than a street. The original distinction between a 'road', which was an unmade way along which horses were ridden, and a paved 'street' lasted until at least the end of the Middle Ages. 'A main road' tends to be a descriptive phrase rather than a name.

Early English street names commented on their relative positions, as in **North Street,** etc, **Upper Street** and **Nether** ('lower') **Street;** on their surfaces, as in **Chiswell** ('pebble') **Street** and perhaps **Featherbed Lane,** a reference to soft mud. **Summer Road** in Thames Ditton would have been **Summer Lane** or **Summer Street** in medieval times, but the meaning would have been the same—a road which was unusable in winter. Other old names were of the type **Bollo Lane,** where a 'bull hollow' is referred to, and **Woodgate,** a road along which wood was transported. Commodities sold in the streets often gave those streets their names, the usual items being salt, pepper, milk, fish and bread.

There were formerly several **Love Lanes** in London, and as in any city these also referred to something being sold rather than a romantic lovers' walk. In his *London Lanes* Alan Stapleton suggests humorously that **Huggin Lane,** which was near a Love Lane, might be connected with it and not derive its name from an early resident called Huggin or from the sale of hogs. In several towns there is a **Grope** or **Grape Lane,** which really is a synonym for Love Lane. One writer has explained the name as 'a dark, narrow alley through which one groped one's way', but the full medieval forms of the name make it quite clear that another meaning was intended.

Other common street names in medieval times mentioned where the street led, including either a place name or a generic term such as 'ferry' or 'castle'. **Gallows Street** survives in some places as a reminder of the grim realities of earlier times, but **Dead Lane,** which has usually been 'lost' as a street name, was a simple reference to a cemetery. The residents of a street were often described in its name, as with **Lombard Street** and **Walker Lane,** the latter being where the walkers, who processed cloth, lived and worked.

These medieval street names throughout Britain have obviously received attention from historical students of place names. They often supply much incidental information about medieval urban life. But relatively few of the names survive in living use. They were bestowed casually by people who always called a spade a spade, and they were doomed when the guardians of public morality began to appoint themselves in the 19th century.

In at least two American cities it is possible to live on *Easy Street* (Boston, Mass and Johnstown, Pa). Three cities have a tongue-twisting *Treat Street*. Of the streets which have Christian names attached to them, *John Street* is the most popular, followed by *Elizabeth Street* and *Mary Street*. I am unable to confirm the report that somewhere in California, because of a prominent member of the Chinese community, there is a *Wong Way*.

London street names

The street names of London, like those of several other European capital cities, have received a great deal of attention. By 'London' the City of London is primarily meant, but several dictionaries have included some of the main suburbs. All writers on the subject begin with a reading of Stow's *Survey of London,* which was first published in 1598. Stow himself knew 16th-century London well, and he was also a student of early records. This showed him that many street names had already changed their form. **Belliter Lane,** for instance, had earlier been **Belzettars Lane,** which indicated more clearly its connection with the bell-makers. There was a large group of such men, for the bells in the many London churches were much used. The lane still exists as **Billiter Street.**

Snow Hill! What kind of place can the quiet town's-people who see the words emblazoned on the north-country coaches, take Snow Hill to be? All people have some undefined and shadowy notion of a place whose name is frequently before their eyes, or often in their ears, and what a vast number of random ideas there must be perpetually floating about, regarding this same Snow Hill. The name is such a good one.

Charles Dickens *Nicholas Nickleby*

The first actual street name dictionary for London, however, appears to have been *London Street Names,* by F. H. Habben. This was published in 1896, so that it had to rely mainly on Stow. In his introductory remarks Habben states sensibly that

In London it is still possible to visit *Bleeding Heart Yard*, though the name is perhaps more interesting than the place. Charles Dickens was attracted to it and featured it in *Little Dorrit:*

The opinion of the Yard was divided respecting the derivation of its name. The more practical of its inmates abided by the tradition of a murder; the gentler and more imaginative inhabitants, including the whole of the tender sex, were loyal to the legend of a young lady of former times closely imprisoned in her chamber by a cruel father for remaining true to her own true love, and refusing to marry the suitor he chose for her. The legend related how the young lady used to be seen up at her window behind the bars, murmuring a love-lorn song of which the burden was, 'Bleeding Heart, Bleeding Heart, bleeding away,' until she died.

Neither party would listen to the antiquaries who delivered learned lectures in the neighbourhood, showing the Bleeding Heart to have been the heraldic cognisance of the old family to whom the property had once belonged. And considering that the hour-glass they turned from year to year was filled with the earthiest and coarsest sand, the Bleeding Heart Yarders had reason enough for objecting to be despoiled of the one little golden grain of poetry that sparkled in it.

Dickens does not mention an even commoner legend concerning Lady Hatton, who sold her soul to the devil. At one time London children knew that as the devil bore her off he dropped her shoe in *Shoe Lane*, her cloak in *Cloak Lane*. Her bleeding heart was found in Bleeding Heart Yard.

As for the truth of the matter, the name certainly derives from an inn sign. There was one which showed the heart of the Virgin Mary pierced with arrows, for instance. The inn sign could also have shown a bleeding 'hart', or male deer. Heraldic experts have been unable to trace a family coat of arms which contains a bleeding heart.

There are perhaps some who will prefer, like the Dickens' characters, to stay with the legends and forget the dullness of reality. As with the explanations of so many romantic names, truth is unfortunately *not* stranger than fiction.

---

names cannot usually be dismissed with a curt etymological sentence and nothing more'. He talks of the 'facts or circumstances round about the name' which need to be given, and he gives them himself.

Nothing is known of Habben, but his frequent quotations of Chaucer, Milton, Longfellow and other poets, and his willingness to guess at an Old Norse personal name origin for names like **Snow Hill** makes one think that the 'B.A.' mentioned on the title-page was probably a degree in English.

Louis Zettersten's *City Street Names* was published in 1917, but the author does not seem to have been aware of Habben's *Dictionary*. Zettersten was a Swedish businessman who worked in London, and once again he was obliged to accept the explanations of Stow and one or two others as facts. His great strength, however, was to produce an attractive little dictionary that could easily be read by a layman, and there seem to be very few instances where he would seriously mislead his readers. In his article on **Fleet Street,** for instance, he says that the name derives from a bridge over the River Fleet rather than the river itself, a comment based on a 13th-century reference to *vicus de Fletebrigge*. As it happens, later writers have unearthed a still earlier reference which would make the explanation 'street leading to the Fleet River', but this is hair-splitting. When a real problem occurs, as it definitely does with the **Snow Hill** (earlier **Snore Hill**) already mentioned, Zettersten makes it clear that there is a problem and that suggestions as to the original meaning can only be tentatively made.

In many ways Zettersten's little book is more satisfying than that of his compatriot, Eilert Ekwall, who published *Street Names of the City of London* in 1954. Ekwall is a pure philologist of the highest quality writing for other specialists, and for him a street name's origin is all that matters. Subsequent associations of a street, which may have given it a meaning that is recognised throughout the world, are totally ignored. He does not mention journalism, for example, when he deals with Fleet Street. He says quite clearly that he is interested only in names 'which go back to medieval times', and could have added that his interest even in those names is highly restricted.

The point perhaps needs stressing for Ekwall, as the heavyweight scholar, has tended to overshadow Zettersten, the intelligent amateur, and others like him. The amateurs respond instinctively to street names and see them as meaningful wholes rather than linguistic specimens under a microscope. I believe very firmly that the 'amateur' approach is the right one, the linguistic facts forming only a part of the whole story.

In between Zettersten and Ekwall several other studies of London street names appeared. These were mostly imitative of the earlier works, but in 1935 E. Stewart Fay published *Why Piccadilly?* in which he abandoned the dictionary style in favour of a discursive work. He begins by writing of **Piccadilly** for three pages, attributing it to the 'pickadills', or ruffed lace collars, made by the tailor Robert Baker in the 17th century. Baker made enough money from these highly fashionable articles to buy a house, which others quickly named **Pickadilly Hall.** The name eventually spread to the area, and has survived several official attempts at various times to change it.

Stewart Fay states his view of street names immediately after the Piccadilly explanation. For him the names lead directly to human anecdotes, the

> 'hundreds of such stories hid behind the often prosaic names of London streets, squares and localities. To search these out is to lay bare a cross-section of the pageant of London from the earliest times down to the living present ... **Spring Gardens** will inform us of a royal practical joke. **Hatton Gardens** conceals a scandal concerning the frailty of Elizabeth...'.

He gives further examples designed to whet the appetite, and it is difficult not to read on. The 'royal joke' he refers to was a sundial which stood in **Spring Gardens.** It had a concealed spring tap nearby on which people stepped when they went to look at the dial. A jet of water would then spurt out and soak them. In spite of this, Spring Gardens is far more likely to have got its name because of the 'spring' of young trees formerly planted there, but who would sacrifice the anecdote? The **Hatton Gardens** story is made into a playlet by Stewart Fay and is rather overwritten, but the essential facts about Elizabeth I and her 'dancing Chancellor' are given. Sir Christopher Hatton danced his way into the Queen's favour, then persuaded her to let him take over most of the Bishop of Ely's house and gardens. Hatton gave his name to the gardens, and later—in rebus form—to a nearby public house, the **Hat and Tun.**

The style of *Why Piccadilly?* is often successful and is a good example of an imaginative writer's approach to names. Although no philologist the author is generally able to sort out fact and fiction in the works he has consulted. On **Snow Hill,** which is always something of a test case, he mentions the story of stage-coach passengers snoring by the time they arrived at the Saracen's Head public house only in order to dismiss it. For a man who was clearly deeply fascinated by names, he also has many sensible things to say about American number names for streets. After praising the functional advantages of the New York system he goes on to say that number names can take on a meaning and value like any other names. Names do not have, he reminds us, 'an inherent stamp of quality; their reputation is derived solely from the nature of their associations'. He gives the example of **Mayfair,** which was notorious at the beginning of the 18th century because of the riotous celebrations which took place at the beginning of May each year but which later changed its meaning completely.

Stewart Fay's discursive method was partly emulated in 1952 by Hector Bolitho and Derek Peel in *Without The City Wall.* Their sub-title refers to 'an adventure in London street names, north of the river', and their aim is to take the reader on a series of excursions—which are mapped out—explaining the names encountered. It is an interesting idea, and shows yet another approach to street names. These authors too make it clear that they are not scholars, but they have gone to respectable

Of all the streets that have been named after famous men, I know but one whose namesake is suggested by it. In Regent Street you sometimes think of the Regent; and that is not because the street is named after him, but because it was conceived by him, and was designed and built under his auspices, and is redolent of his character and time. From this redolence I deduce that when a national hero is to be commemorated by a street we should ask him to design the street himself. Assuredly, the mere plastering-up of his name is no mnemonic.

Sir Max Beerbohm *The Naming of Streets*

In streets, the names of which are matters of history, I should like to see a simple inscription, in full view, within the range of all mental capacities, recording the memorable events or public services connected with the memory of the illustrious man named, or enumerating his literary labours, if an author. Nothing beyond bare facts should be admitted into these inscriptions; and no inscription should be awarded to a man during his lifetime, or to a prince whose dynasty has not expired, so that flattery might not be substituted for history.

Eusebius Salverte *History of the Names of Men, Nations and Places*

sources of information and then applied their own common sense. Wherever possible they checked 'facts' in their own way, so when told that **Chiswell Street** took its name from Old English *ceosel*, 'gravel', they telephoned the Borough Engineer to ask about the geological strata in that area. He confirmed that there were large deposits of flint and gravel there.

And still books on London street names appear. A London taxi-driver, Al Smith, brought out his *Dictionary of City of London Street Names* in 1970. It is a personal selection of historical material gathered from standard sources. Gillian Bebbington's *London Street Names* appeared in 1972. It covers a wider area than previous dictionaries and makes a further useful contribution by displaying the family trees of important landowners. For general reference purposes it is probably the best dictionary of its kind. It has nevertheless been succeeded by *London Street Names*, 1977, by John Wittich and *The Streets of London*, 1983, by S. Fairfield.

Johannesburg street names

An interesting contrast to London street names is provided by those of Johannesburg. They have been carefully studied by Anna H. Smith, whose monumental *Johannesburg Street Names* was published in 1971. At that time the city was still only eighty-five years old, and it might be thought that in such a case there are no difficulties for the researcher. These names were given, however, by a large number of early landowners and surveyors, who usually kept no records of why the names had been chosen. Naming was not taken very seriously, and sometimes the draughtsmen preparing maps were left to select names. They usually made them as short as possible for their own convenience.

Miss Smith omits number names from her dictionary as being self-explanatory, but mentions in her Introduction that there are 'forty or so **First Avenues, Lanes, Roads** or **Streets** in Johannesburg'. This reflects, presumably, the parallel development of different areas by early pioneers. There was certainly no attempt made to evolve an over-all street name system, though the City Council now tries to exercise control.

As with most towns in Britain, a wide variety of people are commemorated in Johannesburg street names. There they include entertainers, admirals, artists, authors, sportsmen, prominent city residents—including landowners, musicians, kings and queens, scientists and inventors, prominent persons in South African history, surveyors and government officials. Street names that link with first names—usually those of women—were often meant to honour the relations of the namers. Place

It was a place of pleasant sounding old names, richly English, and romantic. The names of the streets fascinated Christopher: Green End, Lombard Street, Baileygate, Golden Hill, The Tything, Market Row, Vine Court, Barbican, Angel Alley.

Warwick Deeping *Sorrell and Son*

names are usually meant to be reminders of the pioneers' home-towns. One pioneer, at least, must have come from very close to where this book is being written, for he named an **Esher Street** and **Surbiton, Kingston, Hampton, Molesey** and **Ditton Avenues**, all of which places are within a mile or two of my house.

Other names linked to the street names include those of battles, churches, companies, farms, hotels, mines, mountains, mythological figures, rivers, saints and ships. Transferred names from ships show particularly well the dangers that lie in wait for a researcher less thorough than Miss Smith. **London Street, Suffolk Road, Dunrobin Street, Ivanhoe Street, Mars Street** and **Zebra Street** are names that one would naturally be inclined to explain as being other than ship names, which they happen to be. It is never possible to take a name purely at its face value. Even **Winning Way** turns out to be named after a Mr Winning.

Other street name dictionaries

In a more modest way, there is great scope for local historians and others to compile street name dictionaries in their own areas. An excellent method is to make use of the local newspaper, publishing a series of articles street by street giving the facts so far known. Earlier forms of older names are vital, and with more modern names it is essential to know when the names were given. Local residents will usually respond by giving further information which can be included when the material is published later in more permanent form.

The earliest example I have seen of such articles, leading to a discursive work in this case rather than a dictionary, is *Greenock Street Names*, by Gardner Blair. This was published by the *Greenock Herald* itself in 1907. A more recent example is *Warrington and the Mid-Mersey Valley* by G. A. Carter. Several newspapers are currently publishing articles about local street names. The *Winnipeg Tribune*, for example, has a long-running series written by Vince Leah. It is quite clear that readers of the *Tribune* enjoy having their memories stimulated by such articles.

Local historians working independently have produced very satisfying street name dictionaries for places like Lewes, Bristol, Watford, Stevenage, Acton and Shrewsbury. Articles on the street names of other areas have appeared from time to time in specialised magazines. In the *Maryland Historical Magazine* for June, 1948, for example, is an article by Douglas H. Gordon, *Hero Worship As Expressed in Baltimore Street Names*. Similar topics have been discussed in *Names*, the journal of the American Name Society. Public libraries often have a collection of index cards on which street name information is given, but in other areas the basic research has still to be done.

I have no doubt that it is worth doing. Sir Max Beerbohm once wrote that every street had its character, like individual human beings, and that he was affected by that character when he walked there. In older towns and cities especially, the names of the streets have character, and they are well worth investigating.

Minto Square, Great Clive Street, Warren Street, Hastings Street, Ochterlony Place, Plassy Square, Assaye Terrace ('Gardens' was a felicitous word not applied to stucco houses with asphalt terraces in front, so early as 1827).

William Thackeray *Vanity Fair*

A street by any other name

Many of the following words occur in street names as substitutes for the word 'street' itself. In some cases the original meanings of the words have been considerably stretched, but others are genuine synonyms.

Acre(s)
Alley
Approach
Arcade also used of an avenue of trees forming an arch.
Archway
Ascent
Avenue
Backs behind buildings.
Bank a raised shelf or ridge of land.
Bend
Billet
Bluff
Bottom land in a valley.
Boulevard
Broadway
Bullring
Butts usually transferred from a field name where it referred to land at the boundary of the field, or land covered with tree-stumps.
By-Pass
Carfax from Latin *quadrifurcus*, 'four-forked', used where four or more roads meet.
Causeway raised way across a marsh or a paved way.
Centre
Chase originally unenclosed land reserved for hunting.
Circle
Circus where there is a circular ring of houses.
Cliff
Close an entry or passage.
Common(s) common land.
Coombe a small valley.
Coppice plantation of young trees.
Copse=coppice.
Corner
Cottages
Court
Covert
Cranny a narrow opening.
Crescent
Croft an enclosed field.
Cross for a cross-roads.
Cut where an excavation has been made to allow road to pass.
Cutting=cut.
Dale a valley.
Dell
Dene (also *Dean*) a wooded valley.
Drang (dialectal) an alley.
Drift a track.
Drive
Droke (dialectal) a narrow passage.
Drove a road along which cattle was driven.
Embankment
End
Esplanade=promenade.
Estate
Expressway (USA)
Extension (USA)
Fair on former fair-ground.
Farrow a path.
Fennell (dialectal) an alley.
Field(s)
Flyover
Fold
Freeway
Front
Furlong
Gardens
Garth (dialectal) an enclosure.
Gate Old Norse *gata*, 'road'.
Ginnel (dialectal) narrow passage.
Glade
Glebe land assigned to a clergyman.
Glen
Green
Ground
Grove
Gully
Hangings a steep slope on a hill.
Harbour
Hard a sloping roadway or jetty.
Hatch fenced land.
Hays
Hey fenced land.
Highway
Hill(s)
Hollow
Houses
Hundreds
Jigger (dialectal) an alley.
Jitty (dialectal) an alley.
Knoll
Lane
Lawn='laund', a stretch of untilled ground.
Lea untilled land.
Line (USA)
Link
Loke (dialectal) an alley.
Main
Mall where pall mall, a game with mallet and ball, was played.
Marina
Market
Mead=meadow
Meadow(s)
Mews stables.
Midway (USA)
Mile
Moat
Motorway
Mount
Narrows
Nook
Ope an opening.
Orchard
Oval
Paddock
Pantiles properly roofing-tiles but sometimes used to describe paving-tiles.
Parade
Park
Parkway
Pass
Passage
Pastures
Path(way)
Pavement a roadway in USA.
Pickle a small enclosure.
Piece
Pightle=pickle.
Pike
Pines
Place
Plain
Plaisance (USA) a pleasure-ground.
Plaza (USA) Spanish, 'market-place'.
Pleasaunce
Poultry a poultry market.

Promenade
Prospect a place affording a view.
Quadrant a square.
Quay
Range
Retreat a secluded place.
Ride
Ridge
Riding(s)
Ring
Rise
Road
Roundabout
Row
Rue (USA)
Scarp the steep face of a hill.
Side
Skyway (USA)
Slip
Slope
Slype a covered way, especially one leading from the cloisters of a cathedral.
Sneck (dialectal) a narrow passage.
Sneckett=sneck
Snicket=sneck
Square
Steps
Strand
Sward
Sweep
Terrace
Thoroughfare 'thorough' is an old form of 'through'.
Throughway
Tollway (USA)
Turn
Turnpike a toll-gate.
Twitchel (dialectal) a narrow passage.
Twitchet=twitchel.
Twitten=twitchel.
Twitting=twitchel.
Tyning land enclosed with a fence.
Usage a public right of way.
Vale
Valley
Viaduct
View
Villas
Walk
Wall a footpath next to a wall.
Way(e)
Wharf
Wood
Wynd (dialectal) a narrow street.
Yard

A selection of London street names

Adelphi Terrace from the group of buildings The Adelphi (Greek *adelphoi*, 'brothers') designed by the Adam brothers.
Aldwych possibly 'old wick' or settlement.
Baker Street after William Baker, once controller of the Marylebone estate. Sherlock Holmes lived at 221B according to Conan Doyle.
Barbican a word brought back from the Crusades. An outer defensive wall and watch-tower.
Bayswater Road Bayard's (or Baynard's) watering-place.
Belsize Square from the manor of Belassis, 'beautifully situated'.
Berkeley Square where the nightingale sang. Baron Berkeley had a house there.
Bevis Marks earlier Beris Marks. Land within the marks 'boundaries' of the Abbots of Bury.
Birdcage Walk where Charles II kept birdcages.
Blackfriars Road for the Dominicans who settled there.
Bow Street the famous police court is in this street shaped like a bow.
Cannon Street formerly the street where the candle-makers lived.
Carmelite Street the friars of Our Lady of Mount Carmel, or 'Whitefriars' lived there.
Carnaby Street famous in the 1960s as a fashion centre. From Carnaby in Yorkshire (?).
Charing Cross Road 'Charing' refers to a turning of the Thames; the cross commemorated Queen Eleanor, whose funeral procession passed this way.
Clerkenwell Road a well where parish clerks gathered annually.
Cockspur Street in the days of cockfighting the cocks wore spurs, which were sold in this street.
Cornhill a hill where corn was grown.
Dean Street for the Dean of the Royal Chapel.
Downing Street the official residence of the Prime Minister. Sir George Downing, an unpopular diplomat, was an early leaseholder.
Farringdon Street from the surname of an early Sheriff of London.
Gower Street for the first Earl Gower.
Gracechurch Street the church was St Benet's; 'grace' was formerly grass, perhaps with reference to a turf roof, or to a fodder market.
Gray's Inn Road The inn was a hostel for law students owned by the Grey family.
Great Windmill Street a windmill was there in the 17th century.
Grosvenor Square otherwise 'Little America' because of the Embassy, etc, was owned by the Grosvenor family.
Hanover Square honoured George I, son of the Elector of Hanover.
Harley Street famous as a gathering-place for the élite of the medical profession, is on an estate owned by the Harley family.
Haymarket was a hay market.
High Holborn from the bourne ('stream') in the hollow.
Kingsway for Edward VII.
Leadenhall Street for a hall that had a leaden roof.
Liverpool Street in honour of Lord Liverpool.
Marylebone High Road the church St Mary Bourne, the 'bourne' being the Tyburn stream. Later thought to be *Mary la Bonne*.
Middlesex Street the official name that is rightfully ignored by every Londoner, who knows that petticoat-makers who worked here in the 17th century caused the street to become Petticoat Lane.

Moorgate a gate led to the moor, 'marshy wasteland', outside the north wall of the City.

Old Bailey often used as a synonym for the Central Criminal Court which is situated there. The bailey was once a mud rampart just outside the city wall.

Old Bond Street after Sir Thomas Bond, who owned the land.

Oxford Street formerly **Tyburn Way,** leads to Oxford but was named after Edward Harley, second Earl of Oxford, the landowner.

Park Lane runs beside **Hyde Park,** once a 'hide' or measure of land.

Pentonville Road was owned by Henry Penton.

Petticoat Lane see *Middlesex Street.*

Piccadilly see page 123.

Portland Street the Dukes of Portland owned land here.

Portobello Road to commemorate the capture of Porto Bello in the Gulf of Mexico, 1739.

Praed Street after the banker William Praed.

Procter Street after a former inhabitant, Bryan Procter, solicitor and poet.

Regent Street after the Prince Regent, later George IV, and meant to link Carlton House and Regent's Park.

Rosebery Avenue the fifth Lord Rosebery was the first Chairman of the London County Council, and this street was named after him.

Russell Square owned by the Russell family, Dukes of Bedford.

St Giles High Street a leper colony was established here in medieval times, the hospital and church being dedicated to St Giles.

St James Street from a hospital dedicated to St James.

Shaftesbury Avenue in honour of the seventh Earl of Shaftesbury who did much philanthropic work for the people who formerly lived in this area.

Sloane Square after Sir Hans Sloane, a distinguished physician whose library formed the nucleus of the British Library.

Soho Square 'So-ho' was a hunting cry like 'tally-ho'. There may have been an inn in this area which took the cry as an incident name.

Southampton Row the owner was Thomas Wriothesley, Earl of Southampton.

Theobalds Road led in the direction of Theobalds, in Hertfordshire, where Lord Burghley had his home and lavishly entertained Elizabeth I and James I.

The Strand was formerly the 'strand', or shore of the Thames.

Threadneedle Street from a sign of a house or inn with three needles on it, perhaps the arms of the Needlemakers' Company. But one writer mentions the folk-dance Threadneedle, where dancers form arches for one another.

Tottenham Court Road the court of 'Totta's ham' or village.

Wardour Street now mainly linked with the film industry. Sir Edward Wardour was former owner.

Watergate a rather insignificant London street bears this highly significant name. There was once a gate giving access to the Thames.

Whitefriars Street see *Carmelite Street.*

Whitehall Cardinal Wolsey owned the palace of this name, which passed to Henry VIII.

Wigmore Street one of the Harley family, the landowners, was Baron Harley of Wigmore, in Herefordshire.

'When I [ie Sherlock Holmes] first came up to London I had rooms in Montague Street, just round the corner from the British Museum. . . .'

A Conan Doyle *The Musgrave Ritual*

---

11 Signing a name

Visitors to Britain have for centuries been making favourable comments about the public houses they find on all sides. Britain has some fifty-five thousand 'pubs'. The earlier terms 'inn' and 'tavern' appear to have referred originally to different kinds of pub. The inn was obliged to remain open at all hours in order to receive guests. Taverns were for casual refreshment and were obliged to close at a certain hour. But the two terms became confused at an early date, and few modern writers on the subject use them consistently with their original meanings. Both have in any case been replaced by 'pub' in normal speech, so we will refer to pubs and their names throughout this chapter.

Pubs carry on a tradition of convivial hospitality which began to be established in the Middle Ages. Many writers have written eloquently about their charms, but we must concern ourselves here with their names. These are often distinctive and intriguing in themselves but they have, of course, another famous characteristic. Each name is usually accompanied by its visual representation, its sign. Pub names and signs together add to the interest of any journey through Britain, and this interest can only be deepened when one looks into the past to see how and why the names and signs arose.

The ale-stake

The classic writers on signboard lore, Larwood and Hotten, conclude that our medieval ancestors must have imitated the Romans when they began to make use of trade signs. The Romans certainly identified their various tradesmen by symbols. A tavern keeper would tie a bunch of evergreens to a pole, the 'ale-stake', and display it in the street. He was crudely honouring Bacchus, the god of wine, who was always shown with ivy and vine leaves. The **Bush** appeared in medieval England as a pub sign and is still to be found as such.

The Bush is technically a generic sign, rather like the three balls that symbolise any pawnbroker or the red and white striped pole that still sometimes announces the presence of a barber. In a street where each establishment carries on a different trade such signs are adequate, but the custom whereby particular trades were associated with special streets seems to have begun early. As soon as there were several butchers, bakers or whatever next door to one another in a medieval street it became necessary to distinguish them more individually. Today in such a situation we would do it very simply, by showing the different shop names. At a time when hardly anybody could read, shops needed names for spoken use but signs that could be used for visual identification.

It is important to realise that for several centuries city streets in Britain were filled with signs of all kinds, not just pub signs. All tradesmen needed them, and even private householders found them necessary. This was an age when there were no numbered houses, and one's address was a descriptive phrase that made use of any convenient landmark. Many people found it easier to display a personal sign outside their houses so that they could speak of living 'at the sign of the **Star**' or something similar. Some surnames derive from these sign names, which came into use at the end of the surname period.

Influence of emblems

But did the use of signs consciously imitate the Romans? They could just as easily have come upon the scene as a natural reflection of medieval life. People could not read or write but they could recognise simple pictures. One might say that they were trained to do so. One of the greatest educational influences of the era was the Church, which itself used a system of name signs.

In his *Introduction to Inn Signs*, Eric R. Delderfield writes:

In the coaching era there were two inns at Stony Stratford (Bucks), the Cock and the Bull, and between them a fierce rivalry existed. As the coaches arrived from different directions, the gossip of the road was exchanged, and lost nothing in the telling. So much so that anything which resembled a gross exaggeration or was obviously distorted became known as a 'Cock and Bull story'.

Mr Delderfield has at least provided an excellent example of a cock-and-bull story, which has come to mean 'a foolish story told as if it were true'. The expression was in use long before the coaching era, and there is strong linguistic evidence which connects it with the French *coq à l'âne*. It originally referred to any story which passed incoherently from one subject to another.

These name signs are still to be seen in churches but few of us are now very adept at 'reading' them. The medieval church-goer, by contrast, would look at a stained-glass window which showed a woman holding a basket of fruit or flowers and know immediately that this was St Dorothy. A nearby statue of a man holding a key or keys was St Peter. The saints were known by their *emblems* which performed much the same function as name plates might have done. By the end of the 14th century many of these emblems had become standardised throughout western Europe.

Some of them were highly individual, others had more in common with the Bush in that they were symbolic in a general way. A book might be held not only by the Evangelists but by any saint who had a reputation for learning or devotion to the liturgy. A sword was a symbol of execution and a palm indicated martyrdom by other means. All of these and many more the ordinary person was able to interpret. He went to church often and was frequently told the stories behind the emblems. They came to form a simple kind of hieroglyphic language.

Today we think of pictures of any kind as adjuncts to words and names. If we see a pub with even the simplest of signs outside it, such as a **Red Lion** or **Plough,** we still expect to see the name written with it. A complex sign outside a private house, say, with a sheaf of rye to be seen and a hare near it, the sun shining in the background, would baffle us completely. Even if we knew that the people living there were called **Harrison** we would still not make the 'hare-rye-sun' connection. A few centuries ago we would have been far more practised in deciphering such 'silent names', as Camden calls them when he gives the Harrison example. We would have had to be, for the signs of the time did not bother to give the verbal forms of the names.

After being originally christened The Hospice, and degenerating into its present name, The Ostrich, no wonder the house hangs its head today.

Cecil Aldin *Old Inns*

Mistaken interpretations

This is not to say that all men would immediately have seen the point of the Harrison rebus. There is ample evidence that many signs have been misinterpreted in the past. The mistakes began with the saintly emblems, with new explanations for them being invented by fertile minds. St Denis was usually shown holding his head in his hands, for example, as a reminder that he had been decapitated. A myth soon arose to the effect that he had walked from Montmartre to the place of his burial carrying his head.

Out in the street the signs were often poorly painted, and artists might not manage to convey the impression they wished. A sign which was meant to announce the **Coach and Horses** pub might become the **Coach and Dogs** by a brutal piece of art criticism. A **Black Swan** could likewise become the **Muddy** or **Mucky Duck.** The **Heedless Virgin,** corrupted by folk-etymology to **Headless Virgin** and shown on a sign as a decapitated saint, could accidentally or deliberately be interpreted as the **Silent Woman,** implying an 'at last!'.

Misinterpretation of this kind sometimes led to establishments being known simultaneously by more than one name. The **Rose,** in Bristol, was also known to local people as the **Cauliflower.** The **Swan and Lyre** could be referred to as the **Goose and Gridiron.** When the alternative name became widely known it was sometimes thought desirable to keep it and create a new sign that intentionally matched it.

Influence of heraldry

Another kind of name sign that came into being for practical reasons during the Middle Ages was the coat of arms. Men went into battle heavily armed and were difficult to recognise. It became the custom for them to adorn their shields and to decorate their helmets with distinctive crests. As an idea this was not new, for the Greeks and Romans had fought behind shields painted with animals and the like, but these do not seem to have become conventional symbols, always associated with one family. Coats of arms accompanied the development of surnames in Britain, becoming hereditary in the same way.

It would have been logical for coats of arms to take over the designs used on seals, which were used to authenticate documents in Britain from the 11th century onwards, but the opposite seems to have happened. The seals were again name signs, the upper-class equivalent of the X that was used as the mark of more humble men who could not write. At first they were freely chosen signs used by individuals, but they later reproduced the coats of arms. As F. J. Grant says in *The Manual of Heraldry*: 'but for the fact that few persons were able to write and had to authenticate all deeds and transactions they entered on with their seals, we should not now have these records of the early armorial designs.'

General illiteracy, then, led to names being represented pictorially at all levels of medieval society. Sign names were to remain in practical use for several centuries. They are now little more than decorative fossils, whether coats of arms or pub signs, but they attract in both forms enthusiastic modern students. It is the pub signs with which we are now concerned but that does not mean that we can immediately put heraldry to one side. A large number of pub signs, and therefore pub names, derive from coats of arms. The **Red Lion** and **White Hart** are probably the best known of these, the first referring to the coat of John of Gaunt, the second to that of Richard II. The word 'arms' itself was later to become so strongly associated with pub names that it became almost a synonym for 'inn', 'tavern' or 'pub'. Modern names such as the **Junction Arms, Bricklayers' Arms, Platelayers' Arms** and **Welldiggers' Arms** show the trend.

Sign names

There is a marked difference between most of the pub names that came into existence before the late 18th century and those that have appeared since then. The earlier names may well have been the names of the signs themselves. When the Knights Templars established a hostel for pilgrims and others and identified it by a sign that showed an angel, it is unlikely that they thought in terms of 'naming' what was in effect a primitive pub. They would have wanted an appropriate sign to indicate that the hostel was under divine protection and which was easily recognisable as a generic symbol. The name **Angel** would only occur later, when people shortened the phrase 'at the sign of the Angel' or 'the Angel sign' to 'the Angel'.

Similarly, the signs that indicated loyalty to the throne were meant to do precisely that, but not necessarily to create such names as the **Crown, Sceptre, King's Arms** and **Queen's Arms.** Such

---

At Grantham, in Lincolnshire, from the eccentricity of the lord of the manor, who formerly possessed the majority of the houses in the town, there is at the present time the following inns that have the word 'Blue' attached to their signs: viz.—Blue Boat, Blue Sheep, Blue Bull, Blue Ram, Blue Lion, Blue Bell, Blue Cow, Blue Boar, Blue Horse and Blue Inn.

By way of completing this catalogue, a wag, whose house belonged to himself, and who resided near the residence of his lordship, a few years ago actually had the Blue Ass placed on his sign.

The Mirror, 1833 quoted by Rowland Watson *A Scrapbook of Inns*

---

signs were especially useful in being widely known. The names that derived from them could be classed as descriptive, but once again descriptive of the signs rather than the places.

Many heraldic signs were subjected to a kind of visual folk-etymology. What was perhaps meant to be interpreted as the **Warwick Arms** became the **Bear and Ragged Staff.** The **Prince of Wales** might emerge by a similar process as the **Feathers.** Such names seem to indicate that familiar as certain famous coats must have been in former times, ordinary men could not interpret them as easily as the saintly emblems. These names also show quite clearly that the signs came first, the names afterwards.

One class of pub names, however, which appeared early definitely began as names and were then deliberately converted into visual form. These were often surnames which ended in '-ton' and were easy to illustrate by means of the tun, the large cask in which beer was stored. A lute, thorn, ash tree and the like could be shown with it to pun on **Luton, Thornton, Ashton,** etc. The pub names would nevertheless emerge as the **Lute and Tun** type. The **Tun and Arrows,** for instance, was meant to be the **Bolt in Tun** for **Bolton.** The **Hand and Cock** was similarly the sign used by a publican called **Hancock.** In spite of the punning intention, these remain descriptive names.

Shop sign names

Names chosen in modern times differ from the original sign names in that the names almost always come first, the signs afterwards. A point was reached where the signs were in danger of being abandoned altogether, the names having taken complete precedence. Before this happened, however, the density of signs and names in large cities had become very great, and the signs constituted a public nuisance. They blotted out the daylight from the narrow streets, made a continual creaking noise by swinging back and forth, and occasionally caused accidents. There was a notorious incident in London in 1718, when a heavy signboard pulled down the wall to which it was attached, killing some passers-by.

The density of sign names had also caused them to change in kind. The early signs had always been familiar objects or symbols, but there was only a limited supply of these and they were quickly used up. Partly in an effort to avoid duplication, sign names were formed by deliberately combining elements, such as the **Whale and Crow,** the **Frying Pan and Drum.** Such names could also arise, however, when a publican or shopkeeper went to a new establishment. He would want to take his personal sign with him but retain the goodwill associated with the existing sign, so he would combine the two.

In a famous *Spectator* essay of 1710 Addison commented on street signs of his time and gave in passing another possible explanation of the combination names:

> 'Our streets are filled with **Blue Boars, Black Swans** and **Red Lions,** not to mention **Flying Pigs** and **Hogs in Armour,** with many creatures more extraordinary than any in the deserts of Africa. . . . I should forbid that creatures of jarring and incongruous natures should be joined together in the same sign; such as the **Bell and the Neat's Tongue,** the **Dog and the Gridiron.** The **Fox and the Goose** may be supposed to have met, but what has the **Fox and the Seven Stars** to do together? And when did **Lamb and Dolphin** ever meet except upon a signpost? I must, however, observe to you upon this subject that it is usual for a young tradesman at his first setting up to add to his own sign that of the master whom he served, as the husband after marriage gives a place to his mistress's arms in his own coat. . . .'

Addison uses heraldic terms metaphorically, of course, but at the back of many shop and tavern-keepers' minds must have been the wish to become known by a sign that would act in the same way as a coat of arms.

The Pelican at Speenhamland
It stands upon a hill.
You know it is The Pelican
By its enormous bill.

quoted by Cecil Aldin *Old Inns*

Appropriate sign names

A century before Addison wrote his essay Thomas Heywood had lightheartedly commented on the way different pub signs attracted different kinds of customer. The gentry, he wrote, would go to the **King's Head,** the bankrupt to the **World's End,** the gardener to the **Rose,** the churchmen to the **Mitre,** etc. An extended version of this appeared in the *Roxburgh Ballads.* It was said, for instance, that the drunkards by noon would go to the **Man in the Moon**, while

> The Weavers will dine at the **Shuttle,**
> The Glovers will unto the **Glove,**
> The Maidens all to the **Maidenhead,**
> And true lovers unto the **Dove.**

Addison turned the whole idea round and commented on the relationship between the namer and the sign name: 'I can give a shrewd guess at the humour of the inhabitant by the sign that hangs before his door. A surly, choleric fellow generally makes choice of a **Bear,** as men of milder dispositions frequently live at the **Lamb.**'

'What are we?' said Mr Pecksniff, 'but coaches? Some of us are slow coaches; some of us are fast coaches. We start from The Mother's Arms, and we run to The Dust Shovel.'

Charles Dickens *Martin Chuzzlewit*

There is obviously a serious point underlying both of these approaches to sign names, or any names for that matter, but the majority of signs in Addison's time gave little indication that they had been carefully chosen. The sheer size of a sign became the most important factor in some cases, or the extravagance of its supporting ironwork. All the time they were becoming more purely decorative, since standards of literacy were rising and names could be interpreted in their linguistic form.

By the 1760s official action was taken against street signs. In many areas it was forbidden to have signs that projected into the streets. Number names of houses and shops were to become compulsory before long, again making the sign names superfluous. Inevitably they began to disappear from the streets, and might have done so totally but for their survival as pub signs, and in a different way as trade marks. Pub signs survived for several reasons. From the 15th century onwards publicans had been required to display signs by law, so that the tradition of signs and sign names was particularly strong in their trade. The shopkeepers had never been under such an obligation. There was also a difference for a long time between taverns in the cities and inns elsewhere. For the inns on the coaching roads a sign was not lost among a hundred others but was something of a landmark in itself. Even today signs are still more frequent in the country than in the towns. Finally, the withdrawal of street sign names by the shopkeepers gave a new kind of meaning to those that remained. The mere presence of a sign now had the same generic significance as the early ale-stake as well as a more individual meaning.

Types of pub names

All that has been said so far about the general background to pub signs has been necessary in order to explain pub names as they exist today. The nomenclature has unique characteristics which can only be explained by reference to a time when it was desired not so much to create a name as to allow a locative phrase, 'at the sign of...', to come into being. In modern times the usual processes that affect name systems have come into operation. Many names are transferred to new pubs because they are felt to be unambiguously pub names. Others are created to fit into the traditions established by the early names. The **Air Hostess** and the like are converted names, while the **Sherlock Holmes** and **Sir Walter Scott** are normal transfers. The pub signs give visual support to the names.

Other categories of names are also found. Names that described the pubs themselves rather than the signs naturally became more common when projecting signboards were banned, but a few had existed previously. Publicans sometimes looked at the characteristics of the buildings they occupied and described these in the name. The **White House, Red House, Blue House** and the like may have been deliberately arrived at by painting the buildings for the purpose, or they may simply have reflected what was there. This was almost certainly the case with names such as the **Green Lattice,** a lattice being fixed across a pub's open windows to give those inside the building some privacy. When the lattices gave way to the more usual windows the word was likely to be misunderstood. In at least one instance a **Green Lettuce** later came into being.

By metonymy objects directly associated with the pub could be used for its name. The **Brass Knocker** is one kind of example, while the food offered inside the pub accounts for names like **Round of Beef, Shoulder of Mutton, Boar's Head, Cheshire Cheese** and so on. Drink was obviously not forgotten and led to the **Jug and Glass, Foaming Tankard, Malt and Hops, Full Quart** and many more. The **Black Jack,** for instance, was a primitive kind of leather bottle, sometimes lined with metal. A fashionable drink of the past is remembered in the **Punch Bowl** and other names that mention 'punch', though the nearest pub of this name I can actually get to derives its name from The Devil's Punch Bowl, a metaphorically named hollow in the hills.

The inn-keepers

Even nearer, however, is one of my 'locals', the **Swan.** In the early 19th century it was kept by John Locke who had a wife 'absolutely incomparable in the preparation of stewed eels, and not to be despised in the art of cooking a good beef-steak or a mutton-chop'. So wrote William Hone in 1838, while a few years earlier Theodore Hook sat in a punt on the Thames and wrote a poem about the pub. He also mentioned the inn-keeper's wife, being struck by her 'bright blue eyes' as much as her cooking.

A pub's dependence on its landlord and landlady has long been recognised. In many areas it leads to the unofficial renaming of a pub by its publican's name. Edinburgh, for example, formerly had many establishments known by such names as **Lucky Middlemass's Tavern** and **Jenny Ha's Change House.** 'Lucky' was a pleasant way of addressing a woman, especially a grandmother, and it became the specific term for the keeper of an ale-house. Jenny Ha's was a reference to another 'lucky', Janet Hall.

It is largely due to the inn-keepers, one imagines, that the pub has survived as a national institution in Britain. They have helped to give familiar names like the **Rose and Crown,** the **Bell, George and Dragon, Wheatsheaf, Coach and Horses, Talbot** and **Ship** a very special meaning, an accumulated goodwill built up by centuries of relaxed social gatherings. There are not many names among the millions in existence to which such a remark could apply.

Other pub names

Mention of landlords and their ladies has taken us inside the pubs, and while we are there we can look at some of the names we find. Often, for instance, the individual rooms have names. The well-known **Shakespeare Hotel** in Stratford-on-Avon has rooms named after the plays. A member of The Names Society once told me that she was a little disconcerted, when staying there with her husband, to learn that they would spend the night in a room called **The Taming of the Shrew.** The **Mouth,** a pub mentioned by Taylor, the Water Poet, had rooms called the **Pomegranate,** the **Portcullis, Three Tuns, Cross Keys, Vine, King's Head, Crown, Dolphin** and **Bell,** all of which could occur as pub names in their own right.

Also within a pub are to be found the vast number of names for the various drinks. Gin, for instance, has also been known at various times as **Cuckold's Comfort, Ladies' Delight, Gripe Water, Eyewater, Blue Ruin, Mother's Ruin, Flash of Lightning, Lap, Last Shift** and **No Mistake.** These are only a few of its nicknames. Beer has also come in for unofficial renaming, ranging from **Jungle Juice** to **Belly Vengeance** and **Dragon's Milk.** If one adds the nicknames of the inn-keepers, such as **Mother Louse** who kept an ale-house near Oxford in the 18th century, it is clear that one could fill a book very easily with pub names and those names that are connected with pubs.

Australian pub names

A list of popular and curious pub names, together with their explanations, is at the end of this chapter. They give a general idea of the types of names found in Britain today. But Britain is not alone in having pubs. They appeared in Australia at the end of the 18th century, for instance, and spread throughout that continent. In many places there pubs came before private houses, and in their relatively short history they have played a remarkable part in the country's social development. Pubs have served as churches, town halls, post offices, surgeries, and theatres. The first Australian zoo was at the **Sir Joseph Banks** in Botany Bay. The whole story is well told in Paul McGuire's *Inns of Australia.*

McGuire remarks specifically that 'most' Australian pub names 'were brought from Britain', but his book makes it quite clear that they quickly took on their own characteristics. One of the first pubs in New South Wales, for instance, was the **Three Jolly Settlers.** The **Bulletin** in Sydney was named after the Australian weekly newspaper as soon as it appeared, which may have been an innovation in pub-naming. There are pubs in Britain with names like **Express** and **Mail** but they were named after coaches.

One man who arrived in Australia in a ship called the **Buffalo** founded a pub called the **Buffalo's Head.** A model of the ship's figurehead was used as a sign. Pub signs therefore established themselves in Australia along with the names, but the many photographs in McGuire's book make it clear that not many pubs used them. They had none of the long history behind them to make them traditional, and they served little practical purpose. The fact that they were used at all merely reflected the vague feeling of British settlers that pubs should have a sign.

The Buffalo's Head, mentioned above, later became the **Black Bull** and acquired a double-sided signboard. A peaceful bull was shown on one side, a raging bull on the other. An inscription read:

> The bull is tame, so fear him not
> So long as you can pay your shot.
> When money's gone, and credit's bad,
> That's what makes the bull go mad.

Name, sign and inscription have unfortunately since been removed.

Australian **Halfway Houses** sprang up spontaneously (and optimistically in some cases) and cannot be said to be transfers from Britain. Another entirely Australian pub name, in origin at least, is the **Tiger** in Tantanoola. The tiger turned out to be a wolf, now stuffed and displayed in the bar. A man who traded on the 'tiger's' reputation for sheep-stealing in order to establish a private butchery in the bush was later sent to prison for six years. Two other pub names, **McDonald's** and the **Glenrowan,** have now become totally Australian and Ned Kelly's.

Inside the pubs the food and drink appears to have taken on a national flavour as well. At **Scott's,** which was a club rather than a pub, one could eat Kangaroo Tail Soup, Curried Bandicoot, Parroqueet Patties and Aspic of Native Pigeon. In more ordinary establishments drinks—or 'throat-scrapers' and 'eye-openers'—with names like **Spider** (lemonade and brandy), **Maiden** (peppermint and cloves) and **Catherine Hayes** (claret, sugar and orange) were consumed. All in all it seems safe to say that Australian pubs, and the names that were attached to them in various ways, were well and truly Australian from the beginning.

Conclusions

Pub names have something for everybody. My own special interest lies in their complex relationship with the signs that accompany them. The only parallels that come to mind are certain American place names such as **Straddlebug Mountain** and **Ucross** which derive from brand marks on cattle. For others the appeal lies in the anecdotal explanations of many a curious name. And who could not be curious, for instance, about a name like the **Drunken Duck?** This pub in Westmorland is famous for the story of a former landlady who once found her ducks lying in the road. She thought they were dead and began to prepare them for dinner, but they turned out to be in a drunken stupor. Beer had drained into their feeding-ditch. The ducks were reprieved and allowed to sober up, and one hopes that they lived long and happily.

The Cooney brothers encircled me in the back bar of the Ultima Thule [a pub in Australia]. This had recently been renamed the Whingeing Pom, in deference to the disposition of its clientele.

Howard Jacobson *Redback*

A cocktail by any other name

It is possible that 'cocktail' began as the proper name of a particular mixed drink, then went on to become the general term. Whatever its origin, it remains a fanciful word for something that traditionally attracts fanciful names. The following are a small selection.

Amour
Angel's Kiss
Appendicitis
Atta Boy
Banco
Between the Sheets
Biter
Black Baby
Blonde
Blood Transfusion
Blue Monday
Boomerang
Brainstorm
Buster Brown
Cameron's Kick
Caresse
Cat's Eye
Champs-Elysée
Charleston
Clap of Thunder
Clover Club
Corpse Reviver
Cowboy
Damn the Weather
Depth Bomb
Devils
Earthquake
Eclipse
Elektra
Elixir
Eye-Opener
Fair and Warmer
Fascinator
Favourite
Five Fifteen
Flu
Forty-Seven
Four Flush
Fourth Degree
Frantic Atlantic
Full House
Gimlet
Gin N Sin
Glad Eye
Gloom Chaser
Gloom Raiser
Golden Glow
Good Night Ladies
Grand Slam
Great Secret
Green-Eyed Monster
Hanky-Panky
Hasty
Hell
Hesitation
Hole in One
Honeymoon
Hoopla
Hoots Mon
Hula Hula
Hundred Per Cent
Hurricane
Income Tax
Jabberwock
Jack in the Box
Jupiter
Kicker
Knickerbocker
Knock Out
Last Round
Leap Year
Leave it to Me
Lovers' Delight
Lucifer
Macaroni
Maiden's Blush
Maiden's Prayer
Manhattan
Marmalade
Merry Widow
Moonlight
Moonraker
Moonshine
Morning After
Mule
Mule's Hind Leg
Napoleon
New Arrival
New Life
Nineteenth Hole
Nine-Twenty
Oh Henry
One Exciting Night
Pansy
Paradise
Perfect
Ping-Pong
Poker
Pooh Bah
Poop Deck
Presto
Prohibition
Queen of Sheba
Reinvigorator
Resolute
Rolls Royce
Rusty Nail
S.O.S.
Screwdriver
Self-Starter
Sensation
Seventh Heaven
Sidecar
Six Cylinder
Slipstream
Snowball
Soul Kiss
Stinger
Strike's Off
Sweet Potato
Swizzles
Tempter
Third Degree
Third Rail
Thunder
T.N.T.
Torpedo
Tropical
Twelve-Mile Limit
Twelve Miles Out
Twentieth Century
Upstairs
Velocity
Ward Eight
Wedding Bells
Welcome Stranger
Whizz Bang
Whoopee
Widow's Kiss
Wow

A selection of pub names past and present

Many names have more than one possible origin and these are indicated. For heraldic names the immediate source rather than the ultimate origin is given. Some ten thousand British pub names are fully explained in *A Dictionary of Pub Names*, by Leslie Dunkling and Gordon Wright (Routledge and Kegan Paul, 1987).

Adam and Eve popular figures in medieval pageants; arms of Fruiterers' Company.

Air Balloon often commemorates first ascent at Versailles in 1783 with animals as passengers.

Alice Hawthorn a famous racehorse.

Alma for the Battle of Alma, 1854, in the Crimea. A river name.

Anchor an easily illustrated sign; often a retired seaman as landlord.

Axe and Compass arms of Carpenters' Company.

Bag O'Nails reputedly a corruption of Bacchanals; actually the sign of an ironmonger.

Bear where bear-baiting took place; occurs in many coats of arms.

Beehive a convenient 'object sign'. One pub so named had a living sign, occupied by a swarm of bees.

Bell used by bell-ringers or bell-makers; near a bell-tower.

Bible and Crown a common toast of the Cavaliers.

Bird in Hand a joking reference to the proverb, especially if a Bush was near by; a falcon on a gauntlet is common in heraldry.

Bleeding Heart a reference to the Virgin Mary; arms of the Douglas family.

Blue Boar arms of Richard, Duke of York. Corrupted to **Blue Pig** in one instance.

Blue Boys Bridewell boys—orphans and foundlings—dressed in blue; scholars of Christ's Hospital; postilions of George IV (whose coach stopped at an inn of this name).

Blue Vinny a Dorset Cheese.

Brockley Jack a notorious highwayman.

Bull often because bull-baiting took place before it was forbidden in 1835.

Bull and Mouth commemorates Henry VIII's victory at Boulogne Mouth, or is a corruption of 'bowl and mouth'.

Canopus after a flying-boat.

Cardinal's Error referring to Wolsey's suppression of Tonbridge Priory.

Case is Altered local anecdotes account for different instances, eg a pub replaces something less desirable; departure of a military camp causes loss of trade; new landlord cancels outstanding debts. Ingenious but highly unlikely explanations include a corruption of Casey's Altar or *Casa de Saltar* ('house of dancing').

Castle and Ball perhaps a corruption of Castle and Bull in arms of Marlborough family.

Cat and Fiddle usually a joking reference to the nursery rhyme. Corruptions of *La Chatte Fidèle* ('the faithful cat'); *Caton le Fidèle* (the governor of Calais) and *Catherine la Fidèle* (Catherine of Aragon) have also been suggested.

Cat I' Th' Window a Catherine Wheel window; from a stuffed cat placed in the window.

Charles XII a racehorse.

Chequers formerly emblem of money-changers; indication that draughts or chess could be played; common element in coats of arms; from a simple decorated post used as sign.

Church Inn near a church, though Defoe described one inn of this name as the Devil's Chapel, with a larger congregation than the church itself.

Clickers for the shoemakers.

Clipper's Arms referring both to a ship and sheep-clippers.

Coach and Eight in one instance the reference is to rowing.

Cock and Bottle the 'cock' being a spigot, indicating that draught and bottled beer was sold.

Comet a stage-coach name.

Compleat Angler for the book by Izaak Walton, 1653.

Cow and Snuffers occurs in an early play as a satirical example of a pub name and perhaps taken from there. Another source says it was the result of a bet to find an incongruous name.

Cromwell's Head an oblique reference to the Restoration.

Crooked Billet a shepherd's crook; a weapon; a yoke; bishop's crosier; part of tankard; arms of Neville family.

Cross Foxes arms of Williams-Wynn family.

Crown formerly Crown property; showing allegiance to king.

Cutty Sark the short shirt worn by men and women in the Border Country; name of ship.

Curiosity for its collection of curiosities.

Daniel Lambert a man who died in 1809 weighing fifty-two stone.

Dirty Dick Nathaniel Bentley was so called in the 18th century. He lived as a hermit after his bride-to-be died on wedding-day.

Discovery after Captain Scott's ship.

Doff Cockers an invitation to locals to take off their leather gaiters.

Dog and Duck spaniels were set to chase ducks on nearby ponds.

Dolphin and Crown arms of French Dauphin.

Duke of York after the battleship in one instance.

Eagle and Child arms of Earls of Derby.

Eagle and Lion arms of Queen Mary.

Eclipse usually transferred from the racehorse rather than an actual event.

Elephant and Castle for the Cutlers' Company; often falsely said to be corruption of *Infanta de Castile*.

Falcon a frequent element in coats of arms; formerly a popular bookseller's sign.

Falstaff after Shakespeare's much-loved rogue.

Fifteen Balls Cornish coat of arms.

Fighting Cocks for a 'sport' abolished in Great Britain in 1849.

First and Last usually refers to location of pub at edge of town or village.

Fish and Ring a reference to St Kentigern's having his ring returned to him by a fish when he dropped it into a stream.

Five Alls usually a king, parson, lawyer and soldier who say they rule, pray, plead and fight for all, plus a taxpayer who pays for all, or a devil who takes all, etc.

Fleece for those in woollen industry.

Flower Pot such signs often showed lilies originally, referring to the Virgin Mary.

Flying Bull after Fly and Bull, two stage-coach names.

Flying Dutchman usually after the racehorse of this name.

Flying Horse Pegasus; from roundabout on nearby fairground.

Fox and Grapes Aesop's fable; two signs combined.

Frighted Horse formerly Freighted Horse, a pack-horse (?).

Gate near a church gate, toll-gate, prison gate or gate-keeper's lodge.

George and Dragon to proclaim English patriotism.

Goat in Boots as a caricature of a Welshman; sometimes explained as corruption of Dutch *Goden Boode*, a reference to Mercury.

Goat and Compasses arms of Wine Coopers' Company; a legend that it is a corruption of 'God encompasseth us' is widely believed.

Green Man for foresters and woodmen; for Robin Hood; for May King, Jack-in-the-green.

Greyhound usually a stage-coach name.

Gunners nickname of Arsenal Football Club.

Hammers nickname of West Ham United Football Club.

Hat and Feathers early 17th century reference to fashion in plumed hats.

Hole in the Wall local anecdotes account for the name, eg a debtor's prison that became a pub had a hole through which food was passed; pub is reached by passing under viaduct arch that looks like a hole in the wall.

Honest Lawyer a joke name, usually showing a headless lawyer unable to speak.

Intrepid Fox after Charles Fox, not the animal.

Iron Devil plausibly a corruption of *hirondelle* ('swallow') on arms of Arundel family.

Jacob's Well a biblical joke. for 'whosoever drinketh of this water shall thirst again'.

Key for locksmiths; Jane Keye kept an inn of this name in the seventeenth century.

Labour in Vain originally religious, for Psalm 127 says: 'Except the Lord build the house, they labour in vain that build it.'

Lamb and Flag formerly a religious reference to the Holy Lamb with nimbus and banner; arms of Merchant Taylors.

Lamb and Lark proverbially one should 'go to bed with the lamb and rise with the lark'.

Leather Bottle formerly much used by shepherds.

Lion and Antelope arms of Henry V.

Lion and Bull arms of Edward V.

Lion and Unicorn arms of James I.

Little John variant of Robin Hood, itself often used as a pub name.

Little Wonder a racehorse.

Live and Let Live usually a comment by a landlord on competition which he considers unfair.

Mad Cat probably from a badly painted heraldic fox.

Mall Tavern from the game of pall mall (or pell mell), played with a mallet and ball.

Man with a Load of Mischief a famous sign reputedly by Hogarth shows him with a woman, a monkey and a magpie among other things.

Master Robert a steeplechaser.

Mermaid a popular sign, easy to illustrate.

Moon and Sun a rebus for the Monson family.

Mother Redcap a legendary woman who lived to be 120 'by drinking good ale'.

Nag's Head one sign shows a woman's head; usually a horse.

Naked Man formerly a tailor's sign; sometimes meant to be Adam; in one case said to be for a tree struck by lightning that then resembled a man.

New Inn usually of great age.

Noah's Ark formerly sign of dealer in animals.

No. Ten and other examples such as No. Five, No. Seven refer to houses that had only number names when granted a licence.

Oliver Twist one pub of this name is in Oliver Road, which has a bend or twist in it.

Ordinary Fellow in honour of King George V, who once described himself in this way.

Pewter Platter for Pewterers' Company; to show that food is obtainable.

Pig and Whistle almost certainly a corruption, but origin not clear. A 'peg' was a measure of drink, a 'piggin' a drinking-vessel. 'Wassail' in one of its several meanings may have been origin of 'whistle'.

Pin and Bowl where ninepins and bowls could be played.

Pride of the Valley a reference to Earl Lloyd George.

Printer's Devil frequented by printers' apprentices.

Ram arms of Cloth Workers.

Ram Jam a kind of drink; legend says landlady made to ram and jam holes

---

A remark by Sherlock Holmes to a German spy, who says that he will shout for help: *'My dear sir, if you did anything so foolish you would probably enlarge the limited titles of our village inns by giving us The Dangling Prussian as a sign-post.'*

A. Conan Doyle *His Last Bow*

Professor W. E. Kershaw points out that in rural areas the sign Cock and Bottle is far more likely to refer to a haycock, a small heap of hay, and a 'bottle' of hay, where *bottle* refers to a bundle, not a glass container.

in barrel with her thumbs by trickster who left without paying bill.

Rampant Cat a reference to a heraldic lion by irreverent locals.

Red Cat for a badly painted lion.

Ring o' Bells usually for hand-bell ringers.

Rising Sun heraldic reference to House of York.

Rose Revived reference to Restoration of Charles II; a Rose re-opened after closure.

Royal Mortar probably Royal Martyr.

Running Footman whose job was to run before a coach to clear the way.

Saracen's Head variant of Turk's Head when Crusades made the Turks common topic of conversation.

Sedan Chair introduced to England in 1623.

Seven Stars a reference to the Virgin Mary; the Plough constellation.

Ship an easy to illustrate sign, popular everywhere; in some instances meant to be The Ark.

Ship and Shovel used by coal-heavers who came from nearby ships and left their shovels at the door.

Silent Whistle a former Railway Hotel where branch line was closed.

Silver Bullet a locomotive name.

Sky Blue in honour of the local football club colour (Coventry).

Smoker a racehorse name.

Star referring to Star of Bethlehem or to the Virgin Mary; a simple visual symbol.

Stewpony corruption of Estepona, birthplace of landlord's wife.

Swan and Antelope arms of Henry IV.

Swan With Two Necks probably badly painted sign of two swans originally. Often explained as 'swan with two nicks' on bill to show that it belonged to Vintners, but this would have made a difficult-to-identify sign.

Tabard a sleeveless garment worn outdoors by monks, soldiers, etc.

Talbot breed of hunting-dog used in arms of Earl of Shrewsbury.

The Sparkfold name of a hunt.

Three Compasses arms of Carpenters and Masons; sometimes accompanied by advice 'to keep within compass'.

Three Tuns arms of Vintners, said to be an unlucky sign associated with tragedy.

Tumble-Down Dick a reference to Richard Cromwell; to an 18th century dance; to Dick Turpin.

Two Angels arms of Richard II.

Unicorn formerly sign of goldsmith or apothecary.

Waltzing Weasel weasels actually 'waltz' round their victims.

Why Not a racehorse name.

World Upside Down popular when Australia was being discovered.

Yorker a cricketing reference to the type of delivery perfected by Spofforth, the bowler.

12 Home-made names

It has often been said that man has a 'need to name'. House names may sometimes owe their existence to this aspect of human nature, but they reflect also something that is less often mentioned—man's 'right to name'. An inventor who creates something new is thought to have the right to name it; a botanist has the right to name the new species he has identified. Whatever the legal technicalities, it is now usually looked upon as a mother's right to name the children. The situation where someone finds that he has this right to name does not often occur, and when is does it is not lightly thrown away. It is not surprising that many householders in Britain—for it seems to be in the English suburbs where house-naming most frequently occurs—decide to use their prerogative and name their own houses.

Most houses, of course, already have a number name, and full use is often made of it. The previous owner of my former house had **Seven** made up in wrought iron and displayed it on the gate. I thought it an excellent name and gave it even more prominence on the wall. Most suburban streets show similar examples of number names that have been put into verbal form and carved or painted on attractive boards. Higher number names can be dealt with in **One Three Six** style.

Touches of individuality are often added to number names by varying the spelling. **Numbawun, Nyneteign** and the like show a perfectly understandable determination to individualise common names. Synonyms of number names sometimes occur, as in **Gross House** and **Century House,** and they appear in translated form as **Douze** (12) or whatever. Associations of a number can lead to names like **Sunset Strip** for '77'. An occasional name is added as a phrasal complement to the existing number name, the outstanding example being **Ornot** shown alongside '2B'

Number names can be humanised, then, if this is felt to be necessary, but possibly the common objection to them is caused by the fact that they are imposed from outside by an anonymous authority. The house-owner feels that his right to name is being usurped. In some areas, especially those where all the houses are privately owned, the objection to imposed names may extend to the street names. Residents rightly feel that they, and not the local authority, have the right to choose the name. In other areas where there is a mixture of privately owned houses and council houses, house names may be used as an outward sign that the houses concerned *are* privately owned. As it happens, tenants of council houses could almost certainly bestow names on them if they wished. They would probably not be allowed to fix name-boards to the walls, but they could put them on posts in the garden. The only problems then would be the comments of the neighbours about snobbishness.

Snobbish names

The fairly widespread feeling that it is snobbish to name a house has partly come about because of inappropriate names that have been given. Flora Thompson smiles gently at **Balmoral** in Chestnut Avenue in her *Lark Rise to Candleford*, a book which itself led to **Lark Rise** becoming a popular house name. And to stay with literature—which is safer for the moment—one thinks naturally of **Dotheboys Hall.** Nicholas Nickleby (Knuckleboy as he was for Mrs Squeers) was given a lesson about house names when he arrived in Yorkshire:

'Is it much farther to Dotheboys Hall, sir?' asked Nicholas.

'About three mile from here,' replied Squeers. 'But you needn't call it a Hall down here.'

Nicholas coughed, as if he would like to know why.

'The fact is, it ain't a Hall,' observed Squeers drily.

'Oh, indeed!' said Nicholas, whom this piece of intelligence much astonished.

'No,' replied Squeers. 'We call it a Hall up in London, because it sounds better, but they don't know it by that name in these parts. A man may call his house an island if he likes; there's no Act of Parliament against that, I believe?'

'I believe not, sir,' replied Nicholas.

'Hall' carries a definite suggestion of historic grandeur, but the English language manages to make even 'house' snobbish if it becomes a house-name element. Just as the street I live in would be down-graded by being called **Speer Street** rather than **Speer Road,** so my house would be considerably overgraded if I called it **Speer House.** 'Cottage' is still defined in the dictionary as 'a small or humble dwelling', but it probably has a positive cash value if it can be applied with reasonable appropriateness to a house.

The charge of snobbishness about house names is usually applied when a house also has a number name. If a house has no other kind of identification, the need for a name is accepted. Even then, villagers are likely to smile to themselves when a newcomer puts up a board with his own choice of name over the house he has just bought. If the house has been there for some time it will already have a name. This will remain in general use, or the name of the new owner may become attached to it. Local people will not easily allow a stranger to affect their linguistic habits.

A house which has no number name is normally in the country rather than the town, which gives it immediate status in the eyes of many town-dwellers. It is also often larger than the typical suburban 'semi'. Accusations of snobbishness aimed at someone who has added a name to his house are therefore accusations of misrepresentation. As with Squeers, it is felt, an attempt is being made to profit unfairly by favourable associations.

Defensive names

A defensive reaction to this situation can be seen in many house names which actually belittle the houses concerned. Favoured words like 'manor', 'grange' and 'cottage' are left aside and a house becomes **The Shack, The Igloo, The Hut, Little House. The Bothy** is less obvious, but its specific sense was once a one-roomed hut in which unmarried labourers lodged together. **The Hole** and **The Hovel** are hardly more complimentary, and the Australian **Wurley,** 'an Aboriginal's hut', is again modest to say the least.

A similar type of name refuses to comment on a pleasant view or something of the kind, emphasising instead the house's exposed position. **Windy Walls, Windswept, All Winds, High Winds, Wild Winds** and dozens of others have an admirable honesty about them that would have horrified Squeers. In Bermuda there is a **Rudewinds.** Bermuda, one should mention, has no number name system for its houses and is something of a happy hunting ground for house name enthusiasts. I have not had the pleasure of a personal visit, but the *Bermuda Telephone Directory* is one of my favourite books.

Other 'windy' house names include **Bicarbonate** and **Dambreezee,** the latter occurring in several spellings. There is no joking, however, with **Cold Blow, Gale Force, Western Gales.** It should not be forgotten that the winds themselves have names, **Zephyr** being the best known. This occurs as a house name but is complimentary, since the west wind is normally light and pleasant. **Mistral,** a cold north-west wind in France, has been borrowed as an English house name, and a correspondent who lives in Edinburgh tells me that his house name, **Snelsmore,** is a wind in that area.

Bleak House is hardly a complimentary name, though it has acquired a new meaning thanks to Dickens. He did not invent it, for old directories show that many such houses were in existence before he wrote his novel, but he chose the name with a sure touch. It is hard to imagine a starker name. It has the naturalness of country speech about it, though, not the appearance of consciously invented names. The latter can be seen in **Dryrotia, Dry-Az-Ell, Lean Tu** and **Isor** ('eye-sore') which relieve the negativeness with a touch of humour.

An anthropologist might want to link this deliberate denigration of a house with the custom in some tribes of naming a child negatively. The usual wish is to convince the gods that the child is worthless, for if the opposite impression is given the child might be snatched away from the parents in an early death. In British society the gods are the evil spirits of rumour and gossip who will drag down anyone who tries to stand higher than the rest. The house name is therefore made into an acknowledgment of lowliness, either of the house or its occupants. This may seem extraordinary, but the house names sometimes appear to support such an argument. **On the Rocks, Overdraft, Skynt, Stony**

Broke, Haz-a-Bill, The Bank's, Little Beside and many similar names show a healthy contempt for, but an awareness of, keeping up appearances. A pair of jerry-built houses proclaim **Ibindun** and **Sovi.** Other names publicly announce that inside the house there is **Chaos, Bedlam, Pandemonium, Panic.** More names which have a confessional quality include **Drifters' Lodge, Fools' Haven, Hardheads, Hustlers' Haunt, Paupers' Perch, The Monsters** and **Ellinside.**

An alternative explanation for such names is that the householders are extroverts who are not so much naming a house as putting up a notice for the public to appreciate. A 'graffito instinct', as one might call it, is emerging. It is seen even more clearly in house names which have nothing to do with the house and very little to do with the householder, unless they can be said to reflect his philosophy of life. **Rejoice** and **Wiworry** say such house names, or as D. H. Lawrence discovered in Australia, **Wyework.** They may also throw out a greeting: **Ahoy, Cheers, Hey There, Yoo Hoo.** Next door to the last named, in Bermuda, is **Yoo Hoo Too.**

Houses with names like these need to be publicly situated, perhaps in a seaside town that attracts many visitors. They tend to be in such towns for another reason; the householders there are exposed to nomenclatures where frivolity is a tradition. The names of small boats and beach-huts are especially humorous. In quieter suburbs statement-type house names are neighbourly invitations, such as **Kumincyde, Popinagen, Popova** and **Havachat,** or they are quiet murmurs of satisfaction: **This'll Do, Thistledew, Sootsus, Dunbyus, Welemed.**

A small group of these names are rather aggressive. **Llamedos** on a house in Loughborough is not a Welsh name but a back-spelling. It was chosen, so I was told on the doorstep, because the family were feeling generally fed-up when they moved in. Mrs E. Luhman has written to me in the past about the time she and her husband moved into a bungalow in Essex. A local busybody descended on them 'and after many questions as to who we were and where we previously lived, loftily enquired "What are you going to call this place?" My husband, who was by then exasperated, replied, "We were thinking of calling it **Oppit.**" So Oppit it became.'

Other correspondents have written to me about **Fujia,** a reference to the householder's being all right regardless of Jack's condition, and a dual-purpose house name, **Wypyafeet.**

We were saying earlier that naming a house says in effect that the house is privately owned. Some people feel that the point needs emphasising: **Itzmyne, Myholme, Myonwna Lodge, Ourome, Ourn, Jusferus.** Link names such as **Barholme,** where the family name is Bar, **Ednaville, Helenscot, Lynsdale, Silvanest**—for a De Silva family in Bermuda, serve a similar purpose. **Morgan's Cottage,** actually based on the wife's first name, caused her to be addressed as Mrs Morgan by the neighbours, with a moment of embarrassment all round when she explained that she was Mrs Dunstan.

These link names do not always emphasise ownership. They can become in-jokes for those who happen to know the owner's name. Thus, a **Bird Song** in Middlesex picks up on the surname Bird, **Cornucopia** on Le Cornu (in Jersey), **Deer Leigh** on Deering, **Emblur** on Bulmer, **Little Parkin** on Parr, **Seltac** on Castle, **The Eddy** on Edwards, **The Huddle** on Huddy, **The Nuttery** on Nutt. **Little Manor** is a clever link with the surname Littman.

House-owners' names can also lead to house names without actually being linked to them. **Sixpenny House** was almost inevitable for the Tanner family in pre-decimal currency days, though the surname's origin was nothing to do with money. A Robin and Marion decided they had to live in **Sherwood,** and families with animal surnames, such as Fox and Lyon, are likely to live in **The Lair** or **The Den.**

Blends

It is in the house name system that blends come into their own. A blend is the special type of link that is built up with parts of more than one name, especially the names of the family members. These names clearly have very great significance as a group to the family concerned, and it is natural that people should think of symbolically combining them to represent the family group.

A simple blend may 'marry' the first names of the husband and wife. Barry and Wendy form the name **Barwen;** Mary and Tony decide on **Marony.** Less often the two family names are blended to give names like **Shorrlin** from Shortland and Ling, **Kenbarry** from Kenyon and Barry. One trouble with blended names is that they often fail to conform to the normal rules of the language. It is quite obvious that **Lynmar** *is* a blend, from the daughters' names in this case. Similarly, **Margrek, Dorsyd, Lespau** and the like stick out like linguistic sore thumbs.

'We shall 'ave to call this little 'ouse by a name. I was thinking of 'Ome Cottage. But I dunno whether 'Ome Cottage is quite the thing like. It's got eleven bedrooms, y'see,' said Kipps. 'I don't see 'ow you call it a cottage with more bedrooms than four. Prop'ly speaking, it's a Large Villa. Prop'ly it's almost a Big 'Ouse. Leastways a 'Ouse.'

'Well,' said Ann, 'if you must call it Villa—Home Villa.'

Kipps meditated.

'Ow about Eureka Villa?' he said.

'What's Eureka?'

'It's a name,' he said.

Ann meditated. 'It seems silly like to 'ave a name that don't mean much'.

'Perhaps it does,' said Kipps. 'Though it's what people 'ave to do.'

He became meditative. 'I got it!' he cried.

'Not Ooreka!' said Ann.

'No. There used to be a 'ouse at Hastings opposite our school—St Ann's. Now that—'.

'No,' said Mrs Kipps with decision. 'Thanking you kindly, but I don't have no butcher-boys making game of me . . .'

H. G. Wells *Kipps*

By contrast, blends can resemble words too closely and convey a meaning which is not intended. **Maveric,** for instance, and **Maudlyn** come far too close for comfort to 'maverick' and 'maudlin'. It is even possible for the namers to form a real word without knowing it. In *English House Names* I quoted the example of a Renee and Albert who called their house **Renal,** not realising that this means 'of the kidneys'.

Blended house names often confuse the passer-by, who is likely to be an amateur etymologist. Some householders have overheard remarkable explanations of the names they themselves formed, with people stating confidently that they have visited the places so named. Mrs M. Evans also told me in a letter about the vicar's interpretation of **Maralan,** which derived from Margery and Alan. 'Ah! Latin *mare*, "sea", and Welsh *a-lan*, "high".' Mrs Evans adds: 'As we were in the middle of a coal-field, with a view of coal-tips, I was speechless.'

A name blending more than two names may take only the initial letter of each. In **Kahne Lodge** the first word is for a Kathleen, Amber, Harry and Norman Ellis. An Australian **Kenjarra** is felt to honour John, Eric, Kenneth, Audrey, Joyce, Ross and Keith. One cannot help feeling that the most successful names of this type manage to build in more than one meaning. **Montrose** can thus be a transferred place name and a blend of Tom, Rose, Sheila and Tony at the same time.

It is not only family names that form the basis of blended names. **Tarrazona** is a reminder of two hotels where the householders spent their honeymoon; **Neldean** is from the song 'Nellie Dean' made famous by Gertie Gitana; **Lacoa** commemorates Los Angeles, City of Angels for someone who lived there for several years; **Hillside** includes elements from two previous house names; **Duke Leigh** is for HMS *Duke of York* and a naval base. If the last example seems a very masculine one it is only fitting, for it seems to be the husband who more often than not names the house.

But why, one may ask, do some people instinctively turn to the idea of blending names while others would never dream of doing it? Whatever the conscious reason for choosing a name of this type there appear to be signs of name magic revealing themselves again. For me at least there is a parallel between blending names and the practice of mixing ingredients of special significance to arrive at a powerful potion. I do neither of these things personally, but the more I look at the naming practices of my fellow men, the more I detect these deep-rooted beliefs in name magic.

Transferred house names

Surveys I have made on large estates in the Midlands and South of England show that 32 per cent of suburban house names are transferred from other nomenclatures. The largest group consists of transferred place names, which are usually borrowed because of sentimental associations. The place mentioned may be a birthplace, where a couple met, became engaged, spent a holiday or honeymoon, or formerly lived. An Italian place name I once asked about was where the son of the family had been killed during the war. When you see tears in someone's eyes on an occasion like that you become aware of a name's private meaning in a way that no amount of abstract thinking could achieve.

A house which was 'bought for a song' in the village of Angmering, Sussex, was named *Arches*. The owner was the music-hall entertainer Bud Flanagan who, together with his partner, Chesney Allen, made a fortune from their song 'Underneath the Arches'.

Other reasons for place name transfer—leaving aside the large country-houses which are known by the name of the nearest village—include a liking for a song (**Sorrento**), a wish to honour a clan chief (**Rossdhu**), a combination of favourite hymn tune and holiday associations (**Melita**). Often it is only the namer who can explain the thought process that led to the transferred name, as with **Clairvaux** 'because it is associated with St Bernard and our wedding day was his feast day'; **Pitcairn** because the couple met on a ship the day it arrived there; **Culloden** because the English wife and Scottish husband thought it appropriate to use the name of a battlefield where their nations once fought. I admit to having made completely wrong guesses about two other place names that have been used as house names—**Littleover** and **Knockmore.** Both turned out to have been chosen for the usual sentimental reasons, though I had thought the first a member of the 'money reference' group, the second a 'statement' name.

Transferred field names form another worthwhile group of house names. **Copstone, Pottersfield, Stone Brigg, The Gowter, The Yeld, Venborough, The Wainams** and **The Spawns** are some examples. It seems fitting that fields which are built on should at least leave their names in the area. Many live on by becoming street names; others have to wait for householders with a feeling for the past to rescue them from old documents. Street names themselves lead to house names, as do ship names, pub names, any names that exist. One couple met in a hospital ward, so the name of the ward became their house name. Famous racehorses such as **Arkle** and **Bandalore** have brought winnings to many and given house names to a few grateful backers. **Tia Maria** was suggested by a liqueur bottle, **Sunderland** not directly by the place but by the name of an aircraft flown during the war. Finally, some house names—but not as many as one might expect—are simply the family names of the people living there.

Descriptive house names

The householders who link and transfer names are probably sentimentalists; the down-to-earth prefer a no-nonense, factual name. The house is on a hill, so let it be **Hilltop** or **Hillside.** It's a **Corner House,** has **Twin Chimneys, Blue Shutters** or is at the **Heathside:** the house names itself.

House names like these are obviously very sensible if they are given to houses which have no number names. They are the nearest verbal equivalent to number names—utility names. Activity names such as **The Vicarage** belong here, and little more need be said about them.

To his matter-of-fact home, which was called Stone Lodge, Mr Gradgrind ('Facts alone are wanted in life') directed his steps.

Charles Dickens *Hard Times*

Other descriptions are by no means as functional. **Sunnyside** and **Dawnside** can hardly be put into the same category as **Barnside.** Nor are the metonymic descriptions which make use of flowers or trees that happen to be growing in the garden as practical as the **Blue Gates** type of name. **Roseleigh** and **Oak House** show the most common elements of this kind of name. Animals and birds are often mentioned in house names, including **Dog Cottage.** This is one instance where the use of 'house' would have been humorous instead of snobbish.

Many names are actually of the **Woodside** type in that they describe the house's position in relation to something nearby, but the connecting element is omitted. **Rill Cottage** and **Bonny Brook** are examples of such names. The use of 'view' in a name implies nearness to whatever can be seen, but once again such names are not functionally descriptive. **Castle View** and the like are outward descriptions which by no means identify the houses concerned. Such names are really as vague as **Sunset View.**

Examples of environmental descriptions have already been given with the 'wind' names. 'Sunny' names are of the same kind, though clearly more positive in outlook. Names like **Sunshine** and **Sunnyhurst** may slip into the commendatory class, expressing what is hoped for rather than describing a real situation. They are commendatory in another sense when they are used for seaside boarding-houses along with such names as **Seascape** and **Seaview.**

We must consider as descriptive names those which describe the occupants of a house. The number of people in the family is often indicated as in **Izaners, Triodene, The Foursome, Fyve Fold, Us Lot.** The fact that the householder is retired is indicated in many names, especially the **Dunroamin** type, eg **Dunskruin** for a retired prison warder. Many converted names are also a direct reflection of the occupants' pastimes. **Extra Cover, Double Oxer** and **The Bunker** are probably as effective as any descriptions could be of someone's cricket, show-jumping and golf interests. Music-lovers are likely to choose names such as **Harmony** or transfer the names of composers or pieces of music to their homes. A love of literature leads to transfers from characters and titles of novels, but conversions such as **Brillig,** from the Lewis Carroll poem, also occur. One **House at Pooh Corner,** however, is because of a nearby sewage-farm.

Sometimes the house names which say most about the occupants are not those which do so deliberately. Names like **Cosynest** and **Merriland, Sheerluck** and **Joys** are especially revealing of attitudes and philosophies, though names of all kinds do this to some extent. An astute door-to-door salesman, one would think, might be able to plan his opening remarks on the basis of the house name, which hints strongly at the character of the namer.

Apart from the category of name that is chosen, its form can reveal still more about the namer. Names in foreign languages are especially interesting in this respect. Why was **Chez Nous,** for instance, once *the* typical English house name, when many English people would have had no idea how to pronounce it and would not have been able to translate it? *Chez* represents an Old French *chiese*, Latin *casa*, originally a 'shepherd's hut'. *Chez nous* is a curious fossil in modern French, to be translated 'at our house', but it is even more curious that it should have appeared in countless English streets. It is now disappearing, though occasionally made a joke of in the form **Shay Noo.**

All the name was meant to do for the occupants of the house, we must assume, was to show knowledge of a foreign language. This would in turn hint at a good education and foreign travel. Knowledge of foreign languages and travelling abroad are no longer the status symbols they once were, though an amazing number of **Casa Nostras** have appeared since package tours began.

'How do I find the blasted house?'
'The name's on the door.'
'What is the name?'
'Wee Holme.'
'My God!' said Frederick Mulliner. 'It only needed that!'

P. G. Wodehouse *Portrait of a Disciplinarian*

Names in Welsh, Gaelic, Manx, Cornish, Maori and Australian Aboriginal are obviously different in character. They show a national pride which is nothing to do with impressing the neighbours. Latin names are of several sub-categories, such as religious, botanical and learned. With these, and with Greek names, one is somehow far less suspicious of an urge to impress others. The names usually have some point to them and genuinely reflect the background or interests of the namers. Names in other languages—and The Names Society's files contain house names in at least forty-five languages—are often linguistic souvenirs after residence abroad or a sign that one of the occupants of the house is from the country concerned. Since they are so rarely understood by passers-by, they contrast strongly with the public-statement type of name we were looking at earlier.

Another form a name may take is a back-spelling. The motivation behind such names is difficult to understand but they undoubtedly please many people. Those who are reluctant to put their family names above the porch in its normal form are often quite happy to put it there spelt backwards. I suggest you try reversing your own name to get an idea of the dreadful results this usually achieves. **Gnilknud** is no worse than many which are to be found in suburban streets.

As house names, however, they are part of the rich variety of names that are there for the consideration of a suburban stroller. They add the final personal touches to the historical anecdotes contained in place names, street names, pub names and the like. They have what one might call a language of their own which one must be prepared to study a little. It amply repays the effort.

Beach-hut, caravan and houseboat names

Those who do not live in suburban streets need not feel left out. A holiday stroll along the beach can often be enlivened by the names of those mini-houses, the beach-huts. Monstrous puns and jokes strike exactly the right note as the children play noisily in the background: **RR's by the Sea, Strip and Dip, The Winkle, Avarest, Taconap, Linga-Longa, Thut, Bikini Bay, Lang May Your Lum Reek, Brewden, Dormat, Bunk House** and **Hereur.** I once paid an out-of-season visit to a caravan site in order to collect similar names there. This led to my being arrested by a police dog (whose superb name turned out to be **Justice**), but I managed to note down such caravan names as **Brief Encounter, Cara Mia, Kip Inn, Pent House** (a marvellous comment on the confined space), **Tin Ribs** and **Leisure Daze.**

Houseboats provide a further field for investigation. Kelsie Harder has aroused my envy with a report of some name-collecting he did in the Valley of Kashmir, which has many houseboats bearing English names. Floating along on a lake in such a beautiful place must make one's investigations particularly pleasant. The names Professor Harder collected included many transferred girls' names, flower names and bird names. **Cutty Sark, Miss England, Highland Queen, HMS Pinafore, Dream Boat** and **Buckingham Palace** hint at the wider range of names used.

The houseboats are often let to tourists, and carry announcements to that effect. On one occasion when Mr Khrushchev was in Srinagar a river-boat procession was arranged which passed by two such boats. They carried large signs which read: '**Miss America:** Running hot and cold: Ready for Possession' and '**Miss England:** Sanitary fitted: Ready For Occupation.' Mr Khrushchev is said to have been highly amused.

Let Miss England bring us back to that country for a brief summary of its house names. They are thick on the ground in the South, but thin out as one travels northwards. There are more of them on the coast than inland. They are mainly transferred, linked or are descriptive, but they are also a fine repository of folk-humour. The humorous names are again found mainly in the South. Northern names are more dignified, as are Welsh and Cornish names.

As a naming system, house names have their own characteristics, which I hope have emerged in this chapter. They have a distinctive quality, a unique taste. Perhaps this is what we should expect. They are, after all, home-made names.

Sabine Grossenwahn, divorced niece of Boone Havock, whose Louisiana-plantation-style bungalow was known as Alimony Hall.

Sinclair Lewis *Cass Timberlane*

Following the ancient custom by which the Englishman strives to preserve the sanctity of his castle from strange visitors by refusing to give it a street number, hiding it instead under a name like Mon Repos, Sea View, The Birches, Dunrovin, Jusweetu, and other similar whimsies, the demesne of Mr Hogsbotham was apparently known simply as The Snuggery.

Leslie Charteris *Follow the Saint*

The house was called Dilkhush, 'to make the heart glad'; that was as common a name for a house in India as Fairview or Mon Repos in Europe.

Rumer Godden *Kingfishers Catch Fire*

A house by any other name

The words listed below have all been used by house-namers as replacements for the word *house* itself.

Abode formerly a temporary residence, a place where one waited.
Adobe technically a house built with adobe bricks, which are made from sun-dried earth and straw.
Ark figuratively, a place of refuge.
Asylum an inviolable shelter, but jokingly used for 'a mad house'.
Berth usually used by ex-sailors in the sense of 'a comfortable place'.
Billet used by ex-soldiers. *Billet* is French 'note', and the original reference was to the official notice which required a house-holder to lodge a soldier.
Booth a temporary dwelling.
Bothy originally a hut for unmarried workmen.
Box from a 'shooting box', a small country house.
Bungalow originally a Bengal house.
Burrow often used by families called Fox.
Cabin
Cartref Welsh 'home'.
Casa Spanish 'house'.
Castle *Castlette* is also jokingly used.
Châlet
Château French 'castle', also used for country house.
Corner Used in the sense of 'secluded place'.
Cot a cottage. Dialectal cote also occurs.
Cottage
Court jokingly used because the house-holder 'holds court' there.
Cover in the sense of shelter.
Croft a small-holding.
Curatage used for a house where a curator or curate lives.
Deanery sometimes also used by families called Dean.
Den a place of retreat. Favoured by families named Lion/Lyon
Dive used jokingly to indicate that much (disreputable) drinking takes place there.
Domus Latin 'home'. Usually in the phrase *dulce domum*, 'home sweet home'.
Fold a pen for animals, but used with Christian reference, eg John 10:16 'There shall be one fold and one shepherd'.
Folly for a costly structure showing the builder's, or buyer's, foolishness.
Grange originally a granary, now a country house.
Hacienda Spanish 'country house (plus estate)'.
Hall residence of a territorial proprietor.
Hame Scottish 'home'.
Harbourage a shelter.
Haunt a place of frequent abode.
Haven
Hermitage used for a solitary house, or by occupants who prefer their own company.
Hive for a house swarming with people.
Hole for an untidy house.
Holm(e) flat ground near a river, but used as a spelling variant of 'home'.
Home
Homestead implying a fairly large house and estate.
Hoose Dialectal 'house'.
Hovel
Hut
Igloo Eskimo 'house', used for a cold house.
Inn used for a house that welcomes guests.
Keep a stronghold.
Kiosk technically a Turkish or Persian summer house, rather than a newspaper stand. Used for a very small house.
Kot modern variant of 'cot'.
Lair presumably a place where those who feel hunted can be safe.
Lean-to a building with rafters resting against another building.
Lodge especially a keeper's house or an estate.
Maison French 'house'. *Mini-maison* has also been used.
Maisonette
Manor also in joke names such as *Bedside Manor.*
Manse a Scottish ecclesiastical residence.
Mansion
Nest
Neuk a Scottish form of 'nook'.
Nook a sheltered place.
Ohm used for 'home' by an electrician.
Palace
Parsonage
Penthouse originally a lean-to. Now an additional structure on a roof, suggestive of luxury. Jokingly used for a house, caravan, etc, where people are pent in.
Place perhaps from references to 'my place'.
Port a shelter from storms.
Presbytery a priest's house.
Rectory
Residence
Rest ie resting-place.
Retreat
Roost used especially for a house which has many women living in it, a hen-house.
Shack
Shanty a cabin.
Shebang the original meaning of the American slang term was a hut or shed.
Shebeen a low-quality public-house in Ireland, used as a house name to suggest conviviality.
Shieling also *Shealing.* Originally a hut erected near pasture land in Scotland.
Shelter
Studio
Ty Welsh 'house', used in names like *Ty Ni*, 'our house'.
Vicarage
Villa a superior mansion.
Ville French 'town', but used erroneously for villa.
Warren for a house likened to a rabbit warren.
Wurly the hut of an Australian Aboriginal.

A selection of house names

Alcrest from the phrase 'after labour comes rest'.

Allways husband used to close letters to his wife with this version of 'always'.

Almost There

Aroma opposite a brewery.

Arden a wartime sign 'Warden' lost its initial letter and was taken to be a house name.

Aurora goddess of the dawn.

Bachelor's Adventure on a holiday cottage.

Bali Hai a house on a hill.

Banshee House a 'banshee' is a female elf thought to wail under the windows of a house when someone is about to die.

Bar None for a home in the style of a ranch house.

Barn Yesterday a converted barn.

Bassetts 'all-sorts' in family (four adopted children).

Beam Ends

Beau Nidle

Bedside Manor the home of a retired doctor.

Belleigh Acres a pun on 'belly-achers', ie 'complainers', a name inspired by unfriendly neighbours.

Bendova home of a retired schoolteacher.

Bethany Biblical, 'house of poverty or affliction'.

Billion Bill and Marion live there.

Birdholme 'holme' means an islet, but is often used as a synonym of 'home' in house names.

Birdhurst 'hurst' can mean hillock or wood.

Bonanza Spanish 'prosperity'.

Boogaroph the opposite of **Kumincyde**.

Brouhaha French 'indistinct noise'.

Brytome 'bright home'.

Buffers on a converted railway carriage.

Ca d'oro name of a Venetian palace ('house of gold'). A sign on the gate of the suburban version says: 'Beware of the Doges'.

Cartref Welsh 'home'.

Chattings

Chippings can refer to a kind of sparrow or squirrel.

Clover used metaphorically, 'to be in clover'.

Cobblers

Cobwebs 'currently owned by Woolwich Equitable Building Society'.

Conkers for the horse-chestnuts that fall into the garden.

Copper Coin all that remained after paying for house.

Copper Leaves a retired policeman lives there.

Copper View opposite the police station.

Copsclose next door to the police station.

Cowries little shells found on nearby beach.

Crackers 'to have bought this house'.

Deriter a back-spelling.

Deroda a back-spelling.

Diddums Den

Dinnawurri another version of **Wyeworrie**.

Dokomin

Doo Town in Tasmania, where all the houses have names like **Yule Doo, Av Ta Doo, Zip Eddie Doo, Doodle Doo, Doo Us, How Doo You Doo, Didgeri Doo**.

Dulce Domum Latin 'home sweet home'.

Dunbolyn A. P. Freeman, the former Kent bowler, lived here.

Dunkillin home of a retired surgeon.

Dunravin home of a retired vicar.

Dunrobin home of a retired lawyer.

Dunwistairs a bungalow.

Elasrofton a back-spelling.

Eleven Plus for the number name **11B**.

Elveston an anagram of 'lovenest'.

Emange M and G.

Emoclew a common back-spelling. Does one receive the reverse of welcome when calling there?

End in View at the end of a lane, inhabitants retired.

Eureka Greek 'I have found it'.

Fair Dinkum to show Australian connections.

Fir Teen the number name 13.

Foon Hai Chinese 'happiness', transferred from a Chow.

Forbidden Fruit on a holiday bungalow.

Fortitoo the number name 42.

Fost Un first house in Foston Avenue.

Four Walls Mr and Mrs Walls and their two children live there.

French Leave a holiday house.

Genista Mrs Broom lives there.

Gnuwun 'new one'.

Gorldy Woods 'worldly goods'.

Halcyon Days 'calm days', a reference to a fabled bird.

Halfdan a Danish wife.

Hangover Hall in Temperance Road.

Happy Landing

Happy Ours

Harfa House a semi-detached house.

Heimat a place name transferred by a trampoline enthusiast.

Hen House a reference to the number of daughters in family.

Highlight

High Loaning 'loaning' is a piece of uncultivated ground on which cows are milked, but the mortgage is also referred to.

Hindquarters for the Hind family.

Hobbs 'half owned by building society'.

Holmleigh usually a fancy spelling of 'homely'.

Hysteria next door to a house called **Wistaria**.

Isor a house which is an 'eye-sore'.

Itzit

Jacquaboo the daughter is Jacqueline, the son's nickname is Boo.

Jayceepayde

Justintime

Justinuff

Kayaness K and S live there.

Kef the enjoyment of idleness, a state of dreamy intoxication usually induced by drugs. An Arabic word.

Koldazel
Kon Tiki because they drifted there.
Kosinuk for 'cosy nook'.
Ladsani a father and two sons.
Lautrec because it has 'two loos'.
Little Boredom Mr Bore lives there.
Loggerheads
Long Odds
Lucky Dip a holiday bungalow by the sea.
Majority the number of the house is 21.
Mascot 'mother's cottage' but also 'anything which brings luck'.
Mews Cottage Whiskers is the name of the occupant.
Mini Bung
Moonshine house first seen in moonlight, and son interested in astronomy.
Morning Feeling Mr Munday lives there.
Mutters the neighbours' reaction when they moved in.
Mylzaway a house which is miles away from anywhere.
Myob '*M*ind *y*our *o*wn *b*usiness.'
Nycere it's 'nice here'.
Obu Garret
Offbeat a retired policeman lives there.
Onaroc a reference to *Luke* 6.48: 'He is like a man which built an house, and digged deep, and laid the foundation on a rock.'
On the Rocks
Osterglay back-slang for Gloucester.
Owzat a cricketer who was stumped for a name.
Pan Yan the occupants of the house are always in 'a pickle'.
Peelers a converted police station.
Pennings because of letters written to builders.
Poodleville for the dog.
Popova
Pretty Penny
Pro Tem Latin 'for the time', ie until a number name is allocated.
Raylvu
Ringside a retired boxer.
Robins Nest the Robinsons live there and hope not to fall out.
Rolyat the Taylor family lives there.
Roundabout Friday from the builder's favourite saying.
Round the Bend for a corner house.
Ruff Roof
Rumbling Winds
Seaview on a house in London, forty miles from the sea.
7777777 the number of the house is 49.
Sherkin
Shieling a rough hut erected on pasture-land in Scotland, or the pasture-land itself.
Shilly Chalet
Sixpence the Tanner family lives there.
SJ619714 the National Grid reference of the house.
Sky Lark on a holiday cottage.
Spite Cottage because of a 'spite wall' built to spoil the neighbour's view.
Spooks across the road from a cemetery.
Stocking Cottage 'stocking land' has been cleared of stocks.
St Onrow a blend of John*ston* and *Row*berry.
Straw Hat a thatched cottage.
Stumbledon when houses were scarce.
Sunny Jim a pun on Sonny Jim, used to address any young boy whose name is not known.
Taintours on a Council estate.
Tamesis an older form of Thames.
Ten Minutes a home ten minutes' walk from the station.
Testoon a coin name used by a numismatist.
The Chimes the Bell family live there.
The Filling for a house sandwiched between others.
The Ginger House because of its orange-brown tiles.
The Halfyard former field name, from a measure of land.
The Hardies next door to **The Laurels**.
The Hive the Honey family live there.
The Jays sometimes refers to birds that visit the garden, more often to members of the family whose first names begin with 'J'. Also a metaphorical reference to people who chatter a great deal.
The Keep the Norman family live there.
The Marbles in Elgin Road.
The Moorings home of the Moore family.
The Pride the Lyons family live there.
The Rashers the Gammon family live there.
The Ripples it has a corrugated-iron roof.
The Speck one meaning of the word 'speck' is a small piece of ground.
The Stumps a dentist lives there.
39 Steps
The Toucans Mr and Mrs Cann live there.
The Tops
Three-O for the number name 30.
Tiedam a back-spelling.
Tivuli a back-spelling.
Top Notch
Touche Bouais Jersey French 'touch wood' because the number is 13.
Touch Me Pipes from a Cornish miner's expression meaning 'to rest and have a smoke'.
Traynes near the railway.
Tre-Pol-Pen to show that the occupiers are Cornish.
Triangle House for the Corner family.
Troy Hector is the husband's name.
Tuksumduin
Tusikso the number is 260.
Tu-Threes the number is 33.
Twa Lums for the 'two chimneys'.
Tympcasa tympana (which the owner plays) + *casa*, 'house'.
Uno (United Nations Organization) husband and wife of two nationalities, children born in other countries.
Uprising Twenties the number is 21.
Up Si Daisy
Valhalla in Teutonic mythology the hall where Odin held court.
Venetia named for the Venetian blinds.
Weemskat a dialectical form of 'we're broke'.
Well Away a holiday bungalow.
Wevernder
Whooff for the dog.
Widdershins also withershins, for a house facing in the opposite direction from those round it.
Wiktro '*w*ell *i*t *k*eeps *t*he *r*ain *o*ff'.
Wom dialectal for 'home'.
Wun Tun the number of the house is 100.

Popular house names

In 1988 the Halifax Building Society ran a computer check on over fifteen million addresses of investors and borrowers. The most popular house names in Britain, revealed by the survey, are listed below.

Rank	House name	Number
1	The Bungalow	4485
2	The Cottage	4049
3	Rose Cottage	2936
4	The School House	2038
5	Hillcrest	1607
6	The Lodge	1595
7	Woodlands	1391
8	The Coach House	1205
9	Hillside	1162
10	The Gables	1138
11	The Old School House	1080
12	The Vicarage	1059
13	Sunnyside	1045
14	The Croft	1024
	Treetops	1024
16	Ivy Cottage	1012
17	Greenacres	1005
18	Fair View	1002
19	The Willows	973
20	The Firs	902
21	The Old Rectory	877
22	The Old Vicarage	852
23	The Hollies	842
24	The Laurels	804
25	Wood Side	799
26	Hill View	789
27	Orchard House	783
	Yew Tree Cottage	783
29	Wayside	763
30	The White Cottage	742
31	South View	726
32	Windy Ridge	725
33	The Beeches	723
34	Spring Field	722
35	Four Winds	706
36	West View	697
37	The Haven	690
38	Grey Stones	687
39	Orchard Cottage	679
40	High Field	673
41	The Rectory	661
42	The Grange	623
43	The Nook	616
44	The Homestead	595
45	Brookside	592
46	Mill House	571
47	Lyndhurst	565
48	Holly Cottage	556
49	New House	552
50	Lynwood	549
51	Greenways	542
52	Station House	540
53	Sunny Bank	538
54	Rose Bank	526
55	The Elms	525
56	Mayfield	519
57	Oak Dene	518
58	Cartref	507
	Oaklands	507
60	The Orchard	504
61	Pear Tree Cottage	503
62	Tanglewood	502
63	Meadow Wood	495
64	Avalon	494
65	The Poplars	492
66	The Barn	485
67	The Spinney	483
68	The Manse	481
69	Cornerways	472
	New Lands	472
71	Brook House	467
72	Hilltop	453
73	The Limes	450
74	Hill House	447
75	Keepers Cottage	445
76	Willow Cottage	444
77	White Lodge	443
79	Wind Rush	437
79	Conifers	435
80	Park View	427
81	April Cottage	425
	Garden Cottage	425
83	The Oaks	422
84	Bridge House	421
85	Fairfield	417
86	Fairways	416
	White Gates	416
88	The Mount	409
89	Park House	401
90	Lyndale	396
91	Hazeldene	394
92	The Pines	393
93	Braeside	392
94	Belmont	390
95	Church Cottage	388
	Rosedene	388
97	Cherry Trees	387
98	The Old Post Office	386
99	Oak Cottage	385
100	Beechwood	384
101	Lilac Cottage	381
102	Corner Cottage	375
103	Spring Cottage	369
104	The Paddock	366
105	Field House	360
106	Brook Cottage	358
107	Byways	357
	High Trees	357
109	Lynton	355
	Manor Cottage	355
	Manor House	355
112	Mount Pleasant	351
113	Tall Trees	348
114	Wood View	344
115	Avondale	343
116	Hollybank	340
	The Cedars	340
	The Manor House	340
119	Meadowcroft	338
120	Mill Cottage	336
121	Beech House	335
122	Brooklands	333
123	Little Orchard	330
124	Primrose Cottage	326
125	Beech Croft	325
126	Cherrytree Cottage	323
127	Hill Croft	322
128	Holly House	320
129	Chapel House	319
130	Oak Leigh	318
131	River Dell	317
132	Glen Dale	312
	Green Acre	312
	Highlands	312
135	Vine Cottage	311
136	Cross Ways	310
137	The Birches	309
138	Ash Lea	306
	Ivy House	306
140	The Hawthorns	304
141	Fern Lea	303
	New Bungalow	303
143	Bank House	301
	Braemar	301
145	West Winds	300
146	West Field	299
147	Brook Field	297
	Jasmine Cottage	297
	North Lodge	297
	Stone Leigh	297
	Woodstock	297

13 Trading a name

On several occasions in previous chapters the question of the 'image' created by a name has been mentioned. Personal names, place names and street names, as we have seen, have all been changed in order to create a different impression of the named entity. In our last chapter we had the example of **Dotheboys Hall** being used for business purposes more than as a house name. When we come to deal with trade names as a group, therefore, we are not moving into a totally new world.

Trade names share the basic characteristics of other nomenclatures and the same categories of names are found. The relative importance of those categories, however, is different. As with house names there are many blends, but invented names play a far greater role in the trade name system than in any other nomenclature we have yet examined.

Types of trade name

The reason for the importance of invented trade names will quickly emerge: first it is as well to distinguish between those trade names which were originally meant to identify one business enterprise rather than another, and those names which are designed to further business *in themselves.* **Guinness** is an example of the former, **Lux** of the latter. Guinness is a transferred surname, representing the Irish *Mag Aonghusa* or *Mag Aonghuis,* 'son of Angus'. **Angus** in turn is usually explained as 'one choice', with 'one' being used in the sense 'unique'. Having passed from family name to company name, Guinness was further transferred to the product, but there was never at any time an intention to make use of an intrinsic 'meaning' in the name in order to attract business.

Lux, however, was clearly a conscious attempt at bringing a name into being that would help to associate the product bearing it with certain desirable concepts, 'luxury' and 'luck'. These ideas are suggested without being stated, while the name itself retains a brevity and force useful for advertising purposes. When one notes, too, that its form almost certainly ensures that it will remain a name and not slip into the general vocabulary, it is seen to combine most of the features a trade name needs. The name even has a respectable etymological background, since *lux* is Latin for 'light'.

Early trade names

In earlier times the respectability of products was thought to be assured if their names were based on Latin and Greek or made historical allusions. A soap powder being advertised in 1907, for instance, was **Phenozone,** which apparently relied on the public's understanding of the 'shining' allusion in the Greek prefix. Madame Downing of Charing Cross Road in London was offering a corset a few years earlier to male readers of the magazine *Society.* She called it **The Kitchener.** Lord Kitchener was still alive at the time and one wonders what he thought of this use of his name. To go with the corset gentlemen of the time were offered a hat known as the **Sans Souci.**

The last example shows how startlingly unsuitable a product name could be at this period. *Sans Souci* is certainly a famous name, and it is sometimes found today as a suburban house name. At least it has some point when it is so used. Frederick the Great gave this name to his palace at Potsdam, which made it well known to European high society. Voltaire, who often visited him there, had his doubts about the name, saying that in spite of its meaning ('without care') 'a certain renowned king was sometimes consumed by care when he was there'. Thackeray made a rather similar comment in his *Roundabout Papers: 'Sans Souci* indeed! It is

In the 19th century, pomposity and prolixity were admired to some extent. This was reflected in many of the trade names of the time. As usual Charles Dickens could be relied upon to note the phenomenon and make fun of it. In *Nicholas Nickleby* Mr Bonney is talking of a proposed new company. It is to be the *United Metropolitan Improved Hot Muffin and Crumpet Baking and Punctual Delivery Company*.

'Why,' says Mr Bonney, 'the very name will get the shares up to a premium in ten days.'

mighty well writing, *"Sans Souci"* over the gate, but where is the gate through which Care has not slipped?'

It is difficult to see how such historical and literary associations, which would have been known to relatively few, could have been thought suitable for a hat. Perhaps the namer thought only of the literal meaning of the words, which he assumed the middle-class public would recognise or would never admit to not recognising. The hat seems to have been a soft one, so that it didn't matter if it became crumpled. It could be carried or worn 'without care'.

Such a thought process is likely to lead to a highly unsatisfactory trade name because it satisfies the namer rather than the people at whom the name ought to be directed. It was probably such names that Claude Hopkins had in mind when he wrote in 1923: 'The question of a name is of serious importance in laying the foundation of a new undertaking. Some names have become the chief factors of success. Some have lost for their originators four-fifths of the trade they developed.' Hopkins's comment needs a great deal of expansion. It applies in particular to converted and invented names, which must be chosen with minute care, but transferred surnames have certain points operating in their favour. In the case of a product a family name can carry with it an implicit guarantee. The name transfer suggests a complete identification of the producer with his product, and hints that a pride in the latter is linked with his fundamental self-respect. There is an uncompromising honesty in pinning one's own name to a business or product that will offset neutral qualities in the name itself. **Dunkling,** for instance, would hardly recommend itself as a linguistic unit to someone who was looking for a trade name, but a former namesake of mine who founded a jeweller's shop in Australia was right to use his name for trade purposes. By doing so he made a statement of good intent.

Surnames as trade names

The fact that **Dunkling** is established as a trade name, in one part of the English-speaking world at least, raises an interesting point. If I wanted to set up business as a jeweller in Australia I might not be allowed to use my rightful name for business purposes. I could be legally restrained from doing so if I implied by means of my name that I was connected with the established business. In Britain Messrs Wright, Layman and Umney Ltd, for instance, obtained injunctions against a Mr Wright which stopped the latter trading under a name containing Wright or Wright's. The company claimed that it had a wide reputation in certain goods under the name **Wright's,** and Mr Wright's similar goods would naturally be confused with theirs.

Surnames occur frequently as trade names, but the use of first names is less common. They are mostly seen as shop names, especially those of hairdressers, but they do not seem to be popular for products launched nationally. Ford tried it with a car called the **Edsel,** the name that Henry Ford had chosen for his son. Many attributed the failure of that particular model to the nature of the name Edsel itself.

Other names become trade names, especially popular place names such as **Oxford** and

When they first began to appear on the social scene, automobiles were given names like *Fidelity, Utility, Safety, Safeway, Gadabout, Bugmobile, Fool Proof*. Compare these with the more recent *Mustang, Cobra, Wildcat, Panther, Cougar, Meteor, Comet* and *Starfire*.

D. B. Graham has commented that modern names convey life-styles. He cites (in his article 'Of Edsels and Marauders') names like *Rambler, Ambassador, Marquis, VIP, Cutlass, Rebel, Valiant, Maverick, Lark, Caprice, Boss, Judge, Grabber, Swinger, Spoiler* and *Marauder*.

Cambridge, but there appears to be a definite preference in modern trade-naming to form new names by various processes. One problem with transferred names is that they are by their very nature shared with another entity. The trade name ideal lies in uniqueness. There are other ideals, of course. The name should catch the attention and be memorable. It should also work below the conscious level of the person who is exposed to it and appeal to the motives which really do cause him to buy a product, though he might be reluctant to admit it. As Vance Packard suggested by the title of his book some years ago, product names should be *Hidden Persuaders.*

Lipstick names

A few years ago, Jill Skirrow looked at the names of some lipsticks that were then on sale to see what characteristics they revealed. The namers, she decided, had thought deeply about what was at the back of a woman's mind when she went into a shop to buy lipstick. She would be thinking about making herself look young, hence **Young Pink.** There would be thoughts of kissing, and **Snow Kissed Coral** could remind her of these thoughts while pretending to talk of something else. 'Snow' would also be suggesting coolness to her, with 'purity' lurking in the background, while 'coral' threw out hints of the South Seas. The combination of ideas in Snow Kissed Coral is illogical if one stops to think about it, but the namers knew that very few customers would try to analyse it. Even if they did it would not matter. As a slight obscurity will sometimes be used by a poet to make the reader or listener pay more attention, so an illogicality in a name may make customers notice it more.

The woman buying lipstick is presumably anxious to emphasise her femininity, the namers think, so they tempt her with **Moods of Red, Porcelain Pink, Tiger Rose, Quiet Flame, E. S. Pink.** Moods of Red, Jill Skirrow says, would appeal to the 'vampire instinct' in a woman, and I must accept her word for it. The 'porcelain' reference certainly suggests high quality and fragility, and E. S. Pink plays on 'extra sensory perception', flattering the feminine illusion about intuition. Tiger Rose and Quiet Flame show the male idea of a woman who wants to be docile yet passionate, and may even reflect the idea some women have of themselves.

The moistness of a lipstick is emphasised in **Dewy Peach,** the 'peach' probably linking with the idea of a 'peach of a girl'. **Pink Whisper** cleverly introduces a suggestion of intimate conversations and softness, while focusing the customer's attention on her mouth. **Gilt-Edged Pink** and **All Girl Gold** cater for the dreams of wealth that are lurking at the back of many a young feminine mind. Perhaps Miss Skirrow goes too far, however, in suggesting that 'gilt-edged' will also hint at excitement because of 'guilt'. The same is no doubt true when she says that names like **Bare Blush** and **Itsy Bitsy Pink** have partly been chosen because the lips are especially used to pronounce them. If she *is* right, then the namers have been too subtle, for when these names are most influencing the customer they are probably not being spoken aloud.

The creators of trade names have long been known for their punning. Some results of their efforts noted by Ellen T. Crawley, editor of the *Trade Names Dictionary*, are:

Lip Lip Hooray for a lip-stick collection.
Line Tamers, *Waist-a-way* and *Sweet Add-a-line* for foundation garments.
Bee Bop for an insecticide.
Prints Charming for stationery.
Eye-gene for eye-drops.
Sweeping Beauty for a make-up brush.
W'eyes Guise for false eyelashes.

Lipstick names make a particularly interesting study because the namers are forced to be right up to date in the associations they build into a name. The customers will not be loyal to a particular lipstick for very long, and it is not really possible for the manufacturers to decide on a few names that they will then try to establish for all time. The namers are faced with a challenging situation in which customers will be running their eyes over a great many similar lipsticks, ready to indulge their whim of the moment in deciding which one to buy. While a customer is examining one colour rather than another, the lipstick names will be doing their work, planting suggestions in her mind. I suspect that they plant them in a man's mind too, for even I find myself going back to certain names again and again as I run my eye down the list. **Apricot Dazzle,** for example, attracts me very much as a name, though I can't begin to analyse why. I don't even like apricots.

Hotel names

At about the same time as Miss Skirrow was making her analysis of lipstick names, I was conducting an experiment into hotel names. I asked a large number of people to look at several names. I then asked them to indicate which hotel of those mentioned they thought they would stay at if they had no other information but the name on which to base a judgment.

Names like **Grand Hotel** and **Queens Hotel** were rejected by many because they 'sounded expensive', but they were chosen by others because the names suggested luxury. The **Seaview Hotel** type of name did rather better than the **Sunshine Hotel** type, the former apparently being taken at its face value, the latter regarded with suspicion. Names which I planted experimentally to see whether they would make an appeal were ignored even more completely than I had expected. These were of the **Summerjoy Hotel, Magic Carpet Hotel** variety. Modern-looking names like **Hotel Two** failed to appeal to young or old, while **White Hermitage Hotel** made a quiet showing with older informants. By far the most popular name, particularly with women, was **Little Orchard Hotel.** I was conducting my survey in the centre of a city and presumably their choice revealed an emotional need for a rural retreat.

Poetical names

'Emotional need' is rather a key phrase in this context. Trade names of the kind we have been discussing are not meant to be prosaic descriptions, satisfying the mind with the facts they supply. If they are to be successful they must be like poetry, and the advertising men who suggest new names are commercial poets in their way. A typical poetical device, for instance, is the deliberate exploitation of polysemy—the different meanings that can be suggested simultaneously by the same word. This is constantly used in trade names. In *Trade Name Creation* Jean Praninskas quotes the example of a popular American detergent, **All.** This manages to suggest that it gets all the dirt out of clothes, that it can be used in all machines for all fabrics, does all cleaning jobs and does the work all by itself. For a simple word of three letters it is surely doing a great deal for the product it identifies. Its conversion to a trade name was a brilliant piece of inspiration.

Other poetical devices seen in trade names include rhyme, hyperbole, personification and metaphor. **Merry Cherry,** another lipstick name, shows the usual end rhyme, but one should include here the initial repetition of sound known as 'alliteration'. **Coca Cola** is an obvious example. Hyperbole is exaggeration that is not meant to be interpreted literally, so **Magi-Stik** does not really lay claim to occult powers. By personification a machine or device can be turned into a human servant, a **Handy Man** or **Brewmaster.** Metaphor simply compares the product being named with something having associated qualities, such as the speed and grace of a **Jaguar.**

Other trade name devices

But if one kind of trade name is a miniature poem, making intensive and subtle use of the language, another kind prefers to play games with the language. The various possibilities for playfulness are seen in names like **Helpee Selfee, Eat-A-Voo, Choc-A-Lot, Get Set** and **Ab-Scent.** Helpee Selfee manages to say to Americans that it is a laundry by implying that it has Chinese connections, although the same name elsewhere might suggest a self-service Chinese eating-place. These national associations are probably worthy of a special study in themselves. We have already noted the value of a Russianised name to a ballet-dancer and a French name to a hairdresser. There are presumably many other ways in which vague national associations can be exploited.

Eat-A-Voo plays on the established 'rendezvous' element in many a restaurant name. Apart from making it clear that an eating-house is referred to the name also emphasises a down-to-earth attitude. 'Never mind the fancy foreign names,' it seems to say, 'we're more concerned with the real business of providing a good meal.' As with all jokey names, there is a suggestion that the namer means to entertain and establish a relaxed atmosphere.

Choc-A-Lot identifies the product and adds a further enticement with its suggestion of quantity. Get Set takes a familiar phrase and deliberately reinterprets it. The reference is to a hair preparation and the joke obviously has point to it. What the name brilliantly implies is that having had one's hair set with this product the customer will then be ready to 'go' in the best sense. Ab-Scent is a deodorant, and the name is etymologically satisfying as well as being a pleasant pun.

Trade name spellings

A problem created by trade names is referred to by my former colleague, Dr Sven Jacobson, in *Unorthodox Spelling in American Trademarks.* As is well known, the lack of relationship between the sounds of English and English spelling already causes great difficulty to children who are learning to read. This difficulty is aggravated when children, and adults for that matter, are constantly exposed to spellings in trade names of the **Sox** and **Kwik** kind. Louise Pound commented on 'The Kraze for "K"' as long ago as 1925 in an article in *American Speech.* Other trade name crazes, as Sven Jacobson points out, include the use of hyphens in names like **Tys-Ezy** (plastic straps), **Sto-A-Way** (tables) and **Shat-R-Proof** (safety glass); the use of letter pronunciations in **E-Z-Chek** (brake gauges) and **Trip-L-Bub-L** (chewing-gum); the use of 'x' for '-cks' in **Clix** (light switches) and **Hanx** (paper handkerchiefs); the use of 'z' for 's', as in **Stripzit** (paint-stripper) and **Kilzum** (insecticide).

Names like **Kehr-Fully Made,** used by Kehr Products Co., and the **Get It Dunn Safely** of Dunn Products are obviously not deliberately reformed spellings. They simply profit by a similarity of sounds that is suggested by existing names. It might be claimed that such names add to the orthographic confusion, but the language itself tolerates such an amazing variety of forms that a few more will probably do no harm. Consider how the same sound is represented, for example, in words like meet, meat, mien, me, seize and foetus.

Trade names are in any case virtually forced to resort to spelling variations as the search for new names becomes more difficult. At least 25 000 new consumer products and services come into being in the English-speaking world each year, and each of them needs a new name. They are not in the happy position of being able to borrow names from a small central stock, nor do they inherit names by family tradition. Their names must not resemble those already in existence for similar products, and there are many other restrictions placed on them.

The most notable restriction, however, is undoubtedly that of transfer within the system. What would be considered to be natural duplication elsewhere—when several namers independently arrive at the same name—is also banned. All names must be registered, and only one namer is allowed to be credited with a name in a distinctive business area. As far as possible, therefore, there is an insistence that a name should be truly individual.

This situation has already led, in the relatively short history of legally registered trade names, to there being more trade names on record than there are words in the English language. In 1961 Lippincott and Margulies, the American industrial design and marketing consultants, stated that a half-million trade names were already registered. At that time there were rather less entries in the mammoth *New English Dictionary.* Supplementary volumes of the dictionary have since been published, but it is inconceivable that the vocabulary of English increases at the rate of fifty or more words a day, which is the rate at which trade names multiply. Many of these names are then pounded into the minds of the public by the use of highly sophisticated techniques. Our medieval ancestors were educated by signs and pictures; we are forcibly given a literal education by way of trade names and advertising slogans.

According to Garson Kanin, in *Moviola,* the actor Ricardo Cortez, born Jacob Kranz, took his stage name from a brand of cigars.

Trademarks still supply a visual accompaniment to many names, but these are becoming design abstractions rather than meaningful symbols. Few companies today try to find a **Nipper** who will sit and listen to 'His Master's Voice' with an appealingly attentive ear, though such emotion-rousers add their own touch of aptness to any name. The tendency now is to favour initials and display them in an interesting way, but one suspects that the results often satisfy professional designers rather more than they satisfy the public. A display of

The names of some of Shakespeare's more famous characters have been transferred to products. *Falstaff* aptly names an American beer, and *Hamlet* now means a cigar to British television audiences. *Romeos,* inevitably, have become prophylactics, and *Juliet* lends her name to a bra. It is also possible to buy *Lear* cigarettes, *Macbeth* glassware and *Miranda* rubber gloves, though the last-named, especially, comes close to being sacrilege.

Famous Brand Names, Emblems and Trade-Marks, by Marjorie Stiling, tells the stories behind many familiar names. *Maxwell House* was the name of a luxurious hotel in Nashville used by presidents, diplomats and the European nobility. It was there that Joel Cheek first tried out his new blend of coffee, subsequently using the hotel name for the coffee itself. *Quaker Oats* were named by a man who was not a Quaker himself, but was impressed by the human qualities the Quakers displayed.

graphical ingenuity is wasted if it is mere self-indulgence.

These initial names are unsatisfying in linguistic terms as well as visual, but as company names they are not obliged, perhaps, to create a public image. The companies concerned present themselves to the public by a wide variety of product and brand names, and a modern multi-national company, which has probably acquired many smaller businesses, is likely to own a very large number of names indeed. The latter represent a new phenomenon, a company nomenclature. This in turn must come to play an important part in the lives of employees, affecting their general use of language. The time will certainly come, if it has not done so already, when larger companies will be obliged to prepare dictionaries of these corporate languages for the benefit of employees.

Trade number names

With a few notable exceptions, trade-namers seem to have steered clear of number names. There is the very well-known **4711**, to which one may add examples like **7-Up** and **Vat 69**. Heinz showed a few years ago that '57' could be given an individual meaning, for that number always appeared in their advertising. Had it been converted to a number name at that point it would have been synonymous with **Heinz** itself. Number names are certain to come into their own before long, given the general situation of dwindling supplies of other names and ever-pressing needs. The first in the field will have a distinct advantage, being able to make use of numbers which carry a favourable meaning to many people. Latecomers might have to contend with **900424214** or something of the sort.

As it happens, it would not be as difficult to establish that number name as it might at first seem. Most of us these days successfully cope with several seven-digit number names, otherwise known as telephone numbers. We think of a certain person and the row of numbers comes into our minds. For anyone in a business where the customers need to telephone, the adoption of the telephone number as a trade name would seem to have several advantages. An advertising jingle could then be devised to fix the number name firmly in the mind.

A point that seems to have been missed where number names are concerned is that they have various verbal translations. The monstrous-looking nine-digit group quoted above could become 'nine hundred, four two, four two, one four' rather than 'nine hundred million, four hundred and twenty-four thousand, two hundred and fourteen'. The former breakdown enables a simple mnemonic to be constructed: 'Nine hundred four two, four two, plus one four you.' It would be possible to fit those words to a catchy little tune and have the entire number name nationally known in a few weeks by means of television advertisements.

The trade-namer is not yet in the position of having to accept arbitrary sets of numbers emerging from a computer as name suggestions, though he has for some years now been turning to a computer for new names. A computer can certainly supply combinations of letters that are 'names' of a kind, but the need is for names that will evoke an emotional response. These are needed, at least, in all those commercial areas where the buying of one product rather than another is likely to be a spur of the moment decision as far as the customer is concerned. Naturally there are many other instances where the price and quality of a product are what count, or where a particular product is uniquely associated with one name. When a customer is in what might be called a 'generic situation' the names come into their own. The customer is thinking: 'I need some soap, or a vacuum-cleaner, or whatever.' The trade name's job is to replace that generic, *without becoming a generic term itself.*

The latter point is reached if a person is able to speak of 'hoovering' the carpet and then use an **Electrolux** or other make of machine to do the job; if he thinks of 'cola' as a kind of drink which equally well describes both **Coca Cola** and **Pepsi Cola.** 'Launderette' may still be technically a trade name, but it has passed into the ordinary language and no longer suggests a particular company. Whoever formed the term forgot to leave a name-identifying element within it, a dash of strangeness that would have enabled it to stand outside the main vocabulary.

These generic replacement names are going to be the ones that are more and more difficult to find in the future. Praninskas concludes that industry 'will see to it that the names of their new products are created by literary artists', and there is much to be said for that argument. It is quite clear, for example, that Dickens would have made a superb creator of trade names. Many trade names discussed in this chapter also reveal, I would have thought, a high literary quality. Namers have already learned a great deal from the techniques of the imaginative writers.

What they need to study now, however, is not literature. Their way ahead lies in a study of other nomenclatures, where a million ordinary people have brought names into being. Transfer *within* the trade name system may not be possible, but transfer into it from other non-commercial systems—avoiding the over-worked first name, surname and place name nomenclatures—is not only possible but increasingly necessary.

There must be relatively few trade-namers, but we are all affected by their work. I have not made a full study of my children's speech, but in spite of restricted television viewing it is quite clear that they are familiar with a large number of commercial names. In the course of a few days I was personally able to write down 400 product names with which I was familiar, including those of many products—such as cigarettes—that I would never dream of using. However, these trade names are part of our lives and language.

Pleasures of trade names

For my own part I try to make the best of the situation and enjoy trade names. I am happy to read the yellow pages of the telephone directories to find **Thun-Thoots** and **Teeny Poons,** which are children's sun-suits and feeding-spoons. I like the **Mity Tidy** shelves and the **Kant Mis** fly-swatters, the **Bug-Shok** insecticide and the delightful **Slug-A-Bug.** I cannot wear **Enna Jettick** shoes, which are for ladies, or **Top Secret,** a hair-tint which presumably calls for a better supply of hair than I can boast, but their names are welcome.

I enjoy, too, the names of shops. The Greater Cincinnati telephone directory lists beauty salons called **Pamper Hut, Kut-N-Kurl, Magic Mirror Beauty Shop.** Some British equivalents are **Beyond the Fringe, The Pretty Interlude** and **The Cameo.** Antique shops are another pleasant group: **The Shop of the Yellow Frog, Granny's Attic, Passers Buy, The Tarrystone, Past Perfect.** A member of The Names Society, Sidney Allinson, reports on Canadian names such as **The Salvation Navy Store, Poise 'N' Ivy, The Bra-Bar, Juicy Lucy's, The Fig Leaf, Leg Liberation, The Wearhouse** and **Undieworld,** all of which sell clothes in Toronto. Meanwhile, the *boutique* game continues in London and elsewhere, with **Bootique, Beautique, Shoetique, Fruitique, Motique** (car accessories), **Junktique, Bespotique** (tailor's) and **Fishtique.**

Some of these names you may consider to be dreadful, but their collective message is clear. Trade name creators have not yet run out of ideas, and the English language is alive and well.

Trade names

Some indications of the various ways in which companies or products have been named are provided by the following examples, many of which are derived from *Dictionary of Trade Name Origins*, by Adrian Room:

Adidas a company founded by Adolph Dassler (1900–78), known to his friends as Adi. He added the first three letters of his last name to his pet name to form the trade name.

Aeroflot Soviet 'air-fleet'.

Agfa from the initial letters of *Aktiengesellschaft für Anilinfabrikation* ('limited company for dye manufacture').

Alka-Seltzer the Alka is an abbreviation of 'alkaline'; Seltzer in general terms refers to fizzy water, or *Selterser wasser*, 'water from Nieder Selters, Germany'.

Ampex founder of the company was Alexander Mathew Poniatoff, who added -ex to his initials (from the word 'excellent').

Andrews Liver Salt from the church of St Andrew, near the head offices of the company.

Aspirin from German *acetylirte spirsäure* ('acetylated spiraeic acid') plus the chemical suffix -in.

Audi a company formed by August Horch. His last name translated into Latin gave *audi*, 'hear!'.

Avro the aircraft company was founded by A. V. Roe. The origin of the trade name is thus clear: it is less clear why Mr Roe's parents named him Alliott Verdon.

Babycham originally for the 'baby chamois' used as an emblem, though a link with 'champagne' rather than a goatlike antelope was inevitable in the minds of customers.

Bakelite invented by a Belgian–American L. H. Baekeland, who added the chemical suffix -ite to part of his name.

Bata the shoe company was founded by the Czech, Tomas Bata.

Bejam from the initials of Brian (brother), Eric (father), John Apthorp (founder of company), Millie and Marion (mother and sister).

Berlei founded by Fred Burley.

Birds Eye from the name of Clarence Birdseye (1886–1956) who devised process for freezing foods in small packages.

Biro invented by the Hungarian Lázló Biró.

BMW made by the *Bayerische Motoren Werke*, Bavarian Motor Works.

Bostik ultimately from Boston (Massachusetts) and 'stick'. The original company was the Boston Blacking Co.

Bovril Latin *bos, bovis* 'ox' gives the first two letters. 'Vril' was a word invented by Edward Bulwer-Lytton in his novel *The Coming Race* (1871). It meant 'an electric fluid, the common origin of forces in matter'. Professor Weekley was probably correct in assuming that this word in turn was derived from Latin *virilis* 'manly'.

Brillo from the word 'brilliant' rather than the Italian *brillo*, 'drunk'.

Cadillac manufactured in Detroit (a small town near Bordeaux), which was founded by a Frenchman who was Sieur de Cadillac.

Calor Latin 'heat'.

C & A founded by the Dutch brothers *C*lemens *and A*ugust Brenninkmeyer.

Carlsberg originally the name of the brewery near Copenhagen which stood on a hill (Danish *berg*). Carl was the name of the brewer's son.

Castrol the product was originally based on castor oil, obtained from castor beans.

Cherry Blossom originally used for a toilet soap, sold in tins such as those later used for the shoe polish.

Coca Cola from the coca shrub and cola nut.

Cow Gum from the name of Peter Brusey Cow, one-time owner of the company.

Cuticura Latin *cutis* 'skin' and *cura* 'care'.

Dan-Air from *D*avies and *N*ewman Ltd, which established an air service; nothing to do with Denmark and the Danes.

Dorothy Perkins the trade name was borrowed from the name of the rose.

Drambuie from Gaelic *dram* 'drink' and *buidh* 'yellow'.

Durex a name which came 'out of the air' to the chairman of the company in 1929. Adrian Room links it with words such as 'endurable' rather than Latin *duresco* 'harden'.

Fanta from the German word *fantasie* 'fantasia'.

Findus an abbreviation of *F*ruit *Ind*ustries.

Frisbee from the name of the Frisbie Bakery in Connecticut. Its pie tins could be thrown much as modern frisbees.

Golden Wonder from the variety of potato, which is, however, not suitable for making crisps.

Granada borrowed from the Spanish province when the group's chairman went on holiday there.

Harpic the inventor was *Har*ry *Pic*kup.

Hovis suggested in a competition to find a suitable trade name by Herbert Grime in 1890. He based it on Latin *hominis vis* 'strength of man'.

Kenwood the company was founded by Ken Wood.

Kia-Ora Maori 'good health'.

Kiwi the shoe polish was marketed by an Australian who named it in honour of his New Zealand wife.

Kodak invented by George Eastman, the photographic pioneer. His favourite letter was K.

Lec originally the Longford Engineering Company.

Lego Danish *leg godt* 'play well'.

Lemon Hart from the name of an 18th-century wine merchant, Lemon Hart. Lemon is more usual as an English last name, deriving ultimately from 'beloved man' or 'sweetheart'.

Lucky Strike introduced during the Gold Rush of the mid-19th century.

Mars the company was established by an American, Forrest Mars.
Mazda name of the Persian god of light.
Meccano from the phrase 'mechanics made easy'.
MG for Morris Garages, set up by William Morris, later Lord Nuffield.
Nivea the feminine of Latin *niveus* 'snowy'.
Ovaltine originally 'Ovomaltine' from Latin *ovum* 'egg', 'malt' and -ine. Shortened to Ovaltine when introduced to Britain from Switzerland.
Pepsi Cola influenced by Coca Cola and intended to relieve dys*pepsia*.
Perspex Latin *perspexi* 'I looked through'.
Quink from 'quick-drying ink'.
Rawlplug invented by John Rawlings.
Rentokil originally meant to be Entokil, from Greek *entoma* 'insects' and 'kill'. The initial R- was added because a name like Entokil was already registered.
Ribena the Latin botanical term for the blackcurrant is *Ribes nigrum*, which suggested this name.
Rolex an arbitrary word of no meaning, invented by Hans Wilsdorf.
Ronson founded by Louis V. Aronson.
Ryvita 'Rye' plus Latin *vita* 'life'.
Schweppes the business was begun by a German, Jacob Schweppe.
7-Up originally called Bib-label Lithiated Lemon-Lime Soda. Its inventor then considered, and rejected, six alternative names before deciding on 7-Up.
Shell the founder of the company, Marcus Samuel, imported shells in the early 19th century.
Sony based on Latin *son* 'sound'.
SR the initials on the toothpaste stand for sodium ricinoleate.
Tesco founded by Sir John Cohen, one of whose earliest suppliers was T. E. Stockwell. The latter's initials plus the first two letters of Cohen led to Tesco.
Typhoo invented by John Sumner in 1863, but of no meaning.
Uhu the German word for 'eagle owl'. Such birds live in the Black Forest, where the German manufacturers of Uhu have a factory.
Volvo Latin 'I roll'. Originally the name of a company making ball-bearings.
Wimpy J. Wellington Wimpy was a hamburger-loving character in the Popeye cartoon strips.

Names of hairdressers

Hairdressers in Britain and Australia are rather fond of giving their establishments punny names. Here is a selection of them taken from telephone directories.

Ahead of Time
Ali Barber
All Ways Ahead
Aristocuts
As You Like It
Back 'n' Front
Barbery, The
Basin Cut
Beyond the Fringe
Blow Your Top
Boldilocks
Bubbles
Busy Scissors
By George
Champu
Chick Hairdresser
Classy Clippers
Clear Cut
Clikkers Hair Studio
Clip Joint
Clipso
Comb Corner
Crazy Curl
Cream of the Crop
Crimpers
Crowning Glory
Curls and Capers
Curl Up And Dry
Curl Up and Dye
Cut Above
Cute Cuts
Cut Loose
Cut 'n' Dried
Cutting Corners
Cutting It Fine
Cutting Room
Do Yer Nut
Fringe Benefits
Frizzy Lizzy
Golden Scissors
Goldilocks
Hair Dinkum
Hair Doo
Hair Force
Hairizon
Hairmania
Hair 'n' Now
Hairobics
Hairpin
Hairport
Hair Today
Hair We Are
Hair We Go
Hazel Nutz
Head First
Head High
Headlines
Headmasters
Head Quarters
Heads together
Heads You Win
Headway
High Lights
Hot Gossip
Jet Set
Klever Kutz
Knots 'n' Tangles
Krinkles
Last Tangle
Light Waves
Look Ahead
Lucy Locketts
Mirror Image
Mad Hackers
Mane Line
Mop Shop
New Wave
Nuts
One Step Ahead
Perm Factory
Prime Cuts
Rollers
Roots
Rough Cut
Scalpers
Shady Lady
Shampers
Shear Genius
Shear Pleasure
Sheik Look
Sherlocks
Shylocks
Simply Scissors
Smart Set
Snip in Time
Snippets
Sophisticut
Soul Scissors
Split Ends
Streaks Ahead
Sweeny Todd's
Szizzers
Through the Looking Glass
Topknots
Tops
Topsy Turvy
Trimmers
Trimplicity
Undercutters
Unwind Ltd
Uppercuts
Vanity Fair
Vizzage
Wavelengths
Y Knot Hair Care

14 No end of names

I borrow my chapter title from Browning. It seems suitable for a chapter in which I want to emphasise that the names enthusiast draws his materials from a well that never runs dry. This book is obliged to be finite; the subject is not.

In ranging over a wide variety of name topics this chapter is likely to resemble a typical issue of *Viz.*, the newsletter of The Names Society. A discussion about names of all kinds went on in its pages for nearly ten years, until rising costs and a lack of voluntary help caused it to cease publication. It was not immediately known as *Viz.* when it began in 1969: that was naturally one of the subjects that came up for discussion—what to call a magazine devoted to names. Suggestions included **Onoma** and **Names**—which were already being used for similar publications—**The Nominist, Nomen, Name, The Onomatologist, Nomina, Namely, The Nomenclator, Philonoma, Nomenalia** and **Notamina.**

Other magazine names

Viz. was only one of countless small magazines that are non-commercial labours of love. Poetry magazines abound, for instance, and have names like **Poetmeat, Nightrain, Bean Train, Wild Dog, Long Hair, Software, Fish Sheets, Circle, Circuit, Nomad** and **Stand.** It would be easy to write a verse about them, for one finds a **Twice, Nice, Vice** and **Spice,** a **Choice** and **Voice, Ambit** and **Gambit.** An ever-increasing band of enthusiasts also collect science-fiction magazines, which usually have names that are suitably out of this world. Some examples are **Bweek, Zot, Erk! Reverb Howl, Kangaroo Feathers, Egg, The Hog on Ice, Son of Fat Albert.** A few have names that could easily be absorbed into the English suburbs as house names, however. **Shangri-La** would certainly be at home there, as would **Soitgoze. Curse You** might cause a few mutterings among the neighbours, but **Powermad** might merely strike them as an honest statement.

'Alternative' publications in recent years have included **Wipe,** printed entirely on toilet paper, and **Arse,** published by the Architects' Revolutionary Socialist Enclave.

Pop group names

Names that share many of the magazine name characteristics are those of pop groups. In pre-pop days there were names like **The Andrews Sisters,** which followed the direct description tradition of the theatre. A dash of self-publicity led to **The Supremes, The Magnificent Men, The Spellbinders.**

Another reminder of trade names in the sixties and seventies comes with respelt names, used by famous groups such as **The Beatles** and **The Monkees**. A vaguely religious set of names was discernible in 1968 such as **The Righteous Brothers, The Apostolic Intervention, The Angels** and **The Spiritual Five.** Names that with a slight change of form could easily have appeared on the covers of poetry magazines were also to be found, and some have endured well: **The Searchers, The Seekers, The Shadows, Saturday's Children.**

Names that showed an aggressive reaction to the Establishment were very similar to those of the alternative and 'underground' magazines. These were the groups called **The Enemies, The Animals, The Rejects, The Freak-Outs, The Barbarians** and the like. The science-fiction magazines translated into pop groups names such as **The Grateful Dead, 3½, The Mindbenders, U.F.O., The Leathercoated Minds, The Happenings, The Mind Expanders.** All of these are meant to be attention-catchers, and

Launce: I think Crab my dog be the sourest-natured dog that lives: my mother weeping, my father wailing, my sister crying, our maid howling, our cat wringing her hands, and all our house in a great perplexity; yet did not this cruel-hearted cur shed one tear.

William Shakespeare *The Two Gentlemen of Verona*

'Has she a dog?'

'A cocker spaniel, Mr I., called Benjy.'

'Conciliate that dog, Bert. Omit no word or act that will lead to a 'rapprochement' *between yourself and it. The kindly chirrup. The friendly bone. The constant pat on the head or ribs. There is no surer way to a woman's heart than to get in solid with her dog.'*

P. G. Wodehouse *Cocktail Time*

some perform that function well. But names like **The Strawberry Alarm Clock** and **The Nitty Gritty Dirt Band**—the latter being rare in that it condescends to admit a connection with music—are like certain paintings. They are fine as exhibition pieces, but would be difficult to live with.

But we shall all, no doubt, get thoroughly used to such names as time passes. There is evidence on all sides of a new adventurousness in names which seems likely to affect a great many nomenclatures. Newly formed football clubs, for instance, are leaving aside traditional name elements such as 'Wanderers', 'Rovers', 'United' and 'Athletic'. There are already local teams called the **Alley Cats, Eskimoes, Stags** and **Juggernauts.** Before very long another generation will be wanting to show *its* individuality, and we must wait to see how that affects names.

Meanwhile, we can look back once again at some of the names given in the past. One area of great interest is the living world that surrounds man, the world of animals and plants. Another is that of man's various forms of transport—ships, locomotives, cars and the like, all man-made objects which are often felt to develop a personality of their own. There is enough material in those areas to fill another book of this size, so we must be brief.

Animal names

By animal names I mean the proper names of individual animals rather than the generic names of species used by a zoologist. We could all write down the names of several individual animals who are as well known to us as people. In many cases a pet is considered to be one of the family. Other animals are internationally famous. **Lassie** is better known in Germany, for instance, than **Leslie**, as I often discovered.

A special group of animal names have become part of the English language. We can refer to a tom cat called **Percy** without it seeming strange, for 'tom' is no longer felt to be a form of **Thomas** in that context. Historians who are cat-owners will know that before Tom came on the scene, **Gib**—from **Gilbert**—was the usual name for a male cat. A 'tabby' looks suspiciously like a corruption of 'tib cat', which in some dialects remains the female equivalent of tom cat, but it has a different origin. Tabby is a striped taffeta and derives from the Arabic name of the place where it was made. A tabby cat was earlier described as 'tabby-coloured'. **Tib** was once the name of a low-class woman, the female equivalent of **Tom,** and was probably a diminutive of **Isabel.**

In medieval times cats and dogs were no doubt referred to by generic names and no others. These days individual names are bestowed on a wide range of pets and often display all the ingenuity we find in other nomenclatures. **Dora,** for instance, was owned by Annabel Bool and therefore known more fully as **Adorabool. Ocky** was **Octavius** on formal occasions and received that name because it was its owner's eighth cat. **Polly**, a corgi, was named from a resemblance to a television announcer of that name, and **Nelson** belonged to a **Hardy** family. Among my own favourite names are **Curlicue** for a curly tailed mongrel. **Edom** for a cat ('over Edom will I cast out my shoe'—Psalm 60), Worthington for a Basset hound and **Rover** for a budgerigar. The last example was intended to be an ice-breaker at parties.

Adrian Room's booklet on *Pet Names* gives many

more examples, some of which have already become minor classics. **Keith** and **Prowse** for a pair of cats are probably the best known, the agency of that name being famous for its advertising slogan: 'You want the best seats, we have them.' But children do a great deal of pet-naming and are not usually quite so subtle. They like incident names or descriptive names especially. My own children were probably typical when they named their white rabbit **Flash** because he was off 'like a flash' the first time they put him down.

Needless to say, these informal pet names are usually different from the registered titles of pedigree animals. I use the word 'title' deliberately, for they are often of the **Duchess of Bolcord, Lady of Arvon** type. A Kennel Club *Stud Book* I have by me shows that even formal names can be interesting, however. Among the bulldogs listed are **Abracadabra, Boom-De-Ay, Bully Boy, Derby Day, Queer Street, Rev. Dismal Doom, Bubbles, Cigarette, How Nice** and **Trifle.** There is even a bitch called **Buttercup**, though this would strike most of us as a typical name for a cow. Perhaps it was a humorous mis-naming, for many owners see no need to be too serious in the names they give. Chows with names like **Chin Chin** and **Yum Yum Victoria** are listed, and there is a Japanese spaniel called **Stoneo Brokeo. Spot XXVIII** is not without a certain humour, and has point in being basically the kind of shoutable name that is necessary for daily use.

She would save a slice for Sunny, the cat—his drawing-room name Sung-Yen had undergone a kitchen change into Sunny.

Virginia Woolf *Between the Acts*

The Buttercup example reminds us of non-domestic animal names, of which once again there are countless thousands. Some are worthy of special note, however. R. D. Blackmore mentions a cow called **Dewlips,** which has a definite charm, and the quinquemammalian cow called **Sanctity** discovered by a member of The Names Society who once looked into the subject would always belong in the Top Ten. Cows usually get suitably feminine names given to them, such as **Candy** and **Marigold,** but **Bullyface, Beefy, Droopy, Hoppy** and **Tango** are among other names that have been bestowed. One cow name that later became nationally known as a trade name was **Carnation.**

National attention was focused in Belgium a few years ago on the name of a donkey. A farmer who was protesting about agricultural policy arrived in Brussels with a donkey who bore the same name as the then minister of agriculture. This kind of satirical naming would probably not be allowed in Britain: it would be considered unfair to donkeys. I see from a show catalogue that British donkeys actually receive names like **Mrs Donk,** which is a fascinating generic link name, **Jack the Ripper, Mockbeggar Gussie** and **The Vicar of Bray.**

Who but Stevenson could have named a donkey Modestine?

John Steinbeck *The Pastures of Heaven*

Different kinds of horses receive names of different kinds, as one would expect. There was formerly a special point to the names of dray-horses, which always worked in pairs. Their partnership was often recognised in pairs of names like **Thunder** and **Lightning, Crown** and **Anchor, Might** and **Main, Time** and **Tide, Rhyme** and **Reason, Pomp** and **Circumstance.** No rules governed such names, such as those which have long been imposed by the Jockey Club on namers of racehorses. The restrictions do not prevent the creation of interesting names for the latter, however. Many are what could be called 'notional blends', a group we have not yet mentioned in connection with any other names.

Notional blends lead to names like **Mickey Mouse** by **Lightning Artist** out of **Cinema, Watchdog** by **Warden of the Marches** out of **Beagle.** A phonetic link may also be present, as in **Dial O** by **Diomedes** out of **No Reply,** and puns are possible: **Sea Pier** by **Duke of Buckingham** out of **Mollusca.** In the 1930s **Buchan** and **Short Story** had many bookish offspring, such as **Portfolio, Bookseller, Bibliograph** and **Birthday Book.**

Once the names come into being, by whatever means, they can exert a great influence on amateur punters. Horses are often backed because their names seem significant to a particular person at a particular time. The names are taken to be omens, in other words. We do not seem to be able to escape name magic wherever we look. One cannot help wondering, in passing, how much money has been lost to all but the bookmakers on poor horses that happen to have had brilliant names.

We must leave the animal world with a brief summary of what we have found, for there are wide areas still to cover. What is important in animal names is not so much the predominance of one class of name rather than another, but the evidence one constantly finds of careful, affectionate naming. The names of pets, especially, have the friendly tone that one would expect and make a pleasant collection.

Flower names

If we turn now to flowers, our expectation might lie in the direction of lovely names rather than friendly ones. Oscar Wilde probably spoke for many people when he made Lord Henry, in *The Picture of Dorian Gray*, say:

> 'Yesterday I cut an orchid for my buttonhole.... In a thoughtless moment I asked one of the gardeners what it was called. He told me it was a fine specimen of **Robinsoniana,** or something dreadful of that kind. It is a sad truth, but we have lost the faculty of giving lovely names to things.'

We have not lost this faculty, as it happens, but one can see what Wilde meant. One has only to glance at a list of botanical names to understand also the remark of the nineteenth-century pamphleteer, Alphonse Karr, that 'botany is the art of insulting flowers in Latin and Greek'. The attractive names of flowers tend to be the folk names: **Sweet William, Jack-Go-To-Bed-At-Noon, Gill-Over-The-Ground, Good King Henry, Bitter Sweet, Morning Glory, Youth-And-Old-Age, Nancy Pretty** (or **None so Pretty**), **Old Man's Beard, Mourning Bride, Coral Bells.** The last named, to take one example, translates into the botanical name *Heuchera sanguinea.*

The botanists might argue, however, that scientific accuracy is of more importance to them than aesthetics. Historically speaking, it was logical for them to turn to classical languages that were internationally understood in order to create descriptive names. Those names may seem barbarous to the average person, but still more people would no doubt be offended if botanists made use of that other international language which begins '1, 2, 3'.

There are many signs that those who name cultivated varieties of flowers, such as the rose, make an attempt to find a name that suggests beauty. Rose varieties include **First Love, Maiden's Blush, Coral Dawn, Alpine Glow, Burning Love, Elegance, Golden Showers, Passion** and **Wildfire** as well as the famous **Peace.** (See also page 12.) Oddities occur, nevertheless. It is strange to find **Atombombe,** for instance, named in 1954 and presumably referring to a mushroom shape. One wonders also whether the reasons for choosing names like **Grumpy** and **Radar** really justified attaching them to roses. A number name that has been used for a rose, **Forty-Niner,** named in 1949, seems to fit in quite well with the names around it.

Scientists now say that there is some point in treating a plant as one would treat an animal, talking to it affectionately in order to make it grow better. We are therefore probably not far from the day when house plants will be named individually by their owners. Until that day comes, plant names remain at the generic level. It is probably just as well, for even at that level there are hundreds of thousands of names.

Apple names

The above statement about the vast quantity of names may be too general to impress itself upon the mind. Let us take a specific example. Whether we are gardeners or not, we all eat an apple from time to time. How many different kinds of apple are there? **Cox's, Granny Smith, Golden Delicious**—any more?

The *National Apple Register of the United Kingdom* lists 6000 more, together with another 1600 names that have been used as alternative descriptions for the same 6000 cultivars. To be fair, many of these variant names are slight respellings of one another, abbreviations and so on. Translations of English names into other languages are also treated as variants. Nevertheless, the Golden Delicious, for instance, has also been known as the **Arany Delicious, Stark Golden Delicious** and **Yellow Delicious,** and other apples have a long string of such genuine synonyms. **King of the Pippins** has such aliases as **George I, Hampshire Yellow, Pike's Pearmain, Princess Pippin, Seek No Further** and **Winter Gold Pearmain.** This is the kind of complexity that lies beneath not only 'apple' but most of the generic terms we use every day.

The apples that were popular in the 17th century were rather different from those in the shops today. One was the **Api,** or **Lady Apple,** carried by ladies in their pockets because it was very small and had no odour. It had been found growing wild in the Forest of Apis, in Brittany, and is known to have been in Louis XIII's garden by 1628. The **Catshead**, which 'took the name of the likenesse' according to a 17th-century writer, was later to be much used for apple dumplings. Particularly interesting were **Costards,** which at one time were sold for a shilling a hundred by costardmongers (the later costermongers). 'Costard' became a slang word for the head and occurred in the phrase 'cowardy costard', later corrupted to 'custard'. As an apple name it had originally referred to the apple's ribbed appearance (Latin *costa*, 'rib').

Another apple name well known in the 17th century was the **Nonpareil,** 'having no equal; peerless'. The word is unlikely to occur in a normal English conversation today, but it might well have done so in Shakespeare's day. He himself uses it in several of his plays—Miranda is said to be a nonpareil in her father's eyes, for instance. If there is ever a comprehensive *Dictionary of Names* which lists names that occur in several nomenclatures, 'Nonpareil' will be a typical entry. It names birds and moths, houses and a size of printing type among other things. In 1580 it became the name of a British warship, though this was renamed the **Nonsuch** in 1603.

Ship names

Since brevity is essential in this chapter, we must allow this mention of ship names to lead us into the world of transport, which we mentioned earlier as another area of great naming interest. We move from the world of living things to one where inanimate objects are constantly being personified. Captain T. D. Manning and Commander C. F. Walker introduce the subject well in their *British Warship Names*:

'... of all creations of men's hands, the ship—and especially the sailing ship—is surely the nearest approach to a living entity, possessing individual traits which distinguish her from her sisters, even of the same class. Small wonder, then, that the sailor, ever a sentimentalist at heart, has always endowed his vessel with an almost human personality and given her a name; or that, deprived as he is for long periods of the society of womankind, that personality should invariably be feminine—though by some illogical thought process he does not demand that the name should follow suit, and sees nothing incongruous in referring to an **Agamemnon** or a **Benbow** as "she".'

The Royal Navy has established over several centuries a stock of names that can be transferred from ship to ship. In this way names such as **Victory, Warspite, Orion, Ajax** and **Greyhound** have figured in great naval combats at widely differing periods. Because the ships were specifically built for these combats from the 16th century onwards, their names were often suitably war-like. **Warspite** probably represents 'war despite', showing contemptuous disregard for the danger of battle. **Dreadnought** speaks for itself, as do **Triumph, Repulse, Revenge** and **Defiance, Swiftsure** is thought to be another contraction, this time of 'swift pursuer'.

In our discussion of place names in the New World we saw the influence of both Charles I and Charles II. The latter turned his attention also to his ships when he returned to England, immediately renaming the **Naseby,** which commemorated a Roundhead victory, the **Royal Charles.** Other ships became, for obvious reasons, **Royal Oak, Royal Escape** and **Happy Return.** The **Cleveland** was named after the Duchess of Cleveland, one of his mistresses. His highly subjective naming continued even with the **Loyal London,** which was paid for by the citizens of the city. The ship was sunk, but later raised and rebuilt. It spite of many hints thrown out by Charles, Londoners were less willing on this occasion to provide the funds. Charles struck out the 'Loyal' and allowed only 'London' to remain as the ship's name.

As Jean E. Taggart points out, in her *Motorboat,*

Ships are not always able to live up to their names. An article in the magazine *Yachting* once pointed out that the *Tarry Not* sailed from Maine in November one year with a cargo of Christmas trees. It arrived in Philadelphia in February. *Big Bonanza* was sold for debt four times in thirteen years, and *Brilliant Sailor* held a record for taking longer to cross the Atlantic than any other ship of its kind. A ship called *Prohibition* had a captain who, notoriously, was hardly ever sober.

Yacht or Canoe—You Name It, the United States Navy now has a logical system for naming ships according to their class. Battleships are named for the states, aircraft carriers are named for famous historical fighting ships, or for important battles. Cruisers take the names of American cities or territories if they are larger. People are commemorated in the names of destroyers, frigates, submarines, etc.

The Taggart book contains much interesting information about ships, but the best book on the subject by far was published in 1974 by Don H. Kennedy. It is called simply *Ship Names*, and on almost every page there is something that I would like to re-quote here. For those interested in ships the book is essential. I would go further and say that anyone who is thinking of writing a book about any naming system should study it closely. Among the Names Society's collection of over six hundred books on names it seems to me to be the one which most satisfyingly deals with a single nomenclature.

Ships have often been given nicknames, especially when their official names are difficult to pronounce. Some examples from the British navy:

Agamemnon 'Eggs and Bacon'
Amphitrite ''Am and tripe'
Ariadne 'Hairy Annie'
Belle Poule 'Bell Pull'
Bellerophon 'Billy Ruffian'
Belliqueux 'Billy Squeaks'
Cyclops 'Cyclebox'
Daedalus 'Deadlies'
Dedaigneuse 'Dead Nose'
Niobe 'Nobby'
Polyphemus 'Polly Infamous'
Temeraire 'Trim yer 'air'
Ville de Milan 'Wheel 'em along'

A reading of *Ship Names* makes it clear that we can safely say that all categories of names are represented on the high seas. There was even, at one time, a remarkable example of a physical blend name to add to the notional blends we found in racehorse names. The **Zulu** and **Nubian** were two destroyers that were both damaged in the First World War. A composite ship was assembled in 1917 using the forepart of *Zulu* and the after portion of *Nubian*. It was then named **Zubian.**

Some ship names, such as **Mayflower, Titanic, Mauretania** and **Cutty Sark** are world famous: at the other end of the scale completely are the names of yachts and smaller boats. Whereas modern ships like the great liners need dignified names, private vessels of all kinds allow whimsicality and humour to appear in their names. *Lloyd's Register of Yachts* for 1968, for instance, lists such examples as **Miss Conduct, Miss Demena, Bung Ho, C'est La Vie** (which I have seen elsewhere in the form **Sail La Vie), Annelory** and **Fairynuff.** The last named roughly translates a name I saw on a French chalet, **Sam Sufy** (*ça me suffit*).

Among other names from various sources are **Miss Mie, Miss Fitz, What Next, Bossy Boots, Koliwobbles, Q. Jumper, Tung Tide, Hare-Azing, Codswallop** and **Honey Don't**. I particularly like the names which link with the generic class name. 'Catamaran' is actually an adaptation of a Tamil word meaning a 'tied tree', but to many punsters who own one it is simply another kind of 'cat'. The names therefore emerge as **Nauticat, Kitti, Wild Cat, Cat Nap, Whiskers Two, Pussy Willow, Puss Face, Seamew, Sly Puss, Dupli-Cat, Show'er Puss** and **Pussy Galore.** 'Solo' class yachts receive names like **Solow, So-So, Soliloquy, Imalone, Solace, Slo Koche, Seule, Lone, So-Long, By Me Sen, Soloist.** In the 'Finn' class one finds names like **Huckleberry Finn, Tail Finn, Finale, Dolfinn, Finnigan, Finess** and **Finnisterre.** Even the National 'Flying Fifteen' class does not defeat the jokers. The two 'fs' in the title are picked up in names of the **Ffancy Ffree** type.

All kinds of names occur, not just the jokey ones, and the standard generally is very high indeed. That is to say that if the namers decide to be witty they are usually very witty, often making learned or polyglot allusions. If they decide to be descriptive, convert words into names, link, transfer or invent names, they also seem to do these things well. There are not many nomenclatures where one finds names of the **Sailbad The Sinner** standard.

Train and locomotive names

The care with which boat-owners do their naming reflects the great enthusiasm the boats themselves arouse. An equal amount of enthusiasm is generated for some people by locomotives and trains, though this phenomenon appears to be almost exclusively British. Perhaps only an Englishman

(Cecil J. Allen) could write that many of the trains described in his book 'have become old friends to me', or that 'the route between Victoria and Dover is anything but easy *from the locomotive point of view*' (my italics). Both remarks occur in *Titled Trains of Great Britain*, a loving account of such trains as the **Broadsman, Flying Scotsman, Master Cutler, White Rose, Mancunian, Red Rose, Welsh Dragon, Capitals Limited, Granite City, Statesman** and **Red Dragon.** The *Statesman* was named because it connected with the sailings of the **United States.** The 'Limited' in *Capitals Limited* perhaps referred to the limited number of stops, or first class seats, and the other names all contain references to the places served.

Apart from named trains, most of the larger steam locomotives once had individual names. The practice was established in the early days of Stephenson's **Rocket** and pioneers such as **Novelty, Sanspareil, Invicta** and **Northumbrian,** but when **Locomotion** commenced work in 1825 it also bore the number name, **No. 1.** The many railway companies that sprang up had their own ideas about identifying locomotives, some considering number names quite sufficient, but the Great Western Railway consistently gave verbal names to its express passenger locomotives from the earliest days. When the railways were grouped into four companies in 1923 such names came back into general favour. Everything was set for the small boys (I was among them) who would later gaze upon the powerful giants with considerable awe and carefully underline those names in little books. Later still, 'enthusiasts' were to go much further, removing the nameplates from the driving wheel splashers completely if the opportunity presented itself.

Locomotive names were often grouped thematically as 'halls', 'castles', 'clans', 'granges', 'manors', 'counties', etc. The LNER named some Pacific locomotives after famous racehorses, though this led to the sight of **Sandwich, Spearmint** and **Pretty Polly** standing at the heads of trains and looking rather sheepish. As more and more locomotives were named, so the names were drawn from yet more sources. Many names were those which seem to be free-floating, likely to turn up in almost any nomenclature: **Atlas, Bonaventure, Pathfinder, Blue Peter, Vanguard, Meteor Sunbeam.** Some names looked back to the immediate source of locomotive names, the stage coaches. These had borne names like **Vivid, Lightning, High Flyer, Nimrod, Royal Sovereign, Talisman, Vixen, Arrow, Dart, Comet, Red Rover.** A famous mail-coach bore the name **Quicksilver.**

We see once again how the world of names consists of countless overlapping nomenclatures. It is impossible to look through a book such as H. C. Casserley's *British Locomotive Names of the Twentieth Century* and not be reminded of ship names, place names, surnames, animal names and a dozen other kinds of name. One feels, too, that every name will have its day sooner or later. The stage coach **Red Rover** may have slipped into obscurity, but its name lives on as a pub name and as the name for a London Transport ticket. **Blue Peter** has earned a new kind of fame in Britain as the name of a television programme. Such names call for an individual approach which allows one to trace their path of transfer into different naming systems after their initial establishment as names. **Blue Peter,** for instance, possibly began as a French place name, **Beaupreau,** 'beautiful meadow'. A fabric made there, a kind of linen, was used to make flags. The fabric was called *beaupers* or *bewpers* in English. Professor Weekley suggested that the second part of this word may have been mistaken for **Piers,** which is another form of **Peter**. 'Beau' could then have been changed to 'blue' to suit the actual colour of the flag. Many well authenticated instances of similar word and name changes caused by folk etymology are recorded.

The railways as a whole were sources of very many names. Nicknames for the railway companies soon came into being, usually being based on the company initials. The London, Midland and Scottish was known by such names as **Ell of a Mess, Let Me Sleep** and **Lord's My Shepherd.** The Great Western became **Go When Ready** or **God's Wonderful Railway,** while the LNER was **Late and Never Early. The Bluebell Line** and **Cuckoo Line** were well known branches of the Southern Railway, and the Waterloo and City line became **The Drain.** Much the same kind of process in the USA led to names like the **Apple Butter Route, Spud Drag, Original Ham and Egg Route, Bums' Own** and **Pennsy.**

Frank McKenna, in his *Glossary of Railwaymen's Talk,* mentions nicknames that were used by the railwaymen themselves. The footplatemen from Yeovil, for instance, were known as the **Apple Corps;** the **Master Cutler** was less reverently known as **The Knife and Fork;** an efficient fireman was **Terror of the Tongs;** the Leeds–Carlisle main line was the **Burma Road** because it was difficult to negotiate. One wonders whether many other occupations, other than military, have produced such collections of names. Mining language must include many examples. Geordie pitmen certainly used to name newly opened 'districts', according to one of my correspondents. **Spion Kop** was named after the battle for that hill had just taken place, and grim irony caused **White City** to be transferred below ground.

Lorry names

In many parts of the world individual vehicles are named, and Philip Riley has written an interesting article about the names of lorries in Malta. He thinks that the custom of giving names began when handcarts were the normal conveyers of goods. They had no registration plates but needed to be identified in some way. It became usual to display on them the nicknames of their owners.

The modern lorries which carry on the tradition of naming 'are almost exclusively privately owned', Mr Riley says, which hints at ownership proclamation as the main reason for them. Most of the names are in English, the language used for educational purposes, but there is interference in the spelling of many names due to the influence of Maltese or Italian. A large group of names—which are apparently carefully painted in 'a spiked and ornate lettering, usually in bright red, yellow and green'—are the names of saints. These may be the patrons of villages where the drivers live or the patron saints of the drivers themselves. Other religious names refer to the Virgin Mary or may be statements of faith: **In God We Trust.**

Another large group of names draws its inspiration from the entertainment world. Song titles such as **Sonny Boy, High Noon, Congratulations, Thunderball** and **April Love** appear, and singers such as **Sandie Shaw** and **Cliff Richard** are honoured. Films have an influence, and **Peter Sellers, Steve McQueen, James Dean** are among those stars who drive round Maltese streets. **James Bond** (together with **007**) and **Goldfinger** are there with them.

A wide range of transferred names is called upon, and lorries called **Wilson** and **Kennedy** are seen beside **New York, Victoria, Melbourne, California** and **Germany.** A few lorry owners continue the former tradition of transferring their own nicknames, such as **Happy** or **Blue Boy**. One group Mr Riley describes as 'prowess names, designed to enhance the owners' reputations'. He includes here such names as **Big Boy, Let Me Pass, Roadmaster, Hercules, King of the Road,** and **Super Power,** which reflect drivers' attitudes with which we are all only too familiar. Some of the animal names, such as **Tiger** and **Lion,** might belong in this group, which are another form of personal trade names in a sense. A few names hint at prowess beyond the realm of driving, Mr Riley suggests. He mentions names like **Lucky Lips** and **Kiss Me,** though these now have a curious innocence about them. They take us back to the 'sauciness' of seaside resorts just after the war.

Names take us everywhere, in fact. Not only into our social history, though they do that particularly well, but into every aspect of human activity. They take us everywhere English is spoken, showing the cultural differences that have evolved over centuries among peoples who often had a common origin.

This chapter, however, and those that have preceded it, are meant to have made that point. I have the consoling thought at the back of my mind that if the words I have written have failed to do it, the names will in any case have spoken for themselves.

Popular dog names

The list below shows the most frequently-used names for dogs in the USA, as revealed by a computer-based study of some 25 000 dog licences.

1 Lady
2 King
3 Duke
4 Peppy
5 Prince
6 Pepper
7 Snoopy
8 Princess
9 Heidi
10 Sam
Coco
12 Butch
13 Penny
14 Rusty
15 Sandy
Susie
17 Duchess
18 Blackie
19 Ginger
20 Queenie
21 Rex
22 Candy
23 Buffy
24 Mitzie
25 Tiger
26 Smokey
27 Charlie
28 Chico
29 Brandy
30 Sheba
31 Fluffy
32 Missy
Toby
34 Lucky
Trixie
36 Mickey
37 Tammy
38 Cindy
39 Pierre
40 Tiny
41 Max
42 Skippy
43 Fifi
44 Champ
45 Fritz
46 Brownie
47 Caesar
48 Boots
49 Kelly
50 Buttons
Tina
52 Sparky
53 Daisy
54 Gigi
Nicky
56 Spot
57 Gypsy
Taffy
59 Tuffy
60 Corky
Skipper
62 Misty
Frisky
64 Cookie
65 Buster
Dusty
Muffin
68 Buddy
Teddy
70 Bruno
71 Barney
72 Sassy
73 Bobo
Joe
Mike
76 Rocky
77 Snowball
78 Benji
Peanuts
80 Laddie
81 Scottie
82 Bridget
Lassie
84 Baby
Jack
86 Midnight
Patches
Poncho
89 Happy
90 Jojo
Mac
Rags
93 Brutus
Bullet
Samson
Shadow
97 Dolly
Gretchen
99 Pal
100 Maggie
101 Poochie
Sugar
103 Baron
George
Gidget
Samantha
107 Major
Tony
109 Bonnie
Bozo
Thor
112 Cleo
Pete
114 Boy
Casey
Mandy
Shep
118 Peaches
Pee Wee
Terry
121 Bandit
Red
Satan
Timmy
Tinker
126 Chichi
127 Cricket
Sport
129 Bobby
Sadie
Thunder
132 Holly
Lobo
Ralph
Shawn
136 Bambi
Blue
Duffy
Sammy
Trouble
141 Jackie
Mimi
Pixie
Ringo
Tanya
146 Honey
Killer
Pudgie
Suzette
150 Chip
Dino
Freckles
Frosty
Pookie
Rebel
Roscoe
157 Fritzie
Goldie
Spike
Tramp
161 Beau
Dobie
Rover
164 Hobo
Joey
Randy
Shannon
168 Babe
Jody
Patty
Star
Tracey
173 Bootsie
Ebony
Jenny
Jet
Judy
Ricky
Sarge
Tootsie
Whiskers
Wolf
183 Chipper
Hans
Lisa
Molly
Skip
Spotty
Sunshine
Whitey
191 Bruce
Cuddles
Foxy
Heather
Peggy
Queen
Shaft
Spooky
Tasha
200 Girl
Kojak
Lance
Patsy
Peanut
Pokey
Snow

Amongst the more individual dog names revealed by the computer print-out were the following:

Adonis
Alabuster
Ambrosia
Arf-Arf
Asphalt
Attila
Avanti
Baby Sister
Bacchus
Bad Boy
Banshee
Barker
Bee
Bent
Beowulf
Bicky
Bikini
Bitch
Blacktooth
Bliss
Blood
Bogart
Bounce
Boz
Breezy
Brick
Bugger
Bully
Bus
Cat
Champagne
Charm
Cheater
Chimney
Chimp
Chop
Chump
Cloud
Cop
Cowboy
Cue
Cupcake
Daddy
Dawg
Ding
Disco
Dollar
Donut
Droopy
Dumbo
Evil
Fag
Fate
Fearless
Flake
Flea-bag
Froggy
Gangster
Garbo
Genius

Goodboy
Gorgeous
Gravy
Grope
Groucho
Guinness
Handsome
Havoc
Heyyou
Hitler
Hornet
Hot Dog
Hound
Huggy
Igloo
Inkspot
Jam
Jelly Bean
Judge
Keeper
Kicksie
Kismet
Knuckles
Kosher
Lamb Chop
Lap
Lash
Leed
Legs
Lemon
Limbo
Lollipop
Lover Boy
Macwoof
Magic
Midas
Might
Milky
Mink
Mixed
Monarch
Monday
Monkey
Monster
Moonshine
Mozart
Mudball
Muggins
Munch
Mustard
Mystery
Nanoo
Nibbles
Nuisance
Nutmeg
Orange
Outlaw
Pardner
Paws
Pest
Pickle
Pilgrim
Playboy
Poorboy
Popcorn
Pounce
Puddycat
Pussy
Radar
Rap
Ratso
Rembrandt
Restless
Rich
Ripple
Rug
Sabre
Saint
Salt
Satchmo
Sausage
Scamper
Scoop
Scout
Scratch
Sentry
Shandy
Sheik
Sheriff
Shivers
Shrimp
Slave
Slipper
Smudge
Sniffy
Snuggles
Sox
Spartan
Spitfire
Streaker
Sultan
Tailstar
Teeny
Titan
Tornado
Trip
Twit
Underdog
Venus
Willow
Wobbles
Woman
Woof
Yippy
Zulu

Popular cat names

A survey of British cat names, commissioned by Spillers Top Cat and carried out by the British Market Research Bureau, revealed the following most popular names:

1 Sooty
2 Smokie
3 Brandy
Fluffy
Tiger
6 Tibbie
Tiggie
Tom
9 Kitty
Sam
Sandy
Tinker
13 Blackie
Susie
Toby
Whisky
17 Ginger
Lucy
Tim
Tiny
21 Charlie
Lucky
Rusty
Snowy
25 Candy
Cat
Flossie
Mitzi
Puss
Sally
Sukie
Tammy
33 Bumble
Cindy
Daisy
Dusty
Fred
Frisky
Honey
Jerry
Katie
Kizzy
Mickey
Nelson
Oliver
Penny
Pepper
Pickles
Purdy
Sammy
Scamp
Shandy
Sherry
Simon
Tabitha
Topsy
Twiggy

Some of the other names revealed by the survey were as follows:

Arthur
Ashes
Bagpuss
Basher
Benjy
Benny
Boofy
Boots
Cheeky
Chichi
Chumpers
Cloe
Crackers
Czumczusz
Dandy
Domino
Eric
Ernie
Fats
Felix
Fifi
Fudge
Ginny
Halfpenny
Heidi
Herby
Inky
Jambo
Japonica Troggs
Jason
Jaybee
Jemima
Jenny
Joe
Katkin
Libby
Lydia la Poose
Lulu
Madam
Marmalade
Maxwell
Moggy
Moody
Mousse
Mrs Puss
Muffin
Muggins
Noddy
Panda
Pepsi
Pippa
Pipsqueak
Podge
Polly
Poochy
Puss Puss
Pussy Cat
Puzzle
Raffles
Refus
Sauté
Scampi
Scruffy
Sebastian
Silky
Smudge
Smutty
Sneeze
Snudge
Soda
Softy
Sparky
Spats
Spike
Tabby
Tatty
Teapot
Tibbles
Tiddle
Tinkie
Titch
Treacle
Troubles
Tumble
Twopence
Vesta
Whiskers
Womble
Zebedee

Dog names in fiction

Novelists sometimes comment on the dog names that occur in their stories. A selection of such comments is given below. (In G. B. Stern's *Dogs in an Omnibus*, the author imagines the names that dogs might give to humans—names like Legs-in-Authority, Savoury-Legs, Green-Silk-Legs, Equestrian-Legs, Shapely Legs, Master-Legs, Supreme-Legs, Chubby-Legs.)

'My dog **Blast**, th' only one saved out o' a litter o' pups as was blowed up when a keg o' minin' powder loosed off in th' store-keeper's hut.'
On Greenhow Hill Rudyard Kipling

Dog was the doctor's golden labrador, so called because the family had never bothered to give him a name. Marshall, who believed that animals had souls which could be developed by human contact, had been greatly concerned by the problem of Dog. A dog with no name could hardly have a developing soul. He solved this problem by elevating the word dog to the status of a name.
Emma With Objects Judith Woolf

Dog, which being interpreted cabbalistically backwards, signifies God.
Antic Hay Aldous Huxley

The choice fell upon **Feng Hou**. That is the name to which, since it is hers and she is all caprice and individuality, she refuses to answer. (The name of a Pekinese spaniel, which 'should, of course, be Chinese and also easily pronounceable'.)
The More I See of Men... E. V. Lucas

'If you name him by his character I should say **Hamlet** would be as good as anything.'
'Hamlet'll do,' said Jeremy comfortably. 'I've never heard of a dog called that, but it's easy to say.'
Jeremy Hugh Walpole

Miss Belle Cunningham—'It's a touching habit', Lucille Christian interrupted, 'papa has of naming dogs after young ladies he used to admire when he was young.'
Night Rider Robert Penn Warren

For years they had a black cocker spaniel which they had named **Nigger** without any thought except that black dogs *do* get called Nigger.
'Makes it worse, calling a *dog* that. We coloured people don't like the word 'nigger', and when you act like dogs and us are just the same. . . .'
Neil was angry. 'All right, all right, we'll change it! We'll call the mutt "Prince"!'
Kingsblood Royal Sinclair Lewis

He had a black spot at the root of his spine.
'He ought to be called Spot,' said one. But that was too ordinary. It was a great question what to call him.
'Call him **Rex**—the King,' said my mother. We took the name in all seriousness.
'Rex—the King!' We thought it was just right. Not for years did I realise that it was a sarcasm on my mother's part.
It wasn't a successful name, really. Because my father, and all the people in the street, failed completely to pronounce the monosyllable Rex. They all said Rax. And it always distressed me. It always suggested to me seaweed, and rack-and-ruin. Poor Rex!
Rex D. H. Lawrence

'He was once a **Toby** of yours, warn't he?'
In some versions of the great drama of Punch there is a small dog—a modern innovation—supposed to be the private property of that gentleman, whose name is always Toby.
The Old Curiosity Shop Charles Dickens

Charles rubbed **Tweed** behind his ears. 'What did you call the puppies?'
'This one's **Dee.** The others were **Don, Tay, Garry, Spey** and **Clyde.** All after Scottish rivers.'
Corrie Leonora Starr

Ulysses—'Is that what you call him? Why?'
'Well, he seemed on the evidence to have led a roving life, and judging by the example we saw, it must have been adventurous.'
Arabella Georgette Heyer

'What shall we call him? Harlequin?'
'No, that's too long, and it must mean something that's lost and all alone,' said Dot. 'Rover would do, only it's so common.'
'Vagabond, Tramp, Waif or Stray,' suggested Donovan.
'Oh—**Waif**—that's beautiful, and so nice to say.'
'Yes, a thing tossed up by chance; it'll just suit the beggar.'
Donovan Edna Lyall

A selection of yacht names

Names that speak for themselves

About Time II
Addynuff
Adorabelle
Allgo
Anuddha-Buddha
Any End Up
Anything
Appydaze
Aquadisiac
Avago
Azygos
Baise Mon Cul
Bald 'Ed
Bawdstif
Beezneez
B'Jabbers
Black Azelle
Blew Moon
Blow Mee
Blow-U-Jack
Blu Away
Bluebottle
Blue Over
Bluesology
Bosunover
Branestawm
Bright 'Un
Brillig
Buzz Off
Captain Cat
Cham-Pu
Chancalot
Clewless
Codswallop
Co Mo Shun
Coweslip
Craft E
Crusado
Cuffuffle
Daisy Dampwash
Dambreezy
Dammit
Dashtwet
Dinah Mite
Dinah Mo
Drip Dri
D Sea Bee
Dumbelle
Du-U-Mynd
Eb 'n' Flo
Elcat
Fair Kop
Fantabulous
Fast Lady
Fijit
First Luff
Flamin-Go
Flipincid
Fluffy Bottam
Flying Sorcerer
Foggy Dew
Forsail
Fred N Sign
Freelove II
Frivulus
Gaylee
Geewiz
Gercher
Get Weaving
Giggles
Gigolette
Gloo Pot
Golden B Hind
Gonpotee
Goonlight
Gozunda
Happikat
Hei Yu
Hell's Belles
Helluvathing
Herr Kut
Hot N Bothered
Hot Potato
Howdedo
Hows Trix
Icanopit
I.C.U.
Idunit
Infradip
Itsallgo
Jack's O.K.
Jest As Well
Jesterjob
Joka
Ketchup
K'Fuffle
Kippin
Koliwobbles
Konfewshun
Koolkat
Kriky
La-Goon
La Poussiquette
L For Leather
Loopey Llew
Luffabuoy
Luff Divine
Luffinapuff
Luft Behind
Maida Mistake
Maid Tumesshure
Mark 10:31
Maykway
Mea Tu
Merry Hell
Mighty Mo
Miss B Haven
Miss Carry
Miss Conduct
Miss Doings
Miss Fire
Miss Isle
Miss Myth
Mister Sea
Moanalot
Mrs. Frequently
My Goodness
Nap Kin
Nautitoo
Neveready
Nhit Wit
Nnay Llas
No Idea
Nowt
Nu Name
Nut Case
Nyctea
Odzanends
Oh-Ah
Ooops
Op-A-Bout
Owdonabit
Pen-Y-Less
Petard
Phlappjack
Phlash
Pink Djin
Plane Crazy Too
Potemkin
Puff-N-Blow
Red-E
Redrump
Reef Not
Rock-N-Roll
Rose Cheeks
Rosy Lee
Sa-Cas-Tic
Sail La Vie
Sally Forth
Scilly Whim
Scubeedoo
Seafari
Sheeza B
Shoestring
Sin King
Sir Fon
Sir Loin
Slo-Mo-Shun
Smart E
Soopurr
So Wet
Spraymate
Sudden Sally
Sue Perb
Sweet Fanny
Teas Maid
Tempers Fugit
Tern Up
The Pickle
Thou Swell
Tishoo
To Be True
Tomfoolery
Too Fax
Too-She
Tri-N-Ges
Tsmyne
Tuchango
Twilgo
Tyne E
Ucantu
U1–C
Up-N-Atom
Uskanopit
Utoo
Wacker Bilt
Waltzing Matilda
Water Lou
Weatherornot
We We
Windkist
Wotahope
Wotawetun
Wot-You-Fink
Wunnalot
Wych Syde
Y Dewin
Y Knot
Zom B
Z-Victor-One

Class names

FLYING FIFTEEN
Crafty
Eleffant
Family Fun
Ffab
Ffanfare
Ffascination
Ffelicity
Ffickle
Ffifi
Ffillipp
Fflagon
Ffirty Ffour
Ffizzle
Fflambuoyant
Fflame
Fflipinelle
Fflotsam
Ffluff
Ffolly
Ffortissimo
Ffreak
Ffroff
Ffun
Fifty Fifty
Flip Flop
Nymff
Sstutter

FINN
Affinity
Beefin
Boffin
Chafin
Chin Fin
Coffinn
Enuffin
Fickanfinn
Finantonic
Finbad
Finnatical
Finnomenon
Finny Hill
Laarfinn
Micky Finn
Muffin
Parafinalia
Skyfinn
Sumfinn
Tiffin

FLYING DUTCHMAN
Dutch Uncle
Fair Phantom
Flying Chum
Flying Fish
Flying Phantom
Flying Scotsman
Ghost
Jinx
Sea Myth
Spectre
The Dutchess
Zeelust

Names that reflect special interests

Arch Maid
Bright Eyes
Concubine
Crumpet
Cuddle
Curvaceous
Dabchick
Dancing Girl
Dead Sexy
Easy Virtue
Enterprising Lady
Fast Lady
Flirt
Geisha
Girl Friend
Glamour Girl
Heart Throb
Honeybunch
Honey Don't
Hot Tomato
Hunnibun
Jezebel
Jucy Lucy
Katy Did
Latin Lover
Lust
Meremaid
Mini The Minx
My Posie
My Spare Lady
Naughtilass
Nickers
Nifty Chick
Oui Oui
Painted Lady
Poppet
Popsitoo
Provocative
Saucy Puss
Sea Mistress
Sea Wife
Sexy
Shady Lady
She's Fast
Slap N Tickle
Slick Chick
Some Chicken
Ta Baby
Tangle Legs
Taylor Maid
Tease
Tempt Me
Temptress
Testbed
Tiller Girl
Wayward Lady

Beer Bottle
Bottoms Up
Brandy Bottle
Brewer's Droop
Bubbly
Bung Ho
Cheers
Corkscrew
Foaming Ale
Gin And Tonic
Half Pint
Hangover
Hot Toddy
Lash Up
Mild And Bitter
Opening Time
Pale Ale
Pick Me Up
Pie Eyed
Pink Gin
Pinta
Plastered
Quick One
Rum Baba
Say When
Scotch Mist
Shandy
Sippers
Soaked
Souced
Sozzled
Spree
Still Sober
Too Tipsy
Whisky
Yo-Ho-Ho

Her name was Diana—Diana not of Ephesus but of Bremen. This ridiculously unsuitable name struck one as an impertinence towards the memory of the most charming of goddesses; for apart from the fact that the old craft was physically incapable of engaging in any sort of chase, there was a gang of four children belonged to her.

Joseph Conrad *Falk*

The captain informed us he had named his ship the Bonnetta, out of gratitude to Providence, for once when he was sailing to America with a good number of passengers, the ship in which he then sailed was becalmed for five weeks, and during all that time numbers of the fish Bonnetta swam close to her, and were caught for food.

James Boswell *Journal of a Tour to the Hebrides*

15 Name games

It says here that we'd make perfect couple
NAME compat-ibility

As we have seen in previous chapters, names offer plenty of material for the serious student of history, language, psychology, sociology and the like who wants to make a scholarly investigation. But names also offer scope for a less serious approach. It is easy to play games with them in various ways, to treat them light-heartedly.

In the formal sense of playing an actual game, my children were fond of some simple name games that could be played on a car journey. One of these we knew as *Animal Names*. They looked at names of all kinds—street names, place names, shop names, pub names, etc—and scored a point for each animal they saw. If they saw **Oxford** they would score one point, the **Fox and Goose** would give them two points, and so on. I would personally allow a point, and perhaps give a bonus, if the 'rat' in **Stratford** was pointed out, and if names are scarce one can also allow puns. I might give a point for 'eel' in **Ealing,** for instance (in addition to the 'ling' that is there), if the child claiming the point knew that he was making a pun. If there are younger children who cannot yet read, one can allow them to score a point for any advertisement, pub sign and the like that shows an animal. They can also look for real dogs, cats, horses or whatever in streets or fields.

A simple street name game for a journey through a city makes use of the street name elements listed on pages 135 and 136. In my family we usually guess how many different words for 'street' we will see between the beginning and end of our journey, but there are many possible variations. One is to look for street names which have both parts beginning with the same letter, as in **Aragon Avenue.**

For longer journeys I once devised for the children's section of a national newspaper a place name game based on name elements. For common elements such as '-ton' or '-by', one point can be allowed. To these can be added three points for a tree, as in **Oakwell,** three for a river, as in **Burton-on-Trent,** and three for a first name, as in **Peterborough.** Five points can be given for colours, as in **Redhill,** fruits, as in **Appledore,** and the animals of **Molesey** and the like. Place names containing a number up to ten, such as **Seven Oaks,** score that number of points, but larger numbers score a maximum of ten points.

A more sophisticated game could easily be devised using the list of place name elements on pages 114 and 115, and there is no need to wait for a long journey. A map in a classroom or at home makes an effective substitute. It is not long before children start to ask questions as to why places have the names they do, and a good teacher will instantly respond to such a cue.

In a less formal sense, adults often play games with their own names, and it is surprising what one can do. Anagrams and name rebus have long been popular, and there are translations to be made, pronunciations to be changed, name files to compile, variant spellings to collect, and in certain cases, select clubs to join. From the point of view of name games, 'what's in a name?' turns out to have a host of new answers.

Onomancy

Yet more answers to that question are possible if one believes in some kind of name magic. Since ancient times people have believed that it is possible to predict a person's future and discover hidden character traits by studying that person's name. Several methods of divination have been used, all of which come under the general heading of 'onomancy'. In name terms onomancy is roughly the equivalent of astrology.

The basic tenet of those who practise onomancy is that a person's name *is* that person, the name is not just a kind of label. Such a belief is common in many primitive societies of the world, often leading to a situation where individuals refuse to reveal their names to those outside the family circle. They fear that anyone who knows their name will have power over their innermost spirit.

In civilised societies people are only too willing to reveal their names; indeed they often spend their lives trying to make their names known as widely as possible. But as several of the literary quotations I have used in this book reveal (and as the letters from my correspondents constantly confirm), the belief that a name *is* a person is widely held. This belief is usually revealed unconsciously, but many will know what Addie means in William Faulkner's story *As I Lay Dying*:

'I would think about his name until after a while I could see the word as a shape, a vessel, and I would watch him liquefy and flow into it like cold molasses flowing out of the darkness into the vessel.'

It follows that if a name *is* the person who bears it, then the investigation of a name is like an investigation of the person. Once that point is accepted, there are at least four ways in which the investigation can be made.

NAME MEANINGS: Roman generals would try to find a soldier who had a good name (one which indicated he was likely to be victorious in life) and put him at the head of the troops as they marched into battle. In Roman times, the meaning of a name was usually more immediately apparent than it is today, but if it is possible to discover the original meaning of one's first name and surname, a symbolic interpretation can be made.

ANAGRAMS: Rearranging the letters of a person's name in order to find meaningful phrases was a popular after-dinner diversion in the 17th century, and has been taken more seriously at different times. The French King Louis XIII, for instance, appointed an official anagrammatist. He was able to find (allowing for the common interchange of 'i' and 'j') the phrase *c'est l'enfer qui m'a crée*, 'it was hell which created me', in the name of Frère Jacques Clement, the man who assassinated Henry III. Most people will want to find rather happier omens in their own names.

NUMEROLOGY: This method of divination gives each letter of a name a numerical value and arrives at three figures, a total for the vowels, a total for the consonants and a total for the name. These figures are then interpreted in their turn, though there is disagreement among the various writers on the subject as to what the figures mean.

LETTER INTERPRETATION: This system again takes note of the letters which form a name, but makes a direct interpretation of what each letter means.

There is no doubt that we interpret names in modern times, though not necessarily using the methods outlined above. We constantly make judgements about the age, ethnic background, religion and social standing of people we come across on the basis of their names. They make similar judgements about us.

Such modern interpretations are largely justified, as it happens. Changes in name fashions do often make it possible to guess a person's age by his name, and the parents' choice of names *can* reveal quite a lot about their social position, religion and even political beliefs. We are naturally on more dangerous ground when we make subjective judgements about pleasant or unpleasant names and assume that the name-bearers will be like their names. Yet this commonly happens, and we share the indignation of Nicholas Nickleby when he learns from Newman that the name of the beautiful girl with whom he has fallen in love is Miss Bobster, rhyming with lobster. Not that Dickens allows this to be the case, of course. It turns out that Newman has made a mistake, and the girl concerned is really Madeline Bray.

As for onomancy, attitudes to it will clearly vary from person to person. Some, like the ancients, will take it very seriously, as they do astrology. Others will treat it as little more than a party game, and then be surprised, as I have often observed, by what their names reveal.

In case you would like to try a name interpretation for yourself—establish a 'name-print'—I provide letter meanings on the following pages. I have taken them from my book on the subject of name magic, *Our Secret Names* (see Bibliography for details). If you are with a group of friends, it may be quicker to restrict the interpretation to their initials.

A

This letter is universally acknowledged to be a symbol of excellence and achievement. It is therefore a sign that a high standard can be reached in the name-bearer's chosen field. It also indicates an insistence on excellence in others, which often means a strongly developed critical faculty. How openly this criticism is expressed depends on other aspects of the name-print. This is also a letter of initiation, showing a person who is keen to do new things. When it is the first letter of a name it is a sign of ambition. Occurring elsewhere in the name it can indicate an unfortunate tendency to be negative about other people's ideas and wishes. As the dominant letter of a name-print, it shows a very great potential for a successful life.

B

This letter indicates the ability to compromise. It reveals a faculty for accepting a majority view and abiding by a general decision. In a positive sense the letter indicates maturity and tact. It has a negative side, which could be interpreted as a lack of will-power or determination. As a dominant letter it hints very clearly at a good team-member, but not a leader. The letter is also connected with domesticity.

C

A sign of steadiness and consistency, both in terms of physical effort that can be applied and emotional commitment that can be made. This letter indicates a good employee, who will eventually settle in one job for many years. More importantly, perhaps, it reveals a steadiness and lack of change in emotional relationships. This positive reliability is counter-balanced to some extent by a certain dullness and lack of imagination.

D

A rather negative symbol which must be fought against by the name-bearer, particularly if it is the dominant letter. It indicates a tendency to give in and not fight for survival. It is the letter of laziness, also of small-mindedness. More positively, the letter is associated with travel, but even this may be a metaphoric kind of travelling, a flight of fancy which represents an attempt to escape from problems. Other elements in the name-print will be able to overcome the influence of this letter, but the name-bearer should guard against apathy and indifference.

E

A symbol of recovery, showing the ability to get back to normal after physical or emotional setbacks. An essential characteristic in most people's name-prints, it includes a certain amount of optimism. When things are going well the letter indicates that the name-bearer will be looking ahead and making plans for improvements. The negative side of the letter can be summed up by the word 'muteness'. This is a tendency to let others have their say but not to speak about one's own views. Nevertheless, as a dominant letter it shows someone who will be able to cope resolutely with the ups and downs of life.

F

The letter contains an indication of violence—perhaps a deep-rooted but strongly suppressed wish to be involved in violent action. It hints at a sadistic streak, which may, nevertheless, be kept tightly under control. Here, too, are signs of a contempt for rules and regulations, and a willingness on occasions to go beyond the law. As a dominant letter F is dangerous, but it can virtually be cancelled out by other personality factors. Coupled with ambition, however, it can lead to ruthlessness. Uncontrolled, the name-bearer will be given to violent changes of mood and sudden rages.

G

Movement is the essential concept contained in this letter. It indicates a restlessness of mind and body, a dissatisfaction with a settled situation. This will be nagging constantly at the name-bearer, causing thoughts of a new job or new partner to be lurking in the mind. As a dominant letter G clearly indicates someone who would be happiest travelling about, and a job which involves mobility would be satisfying. In human relationships the name-bearer may find it difficult to remain faithful to one person. More positively, this letter also hints at speed of thought and action.

H

A determination to achieve success and wealth is the keynote of this letter. It also indicates a yearning for world recognition rather than the satisfaction of personal self-respect quietly enjoyed. This personality trait in its most disagreeable form can lead to the yes-man who will demean himself in any way in order to gain advancement. In a woman it can lead to a deliberate exploitation of bodily attraction. Properly controlled, however, this characteristic can lead to dedicated hard work over a long period, provided that appreciation is expressed constantly by others.

I

This, of course, is the letter which indicates egotism, a supreme interest in one's own affairs at the expense of others. As an element in a complete character-reading it plays a necessary part, for everyone must protect personal interests to some extent. (Absence of this letter in a name-print should therefore be considered significant.) When I dominates a name-print the effect will most clearly be seen on a name-bearer who is young. Others are likely to find such a person oppressively self-centred. Some are able to control this characteristic in themselves, or at least control its public display. But a person who is dominated by I and who appears to be sitting quietly, listening to others, is almost certainly considering how his own interests can be advanced as a result of the conversation.

J

A sign of fair-mindedness and a well-balanced outlook. It indicates a faculty of judgement which others will value. Also inherent in this letter is a concern for the past. Memories are important, and a person whose name-print is dominated by J will probably keep a diary and collect souvenirs. J mostly reveals characteristics that will be valued by others, but the total name-print needs a dynamic element to help counteract the rather static quality that it also suggests.

K

This letter refers exclusively to money and the acquisition of wealth. Other letters contain indications of success, and may well include financial success, but here we are dealing with a naked need for money and the power associated with it. As a dominating letter in a name-print it gives a clear indication of someone who values worldly goods above all else. Coupled with such factors as ambition and ability, it will lead to riches. Lacking the opportunity to acquire wealth, the name-bearer is likely to become soured, being unable to apply other sets of values.

L

A sign of co-ordination, both physical and mental, but perhaps one or the other in an individual. Physical co-ordination may well lead to success in sport or other activities when young. The facility for mental organisation will be very useful for an administrator. The drawback of this letter lies in indecision, for while the name-bearer may be able to cause a group of people to contribute their various skills to a common undertaking, policy decisions at the outset may cause him great problems. Nevertheless, a name-print dominated by this letter shows ability to cope with complex situations.

M

A concern for outward appearance and an appreciation of beauty are amongst the main indications contained in this letter. The former trait may lead the name-bearer to conceal inner thoughts and feelings as much as possible. A certain amount of such concealment is a good ingredient in a well-balanced personality, but it must not be taken to excess. Appreciation of beauty is also useful in many ways, but ideally the domination of a name-print by M should be balanced by indications of sensitivity and deeper understanding. In a negative way, this letter gives signs of snobbishness and pettiness. When coupled with critical ability it hints at a person with highly developed artistic skills.

N

This letter indicates lack of confidence, and a name-print in which it is a dominant letter will usually indicate a worrier, always uncertain about the future. It reveals a slightly pessimistic outlook which may come to the fore on occasions. At other times it can be kept in check by more positive characteristics. A person whose name is dominated by N may also be uncertain emotionally, afraid to make a complete commitment to another person. The basic lack of self-confidence will often be hidden by a superficial show of supreme self-confidence which crumbles away upon close examination.

O

An indicator of emotion, hinting at sensitivity and depth of feeling. A very useful ingredient in a name-print, and only a problem when dominating it too markedly. The problem may lie in an extreme sensitivity to other people's comments and opinions, so that the name-bearer is too easily hurt. The same sensitivity, however, will be an asset when dealing with other people's emotional problems. This letter in a name shows a capacity for delicacy, both in human relationships and in physical movement.

P

This is a conformist's letter, showing someone who is content to merge with the crowd, or finds it safer to do so. There may also be a wish for personal recognition shown in the name-print, but this need for the support of others may lead to an unwillingness to take risks. This letter usefully counterbalances more rebellious influences, but as a dominating letter it can hint at obscurity for the name-bearer. In a woman the letter may indicate loss of personal identity in a marriage or other relationship.

Q

An indication of a temperamental person, someone who is subject to sudden, but short-lived, changes of mood. But this letter also reveals someone who is constantly enquiring into the world about him. It shows the eternal curiosity of the life-long student. As a dominant letter it hints strongly at someone who becomes knowledgeable, and who passes that knowledge on to others. For Q also indicates a facility for communication, either in speech or print.

R

Probably the best letter of all, reflecting sound common sense, a special concern for education and a well-balanced adjustment to life. As a dominating letter this may not suggest a person who will be wealthy or surrounded by possessions, but it hints very strongly at inner richness and contentment. People who have the qualities symbolised by this letter are essential supports to those who are less stable. The appearance of the letter in any name-print should be welcomed as an indication of a solidly-founded character and personality. Those who have R as a dominating letter will be valued friends and colleagues.

S

This letter is associated with moral goodness and virtue. It contains its own opposite; in other words, it can hint at either sharp awareness of what is right or wrong, both in the name-bearer's own behaviour and in his or her judgements of other people's behaviour. If the name-bearer does anything which is wrong, there will be an expectation of punishment—a need for punishment. Certain types of people whose name-prints are dominated by S will be very difficult to live with because of the high moral example and rigid code of behaviour they set themselves.

T

This letter is an indication of fickleness and lack of permanent commitment. It also signifies impatience, an inability to wait for events to take their natural course. A person whose name-print has T as a dominant letter feels under a constant pressure to get things done now, which makes him valuable in certain working environments. The obsession with time will also have a negative effect, making the person worry unduly about growing old. Minute exactness will not concern this name-bearer, though he or she will be able to concentrate on the job in hand for a short period. Soon, however, it will have to be set aside for something new.

U

The sign of a protective person who is able to take care of others. It is also an indication, however, of someone who needs to feel protected by a familiar environment. There is no easy adjustment to new people or situations. Superficially the name-bearer may seem at ease, but beneath the surface there will be worries. Intellectually, the person whose name-print is dominated by U will be capable of absorbing a great deal of varied information. It is mostly a very positive letter, marred only by a certain streak of intellectual snobbishness.

V

A letter of psychic and spiritual importance. It indicates a person whose perception of events goes beyond the normal. This is the letter of instinct, by which things are known by no logical process. Other people will also respond to a mysterious quality in the name-bearer's personality. This response will either be strongly positive or strongly negative, and it may well defy logical explanation. As a dominant letter, V reveals a person of great psychic potential, which may be lying dormant.

W

A letter hinting at solidarity and strength of character. When W dominates a name-print there are strong qualities of self-control in the name-bearer. These may not yet have been tested by events, but they are there in the background. This letter also speaks of an active person who is able to get on with a job. It is an indication of a realist, who is able to turn an abstract concept into something concrete. A W person may be thought of as rather dull and old-fashioned by some people, but others will greatly value his or her dependability.

X

A secretive and mysterious nature is indicated by this letter. This may have been overruled by other character traits, but the name-bearer's natural tendency would be to be uncommunicative about thoughts and feelings. At the same time the letter indicates a need for physical contact with others, especially those of the opposite sex. One partner is unlikely to satisfy someone whose name-print is dominated by this letter.

Y

This letter indicates a concern for others. It hints at a quiet personality, ready to take second place to someone who is a more natural leader. A Y in the name-print reveals someone who looks for a permanent relationship in which mutual support will be given consistently. There may be a lack of excitement and fire, but this is someone who can be relied upon. As a dominant letter Y is rather dangerous because it suggests almost total anonymity, the name-bearer failing to establish a personal identity. As a feature of personality it may well make the name-bearer reasonably popular, as a good listener is popular, but it should be tempered with a degree of self-assertion.

Z

An indication of someone who appreciates the unusual and is particularly glad to get out of a rut, socially or professionally. It is the mark of an individual who will stand out in a crowd. The name-bearer will be happiest in a job which allows personal recognition. Negative associations with the letter include a degree of untidiness, and occasionally a lack of clear communication in speech or writing. The name-bearer will also work at a rather slow speed.

Love letters

By using onomancy you can also find out how much two people have in common with one another, and which personality traits they share. The simple love-letter test outlined below also indicates how their relationship is likely to fare over a long period.

First of all, write down the first name and last name of each person, like this:

SARAH WILLIAMS
DAVID LAWSON

(If the two people share a name, eg parent and child, make use of the middle names instead.)

Now consider each letter of the top name in turn. If it occurs in the name underneath, cross it out in both names and write it down separately, like this:

~~S~~ARAH WILLIAMS S
DAVID LAW~~S~~ON

Do this with each letter in the top name:

~~SA~~RAH WILLIAMS SA
D~~A~~VID LAW~~S~~ON

When you come to a letter that does not occur in the name below, ignore it and pass on to the next one:

~~SA~~R~~A~~H WILLIAMS SAA
D~~A~~VID L~~AWS~~ON

With these two names, this is the eventual result:

~~SA~~R~~A~~H ~~WIL~~LIAMS SAAWIL
D~~A~~V~~I~~D ~~LAWS~~ON

The letters common to both names indicate the personality traits that they have in common (see the meaning of each letter under 'Alphabet Mysticism' above). The number of letters shared indicates the kind of relationship they are likely to have, as follows:

Letters in common

1 the two people have almost nothing in common, but perhaps 'opposites attract'.
2 these two people will find it difficult to sustain a long-term relationship without working at it very hard.
3 the relationship between these two people is likely to become more difficult as time passes.
4 these two people could probably survive together quite well.
5 there is a good chance for a harmonious relationship between these two people.
6 these two people should be able to live and work together quite happily.
7 these two people make a very well matched pair.
7+ an ideal couple.

It was a favourite superstition of Uncle Matthew's that if you wrote somebody's name on a piece of paper and put it in a drawer, that person would die within the year. The drawers at Alconleigh were full of little slips of paper bearing the names of those whom my uncle wanted out of the way. The spell hardly ever seemed to work.

Nancy Mitford *Love in a Cold Climate*

Rebus

A name rebus can look like this: **Eur U** which example is meant to be decoded as 'Lo! "u" is past "eur"', or **Louis Pasteur.** Similarly, **Aristophanes, Lord Tennyson, King Solomon** and **George Washington** are to be found—by those who are ingenious enough—in the following:

Ar	**Y**	**M**	**Gt**
Hes	**L/D Xn**	**K**	**Ge/Gew H**

Two simple rebus that are among my own favourites have a satisfying visual appearance. It was J. Bryan who told me of the horse named **Potooooooooo,** and Mark Lower quotes **ABCDEFGHIJKMNOPQRSTUVWXYZ** in his 19th-century *Essays on English Surnames.* The number of 'o's' is important in the first, of course, as is the letter that is missing from the second.

Pictorial rebus have already been mentioned in connection with sign names, and it can be amusing to think of a way to illustrate one's own name. A suggestion for **Dunkling** was long ago given indirectly, I regret to say, by the boy who sat next to me at school. He delighted in calling out at quiet moments: 'Doesn't dung cling!' Other names may hint at a more pleasant illustration, particularly if it is the bearer of the name who is thinking about it. We tend to play unkind games with other people's names rather than our own. I am reminded of the entry in a parish register by the sexton who dug a grave for a Mr **Button.** He wrote simply: 'To making one button hole: 4s 6d.'

Other name games

Some names translate well into other languages. Joe Green, for example, looks altogether better as Giuseppe Verdi. My former colleague René **Quinault** becomes Mr **Cinema** in Germany, where they pronounce his name as *Kino.* In a vaguely similar way, a Greek friend tells me that shifting the stress on his surname, **Melas,** changes him from Mr **Black** to Mr **Honey.** I can think of no English names that would change their meaning so drastically by an altered pronunciation, but some could perhaps be improved in sound. With some English surnames different families do in fact make use of different pronunciations.

There are those who are greatly offended by what they consider to be a mispronunciation of their name, and even more so by a misspelling. Several correspondents of mine have a more light-hearted approach. They keep a little notebook in which they collect variations of their own name. Their enthusiastic greeting of yet another form takes away all traces of irritation. One can go further and deliberately pun on one's own name. In the past many families did this when they adopted mottoes. The **Manns,** for example, adopted the phrase *Homo sum,* 'I am a man', and the *Festina lente,* 'hasten slowly', of the **Onslow** family is well known.

Another name game of a sort is to compile what

A correspondent in Oxford draws my attention to a kind of name game that was first used in the education of Jewish children. It can be adapted from Hebrew to English, and consists of finding a personal text in the scriptures. Such a text must begin with the first letter of one's name, and end with its last letter. The other letters of the name should be included in the text, preferably in order.

For her own name my correspondent cited a verse in Psalm 51 (in the American Prayer Book version): '*C*re*at*e in me a clean *he*a*r*t, O God, and renew a right spirit withi*n* m*e*.' This seems to link well with the original meaning of Catherine, 'pure'.

For Leslie the Authorised Version yields: '*L*ord, my h*e*art i*s* not haughty, nor mine eyes *l*ofty: ne*i*ther do I exercise myself in great matters, or in things too high for m*e*.' I am happy to accept that, with all modesty, as my own personal text.

might be called a 'name file'. The idea is to collect together all the information one can about one's own surname, including details of other people who have borne the name. Biographical dictionaries and encyclopedias can be consulted, but if no one famous has found his way into the reference books it may be necessary to write around to namesakes mentioned in telephone and other directories. There are those who claim to be the unique bearers of a particular surname, but this rarely turns out to be true when one looks into the matter. A name file, then, is a 'clan scrapbook' in a sense. It makes an interesting personal name project and may suggest something to educationists for classroom work.

There is a slight connection between the 'name file' idea and the Jim Smith Society, which we mentioned previously. Membership of that band is obviously open to all Jim Smiths, and for a fortunate few entry into another happy band may be possible. This is the 'My Name Is A Poem Club', open to those who have names like **Jane Cane, Newton Hooton** and **Nancy Clancy.** The president of the club, according to latest information, is **Hugh Blue.** Such names might be described as collectors' items, for there are many people around who do collect unusual names, eagerly noting those that appear in newspaper reports and the like.

A great collector of the past was N. I. Bowditch, who published his *Suffolk Surnames* in 1858, and an edition seven times larger in 1861. The latter contains a very large number of unusual names that were to be found in America, especially Suffolk County, at the time. Bowditch rarely gives the origin of the names, but strings anecdotes together in a fast and furious way. One moment he is recounting how **Ottiwell Wood** spelt out his name ('*O* double *t*, *i* double *u*, *e* double *l*, double *u*, double *o*, *d*'), and immediately he remarks on the confusion of the sexes in Mr **Maddam,** Mr **Shee** and the like.

More recently we have had the published collections of John Train, in *Remarkable Names of Real People* and *Even More Remarkable Names of Real People*. Mr Train scored by adding a line or two about the persons named: **Chief (Clayton) Crook** is a police chief in Ohio, **Wong Bong Fong** lives in Hong Kong, **Mr Vice,** of New Orleans, has been arrested 890 times and convicted on 421 occasions.

In a sense, autograph hunting is a collection of unusual names. Children can also enjoy collecting what I call nymographs. The object is to collect the signatures of people who bear as many different first names as possible. Only one signature per name is needed, but if one does happen to meet famous people, their signatures can be substituted for the more ordinary bearers of the same first names. The advantage of nymograph rather than autograph collecting is that one can start immediately, and every person met is a potential contributor.

Name pieces

Amongst those who do collect names, many are tempted to make humorous use of them in literary pieces. These may take the form of short stories or poems, and a few examples will quickly make the point. A. A. Willis, for example, who used to write for *Punch* as 'A.A.', showed what a really clever writer could do with place names. In the middle of a longer article on the subject which appeared in *Punch* in October 1936, the following occurs:

> 'By way of light relief from cold classification, I have also compiled from village names a little modern romance. It is a love story of **Harold Wood** (Essex) and **Daisy Hill** (Lancashire), **Loversall** (Yorkshire) with **Pettings** (Kent). Follows naturally **Church** (Westmorland) with **Ring O' Bells** (Lancashire) for the **Bride** (Isle of Man). **Honeymoor** (Herefordshire) is obviously a honeymoon cut short—no doubt because the **New House** (Sussex) was **Fulready** (Warwickshire). Follows even more naturally **Nursling** (Hampshire) with **Cradle End** (Hertfordshire) and **Bapchild** (Kent). After a while Harold, being already very **Clubworthy** (Devon), takes to **Club Moor** (Lancashire), so he and Daisy begin to **Bicker** (Lincolnshire) and even **Wrangle** (also Lincolnshire), and are soon at **Loggerheads** (Staffordshire). She is thus left to her own **Devizes** (Wiltshire) with the result that there presently appears **Bill Brook** (Staffordshire), a **Lover** (Wiltshire) for her to **Skipwith** (Yorkshire). This should be the **Finish** (Ireland), but as I don't play with Irish names and anyway it's a modern romance, Harold treats this as a **Cause** (Shropshire) for Divorce (which unfortunately I **Havant** (Hampshire) been able to find anywhere), and all three end up in **Court** (Somerset).'

Miss Muriel Smith has made use of her extensive knowledge of apple names to compose a similar story incorporating them. In the full version Miss Smith managed to build in no less than 365 different names. The story begins as follows:

'**Mrs Toogood**, whose daughter **Alice** was a **Little Beauty,** but rather a **Coquette,** despaired of ever seeing a **Golden/Ring** on the **Lady's Finger,** although she had been **Queen** of the **May, Dainty** as a **Fairy,** with **Brown Eyes, Golden Cluster** of curls, **Pink Cheek, Sweet** expression (her **Family** called her **Smiler**) and had roused **Great Expectations** when she was a **Pretty Maid** of **Three Years Old,** a mere **Baby,** not out of the **Nursery.**'

In Miss Smith's epic, Alice eventually elopes with **Shannon,** an **Irish Giant.** Another rousing tale, based on the names of moths and assembled by Pauline Quemby, traces the adventures of **Grisette,** a **Small Quaker,** who is saved by a **Cosmopolitan** gentleman from the **False Mocha.** The highlight of this story occurs when a **Scarce Dagger** is plunged into Mocha's heart, causing his blood to flow out in a **Small Rivulet.** The landlord of the inn where this takes place then exclaims: 'Look what tha's done to ma **Ruddy Carpet.**'

Names in verse

From such compositions it is but a short step to writing verses about names. Even great poets like Pope, for instance, could dash off a piece in a lighter moment about a name. In his case he chose to theorise about the name of the **Kit-Cat** Club:

Whence deathless **Kit-Cat** took its name
Few critics can unriddle;
Some say from Pastry Cook it came,
And some from **Cat and Fiddle**...

Pope goes on to give an explanation of the name that is more obscure than the name itself, which derives from Christopher **(Kit) Catling,** the keeper of the pie-house where the Club originally met.

In a similarly relaxed moment, Dryden played with his cousin's surname, **Creed.** After a discussion one evening about the origin of names he is said to have composed the following lines spontaneously:

So much religion in your name doth dwell
Your soul must needs with piety excel.
Thus names, like well-wrought pictures drawn of old,
Their owners' natures and their story told.
Your name but half expresses, for in you
Belief and practice do together go.
My prayers shall be, while this short life endures,
These may go hand in hand, with you and yours;
Till faith hereafter is in vision drowned,
And practice is with endless glory crowned.

By the 19th century James Smith was able to take up this theme of names and natures in his *Comic Miscellanies* and say that 'surnames seem given by the rule of contraries'. Sample verses from his long poem will illustrate his theme:

Mr **Child,** in a passion, knock'd down Mr **Rock,**
Mr **Stone** like an aspen-leaf shivers;
Miss **Poole** used to dance, but she stands like a stock,
Ever since she became Mrs **Rivers.**
Mr **Swift** hobbles onward, no mortal knows how,
He moves as though cords had entwined him,
Mr **Metcalfe** ran off, upon meeting a cow,
With pale Mr **Turnbull** behind him.
Mr **Barker**'s as mute as a fish in the sea,
Mr **Miles** never moves on a journey,
Mr **Gotobed** sits up till half after three,
Mr **Makepiece** was bred an attorney.
Mr **Gardener** can't tell a flower from a root.
Mr **Wilde** with timidity draws back,
Mr **Ryder** performs all his journeys on foot,
Mr **Foote** all his journeys on horseback.

Smith turned his attention to a variety of name topics, not to mention allied subjects such as heraldry. He makes his contribution to the large body of poems about pub names, and is one of the very few writers I can think of who has tackled street names. Once again he was concerned with misnomers, this time of London streets:

From Park Land to Wapping, by day and by night,
I've many a year been a roamer,
And find that no lawyer can London indict,
Each street, ev'ry lane's a misnomer.
I find **Broad Street,** St Giles's, a poor narrow nook,
Battle Bridge is unconscious of slaughter,
Duke's Place cannot muster the ghost of a duke,
And **Brook Street** is wanting in water.

Several more verses follow in a similar vein, and Smith does have the grace to admit that, even if he has proved 'That London's one mighty mis-nomer' it is in 'verse not quite equal to Homer'.

Name jokes

Jokes and minor anecdotes based on names have been circulating for a very long time, as William Camden once again makes clear. His *Remains Concerning Britain* contains a whole chapter on name puns, and in this we learn that the Romans, for instance, jokingly changed the name of **Tiberius Nero** because of his drinking habits. They made him **Biberius Mero,** or a 'mere imbiber' if one uses 'mere' in its early sense of undiluted wine. Camden also quotes the famous joke about the Angles ('not Angles but Angels'), which must be almost as well known as 'Thou art **Peter** [which means 'stone' or 'rock'] and upon this rock I will build my church.' Before this the Apostle had been called **Cephas,** the Aramaic equivalent of 'rock', though his real name was Simon.

Archie Armstrong wrote at roughly the same time as Camden, in the early 17th century, but he was far less learned in his *Banquet of Jests and Merry Tales*. His name jokes are not the kind to raise even a smile today, though he was popular at the time. A typical Armstrong joke is about the demand that was current in certain quarters to change Christmas to Christ-tide in order to avoid the Catholic reference to 'mass'. **Thomas,** Archie says, and one can almost feel him holding his sides, is worried in case he has to become **Thomside.** One anecdote in the book does provide additional evidence, if any were needed, about the badly painted name boards that were displayed in 17th-century streets. On a board which had been taken to be a monster, Armstrong says that it is a sign that the painter was an ass.

By the 19th century the standard of name joke had improved somewhat. Bowditch writes of a doctor who, when he learnt that a Mr **Vowell** had just died, instantly remarked that he 'was glad it wasn't *u* or *i*'.

In modern times the best witticisms are probably to be found in the names themselves rather than in anecdotes about them. Personally, I still enjoy coming across a retired teacher of mathematics who is living in a house called **After Math,** and learning that there is a book on chess called *Pawnography*. Surely that is the way the names game should really be played?

Anagrams

A true anagram should use all the letters of one's full name once only, eg William Shakespeare gives 'We all make his praise', Margaret Thatcher gives 'that great charmer'. First names often have their own anagrams, however. In the 17th century the words derived from the names would probably have been thought to give clues to the characters of the name-bearers. Some examples are given below. Names are in bold type and anagrams follow.

Abel able, bale
Adrian radian
Agnes geans
Aidan naiad
Alan anal
Alaric racial
Alban banal
Alberta ratable
Aldred ladder
Alec lace
Alfred flared
Algernon non-glare
Alister realist, saltier
Alma lama
Almeric claimer, miracle, reclaim
Alvin anvil
Amy may, yam
Andrew dawner, wander, warden, warned
Angela anlage
Anna nana
Annie inane
Astrid triads
Avis visa
Bella be-all, label
Bernard brander
Bertha bather, breath
Betsy bytes
Blake bleak
Boris biros
Brenda bander
Brian bairn, brain
Bridie birdie
Caleb cable
Cameron romance
Candide candied
Carlos carols, corals
Carmel calmer
Carole oracle
Caroline acrolein
Cary racy
Cathy yacht
Catrine certain
Charles larches
Chester retches
Cilla lilac
Claire éclair, lacier
Clare clear
Claud ducal
Clea lace
Cleo cole
Clio coil
Cornelia creolian
Cornelius reclusion
Cressida sidecars
Cyril lyric
Dai aid
Damien maiden, median
Damon nomad
Dane dean
Daniel lead-in, nailed
Darien rained
Darius radius
Dave veda
Dean Dane
Deirdre ridered
Delia ailed, ideal
Della ladle
Denis dines, snide
Dennis sinned
Diana naiad
Dodie diode

Don nod
Dora road
Dorian ordain, inroad
Earl real
Edgar raged
Edna dean
Edward warded
Edwin widen, wined
Electra treacle
Elias aisle
Ellis lisle
Elma lame
Elmira mailer
Elsa seal, sale
Elvis evils, lives, veils
Emil lime, mile
Enid dine
Eric rice
Erin rein
Ernest enters, nester, resent, tenser
Ernestine internees
Esme seem
Esther threes
Evan nave, vane
Evelyn evenly
Ewan anew, wane, wean
Ezra raze
Freda fared
Freya faery
Gary gray
Geraint granite, ingrate, tearing
Gerald glared
Geraldine realigned
Gerard grader, regard
Gerda grade, raged
Gina gain
Glenda angled, dangle
Glynis singly
Graeme meagre
Greta great
Gustave vaguest
Hester threes
Horst short
Hortensia senhorita
Ida aid
Ifan fain, naif
Ira air
Isla ails, sail
Isolde soiled
Israel sailer, serial
Ivan vain
Karl lark
Kate take, teak
Kay yak
Laban banal
Lana anal
Lance clean
Laura aural
Laurel allure
Leah hale, heal
Leander learned
Lena lean
Leon lone
Lewis wiles
Liam lima, mail
Lil ill
Lisa ails, sail
Lissa sails
Lloyd dolly
Lois oils, soil
Lorena loaner
Loretta retotal
Lothar harlot
Lottie toilet
Lucian uncial
Luther hurtle
Lydia daily
Mabel amble, blame
Madge gamed
Marian airman, marina
Marianne Armenian
Marina airman
Marlon normal
Mary army
May yam
Medusa amused
Meg gem
Megan mange
Melissa aimless
Mia aim
Miles limes, slime, smile
Mina main
Mirabel balmier
Moira Maori
Mona moan
Morna manor
Munro mourn
Myra army
Nancy canny
Nat ant, tan
Ned den, end
Neil line, Nile
Nigel ingle
Noel lone
Nola loan
Nora roan
Norma manor, Roman
Oberon Borneo
Olaf foal, loaf
Olga gaol, goal
Omar roam
Osbert sorbet
Otto toot
Owen enow
Pat apt, tap
Patsy pasty
Pearl paler
Pedro doper, roped
Perseus peruses
Petra pater, prate, taper
Rab bar, bra
Reg erg
Regan anger, range
Rhoda hoard
Rocky corky
Rodney yonder
Rosa oars, soar
Rosalind ordinals
Rosaline ailerons
Rose Eros, roes, sore
Rosetta rotates, toaster
Ruby bury
Ruth hurt
Ryan yarn
Sadie aside, ideas, aides
Seamus amuses, assume
Selina aliens, saline
Selma lames, males, meals
Seward wadres
Shane ashen
Silas sails, sisal
Simeon monies
Simone monies
Sorel loser, roles
Stan ants, tans
Sterling ringlets, tinglers
Steven events
Stewart swatter
Susie issue
Tabitha habitat
Teresa Easter, eaters, reseat, teaser
Tessa sates, seats
Thea hate, heat
Thelma hamlet
Theresa heaters, reheats
Vera rave, aver
Vida avid
Zelda lazed

A page from a name collector's notebook

The names below were collected by the late George F. Hubbard of New York. All are or were borne by real people.

Henrietta Addition
Cyretha Adshade
Nancy Ancey
Etta Apple
Oscar Asparagus
Orville Awe
Sterling Blazy
Ilse Boos
Philip Brilliant
Duckworth Byrd
George A. Canary
Dina Chill
Columbus Cohen
May Day
Richard Dinners
Upson Downs
Mark Rile Dull
Loveless Eary
Luscious Easter
Lilley Easy
Ophelia Egypt
Ireland England
Alice Everyday
Remington P. Fairlamb
Wanda Farr
Thaddeus Figlock
Charmaine Fretwell
Courter Shannon Fryrear
Yetta Gang
Bess Goddykoontz
Henry Honeychurch Gorringe
Gussie Greengrass
Tommy Gunn
Thomas Hailstones
Ima Hogg
Arabelle Hong
Louise Hospital
Rutgers I. Hurry
Mel Manny Immergut
Inez Innes
Melvin Intriligator
Chester Irony
Frank Ix
Lizzie Izabichie
Hannah Isabell Jelly
Watermelon Johnson
Amazing Grace Jones
Boisfeuillet Jones
Halo Jones
Income Jones
Pinkbloom Jones

Love Joy
Pleasant Kidd
Maude Kissin
Rosella Kellyhouse Klink
Zeno Klinker
Royal Knights
Bent Korner
Joseph Wood Krutch
Rose Leaf
Michael Leftoff
Joan Longnecker
Bernard Darling Love
Logwell Lurvey
Hunt A. Lusk
Sistine Madonna McClung
Raven McDavid
Pictorial McEvoy
Mussolini McGee
Spanish McGee
Phoebe McKeeby
Harry Maleman
Miriam Mates
Marybelle Merryweather
Lilla Mews
James Middlemiss
Maid Marion Montgomery
Malcolm Moos
Seeley Wintersmith Mudd
Harriet Bigelow Neithercut
Savage Nettles
Olney W. Nicewonger
Penny Nichols
Melvin Mackenzie Noseworthy
Louise Noun
Belle Nuddle
Fluid Nunn
June Moon Olives
Ichabod Onion
Memory Orange
Ada Garland Outhouse
Freelove Outhouse
Zoltan Ovary
Victor Overcash
Mollie Panter-Downes
Sirjohn Papageorge
Hector Piazza
Human Piper
Penelope Plum
Omar Shakespeare Pound
George B. Pound
Alto Quack

Florence A. Quaintance
Nellie Quartermouth
Alberta Lachicotte Quattlebaum
Pearline Queen
Flora Rose Quick
Freeze Quick
John B. Quick
Veasy Rainwater
Juanita Rape
Wanton Rideout
Pius Riffle
Murl Rigmaiden
Harry Rockmaker
Sarepta Rockstool
Dewey Rose
Rose Rose
Violla Rubber
Little Green Russian
Louis Shady
Laurence Sickman
Frederick Silence
Bess Sinks
Ester Slobody
Adelina Sloog
G. E. Kidder Smith
Sory Smith
Burt Softness
Minnie Starlight
Sally Sunshine
Daily Swindle
Rose Throne
Yelberton Abraham Tittle
Milton Trueheart
Thomas Turned
Britus Twitty
Nell Upole
Albertina Unsold
Viola Unstrung
Sue Verb
Pleasant Vice
Carrington Visor
Melvin Vowels
Dassah Washer
Burson Wynkoop
Thereon Yawn
Herbert Yells
Romeo Yench
Berma Yerkey
Homer Yook
Ida Yu
April Zipes

Bibliography

Addison, William, *Understanding English Place-Names*, Futura Publications 1979

Akrigg, G. P. & Helen B., *1001 British Columbia Place Names*, Discovery Press 1970

Algeo, John, *On Defining the Proper Name*, University of Florida 1973

Allen, Cecil J., *Titled Trains of Great Britain*, Ian Allan 1953

Ames, Winthrop, *What Shall We Name The Baby?* Hutchinson 1935

Armstrong, G. H., *The Origin and Meaning of Place Names in Canada*, Macmillan 1972

Attwater, Donald, *A Dictionary of Saints*, Penguin 1974

Barber, Henry, *British Family Names*, Elliot Stock 1902

Bardsley, Charles Wareing, *A Dictionary of English and Welsh Surnames*, Genealogical Publishing Co. 1980

Bardsley, C. W., *Curiosities of Puritan Nomenclature*, Gale Research 1970

Bardsley, C. W., *English Surnames*, David & Charles 1969

Baring Gould, S., *Family Names & Their Story*, Seeley & Co. 1910

Bebbington, Gillian, *London Street Names*, Batsford 1972

Bice, Christopher, *Names for the Cornish*, Lodenek Press 1970

Biggs, Thomas H., *Geographic and Cultural Names in Virginia*, Virginia Division of Mineral Resources 1974

Black, George F., *The Surnames of Scotland*, New York Public Library 1971

Bloodworth, Bertha, *Florida Place Names*, Ann Arbor 1959

Bolitho, Hector, & Peel, Derek, *Without the City Wall*, John Murray 1952

Bowditch, N. I., *Suffolk Surnames*, Trübner 1861

Brookes, Reuben S. & Blanche, *A Guide to Jewish Names*, 1967

Browder, Sue, *The New Age Baby Name Book*, Warner Books 1975

Browder, Sue, *The Pet Name Book*, Workman Publishing 1979

Brown, Ivor, *A Charm of Names*, Bodley Head 1972

Camden, William, *Remains Concerning Britain*, E.P. Publishing 1974

Cameron, Kenneth, *English Place Names*, Batsford 1969

Carew, Tim, *How the Regiments Got Their Nicknames*, Leo Cooper 1974

Carlson, Helen S., *Nevada Place Names*, University of Nevada 1974

Casserley, H. C., *British Locomotive Names of the 20th Century*, Ian Allan 1967

Chadbourne, Ava H., *Maine Place Names*, Bangor 1955

Cheney, Roberta C., *Names on the Face of Montana*, University of Montana 1971

Chicheley Plowden, C., *A Manual of Plant Names*, Allen & Unwin 1972

Clarke, Joseph F., *Pseudonyms*, Elm Tree Books 1977

Clodd, Edward, *Magic in Names and other Things*, Chapman & Hall 1920

Coghlan, Ronan, *Irish Christian Names*, Johnston & Bacon 1979

Cottle, Basil, *The Penguin Dictionary of Surnames*, Penguin Books 1967

Coulet du Gard, R. & D., *The Handbook of French Place Names in the USA*, Edition des deux mondes 1974

Dauzat, Albert, *Dictionnaire des noms de famille et prénoms de France*, Larousse 1951

Davies, Trefor R., *A Book of Welsh Names*, Sheppard Press 1952

Delderfield, Eric, *British Inn Signs and their Stories*, David & Charles 1972

Disraeli, Isaac, *Curiosities of Literature*, Moxon 1849

Dixon, Piers, *Cornish Names*, Dixon 1973

Dolan, J. R., *English Ancestral Names*, Clarkson N. Potter 1972

Dunkling, Leslie A., *A Dictionary of Days*, Routledge 1988

Dunkling, Leslie A., *A Dictionary of Terms of Address*, Routledge 1989

Dunkling, Leslie A., *English House Names*, The Names Society 1971

Dunkling, Leslie A., *First Names First*, Dent/Universe 1977; Gale Research 1982

Dunkling, Leslie A., *Scottish Christian Names*, Johnston & Bacon 1978, 1988

Dunkling, Leslie A., *What's In A Name?* Ventura 1978

Dunkling, Leslie A., *Our Secret Names*, Sidgwick & Jackson 1981, Prentice-Hall 1982

Dunkling, Leslie A., *You Name It!* Faber & Faber 1987

Dunkling, Leslie A., and Gosling, William, *Everyman's Dictionary of First Names*, Dent 1983, 1987

Dunkling, Leslie A., and Wright, Gordon, *A Dictionary of Pub Names*, Routledge & Kegan Paul 1987

Dynes, Cecily, *The Great Australian and New Zealand Book of Baby Names*, Angus & Robertson 1984

Ehrensperger, Edward, *South Dakota Place Names*, Vermillion 1941

Ekwall, Eilert, *Street Names of the City of London*, Clarendon Press 1954

Ekwall, Eilert, *The Concise Oxford Dictionary of English Place Names*, Oxford University Press 1966

Ekwall, Eilert, *English River Names*, Oxford University Press 1968

Espenshade, O. H., *Pennsylvania Place Names*, State College Pennsylvania 1969

Ewen, C. L., *History of British Surnames*, Kegan Paul 1951
Field, John, *Discovering Place-Names*, Shire Publications 1971
Field, John, *English Field Names*, David & Charles 1972
Field, John, *Place Names of Great Britain and Ireland*, David & Charles 1980
Field, John, *Place Names of Greater London*, Batsford 1980
Field, Thomas P., *A Guide to Kentucky Place Names*, Lexington 1961
Fletcher, Barbara, *Don't Blame the Stork—The Cyclopedia of Unusual Names*, Rainbow Publications 1981
Franklyn, Julian, *A Dictionary of Nicknames*, British Book Centre NY 1962
Freeman, William, *Dictionary of Fictional Characters*, Dent 1967
Frey, Albert, *Sobriquets and Nicknames*, Whittaker 1887
Fucilla, Joseph, *Our Italian Surnames*, Chandler 1949
Gard, R. E., & Sorden, L. G., *The Romance of Wisconsin Place Names*, New York 1968
Gelling, M., Nicolaisen, W. F. H., & Richards, M., *The Names of Towns & Cities in Britain*, Batsford 1970
Gudde, Edwin G., *California Place Names*, Berkeley 1962
Guppy, Henry B., *Homes of Family Names in Great Britain*, Harrison 1890
Halliwell, Leslie, *Filmgoer's Companion*, Granada 1979
Hanks, Patrick, and Hodges, Flavia, *The Oxford Minidictionary of First Names*, Oxford University Press 1986
Hanson, R. M., *Virginia Place Names*, Verona 1969
Harder, Kelsie B., *Illustrated Dictionary of Place Names*, Van Nostrand Reinhold 1976
Holmgren, E. J. & P. M., *Over 2000 Place Names of Alberta*, Western Producer Book Service 1973
Hook, J. N., *Family Names*, Macmillan 1982
Hughes, Arthur, & Allen, M., *Connecticut Place Names*, Connecticut Historical Society 1976
Jacobson, Sven, *Unorthodox Spelling in American Trademarks*, Almqvist & Wiksell 1966
Johnson, Charles, & Sleigh, Linwood, *The Harrap Book of Boys' and Girls' Names*, Harrap 1973
Johnston, James B., *Place Names of Scotland*, S R Publishers 1972
Joyce, P. W., *The Origin and History of Irish Names of Places*, E.P. Publishing 1972
Kaganoff, Benzion, *A Dictionary of Jewish Names and their History*, Schocken Books 1977
Kane, J. N., & Alexander, G., *Nicknames and Sobriquets of US Cities and States*, Metuchen 1970
Kelly, Patrick, *Irish Family Names*, Gale Research 1976
Kennedy, Don H., *Ship Names*, University Press of Virginia 1964
Kenny, H., *West Virginia Place Names*, Piedmont 1945
Kirke Swann, H., *A Dictionary of English & Folk Names of British Birds*, Witherby/Gale Research 1968
Kneen, J. J., *The Personal Names of the Isle of Man*, Oxford University Press 1937
Krakow, Kenneth, *Georgia Place Names*, Winship Press 1975
Lamb, Cadbury, & Wright, Gordon, *Discovering Inn Signs*, Shire Publications 1968
Larwood, Jacob, & Hotten, John, *History of Signboards*, Hotten 1866
Lawson, Edwin D., *Personal Names and Naming*, Greenwood Press 1987
Leeper, Clare, *Louisiana Places*, Legacy Publishing 1976
Lower, M. A., *English Surnames*, Russell Smith 1875
McArthur, L. A., *Oregon Geographic Names*, Portland 1952
Mackenzie, W. C., *Scottish Place Names*, Kegan Paul 1931
McKinley, R. A., *Norfolk Surnames in the 16th Century*, Leicester University Press 1969
MacLysaght, Edward, *The Surnames of Ireland*, Irish University Press 1969
Manning, T. D., & Walker, C. F., *British Warship Names*, Putnam 1959
Matthews, C. M., *English Surnames*, Weidenfeld & Nicolson 1966
Matthews, C. M., *How Surnames Began*, Lutterworth Press 1967
Matthews, C. M., *Place Names of the English Speaking World*, Weidenfeld & Nicolson 1972
Matthews, C. M., *How Place Names Began*, Hamlyn 1979
Miller, G. M., *Pronouncing Dictionary of British Names*, Oxford University Press 1971
Monson-Fitzjohn, C. J., *Quaint Signs of Olde Inns*, Jenkins 1926
Moody, Sophy, *What Is Your Name?* Bentley 1863
Morgan, Jane, O'Neill, Christopher, & Harré, Rom, *Nicknames*, Routledge & Kegan Paul 1979
Morgan, T. J., and Morgan, Prys, *Welsh Surnames*, University of Wales Press 1985
Mossman, Jennifer, *Pseudonyms and Nicknames Dictionary*, Gale Research 1982
Nath, Dwarka, *Naming the Hindu Child*, Nath 1974
Nicolaisen, W. F. H., *Scottish Place Names*, Batsford 1976
Noble, Vernon, *Nicknames*, Hamish Hamilton 1976
Partridge, Eric, *Name This Child*, Hamish Hamilton 1951
Pawley White, G., *A Handbook of Cornish Surnames*, Pawley White 1972
Payton, Geoffrey, *Payton's Proper Names*, Warne 1969
Phillips, James W., *Alaska-Yukon Place Names*, University of Washington Press 1973
Phillips, James W., *Washington State Place Names*, University of Washington 1971
Praninskas, Jean, *Trade Name Creation*, Mouton 1969

Price, Roger, & Stern, Leonard, *How Dare You Call Me That!* Wolfe Publishing 1966
Pukui, Mary, Elbert, Samuel, & Mookini, Esther, *Place Names of Hawaii*, University Press of Hawaii 1974
Rayburn, Alan, *Geographical Names of New Brunswick*, Department of Energy, Mines and Resources 1975
Reaney, P. H., *A Dictionary of British Surnames*, Routledge & Kegan Paul 1961
Reaney, P. H., *The Origin of English Place Names*, Routledge & Kegan Paul 1969
Reaney, P. H., *The Origin of English Surnames*, Routledge & Kegan Paul 1969
Redmonds, George, *Yorkshire West Riding—English Surnames Series I*, Phillimore 1973
Romig, Walter, *Michigan Place Names*, Grosse Point 1970
Room, Adrian, *A Dictionary of Irish Place-Names*, Appletree Press 1986
Room, Adrian, *Dictionary of Coin Names*, Routledge & Kegan Paul 1987
Room, Adrian, *Place Names of the World*, David & Charles 1974
Room, Adrian, *Place Name Changes Since 1900*, The Scarecrow Press 1979
Room, Adrian, *Pet Names*, New Horizon 1979
Room, Adrian, *Naming Names*, McFarland 1981
Room, Adrian, *Dictionary of Trade Name Origins*, Routledge & Kegan Paul 1982
Rosenthal, Eric, *South African Surnames*, Timmins 1965
Rudnyckyj, J. B., *Manitoba Mosaic of Place Names*, Canadian Institute of Onomastic 1970
Schaar, J. van der, *Woordenboek van Voornamen*, Het Spectrum 1981
Shirk, George H., *Oklahoma Place Names*, University of Oklahoma Press 1974
Smith, Anna H., *Johannesburg Street Names*, Juta 1971
Smith, Elsdon C., *The Story of Our Names*, Harper 1950
Smith, Elsdon C., *Naming Your Baby*, Greenberg 1943
Smith, Elsdon C., *Personal Names—A Bibliography*, Gale 1965
Smith, Elsdon C., *Treasury of Name Lore*, Harper & Row 1967
Smith, Elsdon C., *American Surnames*, Chilton Book Co. 1970
Smith, Elsdon C., *New Dictionary of American Family Names*, Harper & Row 1973
Smith, Muriel, *National Apple Register of the United Kingdom*, Ministry of Agriculture & Food 1971
Stephens, Ruth, *Welsh Names for Children*, Y Lolfa 1972
Stewart, George R., *Names on the Land*, Houghton Mifflin 1967
Stewart, George R., *American Place Names*, Oxford University Press 1970
Stewart, George R., *Names on the Globe*, Oxford University Press 1975
Stewart Fay, E., *Why Piccadilly?* Methuen 1935
Stokes, H. G., *English Place Names*, Batsford 1948
Sturmfels, Wilhelm, & Bischof, Heinz, *Unsere Ortsnamen*, Dümmlers 1961
Swift, Esther M., *Vermont Place Names*, Stephen Greene Press 1977
Taggart, Jean E., *Motorboat, Yacht or Canoe—You Name It*, The Scarecrow Press 1974
Train, John, *Remarkable Names of Real People*, Clarkson N. Potter 1977
Train, John, *Even More Remarkable Names of Real People*, Clarkson N. Potter 1979
Unbegaun, B. O., *Russian Surnames*, Oxford University Press 1972
Upham, Warren, *Minnesota Geographic Names*, St Paul 1969
Urbank, Mae, *Wyoming Place Names*, Boulder 1967
Weekley, Ernest, *Jack and Jill*, John Murray 1939
Weekley, Ernest, *Surnames*, John Murray 1916
Weekley, Ernest, *The Romance of Names*, John Murray 1928
Weekley, Ernest, *Words and Names*, John Murray 1932
Weidenhan, Joseph L., *Baptismal Names*, Gale Research 1968
Williams, Mary A., *Origins of North Dakota Place Names*, Washburn 1966
Withycombe, E. G., *The Oxford Dictionary of English Christian Names*, Oxford University Press 1977
Woulfe, Patrick, *Irish Names for Children*, Gill & Macmillan 1974
Wright, Gordon, *At the Sign of the Flagon*, Frank Graham 1970
Yonge, Charlotte M., *History of Christian Names*, Gale Research 1966
Zettersten, Louis, *City Street Names*, Selwyn & Blount 1926

Surname researchers should remember that useful information about a surname is often to be obtained from a book on place names. For English names the best source of information is always the appropriate county volume of the English Place Name Society. The *Oxford English Dictionary* also provides valuable help with early meanings of words and words now obsolete.

Names Index

A
Aaron 28, 38, 40-4, 49
Abbinett 80
Abbs 81
Abel 32
Aberdeenshire 113
Abiel 32
Abigail 23, 33, 38, 51, 54, 62
Abishag 39
Abner 32
Abraham 32, 38, 41, 43
Absalom 32
Accord 122
Achurch 80
Acres 80
Acton 78
Ada 45, 47
Adah 37
Adair 31
Adam 12, 23, 28, 38, 41-2, 44, 49, 61, 69
Adams 69, 102
Adamson 69
Adcock 69
Adderns 79
Addison 69
Addy 69, 83
Adela 38
Adelaide 33
Adele 33
Adkins 69
Adlai 32
Adlard 70
Adlestrop 112
Adnams 78
Adnil 62
Adolf 54
Adolph 60
Adrian 28, 42, 49
Adshead 78
Agar 82
Agatha 12, 23, 61, 69
Agens 23
Aggass 69
Agnes 12, 38, 45, 47, 55, 61-2, 69
Agnew 72
Ahab 32
Aherne 72
Ahimaaz 62
Aholibanah 39
Aidan 30
Aileen 36
Ailsa 37
Aimee 33
Aine 36
Aisha 36, 48
Aisling 36
Aitken 69
Aitkins 69
Akehurst 82
Akers 81
Alabama 125
Alan 28, 38, 41-4, 49, 69
Alana 37
Alasdair 31
Alaska 125
Albert 28, 41-3
Albut 82
Alcock 69
ALCOHOLIC NAMES 62
Alder 81
Aldermanbury 109
Aldous 82
Aldworth 81
Alec 28
Aled 31
Alex 28
Alexander 12, 28, 40-3, 49, 69
Alexanderina 60
Alexandra 33, 46, 49, 51
Alexia 12
Alexina 37
Alexis 33
Alflatt 70
Alford 74, 79
Alfred 38, 42, 54, 61, 63
Algar 38
Algeria 124
Algernon 23, 55
ALIASES 85-6
Alice 33, 38, 45-7, 49
Alicia 33, 48-9
Alison 33, 46, 49
Alistair 28, 42
Alker 80
Allan 69, 81
Allanson 69
Allbones 76
Allbutt 82
Allcorn 82
Allcott 80
Allen 43-4, 69
Allerton 112
Alleyn 69
Allington 82
Allinson 69
Allison 33, 48
Allman 78
Allnatt 70
Allwright 63
Alma 24, 47, 61
Almond 80
Alonzo 30
Alphonso 30
Alpin 31
Alston 74, 82
Alton 79
Alty 80
Alun 31
Alvah 32
Alvar 70
Alvarez 71
Alvaro 71
Alvin 30
Alwin 38, 70
Amabel 33
Amanda 12, 33, 46, 48-9, 61
Amaziah 39
Amber 33, 39-40, 48
Ambler 83
Amelia 12, 33, 45, 47
America 118
AMERICAN NAMES 30, 36, 67-8, 71
AMERICAN PLACE NAMES 117-22
AMERICAN STATES 126-7
Amery 69, 79
Ames 69
Amesbury 81
Amethyst 39
Amey 80
Amice 38, 69
Amies 69, 81
Amis 69, 81
Amison 69
Amity 39
Amon 32
Amos 32, 41
Amphlett 82
Amsterdam 127
Amy 23, 33, 45-6, 48-9, 60
ANAGRAMS 183, 191-2
Anaktuvak Pass 123
Ananias 62
ANANYMS 62
Anastasia 35
Anderson 69
Andre 30, 44
Andrea 33, 46, 48-9
Andrew 28, 41-4, 49, 69
Andrews 65, 69
Angela 33, 46, 48-9
Angelina 12
Angharad 37
Anglesey 113
ANGLO-SAXON NAMES 38
ANGLO-SAXON PLACE NAMES 108-10
ANGRY NAMES 62
Anguish 76
Angus 31, 55, 113, 160
Anika 33
ANIMAL NAMES 40, 60, 170-2, 177-9
Anita 33
Ankers 78
Ann(e) 25, 33, 45-9, 55-6
Anna 33, 45-8
Annabel(le) 33
Annable 81
Annapolis 119
Annarenia 58
Anne Marie 48
Annemarie 33
Annett 81
Annette 33
Annie 25, 45-7, 55
Anning 79
Annis 69
Annison 69
Anson 69
Antell 79
Anthea 40
Anthony 28, 41-4, 49
Antigua 118
Antoine 30, 44
Antonia 12, 37
Antonio 44
Antony 28
Antrim 113
Anwen 37
Anxious Bay 121
Anyan 81
Aoife 36
ap 67
Ap Rhys 67
Aplin 81
Apperley 80
APPLE NAMES 9-10, 172-3
Applebachsville 122
Applegarth 79
Appleyard 83
April 33, 57, 61
Arch 82
Archer 75
Archibald 55, 61
Ardern 78
Argentina 124
Argyll 113
Ariel 32
Aris 81
Arizona 125
Arkansas 125
Arkell 80
Arkle 81
Arlene 47
Arlott 77
Armagh 113
Armand 69
Arment 69
Armitage 83
Armstrong 77
Arnatt 81
Arney 81
Arnold 30, 40
Arran 31
Arrow 110
Arrowsmith 75
Arscott 79
Arthur 41-4, 49, 60
Arthurton 81
Arwel 31
Arwenna 37
Arwyn 31
Asa 32
Ash 82
Ashby 74
Asher 32
Ashleigh 49
Ashley 28, 42, 46, 48-9, 54, 81
Ashman 81
Ashwell 80
Aspinall 80
Aspinwall 80
Astbury 78
Aston 78
Astra 61
Atarah 37
Athaliah 37
Athens 127
Atherton 80
Athol 31
Atkin(s) 69
Atkinson 69
Atthow 81
Attoe 81
Attrill 80
Audrey 33, 46, 63
Audubon 68
Augusta 108, 119
Augustine 38, 69
Aulay 31
Aurelia 40
Aurora 12, 61
Austen 69
Austin 28, 69
Australia 124
AUSTRALIAN NAMES 49
AUSTRALIAN PLACE NAMES 122
AUSTRALIAN PUB NAMES 143-4
Austria 124
AUTOMOBILE NAMES 161-2
Autumn 33
Averay 70
Averill 82
Aves 82
Avis 38
Avoca 120
Avon 110, 114
Avril 33, 57, 61
Awdry 82
Awen 31
Axe 110
Ayana 36
Ayanna 36
Ayesha 36
Ayles 80
Ayling 82
Aylmer 70
Aylwin 70, 82
Aymes 69
Aynsley 81
Ayrshire 113
Azariah 32
Azaziah 32
Azel 32
Azile 62
Azubah 37
B
Babbage 79
Baber 81
Bacchus 75
Back 81
Backer 75
Bacon 75
Baden 41
Badman 81
Badrick 70
Bagg 81
Baghdad 127
Bagnall 82
Bahrain 124
Bailey 75
Baker 75, 102
Bakewell 82
Balaam 32
Baldey 70
Baldry 82
Balkwill 79
Ball 76
Ballam 79
Ballard 77, 80
Ballinger 80
Balman 70, 79
Balmforth 83
Balsdon 79
Balston 70
Bamber 80
Bamforth 83
Bane 72
Banffshire 113
Banfield 80
Banham 81
Banks 74
Banwell 81
Barabbas 32
Barak 32
Barbara 33, 38, 45-9
Barber 75
Bardon 72
Barfoot 80
Barford 81
Bargo Brush 122
Barham 82
Bark 79
Barker 75
Barling 80
Barnaby 28
Barnsley 79
Barnstable 81
Barnum 68
Barraclough 83
Barrington 81
Barrowcliff 81
Barry 25, 28, 42, 49
Bartholomew 32, 69
Bartle 69
Bartlet(t) 69
Barton 74
Bartram 81
Baruch 32, 68
Barzillai 32
Basford 78
Basham 79
Basil 61
Baskerville 78
Baskeyfield 82
Basnett 78
Bass 77
Bassett 77
Bastable 79
Bastin 79
Bate 69
Bateman 69
Bater 79
Bates 69
Bateson 69
Bather 81
Batho 81
Bathsheba 37
Batkin 69, 82
Batt 69, 81
Battams 78
Batten 69
Batterham 81
Battersby 80
Battiest 120
Battle 121
Batts 81
Batty(e) 69, 76, 83
Bauer 71
Baxter 75
Bayliss 75
Bays 78
Bazeley 81
Bazley 81
Be-Courteous 39
BEACH-HUT NAMES 155
Beadle 79
Beak 82
Beales 81
Beanes 81
Beard 77
Beardall 81
Beardmore 82
Beardsley 79
Beathag 37
Beaton 69
Beatrice 45, 47, 69
Beattie 79
Beatty 69
Beaty 79
Beauchamp 66
Beaulieu 110
Beaumont 110
Beaurepaire 117
Bebb 83
Bebbington 78
Becher 32
Beck 81
Becky 33
Beddall 79
Beddoes 81
Bedfordshire 113
Bedloe 70
Beeby 80
Beecroft 81
Beedell 79
Beer 79, 102
Beet 69
Beeton 69
Beever(s) 83
Beevors 83
Begley 72
Behan 72
Bela 32
Belcham 79
Belcher 77, 87
Belfast 108
Belgium 124
Belgrade 127
Belgrave 110
Belgrove 78
Belinda 33, 49
Bell 77, 102
Bellairs 81
Bellamy 77
Bellars 81
Belle 47
Bellis 83
Belper 117
Belteshazzar 39
Bemrose 81
Ben 42
Benbow 81
Bendall 82
Benedict 23, 28, 38, 69
Benjamin 28, 38, 41-3, 49, 51, 54
Benn 69
Bennett 69, 102
Bennie 30
Benning 78

Benny 78
Benson 69
Benstead 80
Bensted 80
Bent 80
Bentall 79
Bentham 83
Bentley 74
Benton 74
Beornred 109
Berengaria 51
Berenice 60
Berg(er) 71
Berkshire 113
Bermudas 127
Bernadette 36
Bernard 23, 28, 38, 41–3, 49, 60–1
Bernice 37, 60
Berridge 80
Berriman 78
Berrow 80
Berry 60
Berryman 72, 78
Bertha 45, 47
Bertie 41
Bertram 41
Berwickshire 113
Beryl 39, 46
Besent 79
Besley 79
Bess 39
Bessie 47, 61
Best 77
Beth 33, 39
Bethan 37
Bethany 33, 121
Bethell 69
Bethesda 120
Betsy 45
Bett 81
Bettinson 81
Betty 23, 39, 45–7
Beulah 38
Bevan 69, 72
Beverley 33, 46, 49, 52
Beverly 33, 47–8, 52
Bevin 69
Bewick 81
Bewley 110
Beynon 83
Bianca 33, 40
Bibby 69, 80
BIBLICAL NAMES 32, 37, 62
Bice 78
Bickford 82
Bickle 79
Bicknell 81
Biddick 78
Biddle 80
Biggin 79
Biggs 77
Bill 57, 60
Billington 112
Billion 76
Billyard 81
Bing 80
Binge 81
Bingley 81
Binning 81
Binns 83
Bird 102
Birtles 78
Bisdee 81
Bithiah 37
Bjorn 60
Black 77, 102
Blackbird 76–7
Blackman 80
Blackpool 108
Blackshaw 78
Blackwell 74
Blades 81
Blake 77
Blakemore 81
Blakeway 82
Blakey 83
Blamey 78
Blanche 33, 40, 47, 56
Blandford 80
Blanket 76
Blankley 81
Blatchford 79
Blatherwick 81
Bleasdale 80
Bleazard 80
Bleddyn 31
Blencowe 81
Blenkin 82
Blenkiron 82
Bletsoe 80
Blez(z)ard 80
Blossom 39
Blowers 82
Blowey 79
Bloye 79
Blue Mountain 122
Bluebell 39
Blue's Point 122
Blundell 77
Blunt 77
Boaden 78
Boam 79
Board 81
Boase 78
Boaz 32
Bob 57
Boddington 82
Boddy 81
Boden 82
Bodenham 80
Bodle 82
Body 76
Boffey 78
Bolam 81
Bolitho 78
Bolivia 124
Bolshaw 78
Bolt 79
Bolton 74
Bombay 127
Bone 76
Bonfield 80
Bong Bong 122
Boniface 82
Bonn 127
Bonney 80
Bonnie 33, 54
Boon 82
Boorman 80
Boosey 76
Border 81
Borlase 78
Borman 81
Borrett 82
Borthwick 81
Borton 81
Bosanquet 72
Bosomworth 82
Bossey 77
Boston 119
Botany Bay 121
Bothwick 81
Bott 82
Botterill 82
Botting 82
Bottomley 83
Boucher 82
Boughey 81
Boughmore 81
Boughton 78
Bould 82
Boulden 80
Boulter 82
Boulton 82
Boumphrey 69
Bounds 80
Boundy 79
Bourner 82
Bovey 79
Bowditch 79
Bowdler 81
Bowell 76
Bowering 81
Bowers 82
Bowes 82
Bowman 75
Bowmer 79
Bowser 81
Boyd 40, 72
Boyle 72
BOYS' NAMES 28, 30, 32, 41–4, 49
Bracegirdle 78
Bracher 82
Brackenbury 81
Braddock 78
Bradford 74, 112
Bradley 28, 44, 49, 74
Bradridge 79
Bradshaw 74
Brafield 81
Bragg 77, 79
Bramall 83
Brandee 62
Brandi 48, 62
Brandon 28, 44, 74
Brandt 71
Brandy 48, 62
Branson 80
Brasher 75
Brasnett 81
Braund 79
Brayley 79
Brazier 78
Brazil 124
Breach 82
Breakspear 81
Breakwell 81
Brear(s) 83
Breary 78
Breayley 79
Breconshire 113
Breedlove 120
Brenchley 80
Brenda 33, 46–8
Brendan 28, 49
Brendon 78
Brennan 72, 77
Brent 28, 77
Brenton 78
Bretherton 80
Breton 74
Bret(t) 28, 49, 74
Brewer 75
Brewis 81
Brewster 75
Brian 28, 38, 42, 44, 49
Brice 80
Brickell 79
Briddon 79
Bridges 74
Bridget 33, 36, 45
Bridgman 79
Bridstow 109
Brigham 82
Bright 102
Brightman 78
Brightmore 70
Brimacombe 79
Brimble 81
Brindle 80
Brindley 82
Brine 79
Brisbane 127
Brisbourne 81
Bristow 81
Britt 74
Brittany 48
Britten 74, 81
Britteridge 112
Britton 74
Broadbent 83
Broadberry 81
Broadhead 83
Broadhurst 78
Broadley 80
Brocksopp 79
Broderick 31
Brodie 81
Broken Hill 122
Brolly 76
Bromage 80
Bromwich 81
Bronia 51
Bronte 85
Bronwen 37
Brook(e) 33
Brooks 74
Broom 79
Broomfield 80
Broomhead 79
Broster 78
Broughall 81
Broughton 81
Brown 52, 77, 102
Browning 80
Brownlow 81
Bruce 31, 43–4, 49, 72, 79
Brumby 81
Brunger 70
Brunt 82
Brunwin 70
Brussels 127
Bryan 28
Bryant 30, 102
Bryn 31
Brynmore 31
Bryony 33, 39, 51
Bubb 80
Buccaneer Bay 120
Buck 60
Buckeridge 78
Buckinghamshire 113
Buckley 74
Buckmaster 78
Bucknell 79
Budd 76, 80
Budge 78
Buenos Aires 127
Bugg 79, 90
Bugler 79
Bulcock 80
Bull 52
Buller 81
Bullman 79
Bullmore 78
Bulman 79
Bulmer 82
Bunce 78
Buncombe 120
Bunn 81
Burbridge 82
Burch 81
Burchard 70
Burdikin 79
Burdon 79
Burgoin 79
Burgoyne 79
Burke 67, 72
Burkill 81
Burkitt 81
Burma 124
Burnaby 80
Burnett 77
Burns 72, 79
Burrage 70
Burrough 79
Burrow 79
Burston 81
Burton 74
Burward 70
Bushby 81
Buss 80
Buswell 81
Butcher 75
Bute 113
Butler 75
Butlin 81
Butterfield 83
Butters 81
Butterworth 80
Buttery 81
Button 82
Byard 79
Byford 79
BYNAMES 64–5
Byrd 82
Byron 30, 81
C
Cabot 119
Cade 81
Cadle 80
Cadwallader 81
Caer Myrddin 107
Caernarvonshire 113
Caesar 82
Cain 32, 102
Caines 79
Cair Luel 107
Cairns 81
Cairo 127
Caithness 113
Caitlin 48
Cake 79
Calcutt 81
Caldwell 74, 80
Caleb 32
California 125
Callender 79
Callow 80
Callwood 78
Calum 31
Calver 82
Calvin 30
Cambridge 162
Cambridgeshire 113
Camero 71
Cameron 25, 28, 49, 67, 72
Cameroon 124
Camilla 33
Camille 36
Cammack 81
Campbell 25, 31, 72
Campion 75
Campkin 80
Canada 124
Candace 33, 62
Candice 33, 48
Candida 33, 40
Candy 62
Cannell 81
Cannibal Plateau 121
Cannings 108
Cant 79
Cantrell 82
Cantrill 82
Cape Anna 119
Cape Banks 121
Cape Catastrophe 121
Cape Cod 119
Cape Elizabeth 119
Cape James 119
Capes 81
Capstick 83
Cara 33
CARAVAN NAMES 155
Cardell 78
Cardew 72
Cardiganshire 113
Cardwell 80
Careen 54
Careless 82
Carey 81
Carissa 33
Carl 28, 42–4
Carla 12, 33, 46
Carless 77
Carley 33
Carlie 33
Carling 62
Carlisle 107
Carlos 30
Carlson 71
Carlton 30, 74
Carly 33, 46, 49
Carlyon 78
Carmarthen 107
Carmarthenshire 113
Carmel 37, 61
Carmen 12, 36
Carmichael 81
Carne 78
Carnegie 68
Carol(e) 12, 33, 46–9, 61–2
Carolina 33, 119
Caroline 33, 45, 49, 56–7
Carolyn(n) 33, 40, 47–8
Carpenter 65, 75
Carrick 72
Carrie 33, 47
Carruthers 79
Carson 71
Carter 75, 102
Cartier 119
Cartmell 80
Cartridge 82
Cartwright 75
Carver 75, 81
Carveth 78
Carwyn 31
Cary 81
Carys 37
Case 69, 81
Casey 48
Cash 69, 78
Cass 69
Cassandra 33, 40, 69
Cassia 37
Casson 69
Casswell 81
Castillo 71
Castle 74–5
Castleman 75
Castro 71
CAT NAMES 170–1, 178
Catchpole 75
Cater 75
Cathal 30
Catherine 22, 33, 45–9, 61, 188
Catlin 69
Catling 82
Catlow 80
Caton 69, 79
Catrin 37
Catriona 37
Catterall 80
Cattermole 82
Cattling 69
Caunce 80
Cave 77
Cawrse 78
Cawsey 79
Cecil 23, 41, 61
Cecily 69
Cedric 30
Ceinwen 37
Celeste 12
Celine 12, 35
CELTIC NAMES 72
CELTIC PLACE NAMES 106–8
Cemlyn 31
Cent Deux 120
Century 75
Cephas 32
Ceri 31, 33
Cerian 37
Cerise 61
Cerys 37
Chad 28
Chadfield 79
Chafer 75
Chaffe 79
Chaffer 75
Chalker 75
Chalkley 80
Challand 81
Challen 82
Challender 75
Challinor 75
Challis 79
Chalmers 75
Chamberlain 75
Chambers 75
Chamings 79
Chammings 79

Champion 75
Chandler 75
Chandra 36
Chan(n)el 61
Channin(g) 79
Chantal 33
Chantel(le) 33
Chantler 80
Chaplin 75
Chapman 75
Chard 81
Charity 33, 39, 60
Charleen 33
Charlene 33, 46
Charles 23, 28, 41-4, 85
Charles River 119
Charline 33
Charlotte 33, 45-6, 56
Charlton 109
Charlwood 82
Charmain 12
Charmain(e) 33
Charnley 80
Charnock 80
Charterhouse 110
Chartreuse 110
Chatham 120
Chattanooga 127
Chattaway 82
Chatterton 81
Chaundler 75
Chaundy 81
Chave 79
Chavez 71
Chell 82
Chelsea 48-9
Cheney 80
Chennells 80
Chenoweth 78
Cherie 33
Cheriton 79, 109
Cherry 33, 39, 60
Cheryl 33, 48-9, 52, 61
Cheshire 81, 113
Chessman 76
Chester 102
Chesterfield 108
Chesters 78
Chettle 81
Chew 81
Chicago 105
Chilcott 79
Chile 124
Chilton 112
China 124
Chiswick 110
Chitty 82
Chivers 78
Chloe 33, 49
Chobham 117
Cholmondeley 66
Chorlton 109
Chowen 79
Chown 79
Christa 33
Christensen 71
Christian 28, 49, 53, 69
CHRISTIAN NAMES 38-9
Christie 69
Christina 33, 48
Christine 33, 46-9
Christison 69
Christmas 62
Christopher 28, 41-2, 44, 49, 61, 69
Christy 33, 37, 69, 79
Chubb 79, 90, 102
Chugg 79
Churches 81
Churchill 68, 74
Churchman 82
Chuter 82
Ciara 36, 48
Ciaran 30
Cindy 33
Cirencester 110
Clack 64
Clackmannanshire 113
Clair 33
Claire 12, 33, 46, 49, 61
CLAN NICKNAMES 98, 102
Clapham 83
Clapp 81
Clapton 81
Clara 33, 45, 47
Clare 33, 81
Clarence 43
Claridge 78
Clarissa 12, 51
Clark(e) 51, 66, 75, 102
Claxton 81
Clayton 74
Clear 78
Cledwyn 31
Cleeton 81
Clement(s) 69
Clementson 69
Clemms 69
Clem(p)son 69
Clemretta 121
Cleo 12
Clemow 78
Cleveland 114
Cleverdon 79
Clew(e)s 79
Clewlow 82
Clifford 24, 28, 41, 43, 68, 74
Clift 80
Clifton 74
Clinch 80
Clint 61
Clinton 30, 80
Clive 28, 42
Clod 64
Clothier 81
Clough 83
Clowes 82
Cluett 79
Clulow 82
Clumsy 64
Clutterbuck 80
Clwyd 114
Clyde 31
Clyma 78
Coad 78
Coaker 79
Coate 81
Coatsworth 79
Cobbald 70
Cobbity 122
Cobbledick 78
Cobbold 82
Cobden 80
Cobeldick 78
Cobley 80
Cockburn 81
Cockeram 79
Cockram 79
Cockshott 83
COCKTAIL NAMES 145
Coco 61
Codd 81
Coding 82
Cody 44
Coffin 76
Cog(g)an 81
Coggins 81
Cohen 71
Coke 75
Colclough 82
Cole 69
Coleman 38
Coles 102
Colette 33
Colin 28, 42, 49
Colishaw 81
Colleen 33, 48
Collen 78
Collett 69
Collette 33
Colley 69, 83
Collie 76
Collier 75
Collinge 80
Collingham 81
Collins 69
Collinson 69
Collis 69
Colm 30
Cologne 127
Colombia 124
Colombo 118
Colorado 125
COLOUR NAMES 40
COLOURFUL NAMES 61
Colson 82
Columba 24
Columbia 118
Columbiana 118
Columbiaville 118
Columbus 118
Colwill 79
Comely 80
Common 81
Compton 74, 82
Concord 122
Coney 81
Coneybear(e) 79
Congdon 78
Connecticut 125
Connibear 79
Connor 30
Conquest 102
Conrad 28
Constance 38, 46, 69
CONVERTED NAMES 18, 21, 23
Conway 74
Cook(e) 75, 119
Cooling 81
Coombe 79
Cooper 75
Copeman 81
Copenhagen 127
Copestake 79
Copp 79
Coppard 82
Coral 33, 39
Coralie 12
Coralin 12
Corbishley 82
Cordelia 12
Corderey 78
Corderoy 78
Corey 30, 44
Corfield 81
Corinna 40
Corinne 33
Corke 82
Cormac 30
Cornelia 12
Cornelius 30
Cornell 30, 74
Corner 81
Corney 80
Cornford 82
Cornish 74
Cornock 80
Cornwall 74, 113
Cornwallis 74
Cornwell 74
Corp 81
Corringham 81
Cosh 81
Cosmo 31
Cossey 81
Cottingham 81
Cottle 82
Cotton 74, 102
Couch 78
Coulson 69
Coultrip 80
Counsell 81
COUNTY NAMES 113
Coupland 81
Courtice 79
Courtney 33, 48-9
Coveney 80
Coverdale 82
Cowan 81
Coward 80
Cowen 81
Cowing 81
Cowling 78
Cowper 75
Coxall 78
Cozbi 37
Cracknell 82
Crackston 112
Crago(e) 78
Craig 25, 28, 42, 44, 49, 52, 72, 81
Cranfield 78
Crang 79
Cranidge 81
Crapper 83
Crawford 31, 74
Crawshaw 83
Craze 78
Creaser 82
Cresbard 121
CRIMINAL NICKNAMES 98-9
Crimp 79
Crippen 77
Cripps 77
Crisp 77
Crispin 23, 77
Critchley 80
Crockford 78
Crocombe 79
Crofts 82
Cromarty 113
Crompton 80
Cromwell 112
Cronk 77
Crookes 79
Croom 81
Croome 80
Cropley 81
Cropper 80
Crosby 74
Cross 102
Crossman 81
Crowhurst 80
Crowle 78
Crowles 83
Cruikshank 77
Cruise 67
Crump 77, 89
Cruz 71
Crystal 33, 39, 48-9
Cubitt 81
Cuckow 77
Culley 81
Cullimore 80
Culshaw 80
Cumberland 81, 113, 119
Cumberledge 82
Cumbria 114
Cundy 78
Cunliffe 80
Cunningham 72
Cupit 79
Cureton 81
Curling 80
Curning 79
Curnow 78
Currall 82
Curson 81
Curtis 30, 77
Cuss 69, 82
Cussans 69
Cusse 82
Cust 69
Custance 69
Custard 76
Cutforth 81
Cuthbert 23, 53, 55, 61, 63, 81
Cutteridge 70
Cutting 82
Cutts 79
Cynewulf 109
Cynthia 33, 40, 48
Cyril 41, 61
Cyrus 32

D
Dabbs 69
Daffodil 39
Dafydd 31
Dagger 80
Dainty 81
Daisy 39, 45
Dakins 69
Dalby 80
Dale 28, 44, 49
Dallyn 79
Dalton 74
Daly 72
Dalzell 79
Dalziel 79
Damaris 37
Damerell 79
Damian 28, 42, 49
Damien 28
Damon 30
Dampier 81
Danby 82
Dancer 78
Dand 81
Dandy 69
Daniel 28, 38, 41-4, 49, 57, 69
Danielle 33, 46, 48-9
Daniels 69
Dannatt 81
Dannet 69
Dannson 69
Daphne 39
Darch 79
Dare 79
Darius 30, 32
Dark 80
Darlene 48
Darnell 30, 80
Darrell 30
Darren 25, 28, 40, 42, 52
Darrington 78
Darryl 44
Dart 79
Darvell 78
Darvill 78
Darwin 63, 70, 81
Daubney 81
Daved 58
Davenport 74
David 28, 38, 41-4, 49, 61-2, 69
Davidge 69
Davidson 69
Davies 67, 69
Davis(on) 69
Davitt 69
Dawe(s) 69
Dawkins 69, 80
Dawn 33, 46, 48, 52, 61
Dawson 69
Day 52, 69, 75, 102
DAY NAMES 13-17, 62, 109
Dayment 79
De Witt 120
Deadman 76
Deakin 82
Dean 28, 42, 49
DeAndre 44
Deanna 33
Dearden 80
Debbie 33
Debenham 82
Deborah 25, 33, 38, 40, 45-6, 48-9, 51, 60
Debra 33, 40
Decimus 23, 60
Deck 82
Declan 30
Deeley 81
Deinol 31
Deion 58
Deirdre 36, 96
Delaware 125
Delia 40
Delicia 62
Delicious 62
Delilah 37
Delyth 37
Demain(e) 83
Demetrius 30
Denbighshire 113
Denby 83
Dence 74
Dench 74
Denholm 31
Denis 28, 38, 69
Denise 33, 46, 48
Denison 83
Denman 81
Denmark 124
Dennett 69
Denning 81
Dennis 28, 42-4, 49, 74
Dennison 69
Dennis(s) 69
Denns 74
Denny 69
Densem 79
Densham 79
Denton 74
Denver 127
Deon 30
Derbyshire 113
Derek 28, 42, 44
Derman 38
Dermot 30
Derrick 30, 44, 81
Derry 81
Des Moines 127
DESCRIPTIVE HOUSENAMES 153-5
DESCRIPTIVE NAMES 23, 57
DESCRIPTIVE NICKNAMES 97
Desforges 81
Deshawn 30
Desiree 33
Desmond 28
Dethick 110
Devil 76
Devon 113
Dewhurst 80
Dewi 31
Dexter 80
Diamond 40
Dian 12
Diana 33, 40, 48, 51, 181
Diane 33, 46-8
Dianne 33, 49
Diarmid 31
Diarmuid 30
Diaz 71
Dibb 83
Dibble 81
Dick 56-7
Dickens 68-9
Dicker 79
Dickinson 69
Dicks 81
Dickson 69
Diego 71
Digger's Rest 122
Dillamore 78
Dillon 67
Dilnot 80
Diment 81
Dim(m)ock 78
Dimond 79
Dinah 37-8, 45

Dingle 78
Dinning 81
Dinsdale 82
Dion 30
Dionne 36
Diplock 82
Ditton 110
Dix 69
Dixon 69
Dobbie 69
Dobbs 69, 80
Dobie 69
Doble 79
Dobson 69
Docherty 72
Dod 61
Dodd 70
Dodge 70
Dodgson 70
Dodo 32
Dodson 70
Doel 82
DOG NAMES 171, 177-9
Doggett 77-8
Doidge 79
Dolores 47
Dominican Republic 124
Dominic(k) 28
Dominique 48, 61
Dominy 79
Dommett 79
Don 110
Donal 30
Donald 28, 41-4, 49, 69, 79
Donaldson 69
Doncaster 81, 108
Done 78
Donna 33, 46-9
Dook 81
Dooley 78
Doolittle 82
Dora 47
Dorcas 37
Dore 110
Doreen 12, 46
Dorey 79
Dorian 30
Doris 45-7, 51
Dormer 78
Dorothy 33, 45-7
Dorset 113
Dougal 40
Douglas 24, 28, 40, 43-4, 49, 72
Dover 78, 110, 127
Dowdeswell 80
Dowell 80
Dowes 81
Down 113
Downs 74
Dows 81
Dowsett 79
Dowson 69
Doyle 72
Drabble 79
Drackley 80
Drage 81
Drake 102, 119
Drakes 81
Draper 75
Draycott 80
Dresden 127
Drew(e)ry 81
Drewitt 80
Dring 81
Drinkall 80
Dronfield 79
Drudge 80
Drummond 31
Drunkard 64
Drury 81
Drusilla 37
Duane 28
Dublin 108
Duce 81
Duck 76, 82
Duckham 83
Duckmanton 81
Duckworth 80
Dudding 81
Dudley 74
Due West 120
Duffield 81
Dufty 79
Dugald 31, 40
Duggan 83
Duggleby 82
Dulcie 62
Dumbrell 82
Dumbrill 82
Dumfriesshire 113
Dunbarton 113
Duncan 28, 40, 72
Duncombe 78
Dunderdale 80
Dunford 79
Dungey 80
Dunkley 81
Dunkling 73, 86, 161
Dunn 77
Dunstan 78
Dunstone 78
Durand 69
Durant 69
Durden 79
Durham 74, 113
Durose 82
Durrance 69
Durrant 69, 102
Durston 81
Dustin 44
Dutch(man) 74
Dutton 74, 78
Duxbury 80
Dwayne 28, 44
Dwelly 77
Dwight 78
Dyball 81
Dye 81
Dyer 72, 75
Dyfan 31
Dyfed 114
Dylan 31, 49
Dyment 81
Dymond 79
Dyson 69, 83

E
Eade 69
Eady 69
Eamonn 30
Eanwulf 109
Eardley 82
Earl 30, 43, 79
Earle 79
Earnshaw 83
Earthquake 121
Earthy 76
Easterbrook 79
Eastham 80
Eastman 70
Eaton 74, 112
Eatwell 82
Eaves 80
Eayr(e)s 80
Ebenezer 32
Ebony 36, 48
Eccles 80
Eckley 80
Ecuador 124
Edda 61
Eddis 69
Eddison 69, 81
Eddols 70
Eddowes 81
Eddy 70, 78
Eden 78
Edgar 38, 41, 43, 63
Edginton 81
Edinburgh 107
Edis 69
Edison 68-9
Edith 38, 45-7, 56, 69
Edkins 82
Edmans 78
Edmond(s) 69
Edmondson 69
Edmons 69
Edmonton 127
Edmund 25, 38, 41, 63, 69
Edmunds 69
Edna 37, 46-7, 61
Edney 80
Edryd 31
Edsel 161
Edward 28, 38, 41-2, 44, 49, 63, 69
Edwardes 69
Edwards 67, 69
Edwin 28, 41, 43
Edwina 37
Eels 76
Egbert 53
Eggins 79
Eggleston 79
Egham 117
Eglah 39
Eglantine 39
Eglinton 81
Egoniaga 122
Eifion 31
Eileen 36, 46
Eilidh 37
Eilir 31
Einahnuhto Hills 122
Eirlys 37
Eisenhower 68
Ekalaka 119
Ekins 80
El Paso 127
El Salvador 124
Elaine 34, 46-7
Elbourn 78
Eleanor 12, 34, 47, 69
Eleanore 45
Electra 40
Elen 37
Elena 34
Eleri 37
Eley 79
Elfed 31
Elgan 31
Elgey 82
Elgie 82
Elhanan 32
Eli 32, 41
Eliakim 32
Elias 69
Eliezer 32
Elijah 32, 41
Elin 37
Elinor 34
Eliot 69
Elis 31
Elisabeth 34
Elise 49
Elisha 32
Eliza 39, 45
Elizabeth 23-5, 34, 39, 45-9, 51, 55, 69
Elkanah 32
Elkington 82
Ella 47
Ellacott 79
Ellaway 83
Ellen 34, 45, 56, 69
Ellerby 82
Ellicott 79
Ellinore 69
Elliot(t) 69
Ellis(on) 69
Ellwood 70
Elmer 43
Elmitt 81
Elnathan 32
Eloisa 51
Elphee 70
Else 79
Elsegood 70
Elsey 70
Elsie 39, 45-7
Elsmore 82
Elson 69
Elspeth 37
Elston 79
Eluned 37
Elvey 70
Elvidge 81
Elvira 61
Elvis 40
Elworthy 79
Elwyn 31
Embleton 81
Embrey 80
Emerson 68-9
Emery 69
Emily 34, 45, 47-9, 56
Emma 12, 34, 38, 45-7, 49, 54, 69
Emmett 69
Emmott 83
Empson 69
Emrys 31
Emyr 31
Encounter Bay 121
Enda 30
Endacott 79
Endeavour 118
Enfys 37, 61
England 74, 124
English 74
Enid 61
Enoch 32
Enos 32
Ensor 79
Entwis(t)le 80
Eoghan 30
Eoin 30
Ephraim 32
Epping 109
Epton 81
Er 32, 62
Erastus 32
Eric 28, 41-2, 44, 55
Erica 34, 48
Erik 28
Erika 34
Erin 34, 48-9
Erlam 78
Ernest 30, 41-3
Errol 40
Erskine 31
Erwin 70
Eryl 31
Esam 81
Esau 32
Esk 110
Esme 37
Essex 82, 113
Estabrook 79
Estelle 34, 61
Esther 34, 38, 45, 47, 61-2
Etchells 78
Ethan 32
Ethanac 121
Ethel 12, 45-7, 61
Etheridge 82
Ethiopia 124
Ethna 36
Eugene 28, 43
Eugenius 29
Eunice 37
EUPHONY 51
Eurig 31
Euros 31
Eva 45, 47, 78
Evan(s) 69
Eve 34, 38, 62, 79
Eveleigh 79
Evely 79
Evelyn 34, 45-6
Everall 81
Everard 38
Evered 81
Evershed 82
Evison 81
Evodia 37
Evon 22
Ewan 31
Ewer 81
Exe 110
Exeter 108
Eye 76
Ezekiel 32
Ezer 32
Ezra 32

F
Faber 68
Fafa 61
Fagg 80
Failes 81
Faint-not 39
Fairbairn 81
Fairchild 77, 79
Fairclough 80
Fairfax 77
Fairhead 79
Fairthorne 78
Faith 39
Falconer 75
Falkner 75
Fallows 82
Fame 122
FAMILY NAMES 69-73
FAMOUS NICKNAMES 103
Fanny 45, 47
Farley 74
Farmer 75
Farnham 112
Farnsworth 81
Farquhar 31
Farrall 82
Farrar 75
Farrell 72
Farthing 81
FASHIONABLE NAMES 40-51
FASTEST NAMES 60
Faulder 79
Faulkner 75
Fawkes 80
Fay 34, 80
Faye 34
Fazakerley 80
Fear 76, 81
Fearn 79
Fearon 75, 79
Feather 75, 83
Featherstonehaugh 66
Feaveryear 82
Feaviour 82
Felgate 79
Felicia 12, 36
Felicity 23, 34, 39
Felixstowe 109
Felton 81
Fenella 37
Fenner 79
Fensom 78
Fenton 74, 81
Fergal 30
Fergus 31
Ferguson 72
Fermanagh 113
Fern 39, 82
Fernandez 71
Fernando 71
Fewings 79
ff- 66
Ffion 37
FICTIONAL ASSOCIATIONS 54-5
Fidelma 36
FIELD NAMES 111-12
Fields 74
Fife 113
Fifett 79
Fight-the-good-fight-of-faith 39
Figueroa 71
Filbee 81
File 80
Filkins 69
Filmer 80
Finbow 82
Fincham 82
Findlay 72
Finland 124
Finlay 31
Finn 80
Fiona 12, 23, 34, 49
Firkins 82
FIRST NAMES 22-6, 60-2
Firth 83
Fischer 71
Fish 80
Fisher 75
Fisk(e) 82
Fitchett 79
Fitt 80
Fitter 82
Flament 74
Flanders 74
Flannan 30
Flatman 82
Flatt 81
Flavia 40
Fleeming 74
Flement 74
Fleming 74, 79
Fletcher 75
Fleur 54, 57
Flinders 74, 119
Flintshire 113
Flook 80
Flora 12
Florence 45-7, 56, 60-1
Flores 71
Florey 81
Florida 125
FLOWER NAMES 8, 39, 172
FLOWERY NAMES 61
Floyd 30, 43, 81
Fluck 80
Fluvanna 121
Flux 80
Fly-fornication 39
Foal 76
Foale 79
Fogden 82
Folkard 79
Foll 78
Follows 82
Fooks 79
Foot 79
Footit(t) 81
Forbes 31, 72
Forester 75
Forman 81
Forrest 80
Forrester 82
Forryan 80
Forshaw 80
Forster 75
Fortescue 77
Forty 76
Forty Foot 120
Fortymile Creek 120
Foss 79
Foulke 79
Foulkes 83
Fountain 78
Fountaine 78
Fowke 79
Fowler 75
Fowles 81
Fox 102
Foxton 82
France 74, 124
Frances 22, 25, 34, 45, 47-9, 74
Francesca 12, 34
Francis 22-3, 28, 41, 43, 49, 74

Frank 28, 41-4, 49
Frankcom(b)e 82
Frankish 74
Franklin 68
Fraser 31
Freada 58
Frearson 80
Fred 26, 41, 43, 55
Freda 61
Frederick 28, 41-3
Frederick County 119
Fredericksburg 119
Freebody 78
Freegard 82
Freestone 80
Freeth 82
Freethy 72, 78
Fremlin 80
French 74
Fretwell 79
Frewer 70
Frewin 70
Friedman 71
Friend 79
Frisby 81
Frobisher 75
Frogley 78
Frohock 78
Frontenac 122
Frontignac 122
Froome 78
Frow 81
FRUITIEST NAMES 60
Fry(e) 77
Fulcher 82
Fulepet 110
Fullard 78
Fuller 75
Fullman 76
Funnell 82
FUNNIEST NAMES 60
Furber 78
Furneaux 79
Furphy 72
Furse 79
Furze 79
Fyson 78

G
Gabb 82
Gabriel 32
Gabriella 12
Gabrielle 61
Gad 32
Gagg 81
Gail 34, 47-9, 62
Galbraith 72
Gale 72, 102
Gallacher 72
Gallimore 78
Gallon 81
Galloway 82
Galtey 78
Gamble 81
Gammon 79
Gander 82
Ganderton 82
Gapp 81
Garbutt 82
Garcia 71
Gard(i)ner 75
Gare 82
Gareth 28, 42
Garlick 82
Garne 80
Garnham 82
Garrard 69
Garratt 69
Garrett 30, 69
Garrod 69
Garryowen 120
Garside 83
Gary 28, 42-4, 49
Garza 71
Gascoigne 74
Gascoyne 74
Gaskain 74
Gaskin 74
Gatehouse 79
Gates 82
Gateshead 109
Gaunt 81
Gavin 28, 49
Gawain 28
Gay 77
Gayford 81
Gayle 34
Gaynor 34, 52
Gazard 80
Gaze 81
Geach 78
Geake 78
Geary 80
Gedge 81
Geldard 83
Gelder 83
Gelsthorpe 81
Gemma 34, 46, 49
Gemson 69
Genevieve 61
Genge 79
Gent 79
Geoffrey 28, 38, 42, 49, 69
George 19, 23, 25, 28, 39, 41-4, 49
Georgetown 119
Georgia 119, 121, 125
Georgina 34
Geraint 31
Gerald 28, 38, 43-4, 69
Geraldine 12, 34, 47
Gerard 28, 69
Gerlad 31
Germaine 74
German 74, 79
Germany 124
Germing 74
Gerontius 28
Gerry 78
Gershom 32
Gertrude 45, 47, 61
Gerva(i)s 69
Gervase 38
Gervis 69
Gerwyn 31
Gethin 31
Ghey 82
Gibart 69
Gibb(s) 69
Gibbard 81
Gibbin 69
Gibbons 69
Giblett 82
Gibson 69
Giddy 77
Gideon 32
Gidley 79
Gilbert 69
Gilbertson 69
Gilbey 69
Gilchrist 31
Giles 28
Gilham 70
Gilhespy 81
Gill 69
Gillam 70
Gillard 79
Gillbard 78
Gillett 69
Gilliam 70
Gillian 34, 46
Gilliart 81
Gilliatt 81
Gillingham 79
Gillyatt 81
Gilpin 69
Gilson 69
Gimson 69, 80
Gina 34
Ginger 40, 78
Gipp 64
Gipps 69
Gippsland 122
GIRLS' NAMES 33-7, 45-9
Gladwin 38, 70
Gladys 45-7
Glamorgan 113
Glasgow 127
Glasson 78
Gleave 78
Gledhill 83
Glendinning 81
Glen(n) 28, 49
Gloria 36, 47-8
Gloucester 108, 110
Gloucestershire 113
Glover 75
Gloyn 79
Glyndwr 31
Glyn(n) 28
Goacher 82
Godden 80
Goddier 78
Godman 38
Godsall 80
Godsell 80
Godwin 38, 70
Goff 81
Golby 81
Goldbard 70
Goldberg 71
Goldbury 70
Goldhawk 70
Goldsmith 75
Goldstein 71
Goldstraw 82
Goldsworthy 78
Goldwin 70
Goliath 32
Gomesano 71
Gomez 71
Gomm 78
Gomo 71
Gonzales 71
Gonzalo 71
Gooch 81, 85
Goode 81
Gooderham 82
Goodfellow 77
Goodhew 80
Goodier 78
Goodliffe 70
Goodman 77
Goodrich 70
Goodwill 82
Goodwin 70
Goodyear 81
Goolden 77
Goose 81
Gora 71
Gordon 28, 42
Gornall 80
Gorringe 82
Gorst 80
Gorwyn 79
Gosden 82
Gosling 76
Gott 83
Gough 72
Goulder 81
Goulding 80
Goulter 80
Gowan 68
Gower 80
Gowlett 79
Grace 39, 45-7
Graeme 28
Graham 24, 28, 42, 49
Grainger 82
Grainne 36
Granger 82
Grant 25, 28, 77
Grantchester 109
Grantham 140
Gratton 79
Grave 75
Gray 77
Greece 124
Greed 82
Green 74
Greenacre 81
Greenaway 82
Greenhalgh 80
Greenhill 82
Greenwell 79
Greer 69
Gregory 28, 44, 49, 69
Gregson 69, 80
Greig 69
Grendon 79
Gresty 78
Greta 22
Grey 77
Grierson 69
Grieve 75
Grigg 69, 78
Grigson 69
Grimes 82
Grimsbury 118
Grimsdyke 118
Grimsey 82
Grimshaw 80
Grimwood 82
Grist 82
Grose 78
Gross 71
Ground(s) 78
Grove 74, 82
Growcott 81
Grubb 90
Gruffyd 31
Grummitt 81
Guilding 82
Guinevere 52
Guinness 3, 72, 160
Gulliver 77, 81
Gumboil 76
Gummer 70
Gunn 81
Guppy 79
GUPPY'S NAMES 78-83
Gutierrez 71
Guy 28, 43
Gwendoline 46
Gwendolyn 36
Gwent 114
Gwilt 81
Gwilym 31
Gwyn 31
Gwynedd 114
Gwynfor 31
Gwynne 83
Gyda 58
Gynn 78
Gyte 79

H
Haas 71
Habakkuk 39
Hack 80
Hacking 80
Haddad 68
Hadfield 79
Hadingham 82
Hadley 82
Haffenden 82
Hafoc 109
Haggai 32
Haggar 78
Hagger 78
Haggett 82
Hahn 71
Haigh 83
Hainsworth 83
HAIRDRESSERS NAMES 168
Haiti 124
Hakin 80
Hales 81
Haley 83
Halfacre 78
Halford 82
Hall 51
Halliwell 80, 109
Halls 79
Hallworth 78
Halsall 80
Halse 79
Ham 32, 76
Hambleton 82
Hamblin 69
Hambly 78
Hambrook 80
Hames 79
Hamilton 72
Hamish 31
Hamlet 69
Hamley 69
Hamlyn 69, 79
Hammersley 82
Hammett 69
Hammond 69
Hamnet 69
Hamo 69
Hampsall 81
Hampshire 83, 113
Hampson 69
Hampton 74
Hamson 69
Hanan 32
Hananaiah 62
Hananiah 32
Hancock 68-9
Hancorn 80
Handford 79
Hands 82
Handshaker 76
Hankey 78
Hankin 69, 80
Hanks 80
Hann 79
Hannaford 79
Hannah 12, 34, 38, 45-6, 48-9
Hansen 71
Hansford 79
Hanson 69, 71, 83
Harber 82
Hardcastle 83
Harden 80
Harding 38
Hardman 80
Hardstaff 81
Hardy 77
Harker 82
Harland 82
Harle 81
Harman 69
Harmon 69
Harold 41-2, 61, 63
Harper 75
Harpham 81
Harradine 78
Harrianne 40
Harriet 34, 45, 47
Harriman 69
Harris 69, 102
Harrison 69
Harrow-on-the-Hill 109
Harry 41-3, 56, 83
Hartle 79
Hartley 74
Hartman 71
Hartnell 79
Hartnoll 79
Hartop 78
Hartridge 80
Harvey 28, 69
Harvie 69
Hasler 79
Hassall 78
Hassell 78
Hastings 74, 108
Hatch 82
Hatfield 74
Hatherell 80
Hathway 82
Hatt 81
Hauxton 109
HAWAIAN NAMES 121
Hawaii 122, 125
Haward 82
Hawke 69, 78
Hawken 78
Hawkesbury 109
Hawkey 78
Hawking 82
Hawkins 69
Hawksworth 109
Hawley 79
Haworth 80
Hawthorne 68
Hay 81
Haydock 80
Hayes 74
Hayhurst 80
Hayley 34, 46, 49, 52, 57
Hayman 79
Hayne 78
Hayter 79
Haythornthwaite 80
Hayward 75
Hazel 34, 39, 47
Head 82
Heading 81
Headington 78
Headon 79
Health 79
Heaman 79
Heard 79
Hearle 78
Heath 74
Heather 34, 39, 46, 48-9, 61
Heatley 81
Heaver 82
Hebditch 82
Hebron 82
Hector 41
Heddon 79
Hefin 31
Heggadon 79
Heidi 12, 34
Heighway 81
Helen 34, 45-7, 49
Helena 34
Heler 82
Helga 12
Helliwell 83
Helmer 79
Helmheard 109
Helsinki 127
Heman 32
Hembrow 82
Hemus 82
Henderson 69
Hendry 69
Hendy 77
Henery 58
Henley 82
Henrietta 24, 45
Henry 24-5, 28, 38, 41-4, 60, 69
Henryson 69
Henshall 78
Henson 80
Henstock 79
Henwood 78
Heppell 79
Hepple 79
Hepworth 83
Herbert 25, 38, 41-2, 61
Hercule 10
Herd 75
Herdman 81
Herefordshire 113
Heriot 69
Herman 30, 43, 61, 69, 71
Hernandez 71
Hernando 71
Herod 32
Herrick 81
Herring 81
Herrod 81
Hertfordshire 113
Hervey 69
Heseltine 82

HESITANT NAME 62
Hesketh 80
Hesmondhalgh 80
Hess(e) 71
Heulwen 37
Hewer 80
Hewes 69
Hewett 69
Hewitson 69, 79
Hewlet 69
Hewson 69, 81
Hext 79
Hey 83
Heygate 81
Heyward 79
Heywood 79
Hezekiah 32
Hiawatha 120
Hick(en) 82
Hickie 69
Hickin 82
Hickmott 80
Hicks 69
Hickson 69, 78
Hickton 81
Hide 82
Hides 81
Higgins 69
Higgs 69
Higman 78
Hignell 80
Higson 80
Hilary 34, 46
Hilda 45-6
Hildred 81
Hill 74
Hillary 34
Hillson 79
Hilson 79
Hilton 74
Hinchcliff(e) 83
Hindle 80
Hindmarsh 81
Hingley 82
Hinton 74, 81
Hiram 32
Hirst 83
Hitchcock 82
Hitchens 69
Hoadley 82
Hoare 77
Hoath 82
Hobart 69
Hobbs 69
Hobby 80
Hobden 82
Hobgen 82
Hobley 81
Hobson 69, 83
Hockenhall 78
Hockenhull 78
Hockey 82
Hockley 79
Hocknell 78
Hockridge 79
Hod 32
Hoddell 80
Hodge 78
Hodges 70
Hodgkins 82
Hodgkinson 70
Hodgkiss 70
Hodgson 70
Hodiah 32
Hodson 70
Hoffman 71
Hogben 80
Hogbin 80
Hogg 76, 81, 90
Holbrook 74, 81
Holder 80
Holdom 78
Holdsworth 83
Holebeck 112
Holick 82
Hollamby 80
Holland 102
Hollands 80
Holliday 82
Hollie 34
Hollier 80
Hollingsworth 82
Hollington 82
Hollins 82
Hollinshead 78
Hollow 78
Holloway 74
Holly 34, 39, 46
Hollyman 76
Holmes 74, 102
Holness 80
Holroyd 83
Holt 74
Holtom 82
Holton 81
Holyday 82
Homa 56
Home 81
Homer 79
Honduras 124
Hone 81
Honess 80
Honeyfield 79
Honeysett 82
Honniball 79
Honour 39, 81
Hook 82
Hookway 79
Hooley 78
Hooper 75
Hoover 68, 71
Hope 34, 39, 53
Hopkins 69
Hopkinson 69
Hopley 78
Hopps 79
Horace 25, 41, 61
Horne 102
Hornsby 81
Horrocks 80
HORSE NAMES 171-2
Horsey 82
Horsfall 83
Horsley 82
Horton 74
Horwood 78
Hotchkiss 70, 81
HOTEL NAMES 163
Hotten 78
Houlbrook 78
Houldsworth 83
Hounsell 79
Hounslow 109
Housden 79
House 74
HOUSE NAMES 7, 149-59
HOUSEBOAT NAMES 155
Houseman 83
Housley 79
Houston 74
Howard 25, 28, 43
Howel(l) 69
Howes 81
Howett 81
Howey 81
Howie 81
Howitt 81
Howkins 69
Howland 112
Howse 82
Howson 69, 82
Hoyes 81
Hoyles 81
Huband 82
Hubbard 69
Hubert 69
Huddleston 80
Hudson 69, 102
Huggett 69
Huggins 69, 81
Hugh 28, 38, 41, 69
Hughes 67, 69
Hugill 82
Hulbert 70, 82
Huldah 37
Hulland 79
Hullett 69
Hullis 69
Human 76
Humberside 114
Humbley 80
Humphrey(s) 69
Humphries 69
Hundred 120
Hungary 124
Hunt 75
Hunter 75, 102
Huntingdon 113
Hurd 82
Hurley 82
Hurrell 79
Hurren 82
Hurry 78
Hurt 81
Huskinson 81
Hutch 102
Hutchings 69
Hutchins 69, 102
Hutchinson 69, 102
Hutley 79
Hutt 81
Hutton 74, 81
Huw 31
Huxham 79
Huxley 78
Huxtable 79
Hyde 82

I
Ian 28, 42, 49
Ibbotson 69, 82
Ibison 80
Ibson 69
Iceland 124
Ichabod 32
Ida 47, 61
Idaho 125
Iddon 80
Idler 64
Iestyn 31
Ieuan 31
If-Christ-had-not-died-for-Thee-thou-hadst-been-damned 60
Ifan 31
Iles 80
Illecillewaet 122
Illinois 125
Immanuel 32
Ina 37
INCIDENT NICKNAMES 96-7
Incomappleux 122
India 36, 124
INDIAN PLACE NAMES 122-3
Indiana 125
Indonesia 124
Ing 78
Ingall 81
Ingate 82
Inge 80
Ingle 81
Ingleby 83
Inglis 74
Ingram 81
Ingrid 34
Inions 81
INITIALS 24, 51-2
Innes 37, 72
INSECT NAMES 60
Inskip 78
Instone 81
INVENTED NAMES 20, 23
Inverness-shire 113
Iolo 31
Iona 37
Iowa 125
Ira 32
Iran 124
Iraq 124
Ireland 74, 124
Irene 46
Iris 39, 46
Irish 74, 79
IRISH NAMES 30, 36, 66-7
Irvona 120
Isaac 30, 41, 43
Isaacs 79
Isabel 12, 34, 45, 69
Isabella 34, 45, 119
Isabelle 34
Isgar 82
Ishmael 32
Isla 37
Isle of Wight 113
Ismay 37
Isobel 34
Israel 41, 124
Istanbul 127
Isted 82
Ita 36
Italy 124
Ivan 28
Ivatt 78
Iveson 82
Ivey 78
Ivor 61
Ivory 80
Ivory Coast 124
Ivy 39, 45-6, 51, 53
Iwan 31
Izzard 78

J
Jabal 32
Jack 28, 41-3, 56
Jackman 79
Jacks 81
Jackson 51, 69
Jacob 28, 38, 41, 43-4, 69
Jacobson 69
Jacqueline 23, 34, 46-9
Jacques 28, 82
Jade 40, 46, 49
Jagger 83
Jaggs 69
Jago 72
Jaguar Ferrari 60
Jaime 34
Jake 49
Jamaica 124, 127
Jamal 30
James 28, 41-4, 49, 57, 61, 67, 69
Jameson 79
Jamie 28, 34, 42, 48
Jamieson 69, 79
Jane 34, 45-6, 49, 55-6, 78
Janet 34, 46-9
Janice 25, 34, 46-9
Janine 34
Japan 124
Japheth 32
Jaquenetta 12
Jared 28, 32, 44
Jarman 74
Jarrad 49
Jarrett 69, 80
Jarrod 28
Jarrom 80
Jarvie 69
Jarvis 69
Jasmine 48
Jason 28, 42, 44, 49-51, 54
Jasper 78
Jayne 40
Jean 46-7
Jeanette 34
Jeavons 82
Jedaiah 32
Jeeves 69
Jeffcoate 82
Jefferies 69
Jefferson 68-9
Jeffrey 28, 42, 44, 49, 69
Jeffs 78
Jehoshaphat 39
Jehovah 62
Jehudi 32
Jelbart 78
Jelbert 78
Jellis 80
Jelly 76
Jemima 45, 52
Jemimah 37, 40
Jemma 34
Jenkin 78
Jenkins 69
Jenna 46, 49
Jennie 34, 47
Jennifer 34, 46, 48-9, 54, 61
Jennings 69
Jennison 69
Jenny 34, 45
Jensen 71
Jephcott 82
Jephson 69
Jepp 69
Jepson 69, 78
Jeremiah 29, 83
Jeremy 29, 41-2, 44
Jermaine 30, 60
Jermyn 74
Jeroboam 32
Jerome 43-4
Jerram 79
Jerrold 69
Jerry 29, 43
Jeshua 29
Jesse 29, 41, 44
Jessica 34, 46, 48-50, 57
Jessie 37, 45-6
Jesson 80
Jesty 79
Jesus 28-9, 62
Jesus-Christ-came-into-the-world-to-save 60
Jet 39
Jethro 32
Jevons 82
JEWEL NAMES 39-40
Jewett 69
Jezebel 37
Jill 34, 49
Jillian 34, 49
Jillings 82
Jim 57
Jimmy 28
Jimpson 69
Joab 32
Joan 24, 45-9, 56
Joanna 34, 45
Joanne 25, 34, 46-9, 51
Job 32
Jobling 81
Jocelyn 12, 34, 38
Jodi(e) 34, 46, 49
Jody 34
Joel 29, 49
Johanan 62
JOHANNESBURG STREET NAMES 133-4
John 24-5, 29, 41-4, 49-50, 56, 60, 62, 69
Johns 69
Johnson 69, 102
Johnston 79
Joke 60
Jolliffe 77, 80
Jolly 77
Jolyan 69
Jonah 32, 40
Jonas 78
Jonathan 29, 38, 41-2, 44
Jonathon 49
Jones 51, 67, 69, 94
Jonothon 58
Jordan 49, 124
Jordison 82
Jorgensen 68
Jory 72
Jose 78
Joseph 24, 29, 38, 41-4, 49, 62
Josephine 34
Joshua 28-9, 38, 41, 44, 49, 54, 62
Josiah 32, 41
Joule 79
Jowett 69, 83
Joy 34, 39
Joyce 34, 46-8
Joyes 82
Jubb 83
Juby 82
Judah 32
Judith 34, 45-9
Judkins 81
Judson 82
Judy 48
Julia 34, 45, 47, 56
Julian 29, 42, 69, 78
Juliana 69
Julie 34, 46, 48-9, 60
Julien 69
Juliet 34
Julyan 69, 78
June 46, 57, 61
Jupe 82
Justin 29, 42, 44, 49
Justine 34

K
Kalvaitis 68
Kane 29, 49, 102
Kansas 125
Karen 25, 34, 40, 46-9
Karina 34
Karl 29
Karla 34
Kate 34, 45-6, 49
Katharine 22, 34, 46, 69
Katherine 34, 47-9
Katheryne 58
Kathleen 12, 34, 45-9
Kathryn 34
Kathy 48
Katie 12, 34, 46, 48
Katina 36
Katrina 34
Katrine 37
Katy 34
Katz 71
Kaufman 71
Kay(e) 34, 49
Kayla 48
Kayleigh 46, 57
Kayley 57
Keast 78
Keeble 82
Keedwell 82
Keel 82
Keeley 34
Keelie 34
Keeling 82
Keely 34
Keen 77
Keep 78
Keetley 80
Keevil 82
Keightley 80
Keir 31
Keirl 82
Keisha 36, 48
Keith 24, 29, 42, 44, 49
Keli 34
Kellaway 79
Keller 71
Kellett 80

Kellie 34, 49
Kellogg 75
Kelly 34, 46, 48–9, 52, 54, 57, 72, 102
Kelsey 48
Kelvin 30
Kemball 82
Kemble 82
Kemp 75
Kempson 78
Kemsley 79
Kendra 48
Kendrew 82
Kennedy 72
Kennerley 78
Kenneth 29, 42–4, 49
Kent 56, 113
Kentucky 125
Kenward 70
Kenway 70
Kenworthy 83
Kenya 36, 60
Kenyatta 36
Kenyetta 36
Kenyon 80
Kerenhappuch 37
Keri 34
Kerkin 78
Kermode 72
Kerr 72
Kerri 34
Kerrich 70
Kerridge 82
Kerrie 34, 49, 52
Kerrison 81
Kerry 34, 40, 46, 49, 61, 82
Kersey 82
Kerslake 79
Kestle 78
Keswick 110
Ketley 79
Kettle 102
Kettlewell 82
Kettley 79
Keturah 37
Kevern 78
Kevin 29, 42, 44
Keynes 79
Keyonna 48
Keyte 82
Keyworth 81
Keziah 36–8
Kidd 82, 102
Kidner 82
Kieran 29, 42
Kierra 48
Killer 76
Killick 82
Kilminster 80
Kilmister 80
Kilshaw 80
Kilts 120
Kilvington 82
Kim 12, 34, 48–9
Kimball 10
Kimber 78
Kimberley 34, 46, 48–9
Kimberly 48
Kincardineshire 113
Kinch 82
King 102
Kingham 78
Kingman 79
Kingsley 80
Kingsnorth 80
Kingston 81, 109
Kingwell 79
Kinross-shire 113
Kinsley 78
Kipling 82
Kirby 74
Kircudbrightshire 113
Kirk 29
Kirkman 80
Kirkup 79
Kirstie 37
Kirsty 34, 46
Kirton 79
Kish 32
Kisser 76
Kissing Point 122
Kitchener 80
Kitson 69
Kitt 69
Kitto 78
Kittow 78
Kitts 69
Kitty 45
Kizzie 36
Kizzy 36
Klein 71
Kleinville 122
Kline 71
Knaggs 82
Knapman 79
Knapp 74, 82
Kneebone 78
Knibb 82
Knickerbocker 68
Knifton 79
Knight 75, 102
Knightsbridge 109
Knott 79
Knowles 74
Koch 71
Kodak 120
Korah 32
Kovacs 68
Kowalsky 68
Kramer 71
Krause 71
Kristen 48
Kristin 48
Kristine 40
Kristopher 29
Kristy 49
Kruger 71
Kurt 29
Kuwait 124
Kuznetsov 68
Kyla 57
Kyle 42, 44
Kylie 34, 49, 57
Kynaston 81

L
La Fayette 68
Laban 32
Lacey 80
Lachlan 31, 49
Ladds 80
Lagden 80
Laidler 81
Lain 81
Laity 78
Lake 74
Lakeisha 36, 48
Lakin 82
Lala 61
Lamar 30
Lamb 102
Lambrick 70
Lambshead 79
Laming 81
Lamming 81
Lamond 30
Lamont 30
Lamorna 7
Lamplough 82
Lamplugh 82
Lanarkshire 113
Lancashire 113
Lancaster 108
Lance 29
Land 81
Lander 75, 78
Lane 74
Lanfear 78
Lang 71, 77, 79
Langford 74
Langley 74
Langman 79
Langridge 80
Langworthy 79
Lanyon 78
Lara 34
Larcombe 79
Larkin(g) 80
Larkin(s) 69
Larry 43–4
Larsen 71
Larson 71
Larwood 81
Lashawn 36
Laslett 80
Last 82
Latanya 36
Latasha 36, 48
Latisha 36
Latonya 36, 60
Latoya 36, 48
Latrice 36
Laura 12, 34, 38, 45–9, 56, 60
Laurel 39
Lauren 34, 46, 48–9
Laurence 23, 29, 41–2, 69
Laurie 69
Lavender 75
Laverack 82
Laverick 82
Lavington 80
Lavinia 12
Law 69
Lawley 81
Lawrence 23, 29, 43–4, 69
Lawrenson 80
Lawrie 69
Lawry 78
Lawson 69
Lay 78
Laycock 83
Lazarus 32
Lea 34
Leach 75, 102
Leadbeater 75, 80
Leadbetter 75, 80
Leadbitter 75
Leah 34, 38, 49, 78
Leak 82
Leake 82
Lean 78
Leanne 34, 46, 49
Leaper 82
Lear 79
Leather 78
Leaver 80
Leavers 81
Leavey 70
Leavold 70
Lebanon 124
Leckenby 82
Leda 12
Ledbrook 82
Lee 29, 42, 52–3, 74
Leech 75
Leeder 81
Leeds 81
Lees 102
Leese 82
Lefevre 68
Legg 79, 102
Leggett 81
Leggott 81
Leicestershire 113
Leigh 34, 49, 52–3
Leighton 29, 82
Leister 112
Leivers 81
Lemmer 70
Lemon 77
Lemuel 32
Lena 34
Leney 80
Lent 110
Lenton 80
Leo 40, 60
Leon 30, 43
Leonard 29, 40–4, 60
Leonie 61
Leppard 82
Leroy 43
Lerwill 79
Lesley 22, 34, 46, 49, 53
Leslie 22, 24, 29, 41–2, 53–4, 188
Lethbridge 79
Letheren 79
LETTER INTERPRETATION 183–7
Lever 80
Levi 32, 71
Levine 71
Levy 71
Lewell 81
Lewin 70
Lewis 29, 43, 69
Ley 79
Liam 29, 42
Lianne 34
Libby 69
Liberia 124
Liddicoat 78
Lidstone 79
Light 80
Lilian 45–6
Lilith 37
Lill(ey) 81
Lilleyman 70
Lillian 47
Lillie 47
Lilly 45
Lily 39, 45–6
Limb 79
Limbrick 80
Limer 82
Lincoln 68, 74, 112
Lincolnshire 113
Linda 34, 46–9, 61
Lindley 81
Lindop 82
Lindsay 34, 46
Lindsey 12, 34, 48
LINK NAMES 23–4
Linnell 81
Linsay 34
Linsey 34
Lionel 40, 60
LIPSTICK NAMES 162
Lisa 35, 46, 48–9
Lister 75
Litchfield 79
LITERARY NICKNAMES 104
Lithgoe 80
Little 102
Littlechild 80
Littlejohn 69, 78
Littlejohns 79
Littler 78
Litwin 70
Liverpool 127
Livesey 80
Livesley 80
Liz 39, 55
Liza 39
Lizzie 45
Llewellyn 69
Llinos 37
Lloyd 29, 72
Llyr 31
Loaring 74
Lobb 78
Loch Ness 107
LOCOMOTIVE NAMES 174–6
Lodder 79
Loder 79
Lodge 83
Loggerhead 87
Lois 37, 47
Lombardo 68
Lona 37
Londinos 107
London 106–7, 109, 113
LONDON STREET NAMES 130–3, 136–7
Londonderry 113
Long 77, 102
Long Ditton 110
Longbottom 83
Longden 79
LONGEST NAMES 60
Longfellow 68
Longley 82
Longton 80
Longworth 80
Lonsdale 80
Lonsley 78
Look 82
Looker 80
Loosemoor 79
Loosley 81
Loosmoor 79
Lope 71
Lopez 71
Lora 37
Lori 35, 48
Lorimer 75
Loring 74
Lorna 10, 23, 35
Lorraine 35, 46–7, 49, 52, 74
LORRY NAMES 176
Lory 78
Los Angeles 127
Loseby 80
Lothian 113
Louch 81
Louis 24, 29, 38, 43, 69
Louisa 35, 45, 56
Louise 24, 35, 46–7, 51, 56
Louisiana 119, 125
Lovatt 82
Love 80
Lovegod 70
Lovegrove 81
Loveguard 70
Lovelace 77
Lovering 79
Loverock 82
LOVERS NAMES 8
Loveybond 82
Lovibond 82
Loving 120
Lowis 69
Lowri 37
Lowry 69
Loxton 82
Lucas 69
Lucetta 12
Luck 69, 80
Luckett 69, 81
Luckin 69
Lucking 80
Lucy 35, 45–7, 49
Ludlam 79
Ludovic 31
Ludwig 85
Lugg 78
Luguvallium 107
Luke 29, 41–2, 49, 69
Lukin 69
Lulu 47
Lumb 83
Lumsden 81
Lundenceaster 108
Lupe 71
Luscombe 79
Lush 76
Lusty 80
Luther 120
Lutley 82
Luxton 79
Lydia 37, 45
Lyford 78
Lyle 78
Lymer 82
Lyn 35
Lynam 79
Lynda 34, 40
Lyndsay 34
Lyndsey 34
Lynette 35, 49
Lynn 35, 46, 81
Lynn(e) 35, 46, 48–9
Lynsay 35
Lynsey 35, 46
Lyon 80
Lythgoe 80

M
Maachah 39
Maaz 62
Mabbot 69
Mabbs 69
Mabel 45, 47, 69
Mably 78
Macaulay 80
McCormick 68
McFarlane 72
McGowan 66
McGregor 67, 72
Machin 69, 75
Macintosh 67
McIntosh 72
McIntyre 72
Mack 81
Mackaness 81
McKay 72
McKenzie 72
Mackinder 81
Mackley 80
MacLaren 79
McLean 72
McLeod 72
McMillan 72
McPherson 72
Maddaford 78
Maddison 69
Maddiver 78
Maddy 80
Madeleine 35
Madeley 81
Madeline 35
Maden 80
Madge 22, 79
Madison 69
Madrid 127
MAGAZINE NAMES 169
Magdalen 69
Magdalene 37
Maggot 76
Maggs 69
Magnus 31
Magor 78
Magson 69
Mai 37
MAIDEN NAMES 86
Maidens 81
Mailes 80
Main 81
Maine 125
Mainwaring 66, 80
Mair 37
Mairead 36
Mairi 37
Maisie 22
Majella 36
Major 78
Make-peace 39
Makepeace 79
Makins(on) 69
Malachi 32
Malawai 124
Malchiah 32
Malcolm 24, 29, 40, 42, 49
Malden 78
Maldonado 71
Malkin 82
Mallam 79
Malleson 69
Mallett 69, 81
Mallinder 79
Mallinson 83
Mallory 77
Malluch 32

Malta 124
Malvina 37
Manasseh 32
Manchester 114
Mandi 40
Mandy 35, 46, 52
Manitoba 127
Manley 79
Mann 71
Manners 82
Mannington 82
Mansell 81
Manuela 12
Manwaring 80
MAORI PLACE NAMES 105
Mapp(in) 69
Mapson 69
Mapstone 82
Marc 29
Marchant 75
Marchbanks 66
Marchington 79
Marcia 35, 48
Marcus 29–30, 44
Mardell 80
Marfell 80
Marfleet 81
Margaret 12, 22, 25, 35, 40, 45–9, 56, 61, 69
Margerison 69, 80
Margerson 80
Margetson 69
Marginson 80
Margison 80
Margot 57
Margretts 69
Marguerite 35
Mari Dunum 107
Maria 35, 45–6, 48–9
Marianne 35
Marie 35, 46–8
Marie Galante 118
Marilyn 46–9, 61
Marion 46–7, 49, 69
Marisa 37
Marjoribanks 66
Marjorie 38, 45–7
Mark 29, 41–2, 44, 49, 51, 61
Markham 81
Markk 58
Marks 71
Marlena 12, 36
Marlene 47
Marlon 30
Marples 79
Marriage 80
Marriott 69
Marrison 69
Marryat 69
Marseilles 127
Marshall 75
Marsland 78
Marson 82
Martell 69
Martens 69
Martha 12, 35, 37, 45, 47
Martin 29, 41–2, 44, 51, 69, 98, 102
Martina 35
Martindale 79
Martine 35
Martinet 69
Martinez 71
Martland 80
Martyn 29
Marvin 30, 43
Mary 9, 12, 25, 35, 38, 45–9, 52–3, 55–6, 62, 69
Mary Ann 45, 51
Maryat 69
Maryland 119, 125
Mash 80
Mashiter 80
Maskell 80
Maskery 79
Maskrey 79
Maslen 78
Mason 75
Massachusetts 125
Mastin 81
Matcham 80
Matheson 69
Mathieson 69
Matilda 45, 69
Matson 69, 82
Matterson 69, 82
Matthams 80
Matthew 29, 41–2, 44, 49–50, 60, 69
Matthews 69
Matthias 83
Mattin 69
Mattison 82
Matts 80
Maud 38, 45, 47, 61
Maudling 69
Maudsley 80
Maudson 69
Mault 69
Maunder 79
Maundrell 82
Maura 36
Maureen 35, 46, 48–9
Maurice 30, 38, 42–3, 69
Mauritania 124
Mavis 23
Maw(er) 81
Mawdsley 80
Mawle 81
Mawson 69, 83
Maxima 12
Maxine 35
Maxted 80
Maxwell 31, 78
May 25, 45, 47, 61, 102
Maycock 69
Mayer 71, 82
Mayfield 74
Mayhew 69
Maykin 69
Maylam 80
Mayne 78
Mayo 79
Mayor 80
Meaden 79
Meadmore 80
Meadows 74
Meaker 82
Measures 81
Meatyard 79
Medforth 82
MEDIEVAL STREET NAMES 129–30
Medina 71
Meech 79
Meen 82
Meeson 80
Meg 12
Megan 35, 48–9
Meggeson 69
Megginson 82
Meggison 82
Meggs 69
Meghan 35
Megson 82
Meironwen 37
Melancthon 120
Melanie 35, 40, 46, 49, 54, 61
Melbourne 127
Melech 32
Melfyn 31
Melhuish 79
Melinda 12, 49, 62
Melissa 35, 40, 46, 48–9, 60, 62
Melita 62
Mellings 81
Melluish 79
Melody 35
Melsome 82
Melton 74
Melvin 30
Memory Cove 121
Memphis 127
Mentasta 122
Mercedes 12
Mercer 75
Merchant 75
Mercy 39
Merdegrave 110
Meredith 35, 67
Mererid 37
Meriel 37
Merionethshire 113
Merrell 82
Merrikin 81
Merrills 81
Merseyside 114
Mervin 38
Mesha 32
Message 82
Metherall 79
Metherell 79
Metson 80
Mew 80
Mexico 124
Meyer 71
Miami 127
Micah 32
Michael 29, 38, 41–4, 49, 61–2, 69
Michaela 35
Michele 12, 35
Michelle 35, 46, 48–9, 56, 61
Michieson 69
Michigan 125
MIDDLE NAMES 24
Middlemas 81
Middlemiss 81
Middlesex 113
Midgley 83
Midlothian 113
Midwinter 81
Milbank 80
Milborrow 70
Milcah 37
Mildon 79
Mildred 36, 47, 61
Milk 81
Mill 79
Millbank 80
Mille 60
Milledge 79
Millen 80
Miller 75, 102
Millichamp 81
Millington 81
Mil(l)man 79
Mills 74–5
Milne 80
Milner 75
Milsom 82
Milton 30, 74
Mimi 12, 61
Minchin 80
Minett 80
Minneapolis 127
Minnehaha 122
Minnesota 125
Minnie 45, 47
Minns 81
Minshall 78
Minshull 78
Minta 81
Minter 80
Mintey 82
Minton 81
Minty 82
Miranda 23
Miriam 35, 38, 47, 62
Miser 64
Miskin 80
Missing 80
Mississippi 125
Missouri 125
Mitchell 69
Mitchelson 69
Mitchison 69
Mobbs 69
Mogford 79
Mogg(s) 69
Mold 69
Mole Hill 123
Mollison 69
Molyneux 80
Monaco 124
Money 76
Moneypenny 76
Mongolia 124
Monica 35
Monique 12, 36
Monkman 82
Monmouthshire 113
Monnington 80
Montana 125
Montgomery 81
Montgomeryshire 113
MONTH NAMES 61
Montreal 122
Moody 76–7
Moore 77, 102
Moorhouse 83
Morag 37
Morales 71
Moray 113
Morcock 69
Morcom 78
Mordecai 32, 83
Moreno 71
Morgan 31, 67, 102
Morkam 78
Morna 37
Morphett 80
Morrice 69
Morris 69
Morrison 69, 81
Morse 69, 82
Morson 69
Morter 102
Mortimore 79
Mortin 79
Morton 74
Morven 37
Moscow 127
Moseley 74
Moses 32, 41, 83
Mossman 78
Mossop 79
Mott 70, 80
Mottershead 78
Mottram 82
Mould 69
Moule 82
Moulson 69
Moult 69
Mounfield 78
Mounsey 79
Mountain 123
Mountfield 78
Mowbray 81
Moxon 69, 82
Moyle 78
Moza 32
Mudge 79
Mueller 71
Mugford 79
Muggleston 80
Muirne 36
Mullen 71
Mulliner 75
Mullinger 81
Mullock 78
Munckton 79
Mundy 72
Mungo 31
Munich 127
Munn 82
Munro 72
Munslow 81
Murcott 82
Murder 121
Murdoch 31
Murfin 79
Murfitt 78
Murgatroyd 83
Muriel 46
Murphy 72, 102
Murray 31, 72
Murrumbidgee 105
Murton 80
MUSICAL NAMES 61
Musson 80
Mustill 78
Mutton 78
Myatt 82
Mycroft 10
Myers 71, 83
Myfanwy 37
Myrddin 107
Myron 30
Myrtle 39, 61
Mytton 82

N
Naamah 37
Nabal 32
Nadia 35
Nadin 79
Nadine 35, 61
Nahor 32, 61
Nahum 32
Nairnshire 113
Naked 121
Nakia 36
Nakita 36
NAME ASSOCIATIONS 53–6
NAME CHANGING 87–91
NAME COLLECTING 189–90, 193
NAME GAMES 10, 182–93
NAME JOKES 190–1
NAME MEANINGS 183
NAME ORIGINS 6–8
NAME PRINTS 10
NAME STORIES 189–90
NAME STUDIES 11
NAME USAGE 26–7
NAMES AND HOUSENAMES 151–2
NAMES AND SEX 53
NAMES IN VERSE 190
NAMES TURNED INTO WORDS 18
NAMESAKES 88–90
Nance 72, 78
Nancekeville 79
Nancekivell 79
Nancy 35, 45, 47–8
Nankevil 79
Naomi 35, 38, 49
Naphtali 32
Naples 127
Napper 78
Narelle 49
Natalie 23, 35, 46, 49, 57, 61, 62
Natasha 35, 46, 48–9, 62
Nathan 29, 38, 42–4, 49
Nathaniel 29, 41
NATIONAL NAMES 124
NATIONALITY 56
Naylor 75
Neal 29, 58, 69
Neame 80
Nebraska 125
Nebuchadnezzar 32, 39
Negus 72, 78
Nehemiah 32
Neighbour 81
Neil 29, 42, 49
Neilson 69
Nellie 25, 45, 47
Nelly 45
Nelson 69
Neola 120
Nerys 37
Nesling 82
Nesta 37
Netherlands 124
Netherway 79
Nevada 125
Nevell 81
Neville 25
Nevin(s) 81
New 80
New England 119
New Hampshire 125
New Jersey 125
New Mexico 125
New York 119, 125
New Zealand 124
Newall 78
Newby 80
Newcombe 79
Newey 82
Newington 82
Newitt 81
Newsholme 83
Newsome 83
Newson 82
Newth 82
Newton 74
Nia 37
Niall 30
Niamh 36
Nibbs 69
Niblett 80
Nibson 69
Niceville 122
Nicholas 29, 41–2, 44, 49, 69
Nicholson 69
Nickells 69
Nickless 82
NICKNAMES 23, 93, 98–9, 102–4
NICKNAMES, AMERICAN STATES 126–7
NICKNAMES, PERSONAL 93–6
NICKNAMES, POLITICAL 99–100
NICKNAMES, ROYAL 94–5
Nicks(on) 69
Nicky 35, 40
Nicola 35, 46
Nicole 35, 48–9
Nicolson 69
Nielsen 71
Nigel 29, 42, 69
Niger 124
Nigeria 124
Nikki 35
Nina 35
Ninaview 121
Ninel 62
Nixon 69
Noah 32, 38
Nobbs 69
Noble 77, 83
Nock 81
Noden 78
Noel 23, 29, 57, 62
Noelle 62
Nolan 72
Nora 45–6, 61
Norbury 78
Norfolk 109, 113
Norma 47
Norman 29, 38, 41–3, 61, 74
NORMAN NAMES 38
NORMAN PLACE NAMES 110–11
Normand 74

Nornabell 82
Norrish 79
North Carolina 125
North Dakota 125
Northam 79
Northamptonshire 113
Northey 57
Northmore 79
Northumberland 113
Norton 74
Norway 124
Norwood 74, 81
Nosworthy 79
Nottage 80
Nottingham 82
Nottinghamshire 113
Novak 71
Nuala 36
NUMBER NAMES 19
NUMERICAL NAMES 60–1
NUMEROLOGY 183
Nurse 81
Nutter 80

O
Oakden 79
Oakes 78
Oakley 74
Oat(e)s 78
Obadiah 32
Obed 32
O'Brien 72
OBSOLETE NICKNAMES 100–1
O'Byrne 72
Ockey 80
O'Connor 72
Octavia 57, 60–1
Odd 60
ODDEST NAMES 60
Odger(s) 78
Odling 81
ODOROUS NAMES 61
Ody 82
Offen 80
Ogle 81
Ohio 125
Okel 78
Okla 56
Oklahoma 125
Old 78
Oldacres 80
Oldreave 79
Oldrieve 79
Olean 120
Oliphant 81
Olivant 81
Olive 12, 39, 45–6
Oliver 29, 38, 41–2
Olivia 35, 39
Ollerton 80
Olsen 71
Olson 71
Olver 78
Olwen 37
Omar 30
One Hundred and Two River 120
O'Neill 72
Onesiphorous 39
Onions 81
ONOMANCY 182–7
Ontario 127
Onyx 39, 62
Opal 39
Ophelia 12
Opie 72, 78
Oppy 78
Optima 122
Oram 82
Orangeburg 119
Orchard 80
Ordway 70
Oregon 125
O'Reilly 72
Oren 32
Organ 80
Orgee 80
Oriana 61
Oriel 38
Original 23, 62
ORIGINAL NAMES 52–3, 62
Orkney 113
Orla 36
Ormond 83
Ormston 81
Orpe 82
Orpen 80
Orpin 80
Orrick 70
Orson 40, 60, 80
Ortiz 71
Oscar 43
Osker 58
Oslo 127
Osmer 70
Osmund 38
Oswald 63
Oswin 70
Ottawa 127
Otter Point 120
Otto 60
Oulton 78
Ouse 110
Outhwaite 82
Outram 79
Outridge 70
Overell 80
Overett 102
Overton 81
Owain 31
Owen 29, 41, 67
Oxford 161
Oxfordshire 113
Oyler 80

P
Packham 82
Padbury 81
Paddock 81
Paddon 79
Paddy 62
Padfield 82
Padraig 30
Pagan 69
Page 75
Paget 75, 80
Paige 75
Paine 69
Pakistan 124
Palethorpe 81
Palfrey 79
Paling 81
Palk 79
Pallister 79
Pamela 23, 35, 46, 48–9, 62
Paniers 80
Pankhurst 82
Pannel 69
Pannell 80
Panniers 80
Pansy 39
Pantall 80
Panther 81
Paradise 122
Paraguay 124
Paramatta 105
Parfitt 77
Parham 82
Paris 9
Parish 80
Parker 75, 102
Parkhouse 79
Parkin 69
Parkins 80
Parkinson 69
Parks 69
Parnaby 82
Parnell 69
Parr 69
Parrish 80
Parrot 69
Parry 69
Parslow 80
Parson 75
Parsons 75, 102
Parton 82
Pascoe 72, 78
Patchett 81
Pate 76
Patience 39, 53
Patmore 80
Paton 69
Patrice 36
Patricia 35, 46–9
Patrick 29, 42–4, 49, 62, 69
Patten 80
Patterson 69
Pattinson 69, 79
Pattison 69
Paul 29, 39, 42–4, 49, 51, 61
Paula 35, 46
Pauline 35, 46–7
Paulson 81
Pavey 79
Paxman 81
Paxton 81
Payling 81
Payne 69
Paynter 78
Peach 79
Pearcey 79
Pearl 39
Pearn 78
Pears 69, 102
Pearse 69
Pearson 69, 102
Pease 79
Peat 79
Peatfield 81
Pedaiah 32
Pedlar 78
Pedler 78
Peebleshire 113
Peel 83
Peggy 22, 45–6
Pegler 80
Pegrum 80
Pegson 69
Peking 127
Pell 81
Pemberton 80
Pembrokeshire 113
PEN NAMES 85
Pendell 82
Pendle 82, 106
Pendlebury 80
Pendleton 74
Penelope 12, 35, 49
Penfold 82
Pengelly 72, 78
Pengilly 78
Penhill 106
Penn 68, 128
Penna 78
Pennifold 82
Pennsylvania 120, 125
Penny 35
Penrice 82
Penrose 72, 78
Penson 80
Penwarden 79
Pepper 75
Percival 41, 61
Percy 24–5, 41
Perdita 12
Peregrine 10, 29
Perez 71
Perfect 77
Perham 82
Perkin 79
Perkins 69
Perrin 69, 79
Perrot 69
Perry 29, 69
Pershing 68
Person 69
Perthshire 113
Peru 124
Petard 87
Petch 82
Peter 29, 41–4, 49, 69, 78
Peterborough 113
Peters(on) 69
Pether 81
Petherbridge 79
Petherick 79
Pethick 78
Petronella 69
Pettengale 74
Pettingale 74
Pettingell 74
Pettipher 81
Pettit 77
Phelan 60
Phelps 69
Phileas 10
Philip 29, 41–4, 49, 61–2, 69
Philippa 35, 50
Philippines 124
Phillip 29, 49
Phillips 67, 69
Phillipson 69, 81
Philp 78
Philpot 69
Phippen 82
Phipps 69
Phoebe 45
Phyllis 45–8
Pick 81
Pickersgill 82
Pickett 82
Pickin 81
Pickup 80
Pickwell 81
Pidduck 80
Pierce 69
Piers 38
Pike 102
Pilcher 80
Pilgrim 80
Pilkington 80
Pilling 80
Pimblett 80
Pimlott 78
Pinch 78
Pinches 81
Pinchin 82
Pinhay 79
Pinhey 79
Piper 75
Pitchford 81
Pither 78
Pittock 80
Pittsburgh 127
PLACE NAME CHANGES 123
PLACE NAME ELEMENTS 114–15
PLACE NAME TRANSFERS 117–18
PLACE NAMES 60, 105–6, 114–15
PLACE NAMES, ROYAL 118–20
Plackett 79
Plaistowe 78
Pledger 80
Plews 82
Plumbly 81
Plummer 75
Plumtree 81
Plymouth 117, 119
Pochin 80
Pocklington 81
Podmore 81
Poel 69
Poggs 69
Poland 124
POLITICAL NAME CHANGES 84
POLITICAL NICKNAMES 99–100
Polkinghorne 78, 85
Poll 81
Pollitt 80
Polly 12
Pollyanna 10
Pomeroy 79
Pomfret 80
Poore 80
POP GROUP NAMES 169–70
Pople 82
Popplewell 83
Poppy 39
Porrett 82
Porritt 82
Portsmouth 80
Portugal 74, 124
Poskitt 83
Postlethwaite 80
Pottenger 82
Potter 75
Potticary 80
Potts 69
Pow 82
Powell 69
Powlesland 79
Pownall 78
Powys 114
Poyey 78
Pratt 77
Prebble 80
Precious 82
Preece 69
Prescott 74
Preston 74
Prettejohn 79
Pretty 80
Pretty Sally's 122
Prettyjohn 79
Prettyman 77
Price 67, 69
Prickett 69
Priday 80
Priestner 78
Primrose 39
Pring 79
Pringle 81
Priscilla 45
Prisk 78
Pritchard 69
Pritchett 69
Probert 69
Probyn 69
Proctor 75
Prodham 82
PROLIFIC NAMES 61
Proud 79
Proudfoot 77
Prowse 77
Prudence 23, 39
Prudom 82
Psyche 51
PUB NAMES 138–44, 146–8
Puckeridge 82
Puddifoot 77
Puddy 82
Pugh 69
Pugsley 79
Pullen 77
Pullman 68
Pumphrey 69
Purdy 81
Purfleet 108
PURITAN NAMES 39, 119
Purkis 78
Purnell 69
Purser 82
Pursglove 79
Purslove 79
Purssell 78
Puttergill 74
Puttock 82
Puuenuhe 121
Pyatt 82
Pybus 82
Pym 79

Q
Quail 76
Quance 79
Quartermaine 77
Quebec 127
Queenborough 109
Queenie 12
Quelch 79
Quenby 78
Quenell 70
Quentin 30
Quested 80
Quibell 81
Quiggin 72
Quilp 88
Quilter 80
Quinn(e)y 82
Quirk 72

R
Rabbetts 79
Rabjohns 79
Rachael 35
Rachel 35, 38, 40, 45–6, 48–9
RACIALLY MARKED NAMES 60
Raddall 78
Raddle 78
Radley 81
Radnorshire 113
Radway 80
Rafferty 72
Rafter 72
Rainbow 61, 82
Rainford 80
Rains 79
Ralegh 66
Raleigh 66, 112
Ralph 29, 38, 41, 43, 60, 69
Ram 32
Ramirez 71
Ramon 71
Ramos 71
Ramsay 31
Ramsbottom 80
Ramsden 83
Ramsey 74
Ranby 81
Randal(l) 29, 44, 69
Randolph 60, 63, 69
Rand(s) 69
Randy 29
Rangitoto 105
Rank 77
Rankin 69
Ransome 69
Raphael 32
Rapley 82
Rapson 78
Rasheda 36
Rashida 36
Rathbone 78
Ratigan 72
Raughley 66
Rauly 66
Raven 36, 80
Ravenscroft 78
Ravenshaw 81
Raw 82
Rawcliffe 80
Rawdon 10
Rawkins 69
Rawle 69, 82
Rawleigh 66
Rawleleygh 66
Rawley 66
Rawlings 69
Rawlins 69
Rawlinson 69, 80
Rawlison 69
Rawson 69
Ray 43
Rayley 66

Raymond 29, 42-4, 49
Raymont 79
Raymount 79
Read 77
Reading 108
Readman 82
Reagh 72
Reakes 82
REAL NAMES 90, 193
Reavey 72
Rebecca 35, 45-9, 56
Rebekah 39
REBUS 188
Reddaway 79
Reddicliffe 79
Redgate 81
Redman 75
Redmayne 83
Redvers 41
Redway 70
Reece 69
Reed 77
Reeson 81
Reeve 75
Regina 35
Reginald 29, 41-2, 53, 60
Reilly 72
RELIGIOUS NAMES 53
Remlap 120
Remlig 120
Renee 35, 48-9
Renehan 72
Renfrewshire 113
Renita 36
Rennell 69
Rennie 69
Rennison 69, 82
Renshaw 79
Renton 81
Renwick 81
Rere 61
RESPECTABLE NAMES 52
Retallack 78
Retallick 78
Retter 79
Reuben 29, 41
Revell 79
Revill 79
Rew 79
Reyes 71
Reynald 69
Reynolds 69, 102
Reynoldson 69
Rhett 10
Rhiain 37
Rhiannon 37
Rhoades 81
Rhoda 37
Rhode Island 125
Rhodes 102
Rhodri 31
Rhona 37
Rhonda 48
Rhys 31, 49, 69
Rice 69
Rich 60
Richard 29, 38, 41, 43-4, 49, 57, 60-1, 69
Richards 67, 69, 102
Richardson 69
Rickard 78
Rickett 80
Ricketts 69, 80
Rickie 29
Ricky 40, 54
Ridd 79
Rider 82, 102
Riding 80
Ridout 79
Rigdale 112
Rigden 80
Riggall 81
Righton 80
Rimmer 80
Ring 72
Ringer 81
RIOTOUS NAME 62
Rioty 62
Rippon 81
Rishworth 83
Rising 81
Rita 55
Ritchie 72
Rivanna 121
RIVER NAMES 110-11, 115-16
Rivera 71
Rivett 81
Rix 69, 81
Roadley 81
Roads 78
Robbie 69
Robbins 69
Robens 69
Robert 23-4, 29, 38, 41-3, 44, 49, 61, 69
Roberta 24
Roberts 67, 69
Robertshaw 83
Robertson 69
Robey 69
Robin 29, 35, 42, 48
Robinson 10, 69
Robson 69
Robyn 35, 49
Rochelle 35
Rockefeller 68
Rodda 78
Roddam 81
Roddis 81
Rodenhurst 81
Roderick 29
Rodmell 82
Rodney 29
Rodrigo 71
Rodriguez 71
Roebuck 83
Roger 29, 38, 41-3, 70
Rogers 70
Rogerson 70, 80
Roisin 36
Roland 38
Romain 74
Romania 124
Romayne 74
Rome 74, 127
Romeo 7
Romero 71
Ronald 29, 42-4, 49
Ronan 30
Rood 82
Roofe 81
Room(e) 74
Roose 78
Roosevelt 30, 68
Root 80
Rory 29
Rosamund 38
Rosanna 45
Rosbotham 80
Rosbottom 80
Rose 35, 39, 45-7, 52
ROSE NAMES 12, 172
Rosebotham 80
Rosebud 53
Rosemary 35, 46, 49
Rosenberg 71
Roseveare 78
Rosewarne 78
Rosh 32
Rosina 12
Roskelly 78
Roskilly 78
Roslyn 49
Ross 29, 49, 72, 79, 113
Rossall 80
Rossell 80
Rosser 83
Rossiter 79
Rothwell 80
Rounthwaite 82
Rouse 78
Routhwaite 82
Routledge 79
Routley 79
Rowan 31
Rowarth 79
Rowland 74
Rowles 81
Rowlingson 78
Rowntree 82
Rowse 78
Roxana 35, 61
Roxanne 35
Roxburghshire 113
Roy 29, 40, 42
ROYAL NICKNAMES 94-5
ROYAL PLACE NAMES 128
Royce 80
Ruby 39
Ruddle 82
RUDEST NAME 60
Rudyard 107
Ruffle 80
Rufus 32
Rugg 82
Rugman 80
Ruiz 71
Rum Cay 118
Rumbold 80
Rumming 82
Rundle 78
Runnalls 78
Rupert 29, 61
Ruscoe 78
Rushworth 83
Russ 82
Russell 29, 40, 42-3, 49, 77, 102
Ruston 78
Ruth 35, 39, 45, 47-8
Rutland 113
Ruy 71
Ryan 42, 44, 49, 55, 72
Ryder 83
Ryding 80
Rymer 80

S
Sabin 81
Sabrina 35
Sacandaga 122
Saddler 76
Sade 48
Sadie 35
Safe-deliverance 39
Sagar 80
Saint 79
St Kitts 118
St Maur 77
Sallie 35
Sallis 78
Sally 23, 35, 45-7, 49
Salmon 76
Salome 37
Salop 114
Salter 76
Salthouse 80
Sam 41
Samantha 35, 46, 48-9, 54, 61
Samson 32
Samuel 29, 38, 41, 43, 49
Samways 79
San Marino 124
San Salvador 123
Sanchez 71
Sancho 71
Sandbach 78
Sandercock 78
Sanders(on) 69
Sandie 35
Sandra 35, 46-9
Sandry 78
Sands 81
Sankey 81
Santiago 71
Sara(h) 23, 35, 39, 45-9, 52, 62
Sardeson 81
Sare 78
Sargent 76
Sargisson 81
Satchmo 12
Saudi Arabia 124
Saul 12, 32, 38
Saunders(on) 69
Savage 77
Savill 80
Savin 81
Savory 81
Sawyer 76, 82
Say 82
Sayers 82
Scales 81
SCANDINAVIAN NAMES 63
SCANDINAVIAN PLACE NAMES 110
Scantlebury 78
Scarborough 81
Scarlett 54
Scarletta 12
Scarp 88
Scarth 82
Schaefer 71
Schmidt 68
Schneider 71
Schoen 71
Scholes 80
Scholey 81
Schoolcraft 120
Schroeder 71
Schultz 71
Schwartz 71
Schwenkville 122
Scoley 81
Scollan 74
Scoones 80
Scotland 74, 124
Scott 25, 29, 42, 44, 49, 52, 60, 74
SCOTTISH NAMES 31, 37, 67
Scotton 80
Scragg 78
Scrimshaw 81
Scrimshire 81
Scriven 81
Scrivener 78
Scroggs 78
Scruby 80
Scudamore 80
Scutt 79
Scutts 74
Seal 79
Seal(e)y 82
Seamus 30
Sean 29-30, 44
Sear 78
Sears 80
Searson 81
Seath 80
Seavers 70
Seaward 80
Sebastian 29
Seccombe 78
Seddon 80
Sedgwick 83
Sedman 82
Sefton 80
Segar 80
Selby 81
Seldon 79
Selena 35
Selina 35, 45
Selkirkshire 113
Sellars 82
Sellek 79
Sellers 82
Selwyn 54, 80
Senga 37, 62
Sephton 80
Seppanen 68
Septimus 23, 60
Seraiah 32
Sercombe 79
Serena 35, 57
Sergeant 81
Seth 32, 38
Seventy-Six 120
Severs 82
Seville 127
Seward 79
SEXIEST NAMES 61
Seyoyah Creek 122
Sha-Bosh-Kung Bay 122
Shabbona 122
Shackel 78
Shackerley 109
Shacklady 80
Shackleton 83
Shacklock 79
Shakelady 80
Shakespeare 77
Shameless 64
Shane 29, 49, 52
Shanel(l) 61
Shanghai 127
Shanks 81
Shannon 35, 48
Shapland 79
Sharland 79
Sha[illegible]ene 35
Sharon 35, 40, 46-9
Sharp 77
Sharples 80
Sharpley 81
Sharratt 82
Sharrock 80
Shaun 29, 42, 49
Shave 80
Shaw 74
Shawn 29, 44
Shayla 36
Sheard 83
Sheba 37
Sheen 78
Sheena 35
Sheffield 80, 127
Sheila 36, 46, 48
Shelah 32
Sheldrake 82
Sheldrick 82
Shelemiah 32
Shelley 35, 82
Shelly 35
Shelton 74
Shem 32
Shemaiah 32
Shemilt 82
Shenton 82
Shephatiah 32
Shepherd 76
Sheppard 76
Shepperson 78
Sheri 35
Sheringham 81
Sherratt 82
Sherri 40
Sherrill 79
Sherry 12, 48, 62
Sherwill 79
Sherwin 79
Shetland 113
Shield 81
Shields 80
Shiloh 120
SHIP NAMES 173-4, 180-1
Shipley 74
Shipman 80
Shipp 80
Shipton 110
Shipway 80
Shirley 8, 35, 46-8, 54, 82
Shirt 79
Shoebotham 82
Shoebottom 82
Shona 12, 37
Shone 78
Shopland 79
Shore 78
Shorland 79
Shorrock 80
Short 65, 77
Short Leg 64
Shorter 80
SHORTEST NAMES 60
Shorthouse 77
Shortt 66
Shotton 79
Shreeve 81
Shrimpton 81
Shropshire 113
Shufflebottom 76
Shuker 81
Shute 79
Sian 35, 37
Siddons 81
Siddorn 78
Sidebottom 79
Sidford 82
Sidney 25, 41-2, 61
Sierra 48
Sierra Leone 124
Siggers 70
SIGNATURES 92
Silcock 80
Silva 71
Silvana 61
Sim(m) 79
Simeon 29, 62
Simmonds 70
Sim(m)s 70
Simon 29, 41-2, 49, 56, 62, 70
Simone 35, 49, 61
Simpkins 70
Simple 77
Simpson 70
Sinclair 72
Sinden 82
Sine 35
Sinead 36
Singapore 124
Singer 76, 82
Singeton 80
Siobhan 35-6
Sioned 37
Sirene 57
Sirett 78
Sirrell 80
Sisi 61
Sisley 69
Sisson 69
Skeels 78
Skegg 77
Skelton 74
Skerrett 80
Skewes 78
Skidmore 79
Skinner 76
Skipton 110
Skull Creek 122
Skyrme 80
Slader 79
Slater 76
Slatter 76
Slee 79
Sling 64
Slipper 81
Slocock 78
Sloper 82
Sluggett 79
Smale 79
Small 77
Smallbridge 79
Smallridge 79
Smaridge 79
Smart 77
Smedley 79
Smellie 76
Smerdon 79
Smith 66, 52, 68, 76, 87, 102
Smithers 76, 82

Smithin 82
Smoker 76
Smollett 77
Smyth 79
Smythe 76
Sneath 81
Snell 77
Snelson 78
Snitkaw 119
Snow 77, 102
Snowdrop 39
Snyder 71
Soame 81
Sob Lake 122
Soby 79
Solley 80
Solomon 32, 38, 80
Somerset 113
Sonia 35
Sonja 35
Sonya 35
Soper 79
Sophia 35, 39, 45, 47
Sophie 35, 49
Sophronia 60
Soraya 12
Sorcha 36
Sorrell 77, 80
Soso 61
South 80
South Carolina 125
South Dakota 125
Southgate 82
Southon 80
Southwell 80
Spain 74, 124
Spalton 79
Spanier 74
Spargo 78
Sparkes 82
Sparrow 102
Speechley 80
Speed 82
SPELLING 22, 58, 65-6
Spenceley 82
Spencer 29, 76
Spensley 82
Sperling 38
Sperring 82
Spicer 76
Spiers 82
Spink(s) 81
Spittle 76
Spokane 120
Spokes 81
Spooner 76
Spotterswood 79
Sprake 79
Spratt 82
Spriggs 80
Sproston 78
Spurgeon 80
Spurle 79
Spurrell 79
Spurrett 81
Squance 79
Squeaky Creek 119
Squinter 64
Squire 76
Squirrell 82
Stace 80
Stacey 35, 42, 46, 48-9
Staci(e) 35
Stacy 35
Stafford 74
Staffordshire 113
STAGE NAMES 84, 164
Staines 80
Stainthorpe 82
Staite 80
Staley 79
Stallard 82
Stamp 81
Stanbra 81
Stanbridge 78
Stanbury 79
Stand-fast-on-high 39
Standish 112
Stanford 74
Staniforth 79
Stanley 29, 41-3, 74, 77
Stannard 82
Stansfield 83
Stanton 74, 78
Stanworth 80
Staples 81
Stapleton 74
Stares 80
Starkie 80
Starling 81
Stavely 82
Stay 82
Steeds 82
Steele 76, 102
Steggall 82
Stein 71
Stelfox 78
Stella 12, 47, 61
Stendall 81
Stenson 70
Stephanie 35, 46, 48-9
Stephen 22, 29, 41-3, 49, 61, 70
Stephens 70
Stephenson 70
STERTOROUS NAME 61
Steven 22, 29, 42, 44, 49
Stevens 70
Stevenson 70
Stewart 29, 72, 81
Stickles 80
Stidolph 70
Stidston 79
Stimpson 81
Stinchcombe 80
Stinton 82
Stirlingshire 113
Stobart 81
Stobert 81
Stock 80
Stockdale 78
Stockhill 82
Stockill 82
Stockton 78
Stoddard 82
Stokell 82
Stokes 74
Stonehouse 82
Stoneman 79
Stoppard 79
Stops 81
Storer 79
Storm 62
Storr 81
Stowe 81
Strang 77
Stratford 78
Stratton 74
Straughan 81
Straw(son) 81
STREET NAMES 127-37
Stride 80
Stringer 76
Strong 77
Strutt 80
Stuart 29, 42, 49, 80
Stubbins 81
Stuble 81
Stuckey 82
Studley 79
Stunt 80
Stuppies 80
Sturdy 82
Sturgeon 82
Sturt 82
Subligna 120
Suckabone 122
Sudan 124
Suddaby 82
Suffolk 109, 113
Sugden 83
Suggett 82
Suggitt 82
Suicide 121
Sullivan 72, 102
Sully 82
Summer 35
Summerfield 78
Summerhayes 82
Sunderland 83
Sunter 82
SURNAMES 52, 69-72
Surprise 61
SURPRISING NAME 61
Surrey 113
Surtees 79
Susan 12, 35, 45-9, 61
Susanna 39
Susannah 35, 45
Susanne 35
Sussex 109, 113
Suter 82
Sutherland 72, 113, 119
Suzanne 35, 46-9
Swaffer 80
Swaffield 79
Swanton 82
Swarbrick 80
Swearing Creek 120
Sweden 124
Sweet 82
SWEETEST NAMES 62
Sweeting 80
Swetman 82
Swift 77
Swindle 76
Swinton 78
Switzerland 124
Sydney 43, 119
Sylvia 35, 40, 46
Symes 79
Symonds 70
Syratt 78
Syrett 78

T
Taber 80
Tabitha 37
Tabor 80
Tac(e)y 60
Tag 69
Tagg 79
Tait 77
Talbot 77
Tallulah 12
Tamar 37, 39
Tamara 35
Tamasa 110
Tamblin 70
Tamblyn 78
Tame 78
Tameke 36
Tamika 48, 60
Tamike 36
Tamlin 70
Tammie 35
Tammy 35, 48
Tampling 70
Tamsin 35
Tancock 79
Tandy 82
Tania 35, 49
Tanisha 36, 48
Tanner 76
Tanya 35
Tanzania 124
Tapley 78
Tapping 78
Tara 35, 49
Tarn 79
Tarr 82
Tasha 36
Tasman 119
Tassell 80
TASTIEST NAME 62
Tatchell 82
Tatham 83
Tattam 78
Tattersall 80
Taunton 82
Taupo Nui A Tia 122
Taverner 79
Tawan(n)a 36
Taylor 76, 102
Tazewell 82
Teal(e) 83
Teek 82
Tegan 49
Telfer 81
Telford 81
Tempest 62
Temple(man) 81
Tennessee 125
Tennison 82
Tennyson 69
Tenville 36
Terence 29, 42, 49
Teresa 35, 46
Terrance 30, 44
Terrell 44
Terri 35, 46
Terrie 35
Terry 29, 35, 40
Tester 82
Texas 126
Texhoma 121
Thackery 83
Thackray 83
Thackwray 83
Thailand 124
Thames 110
Thames Ditton 110
Thatcher 76
The Paroo 122
The-Lord-is-near 39
Thelma 12, 23
Theodora 34
Theodore 29, 43
Theresa 35, 48
Therese 53
Theyer 80
Thirkell 80
Thisbe 12
Thoday 78
Thomas 23, 29, 41-4, 49, 51, 67, 70
Thomasin 35
Thomason 70
Thomlinson 79
Thompson 70
Thompstone 78
Thora 37
Thoreau 68
Thorington 80
Thornber 83
Thornhill 78
Thornton 74
Thoroughgood 77
Threlfall 80
Thrower 76, 81
Thurlby 81
Thurman 82
Thurston 74
Thwaites 83
Tiara 48
Tibbetts 82
Tibbs 69
Tice 82
Tickle 78
Tickler 68
Tickner 80
Tidy 82
Tierra 48
Tiffany 36, 48
Tiglathpileser 60
Tilbrook 80
Tilgathpilneser 60
Till 80
Tiller 76
Tillett 69
Tilley 69, 82, 112
Tillison 69
Tillman 76
Tillotson 69
Timberlake 78
TIME OF DAY NAMES 61
Timothy 29, 41-4, 49-50
Timperley 78
Tina 35, 46, 48
Tinker 83
Tinkler 79
Tinney 78
Tippett 78
Tipping 82
Tipton 74, 81
Tirzah 37
Titcombe 82
Titley 81
Tittmuss 80
Tiw 109
TO-NAMES 93-4
Tob 32
Tobias 29, 32, 58
Tobitt 82
Toby 29
Todd 29, 44, 49, 60, 76
Toddman 76
Tofield 78
Tofts 80
Tokyo 127
Toll 78
Toller 76
Tolley 69, 82
Tom 41, 56, 78
Tombs 70, 76
Tomes 78
Tomika 36
Tomkin 80
Tomkinson 82
Tomlinson 70
Tommie 30
Tompkins 70, 78
Tompsett 80
Toms 79
Tomsett 70
Tongue 82
Toni 35
Tonkin 78
Tonkins 70
Tonks 70
Tono 121
Tony 29
Toogood 82
Tooley 81
Toon(e) 80
Tope 79
Topp 79
Topping 79-80
Topsi 12
Torpenhow 106
Torquil 31
Torr 82
Torres 71
Tortoiseshell 76
Towes 82
Towndrow 79
Towneley 64
Townend 83
Townroe 79
Townrow 79
Townsend 74
Townson 80
Towse 82
Toya 36
Tozer 79
Trac(e)y 22, 35, 46, 48-9, 51-2, 54
TRADE NAMES 160-8
TRADITIONAL NICKNAMES 98
Trafford 81
TRAIN NAMES 174-6
Trainer 76
TRANSFERRED NAMES 24
Tranter 76
Trapp 76
Travers 76
Travis 29, 44, 49
Trease 72
Treasure 82
Trebilcock 78
Tregear 78
Tregellas 78
Tregelles 78
Tregoning 78
Treleaven 78
Treloar 79
Tremain 79
Tremaine 72
Tremayne 79
Trembath 79
Tremlett 79
Trerise 79
Tresidder 79
Trethewey 79
Trevail 79
Trevean 72
Trever 58
Trevor 29, 42, 49, 72
Treweeke 79
Trewen 72
Trewhella 79
Trewin 79
Tribe 82
Trick 79
Tricker 82
Trickett 78
Trinder 76
Trinidad 124, 127
Tripcony 79
Trippas 82
Tristram 60
Trollope 76
Trotman 80
Trott 79
Trotter 76
Trounson 79
Trowbridge 79
Troy 29, 49
Trude 79
Trudgen 79
Trudgeon 79
Trudgian 79
Truelove 82
Trueman 78
Trumble 70
Truscott 79
Truswell 81
Truth or Consequences 120
Tucker 76
Tuckett 79
Tudge 80
Tudor 83
Tuesley 109
Tuff 80
Tuffin 79
Tuffley 80
Tulip 56
Tully 79
Tunnicliff 82
Tupper 102
Turnbull 77
Turnell 81
Turner 76, 102
Turnock 82
Turrill 81
Turton 79
Turvill 80
Tustain 81
Tweedy 82
Tween 80
Twitchin 80
Tyack(e) 79
Tyerman 82
Tyler 44, 76
Tyley 82
Tym(m) 79
Tyne and Wear 114
Tyreman 82
Tyrer 80
Tyrone 30, 113
Tyrrell 78
Tyson 49

U
Udall 79
Ullyatt 81
Umpleby 83
Una 23, 36
Underhay 79
Underhill 79
UNEXPECTED NAME 62
Unicume 80
UNLUCKIEST NAMES 60
Unworth 80
Uren 79
Uri 32
Uriah 32
Uriel 32
Urmston 78
Ursula 40, 60
Usher 81
Usherwood 80
Utah 126
Utopia 122
Utting 81
Uttley 83
Uzziah 32
Uzziel 32

V
Vale 80
Valerie 46
Vallance 79
VALUABLE NAMES 60
Vancouver 119
Vandermeer 71
Vanessa 23, 35, 49
Vanstone 79
Varley 83
Varney 78
Vaughan 72
Vawser 78
Vazquez 71
Vellenoweth 79
Venezuela 124
Venner 79
Venning 79
Ventress 82
Ventris 82
Venus 40
Vera 46
Verall 82
Vergette 81
Verity 36, 39, 83
Vermont 126
Vernon 29
Veronica 36
Verran 79
Vessy 72
Viccars 78
Vicesimus 60
Vick 80
Vickers 76
Vicky 36, 40
Victor 29, 41-2
Victoria 36, 40, 46, 119
Vienna 127
Vietnam 124
Vigar 82
Vigors 82
Vikki 36, 40
Vimpany 80
Vincent 29
Vinson 80
Vinter 81
Viola 39
Violet 39, 45-6
Violet Town 122
Violette 12
Virginia 36, 47, 49, 126
Vivian 79
Vivienne 36
Vlk 88
Voaden 79
Vodden 79
Vooght 79
Vosper 79
Vowles 82
Vyse 80

W
Wacher 80
Waddingham 81
Wadland 79
Wadley 80
Wadsley 81
Wadsworth 83
Wager 79
Wagner 71
Wagstaffe 77
Waimakiriri 122
Wainwright 76
Wakeford 82
Wakeham 79
Wakely 79
Walburn 79
Walby 80
Walch 74
Walden 79
Walder 82
Wales 124
Walker 76, 102
Wallace 31, 74
Wallbank 80
Waller 76
Walles 74
Wallis 74
Wallwin 79
Walmsley 80
Walrond 82
Walsh 74, 80
Walsman 74
Walter 29, 38, 41-3, 70
Walters 70, 102
Walton 74
Wanamaker 68
Wanda 36
Wanlace 81
Wanless 81
Ward 76, 102
Warden 82
Warder 81
Ware 74, 79
Wareham 79
Wareing 80
Waring 80
Warminster 109
Warnborough 109
Warnes 81
Warr 78
Warren 29, 38, 43, 52, 74, 102, 112
Warrilow 82
Warwick 81
Warwickshire 113
Washington 68, 74, 112, 126
Wass 81
Waterfall 79
Waterhouse 79
Waterman 80
Waters 102
Waterson 70
Watkins 70
Watkinson 70, 83
Watman 38
Watson 70, 102
Watts 70
Waycott 79
Wayman 78
Wayne 29, 42, 49, 52
Wearmouth 79
Wearne 79
Weatherhead 83
Weaver 76
Webb 76, 102
Webber 76
Weber 71
Webster 76
Weddell 81
Weddle 81
Wednesbury 109
Weedon 109
Weeney 72
Weetman 82
Weighell 82
Weighill 82
Weightman 81
Weir 72
Weiss 71
Welburn 83
Welch 74
Welford 83
Wellburn 83
Wellings 81
Wellington 79, 127
Wellish 74
Wells 74
Wellsman 74
Welsh 74
WELSH NAMES 31, 37, 61, 67
WELSH NICKNAMES 94-5
Welson 80
Wenden 80
Wendon 80
Wendy 23, 36, 46, 48-9
Wenham 82
Wennell 70
Went 80
Were 79
Werner 71
Werrett 80
Wescott 82
Wesley 29, 74
West Midlands 114
West Virginia 126
Westacott 79
Westaway 79
Westbrook 74
Westcott 79
Westerby 81
Western 79
Westley 81
Westmorland 113
Westoby 81
Westren 79
Wetton 79
Wey 105
Weybridge 105
Weymouth 105
Whalebelly 81
Whatley 82
Whatman 70
Whearty 72
Wheatcroft 79
Wheaton 79
Wheeler 76, 102
Wheelton 78
Whelan 72
Whetter 79
Whinnett 78
Whipp 80
Whisky 76
Whitaker 74
Whitbread 77
Whitcher 80
White 102
Whiteaway 79
Whitebread 80
Whitehouse 77
Whitehurst 82
Whitelegg 78
Whiteley 83
Whiteside 80
Whiteway 79
Whitley 83
Whitlock 80
Whitlow 78
Whitmore 82
Whitney 48, 81
Whitsed 81
Whittard 70
Whittingham 79
Whittleton 81
Whitton 81
Whitwell 83
Wibberley 79
Wickens 82
Wickett 79
Widdicombe 79
Widdop 83
Widdows 81
Widdup 83
Wigley 79
Wigtownshire 113
Wilberforce 83
Wilberfoss 83
Wilbur 55
Wilcock 70
Wilcox 70
Wild 52, 77
Wilday 82
Wilder 78
Wiles 80
Wilford 80
Wilfred 41
Wilkie 70
Wilkins(on) 70
Willday 82
Willets 82
Willetts 82
Willey 81
William 29, 38, 41-4, 49, 58, 70
Williams 67, 70
Williamsburg 119
Williamson 70
Willie 29, 41, 60-1
Willing 79
Willis 70
Willison 78
Willoughby 74
Willows 81
Wills 70
Wilmer 70, 78
Wilsdon 81
Wilshaw 82
Wilson 70, 102
Wiltshire 113
Winbolt 70
Winbow 70
Winder 80
WINDY NAMES 62
Winifred 25, 45-6
Winmer 70
Winn 81
Winnall 82
Winney 70
Winnipeg 127
Winslade 82
Winslow 112
Winson 79
Winstanley 80
Winston 30, 40, 74
Winstone 82
Wint 82
Wintle 80
Wintour 80
Winwood 82
Wisconsin 126
Wise 77
Witchell 80
Withecombe 79
Witherden 80
Witheridge 79
Withers 85
Withey 82
Witheycombe 79
Withy 82
Witney 81
Witt 80
Witter 78
Witty 83
Woden 109
Wogan 72
Woking 112
Wolton 82
Wombwell 81
Wonnacott 79
Wood 102
Woodall 78
Wooddisse 82
Woodhams 82
Woodhead 83
Woodings 82
Woodland 81
Woodley 79
Wood(s) 74, 102
Woodward 76
Woof 76
Wookey 82
Woolcock 79
Woolgar 70
Woolgrove 81
Woolhouse 81
Woollage 77
Woollam 78
Woollams 78
Woolland 79
Woollard 82
Woollatt 80
Woolston 81
Woombill 81
Woomera 105
Wooster 78
Worcestershire 113
WORDS TURNED INTO NAMES 21
Workman 82
Worledge 77
Wormington 82
Wormleighton 80
Worsley 80
Worthington 74
Wortley 81
Wotton 74, 79
Wragg 79
Wrathall 83
Wray 83
Wrayford 79
Wreford 79
Wren 82, 102
Wrenn 77, 82
Wright 76, 102
Wrighton 81
Wrights 161
Wrightson 83
Wrixon 79
Wroot 81
Wroth 79
Wulmar 38
Wumond 38
Wych 78
Wyles 80
Wyman 63, 70, 81
Wyn 31
Wynn 72
Wyoming 126

Y
YACHT NAMES 180-1
Yackandandah 122
Yah 62
Yahweh 62
Yapp 77
Yarnold 82
Yarrow 78
Yarwood 78
Yates 74
Yeandle 82
Yeend 80
Yehudi 32
Yelland 79
Yemen 124
Yolanda 36
Yonwin 70
York 74, 81
Yorkshire 113
Younger 81
Youngmay 70
Yugoslavia 124
Yukon 127
Yves 36
Yvette 36
Yvonne 22, 36, 38, 46

Z
Zabad 32
Zabdiel 32
Zachary 29, 44
Zadok 32
Zambia 124
Zara 36
Zebedee 32
Zebediah 32
Zechariah 32, 62
Zedekiah 32
Zelda 61
Zephaniah 32
Zero 61
Zilpah 37
Zimmerman 71
Zipporah 37
Zoe 36, 46
Zola 61
Zuriel 32